CLOCKWORK PLANET

VII

STORY BY YUU KAMIYA & TSUBAKI HIMANA
MANGA BY KURO
CHARACTER DESIGN BY SINO

ClockWork Planet
CONTENTS

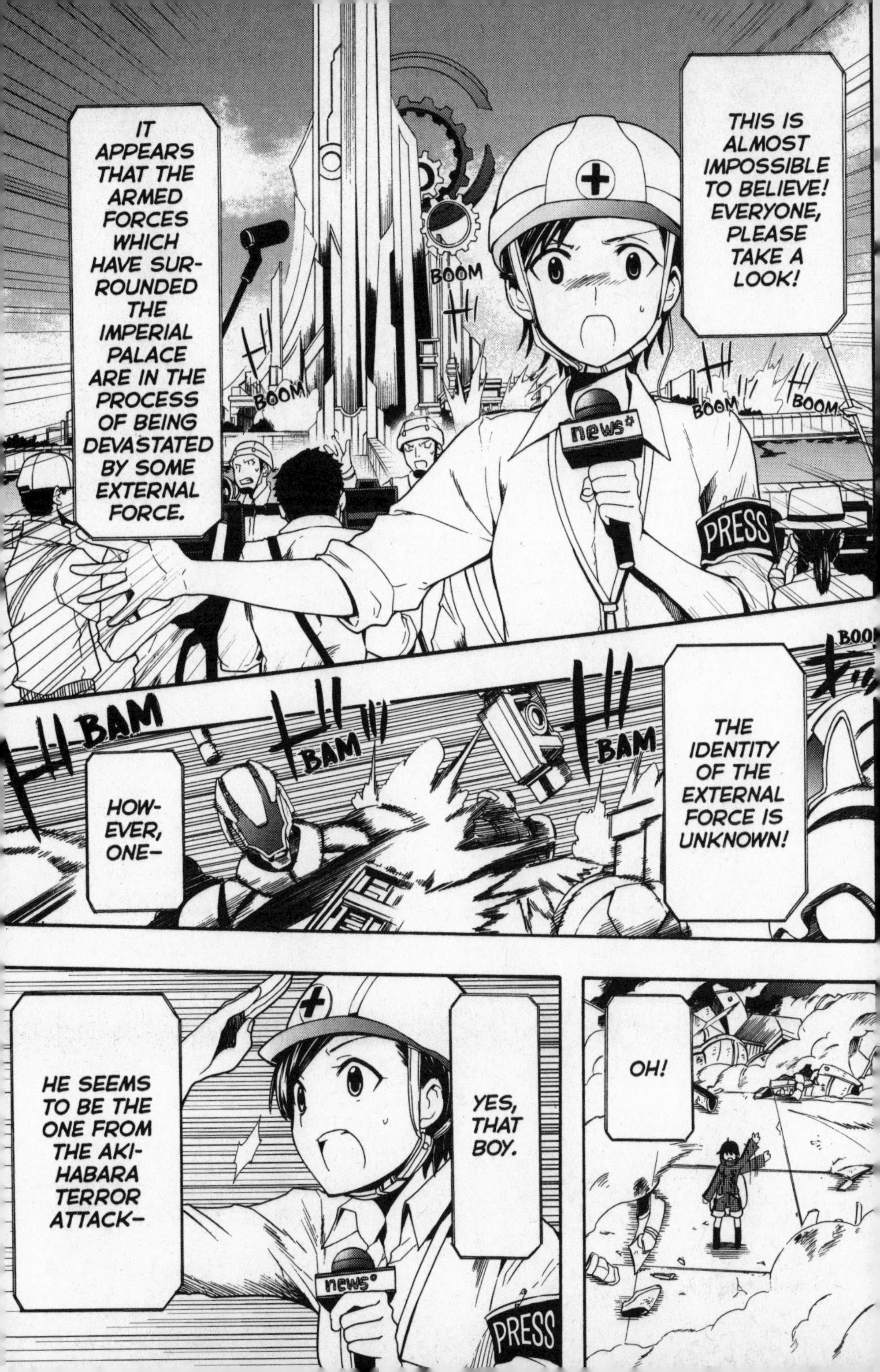
THIS IS ALMOST IMPOSSIBLE TO BELIEVE! EVERYONE, PLEASE TAKE A LOOK!
BOOM
BOOM
BOOM
BOOM
PRESS
news
IT APPEARS THAT THE ARMED FORCES WHICH HAVE SUR-ROUNDED THE IMPERIAL PALACE ARE IN THE PROCESS OF BEING DEVASTATED BY SOME EXTERNAL FORCE.
BOOM
THE IDENTITY OF THE EXTERNAL FORCE IS UNKNOWN!
BAM
BAM
BAM
HOW-EVER, ONE-
OH!
YES, THAT BOY.
HE SEEMS TO BE THE ONE FROM THE AKI-HABARA TERROR ATTACK-
news
PRESS

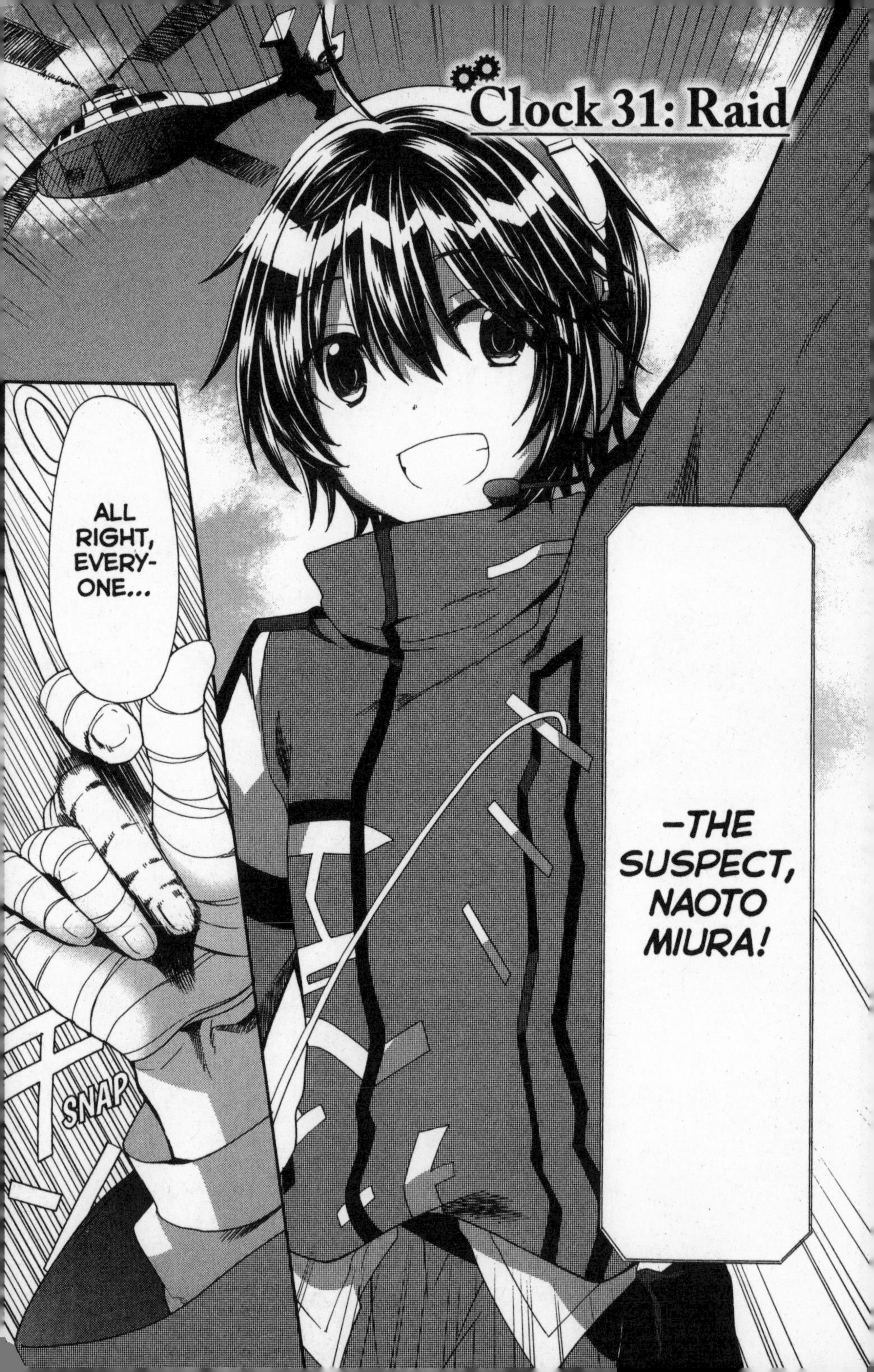
Clock 31: Raid
ALL RIGHT, EVERY-ONE...
—THE SUSPECT, NAOTO MIURA!
SNAP

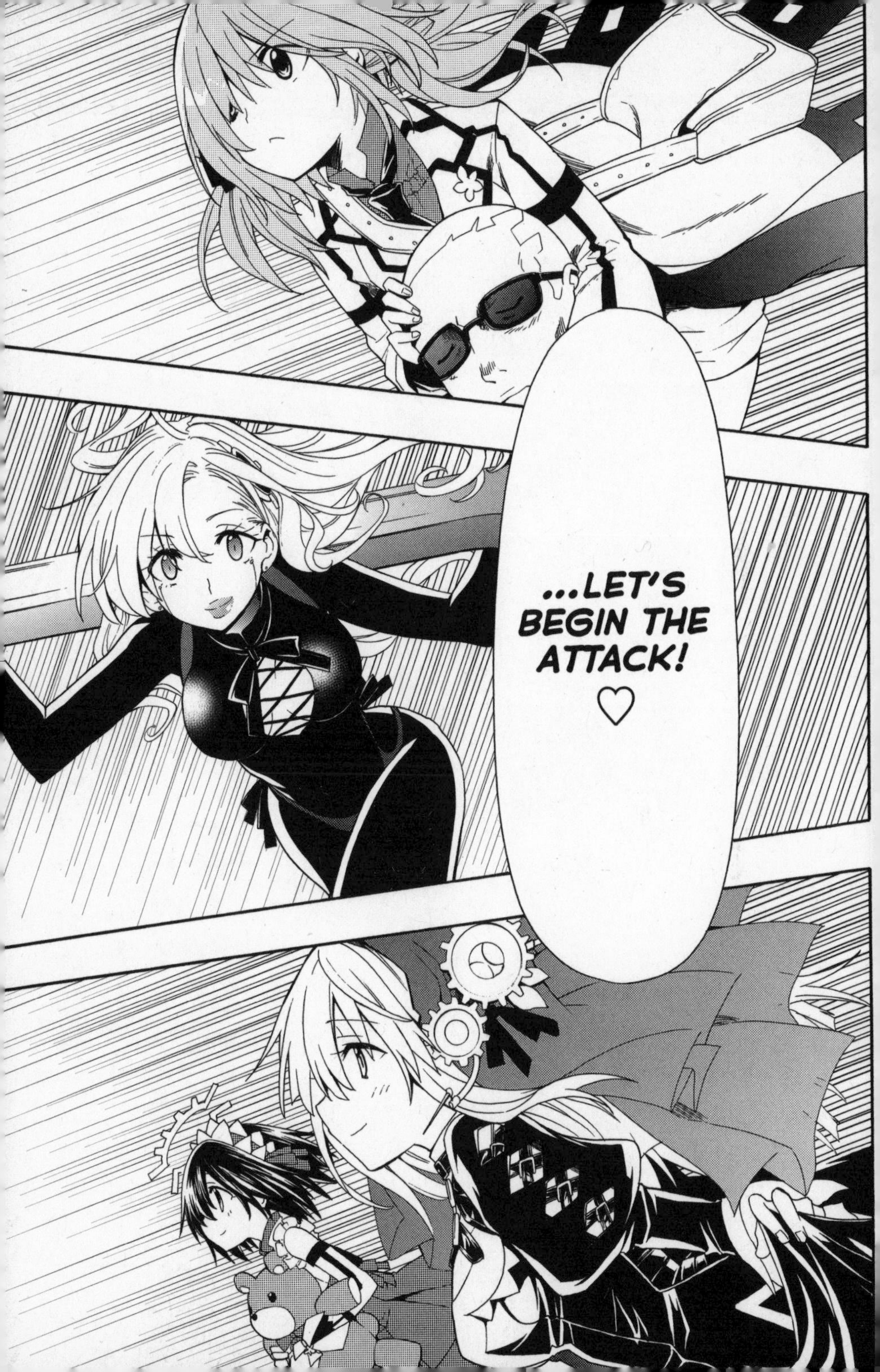
...LET'S BEGIN THE ATTACK! ♡

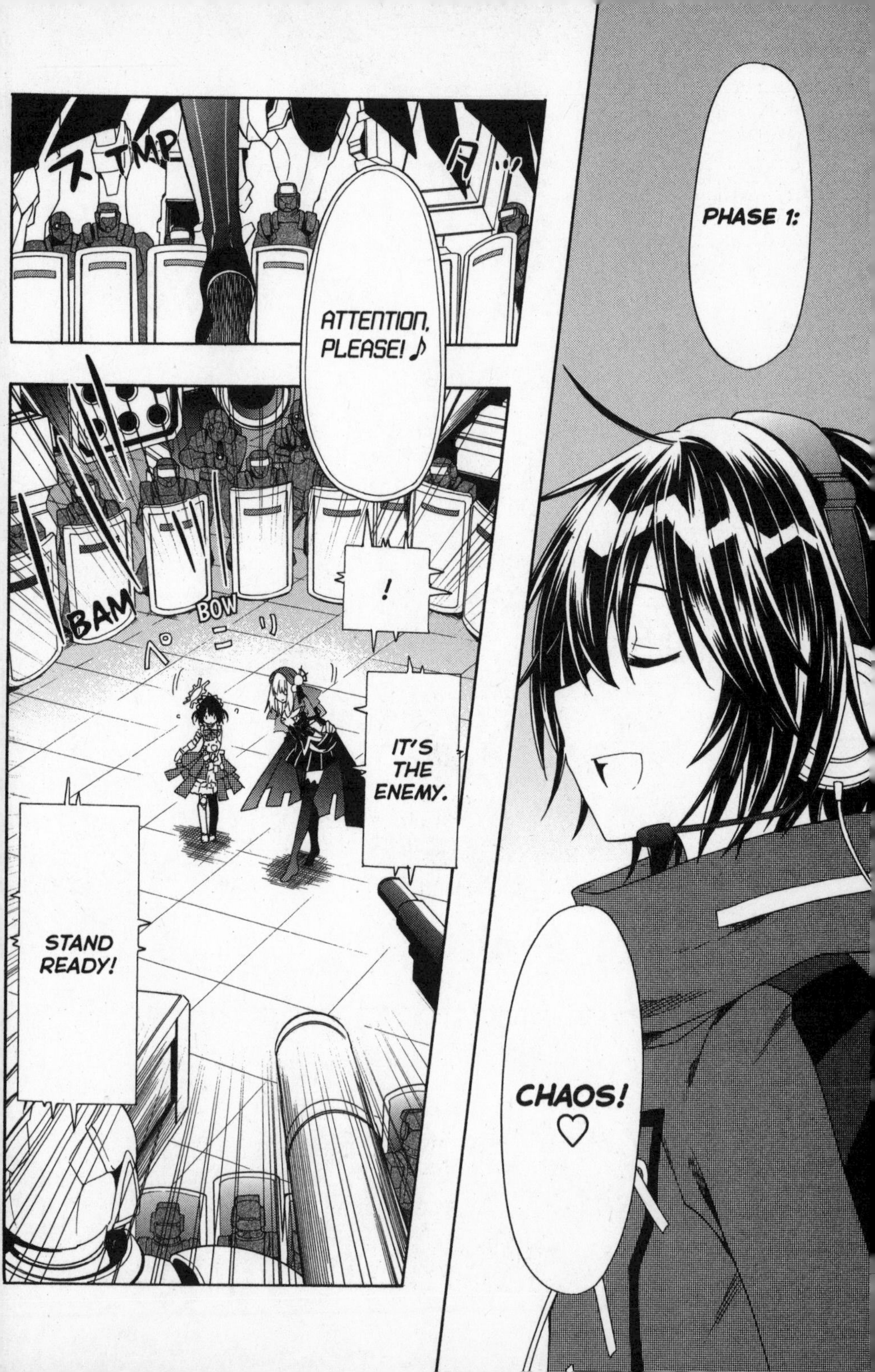
PHASE 1:
CHAOS! ♡
STMP
ATTENTION, PLEASE! ♪
!
IT'S THE ENEMY.
STAND READY!
BAM
BOW

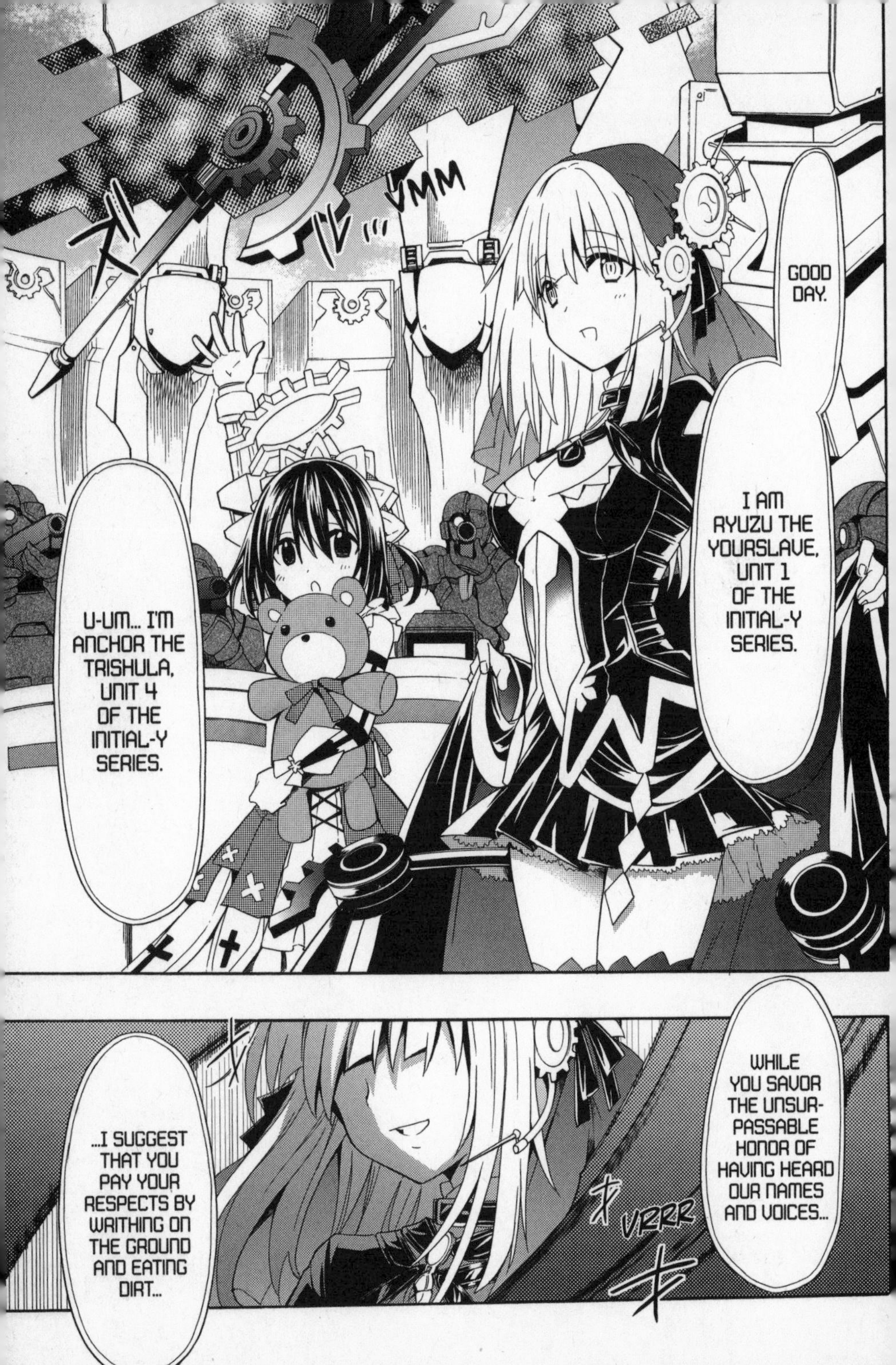
GOOD DAY.
VMM
I AM RYUZU THE YOURSLAVE, UNIT 1 OF THE INITIAL-Y SERIES.
U-UM... I'M ANCHOR THE TRISHULA, UNIT 4 OF THE INITIAL-Y SERIES.
WHILE YOU SAVOR THE UNSUR-PASSABLE HONOR OF HAVING HEARD OUR NAMES AND VOICES...
VRRR
...I SUGGEST THAT YOU PAY YOUR RESPECTS BY WRITHING ON THE GROUND AND EATING DIRT...

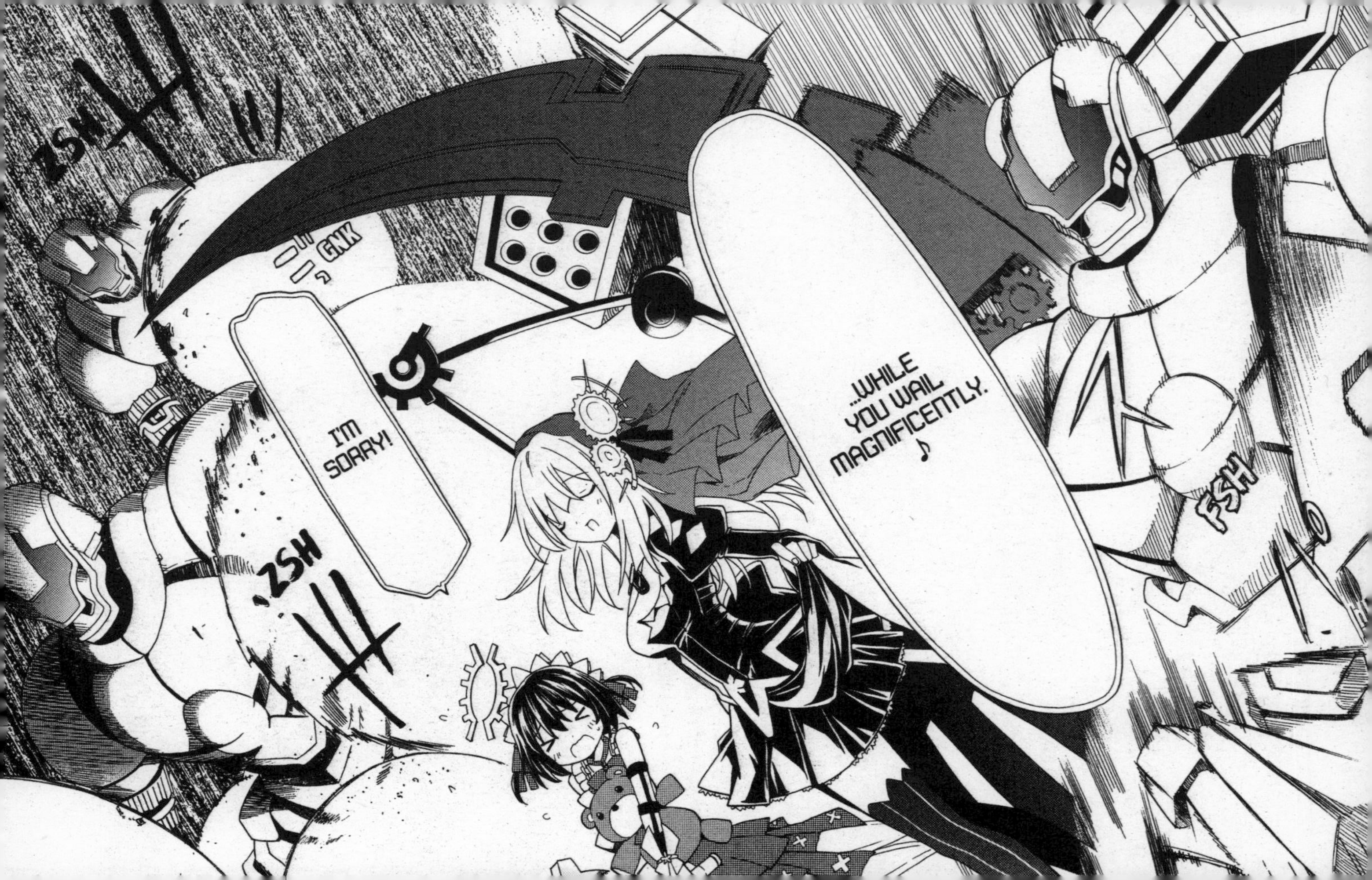
FSH
...WHILE YOU WAIL MAGNIFICENTLY. ♪
GNK
ZSH
I'M SORRY!
ZSH

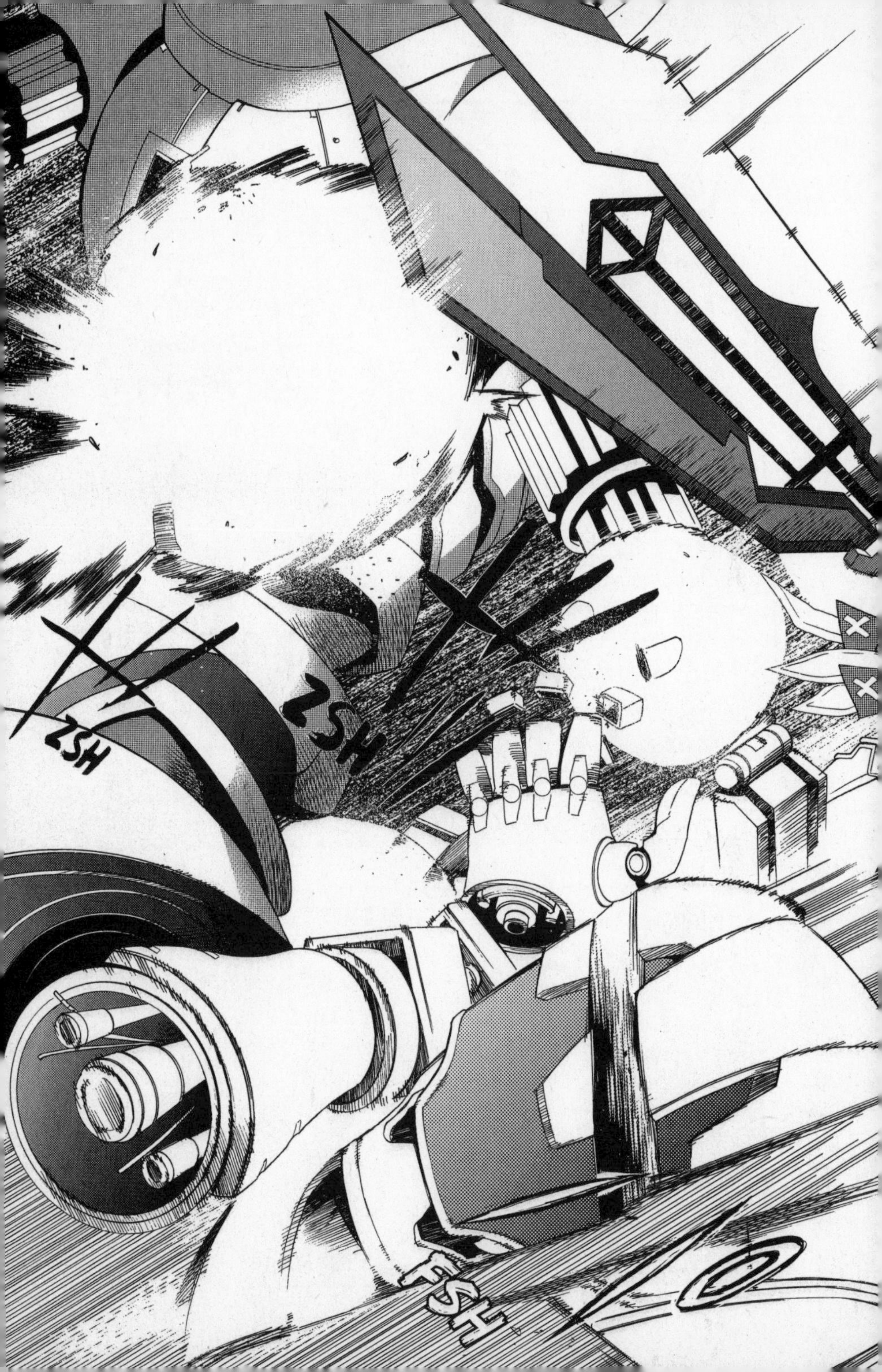
ZSH
ZSH
FSH

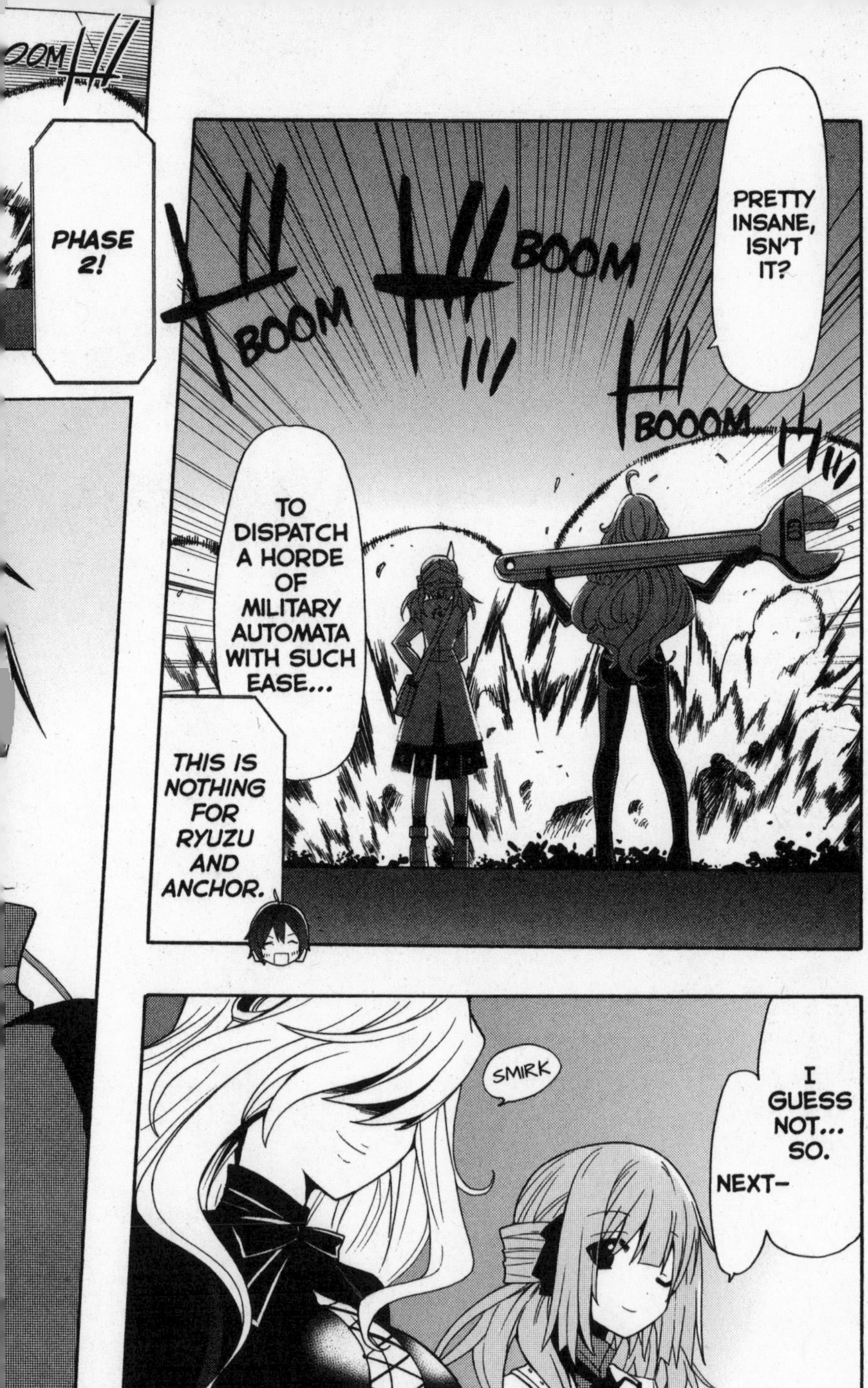
PRETTY INSANE, ISN'T IT?
BOOM
BOOM
BOOOM
TO DISPATCH A HORDE OF MILITARY AUTOMATA WITH SUCH EASE...
THIS IS NOTHING FOR RYUZU AND ANCHOR.
I GUESS NOT... SO.
NEXT–
SMIRK
OOM
PHASE 2!

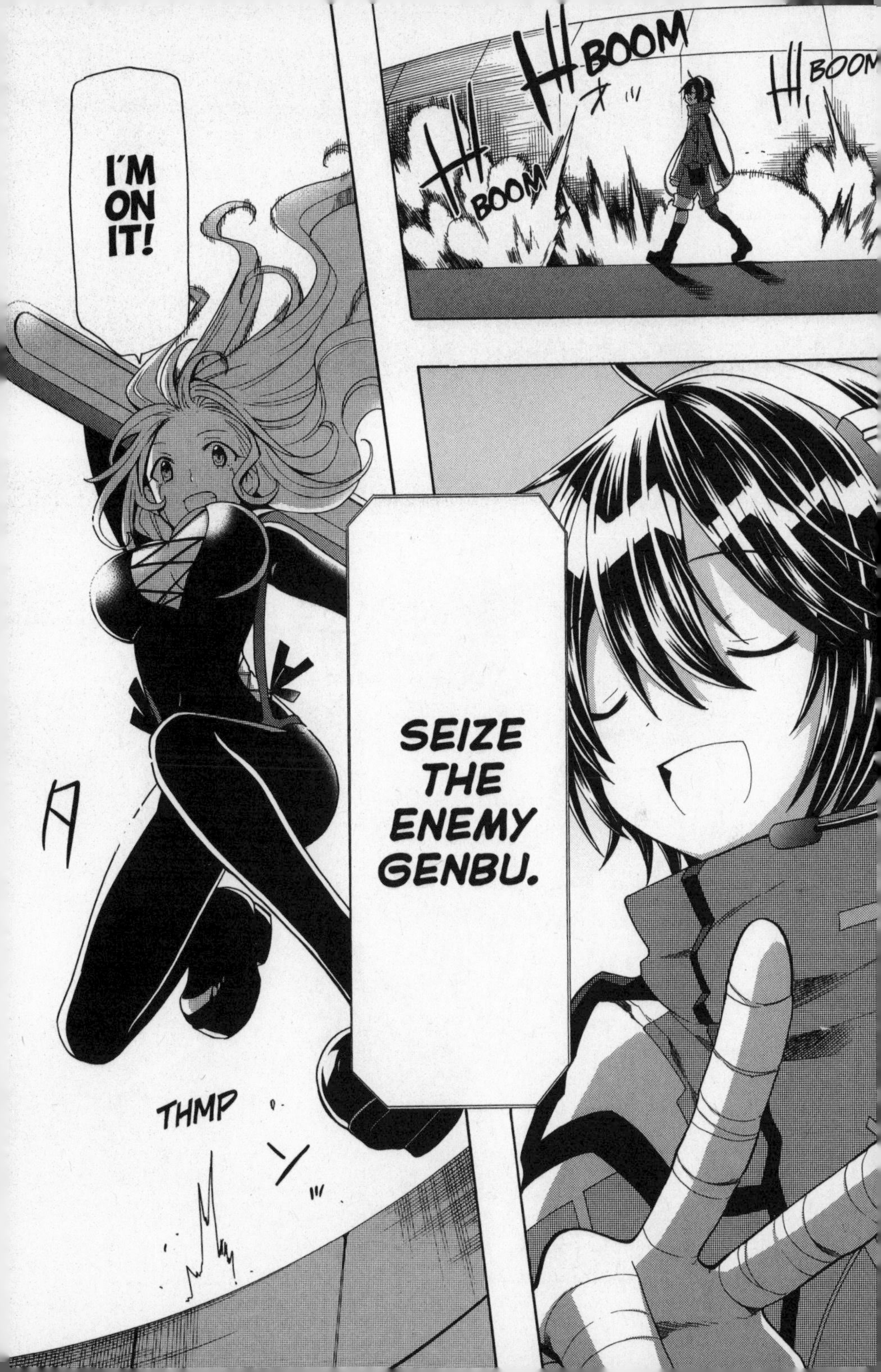
BOOM
BOOM
BOOM
SEIZE THE ENEMY GENBU.
I'M ON IT!
THMP

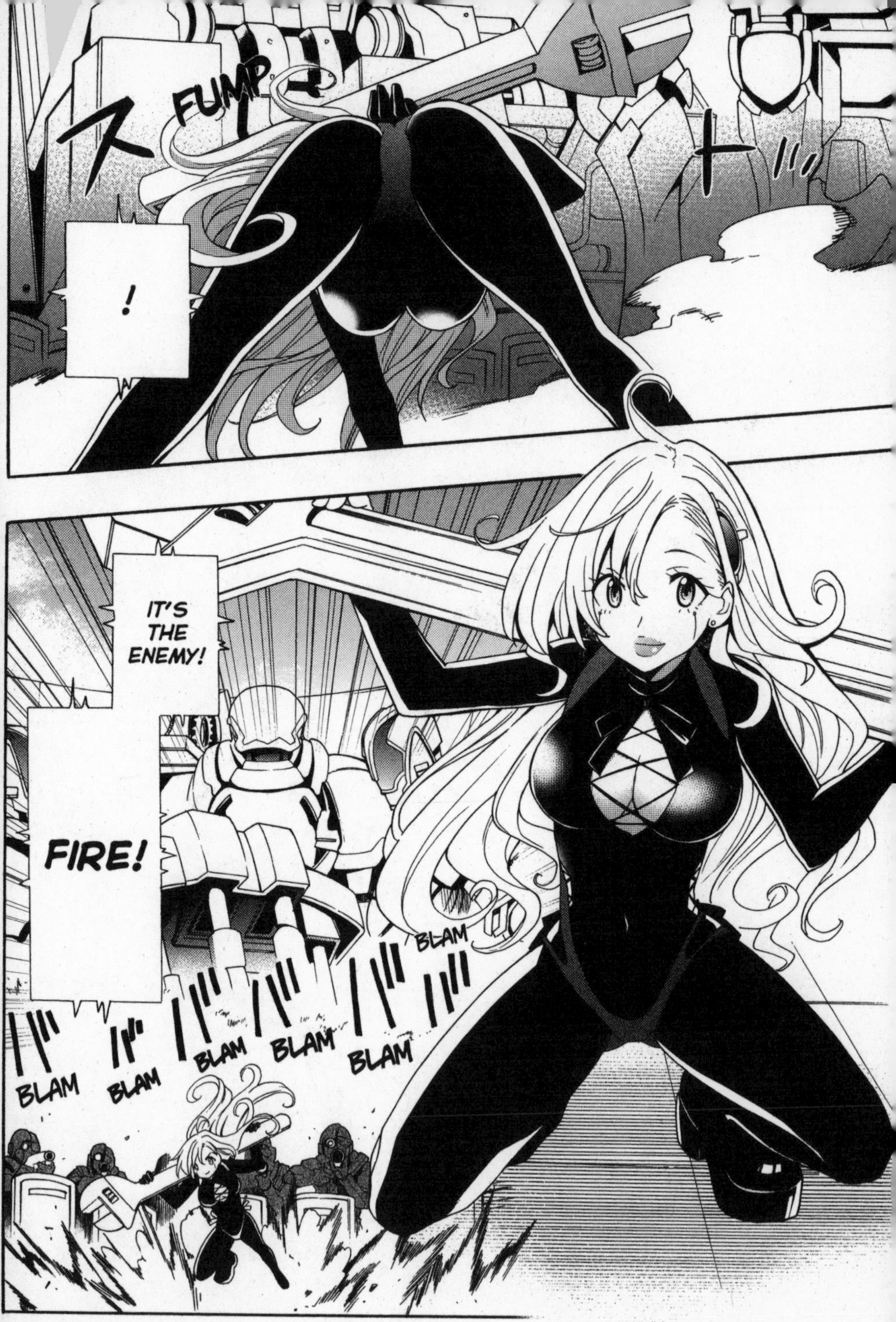

FUMP
!
IT'S THE ENEMY!
FIRE!
BLAM
BLAM
BLAM
BLAM
BLAM
BLAM

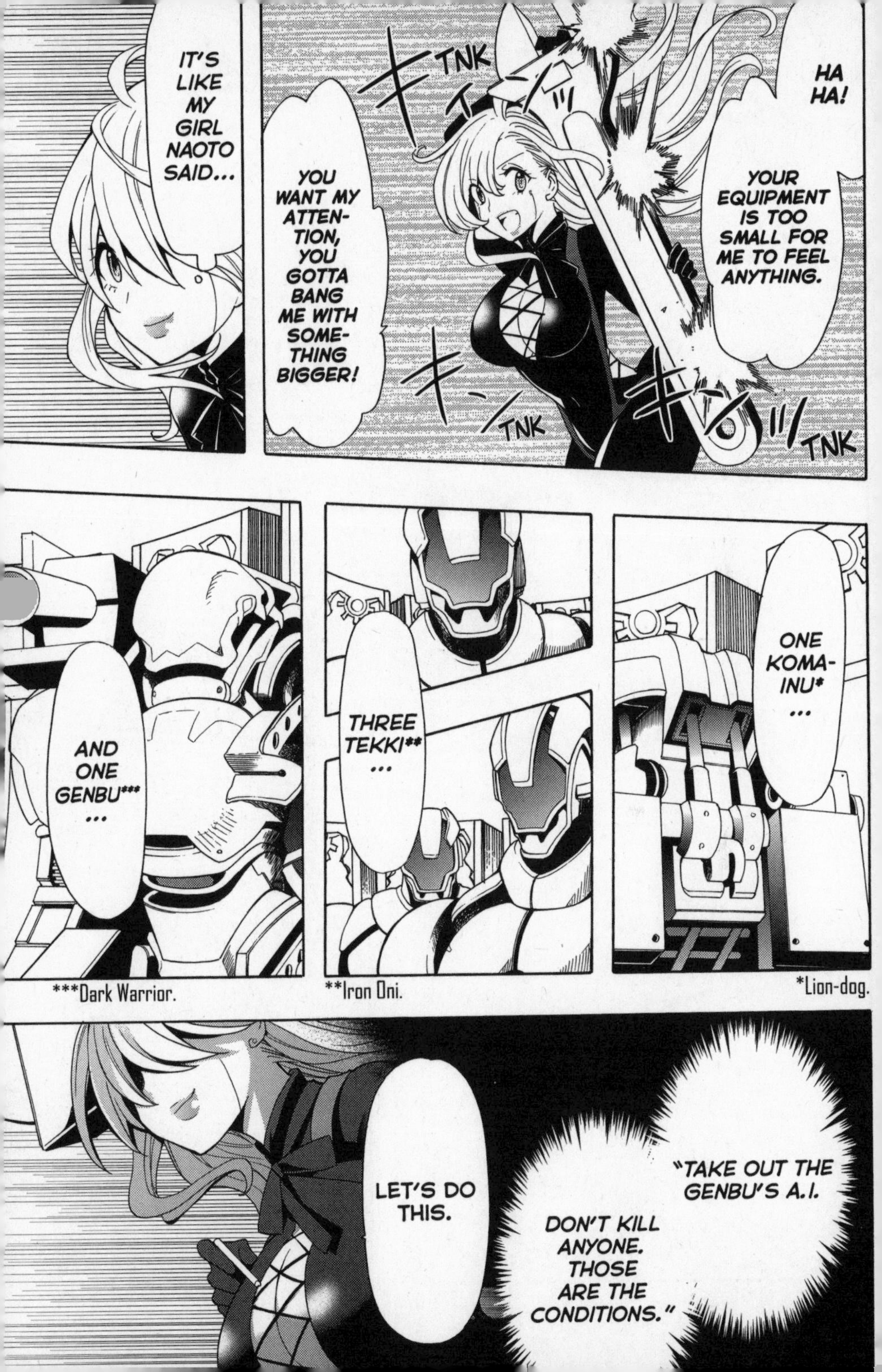
HA HA!
YOUR EQUIPMENT IS TOO SMALL FOR ME TO FEEL ANYTHING.
TNK
TNK
TNK
YOU WANT MY ATTEN-TION, YOU GOTTA BANG ME WITH SOME-THING BIGGER!
IT'S LIKE MY GIRL NAOTO SAID...
ONE KOMA-INU* ...
THREE TEKKI** ...
AND ONE GENBU*** ...
"TAKE OUT THE GENBU'S A.I.
DON'T KILL ANYONE. THOSE ARE THE CONDITIONS."
LET'S DO THIS.

*Lion-dog.

**Iron Oni.

***Dark Warrior.

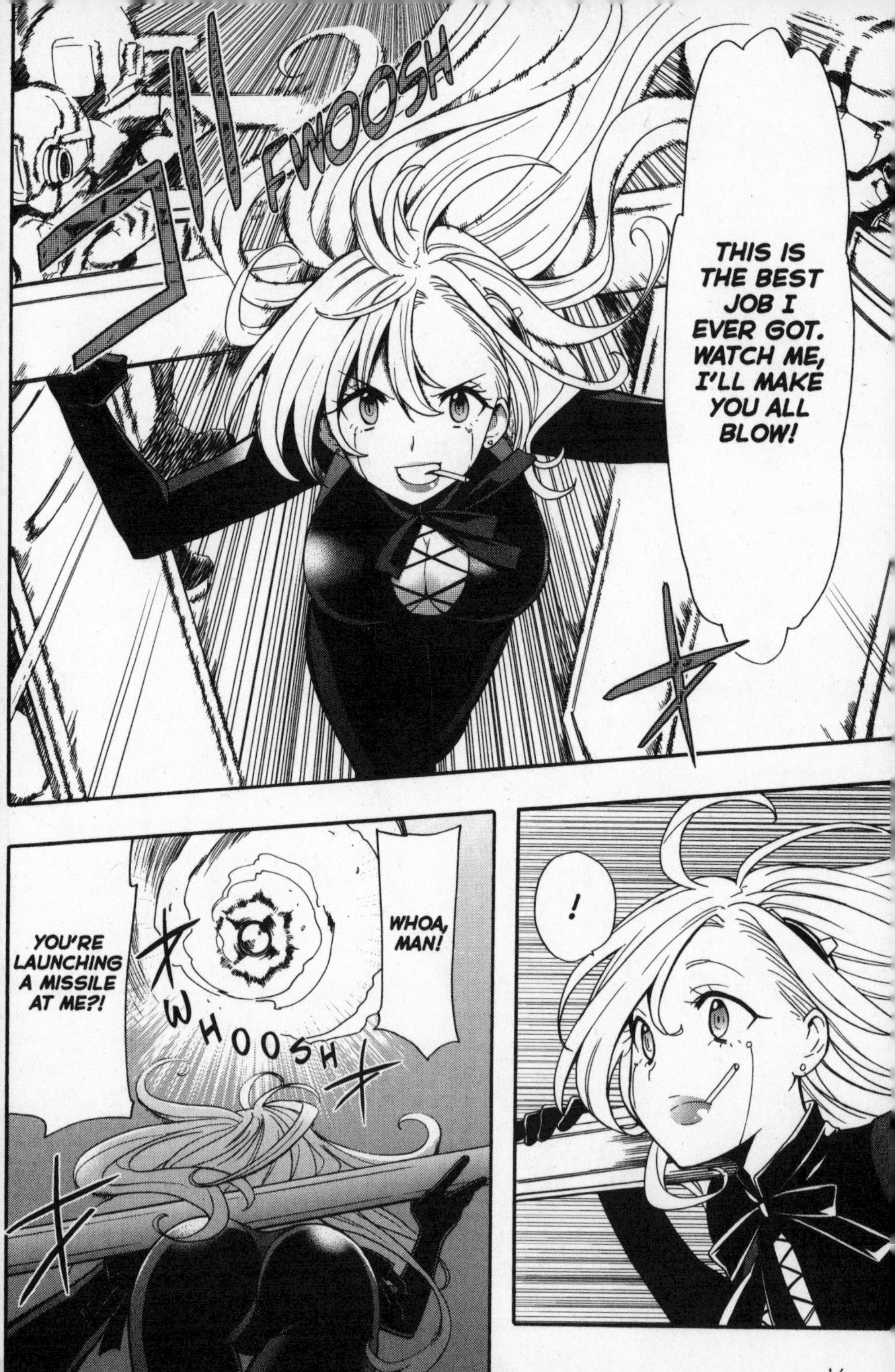
THIS IS THE BEST JOB I EVER GOT. WATCH ME, I'LL MAKE YOU ALL BLOW!
FWOOSH
!
WHOA, MAN!
YOU'RE LAUNCHING A MISSILE AT ME?!
WHOOSH

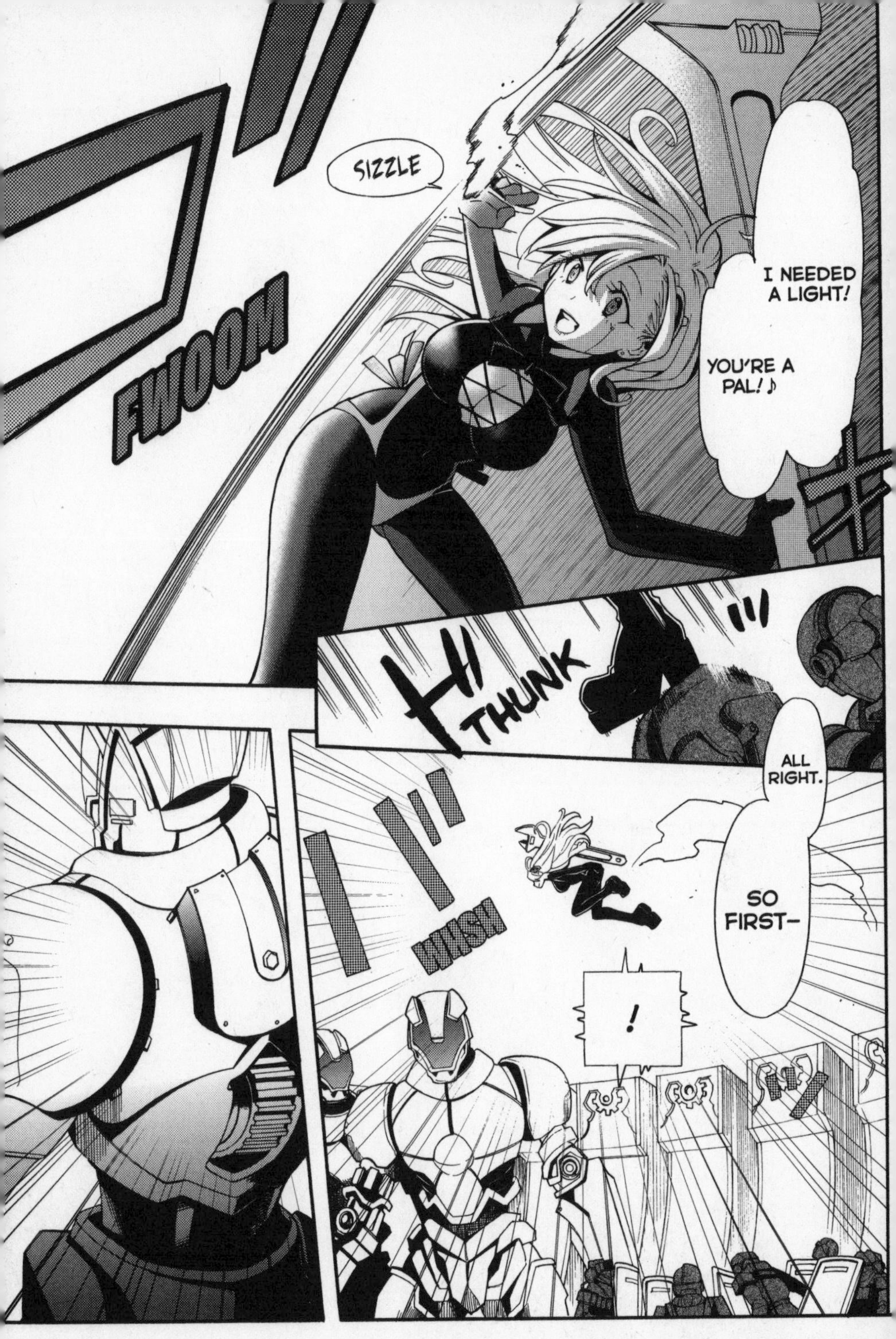
I NEEDED A LIGHT!
YOU'RE A PAL!♪
SIZZLE
FWOOM
THUNK
ALL RIGHT.
SO FIRST–
WHSH
!

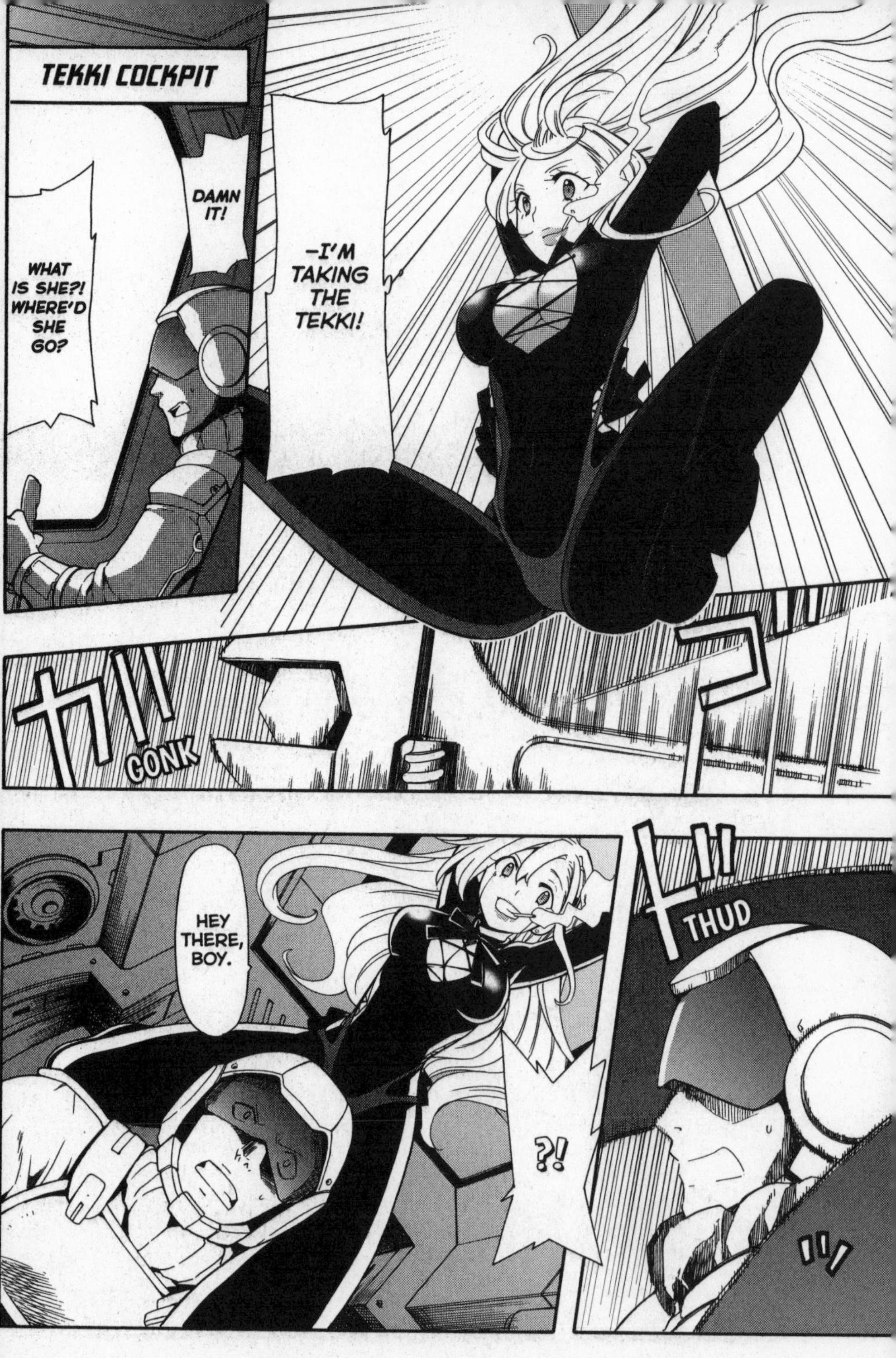
—I'M TAKING THE TEKKI!
TEKKI COCKPIT
DAMN IT!
WHAT IS SHE?! WHERE'D SHE GO?
コッ
カッ
GONK
ドッ
THUD
?!
HEY THERE, BOY.

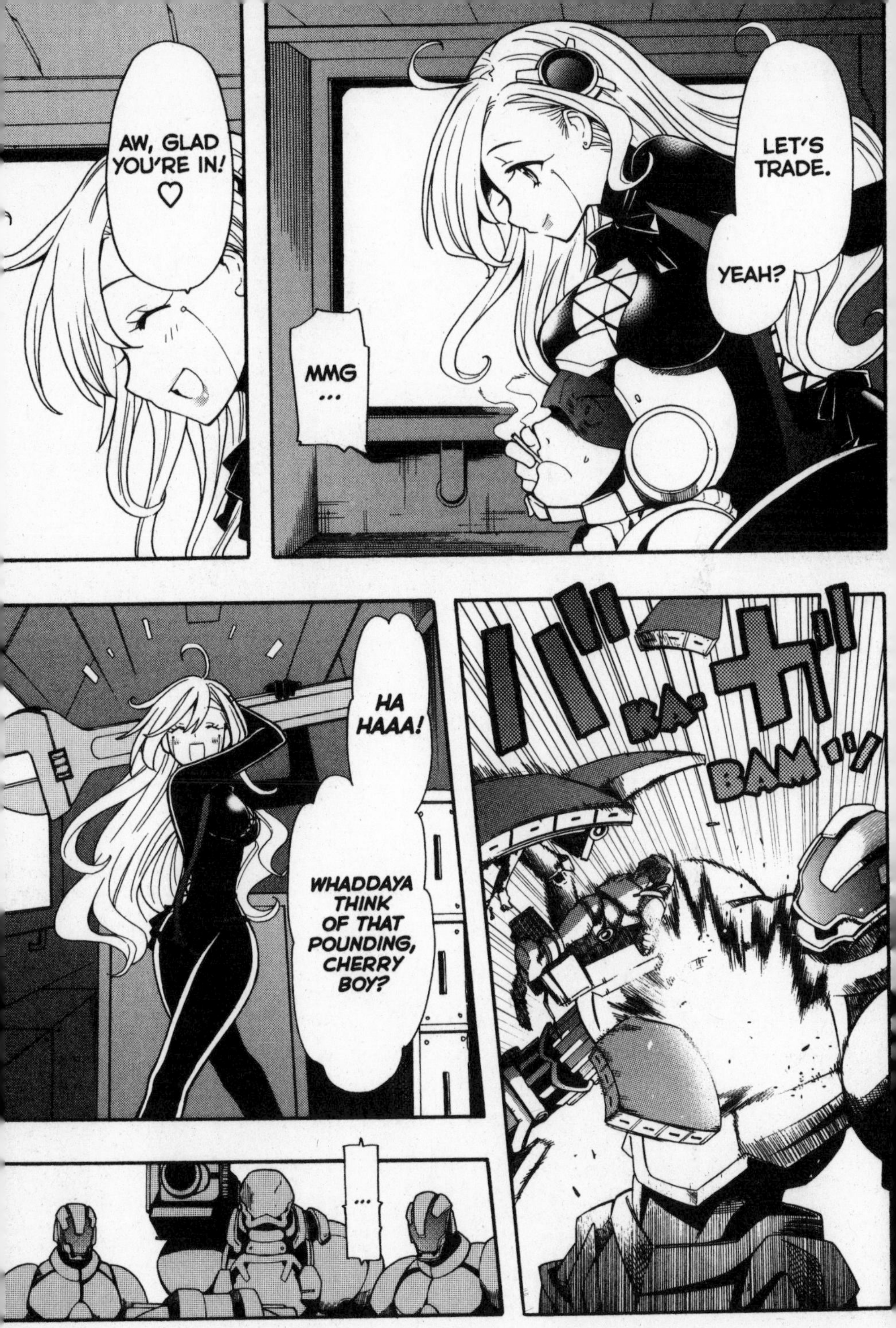
LET'S TRADE.
YEAH?
MMG ...
AW, GLAD YOU'RE IN! ♡
KA- BAM!!
HA HAAA!
WHADDAYA THINK OF THAT POUNDING, CHERRY BOY?
...

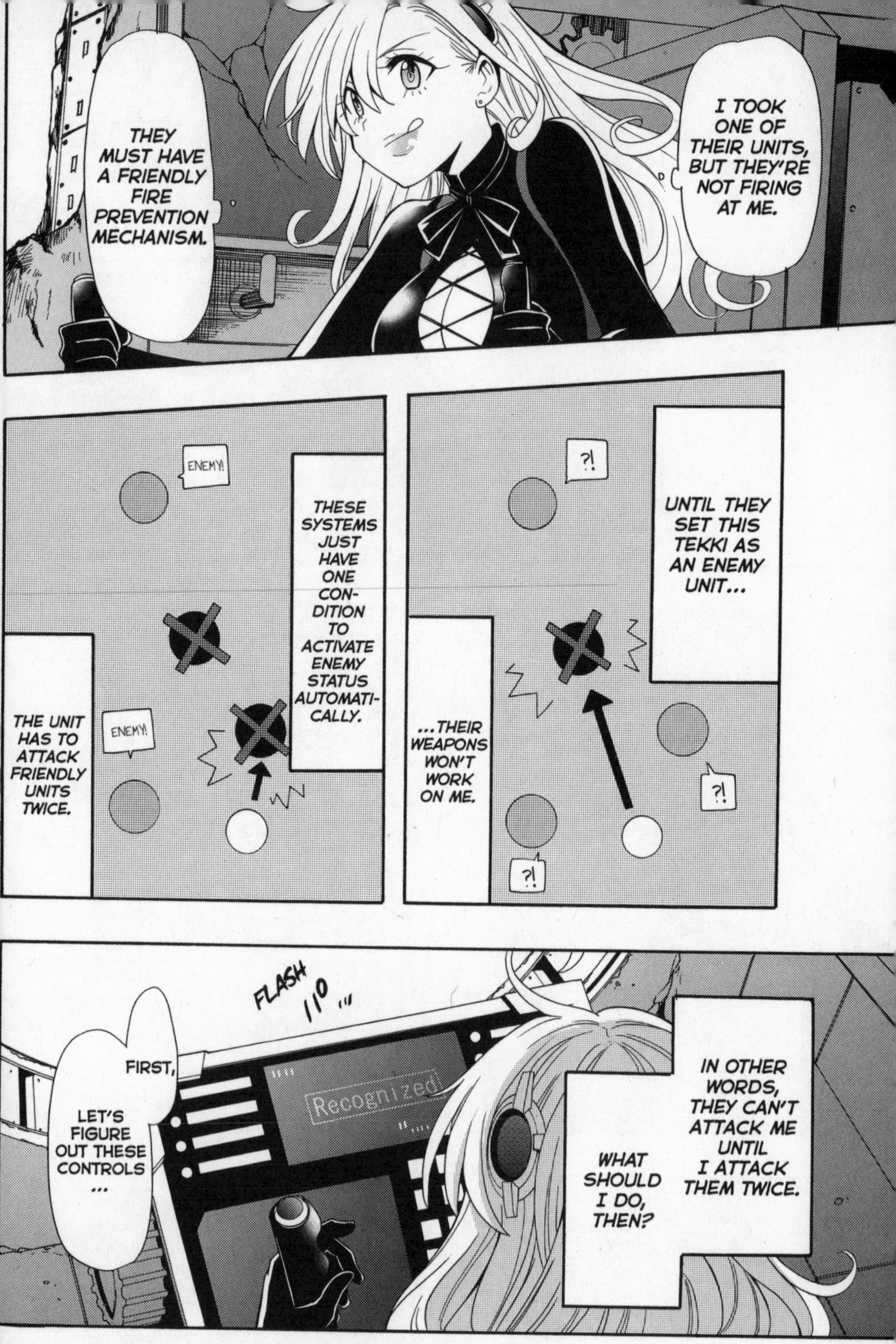
I TOOK ONE OF THEIR UNITS, BUT THEY'RE NOT FIRING AT ME.
THEY MUST HAVE A FRIENDLY FIRE PREVENTION MECHANISM.
UNTIL THEY SET THIS TEKKI AS AN ENEMY UNIT...
?!
?!
?!
...THEIR WEAPONS WON'T WORK ON ME.
ENEMY!
THESE SYSTEMS JUST HAVE ONE CON-DITION TO ACTIVATE ENEMY STATUS AUTOMATI-CALLY.
ENEMY!
THE UNIT HAS TO ATTACK FRIENDLY UNITS TWICE.
IN OTHER WORDS, THEY CAN'T ATTACK ME UNTIL I ATTACK THEM TWICE.
WHAT SHOULD I DO, THEN?
FLASH
Recognized
FIRST,
LET'S FIGURE OUT THESE CONTROLS ...

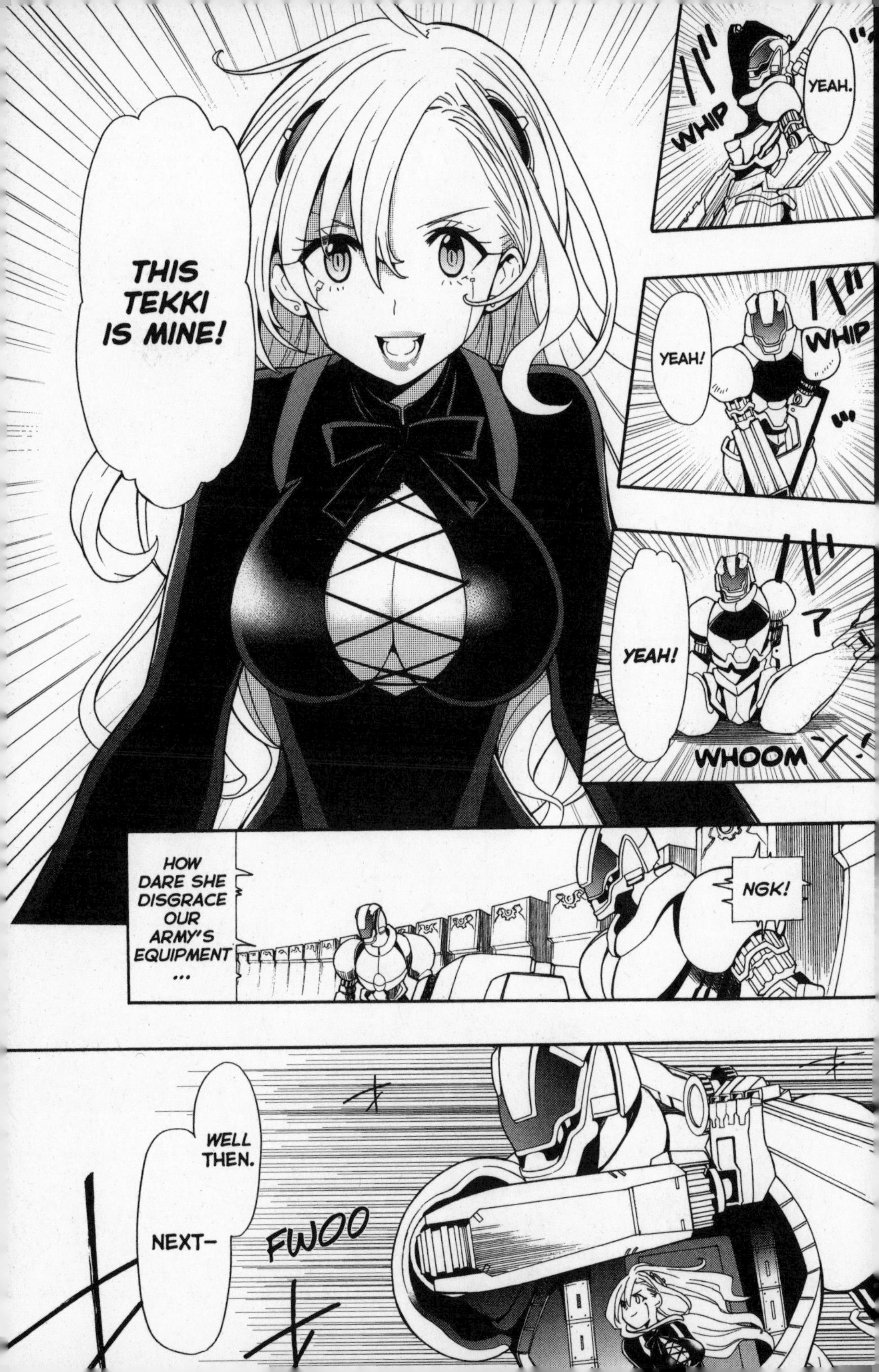
YEAH.
WHIP
YEAH!
WHIP
YEAH!
WHOOM
THIS TEKKI IS MINE!
NGK!
HOW DARE SHE DISGRACE OUR ARMY'S EQUIPMENT ...
WELL THEN.
NEXT–
FWOO

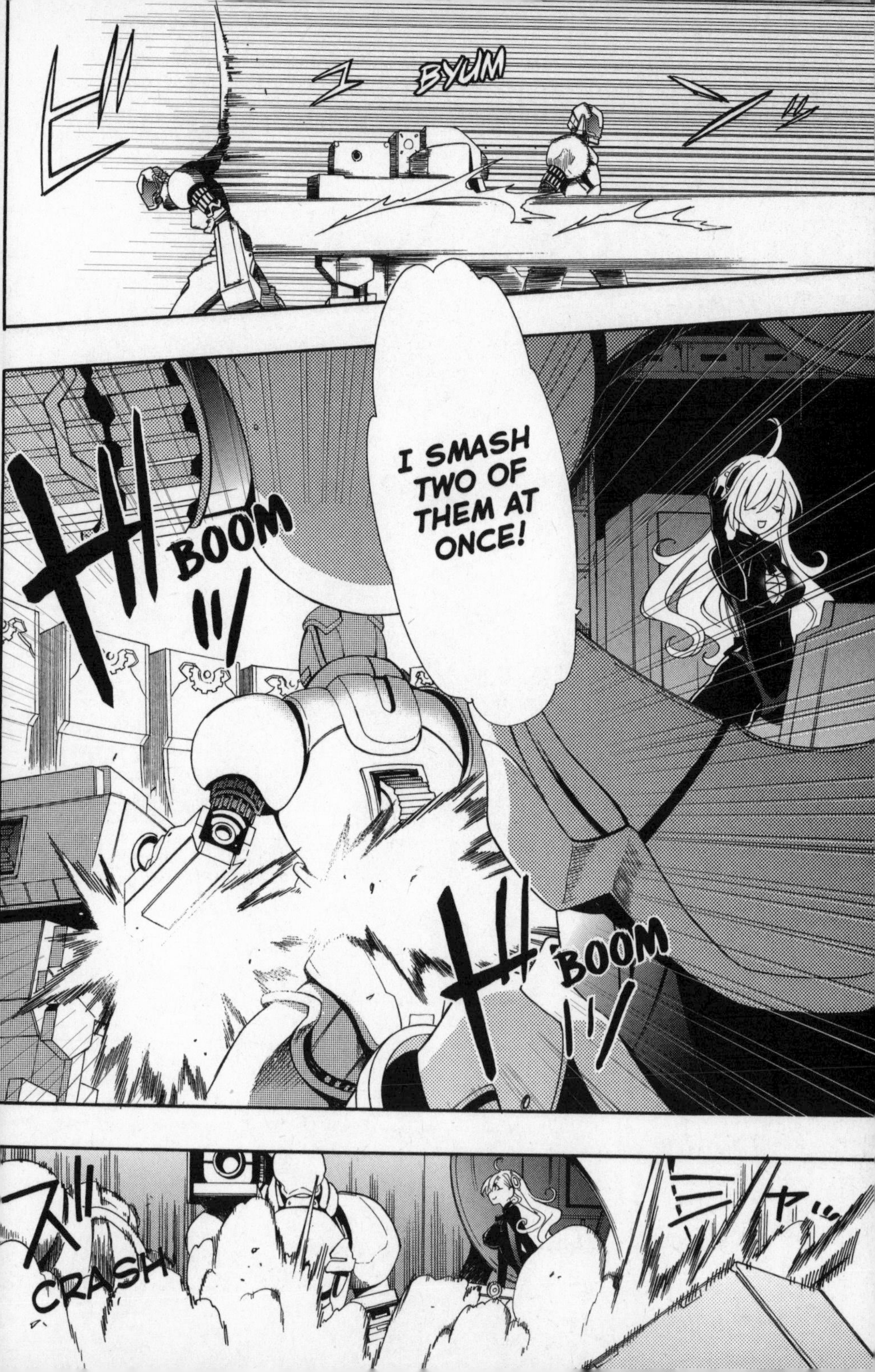
BYUM
I SMASH TWO OF THEM AT ONCE!
BOOM
BOOM
CRASH

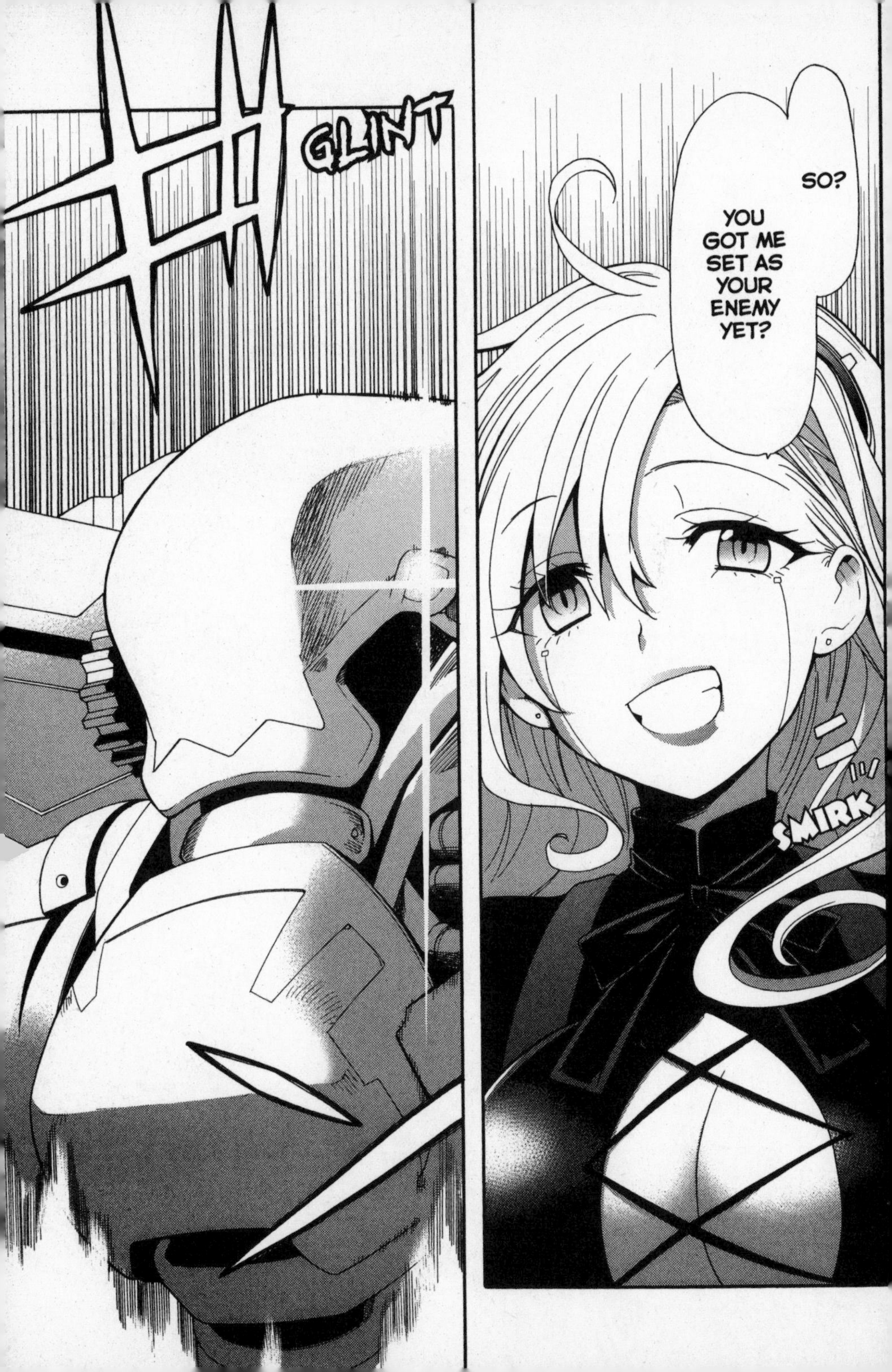
SO?
YOU GOT ME SET AS YOUR ENEMY YET?
SMIRK
GLINT

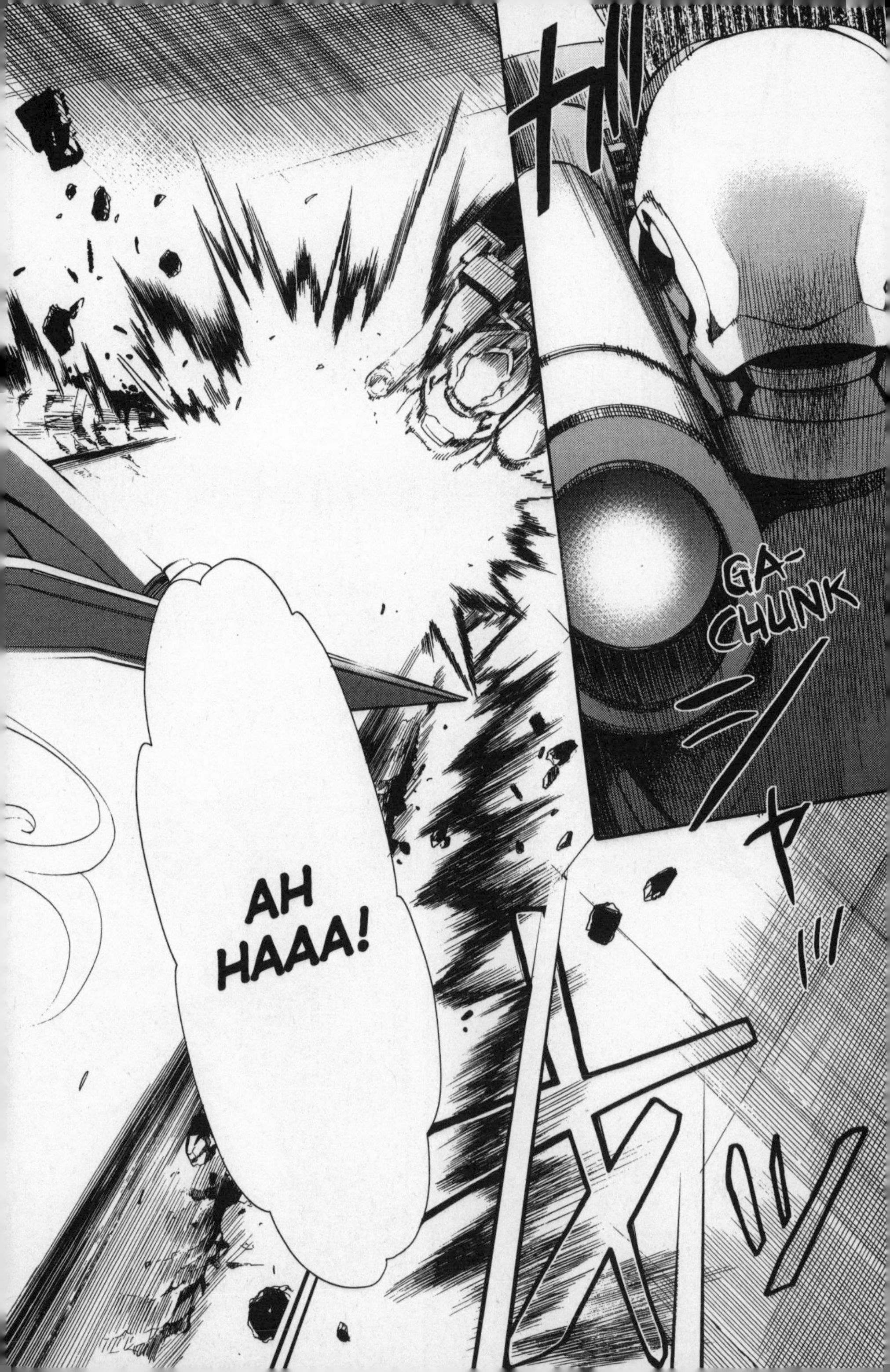
GA-
CHUNK
AH
HAAA!

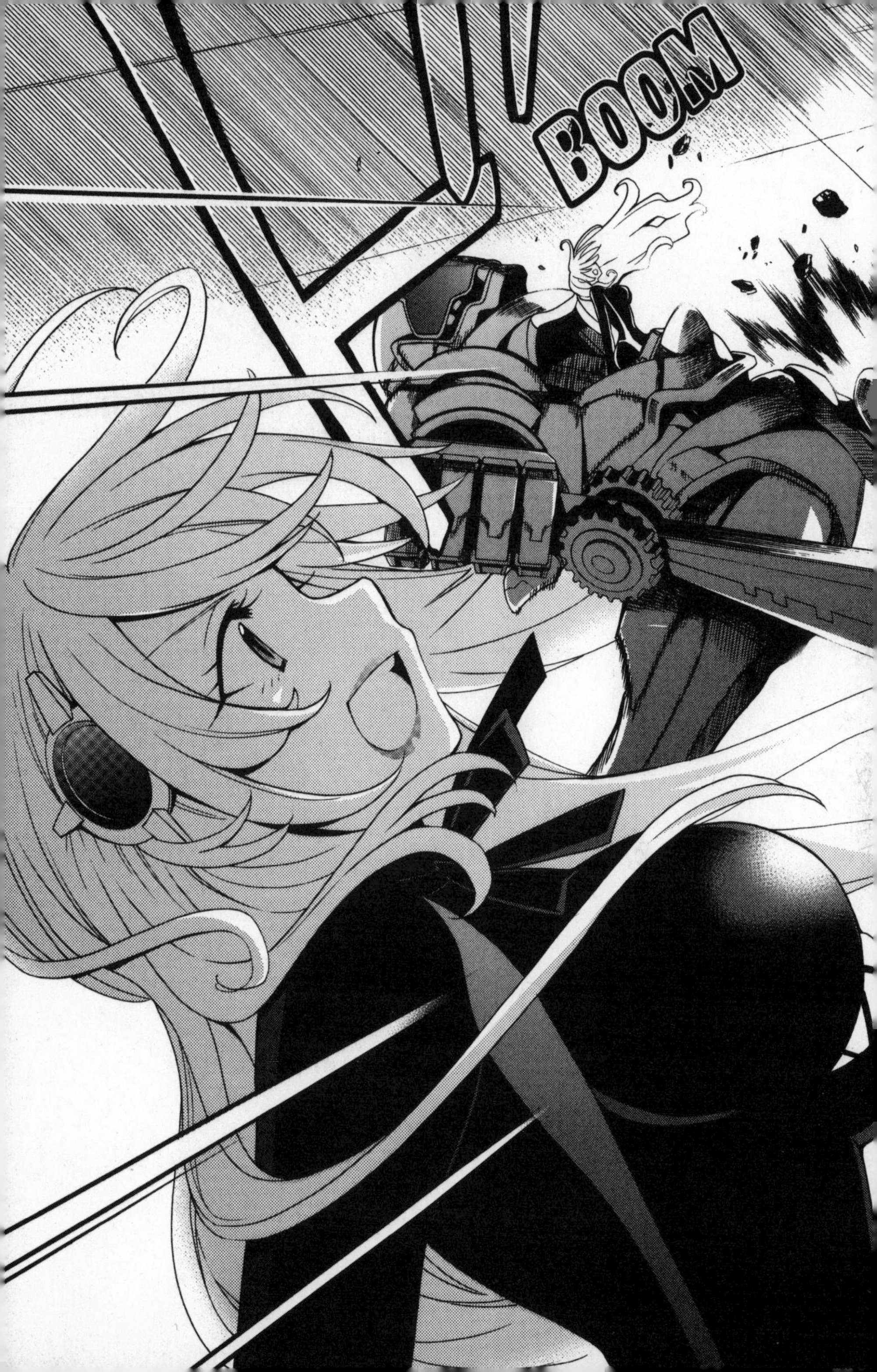
BOOM

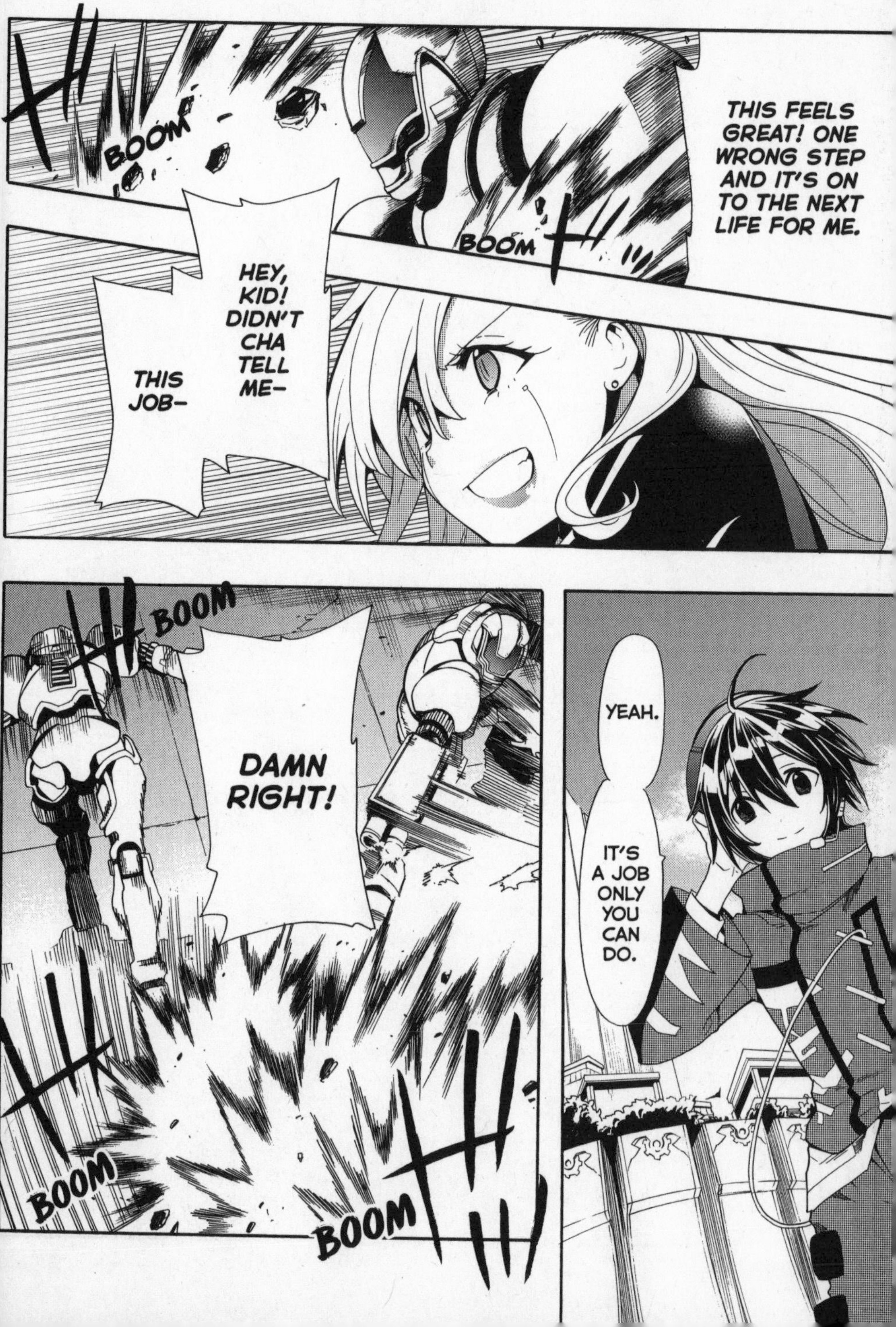
THIS FEELS GREAT! ONE WRONG STEP AND IT'S ON TO THE NEXT LIFE FOR ME.
BOOM
BOOM
HEY, KID! DIDN'T CHA TELL ME–
THIS JOB–
YEAH.
IT'S A JOB ONLY YOU CAN DO.
BOOM
DAMN RIGHT!
BOOM
BOOM

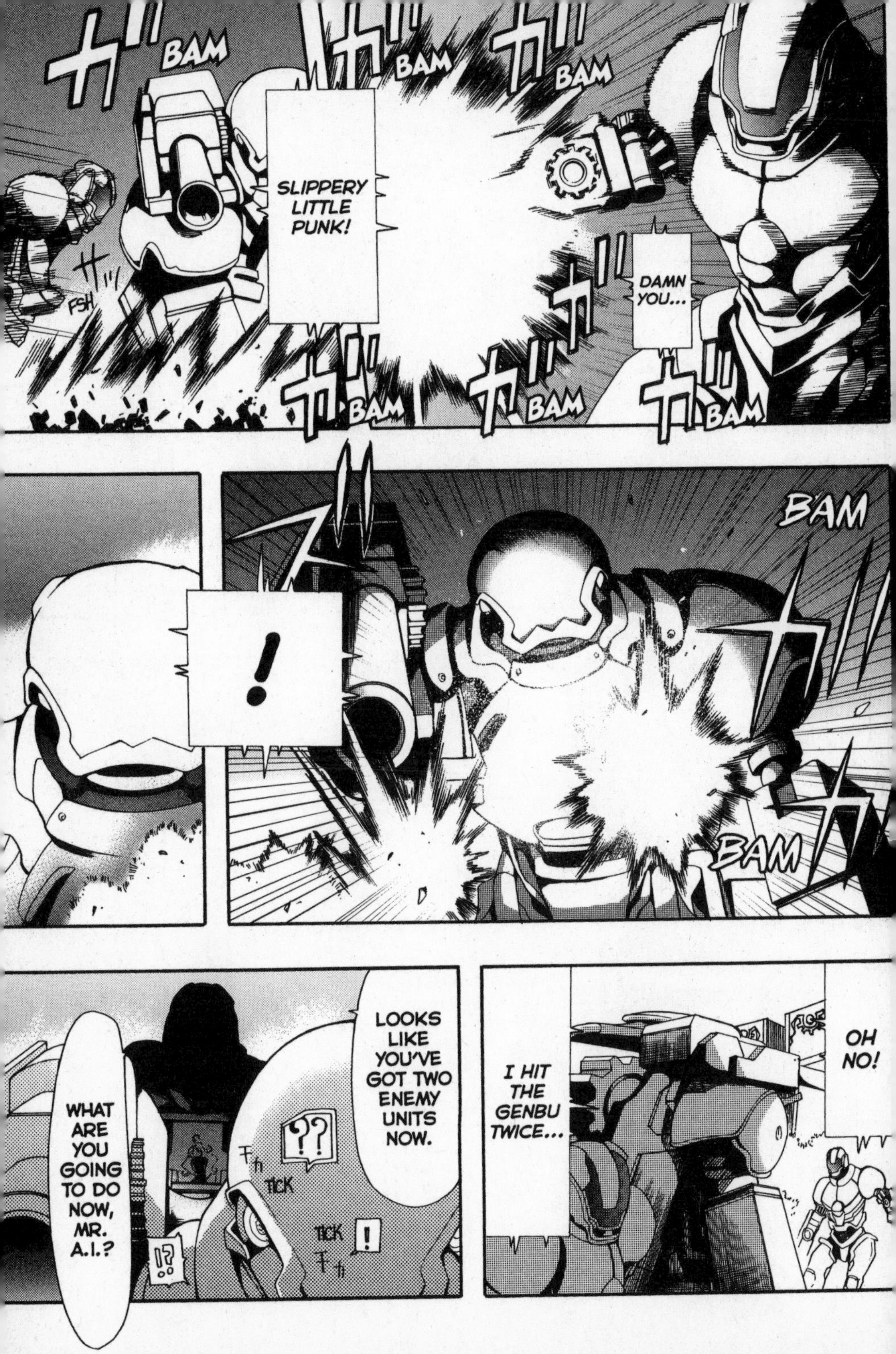
BAM
BAM
DAMN YOU...
SLIPPERY LITTLE PUNK!
BAM
FSH
BAM
BAM
BAM
BAM
!
BAM
OH NO!
I HIT THE GENBU TWICE...
LOOKS LIKE YOU'VE GOT TWO ENEMY UNITS NOW.
??
TICK
!
TICK
WHAT ARE YOU GOING TO DO NOW, MR. A.I.?
!?

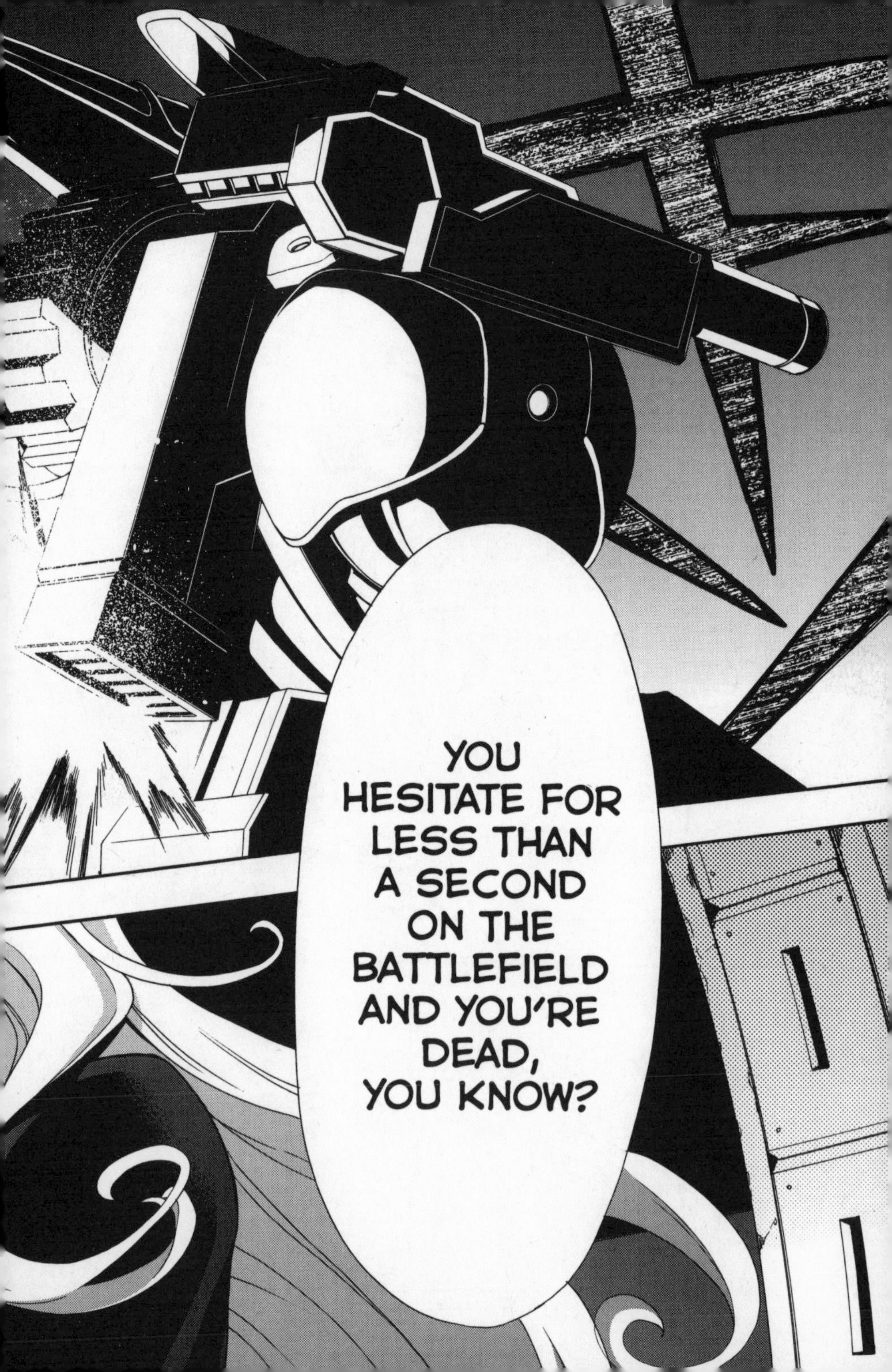
YOU HESITATE FOR LESS THAN A SECOND ON THE BATTLEFIELD AND YOU'RE DEAD, YOU KNOW?

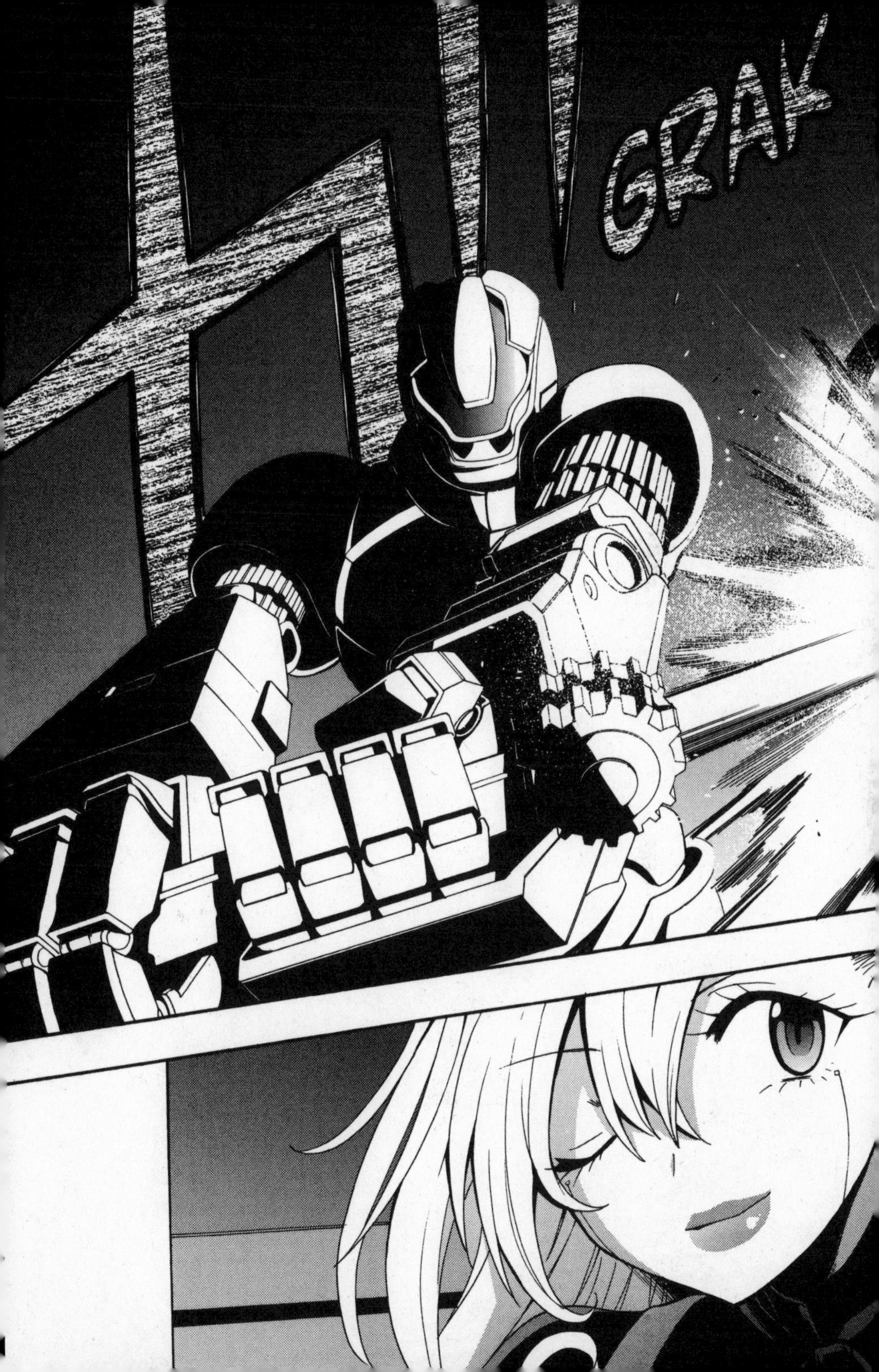
GRAK

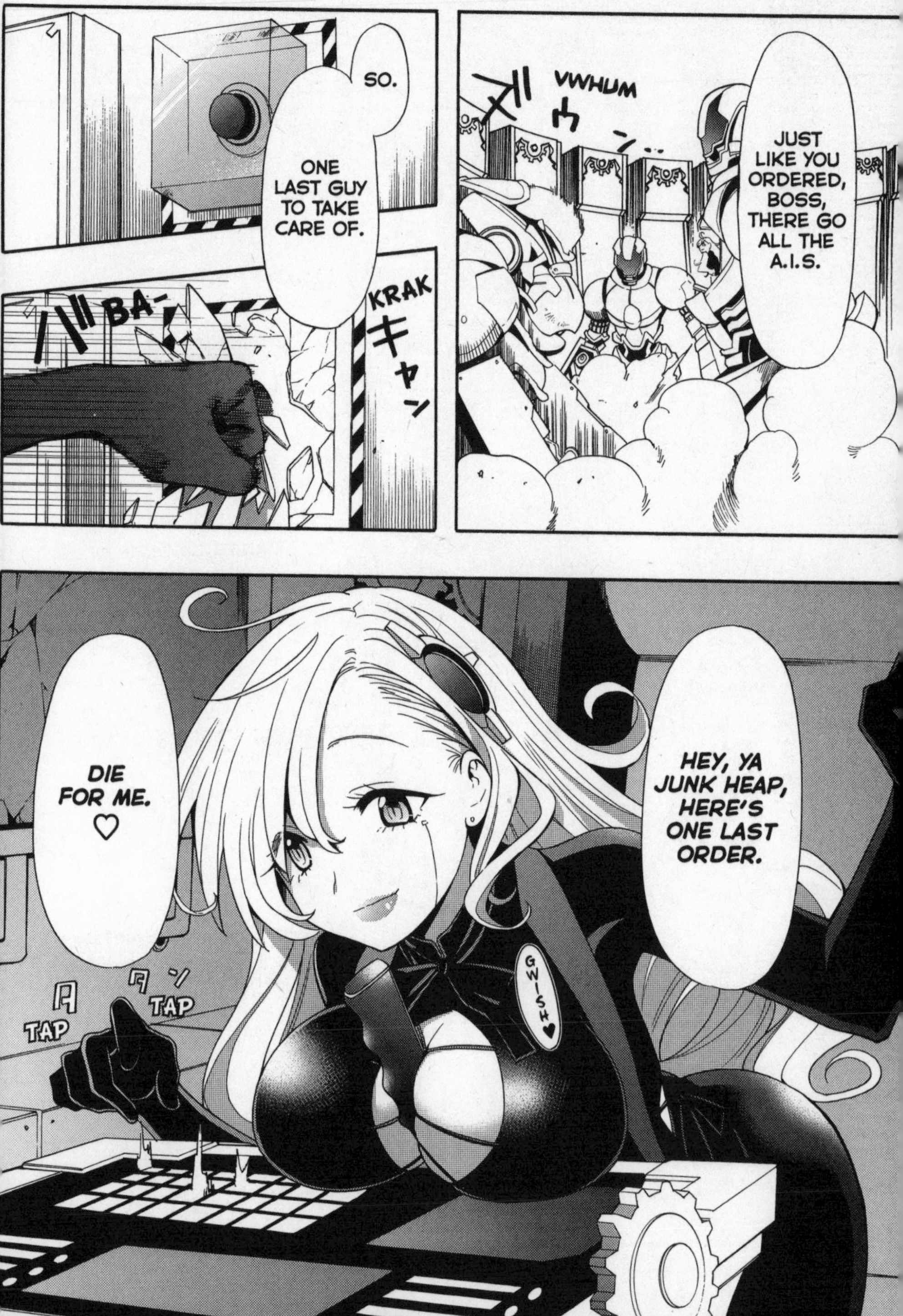
VWHUM
JUST LIKE YOU ORDERED, BOSS, THERE GO ALL THE A.I.S.
SO.
ONE LAST GUY TO TAKE CARE OF.
KRAK
BA-
HEY, YA JUNK HEAP, HERE'S ONE LAST ORDER.
GWISH♥
DIE FOR ME. ♡
TAP
TAP

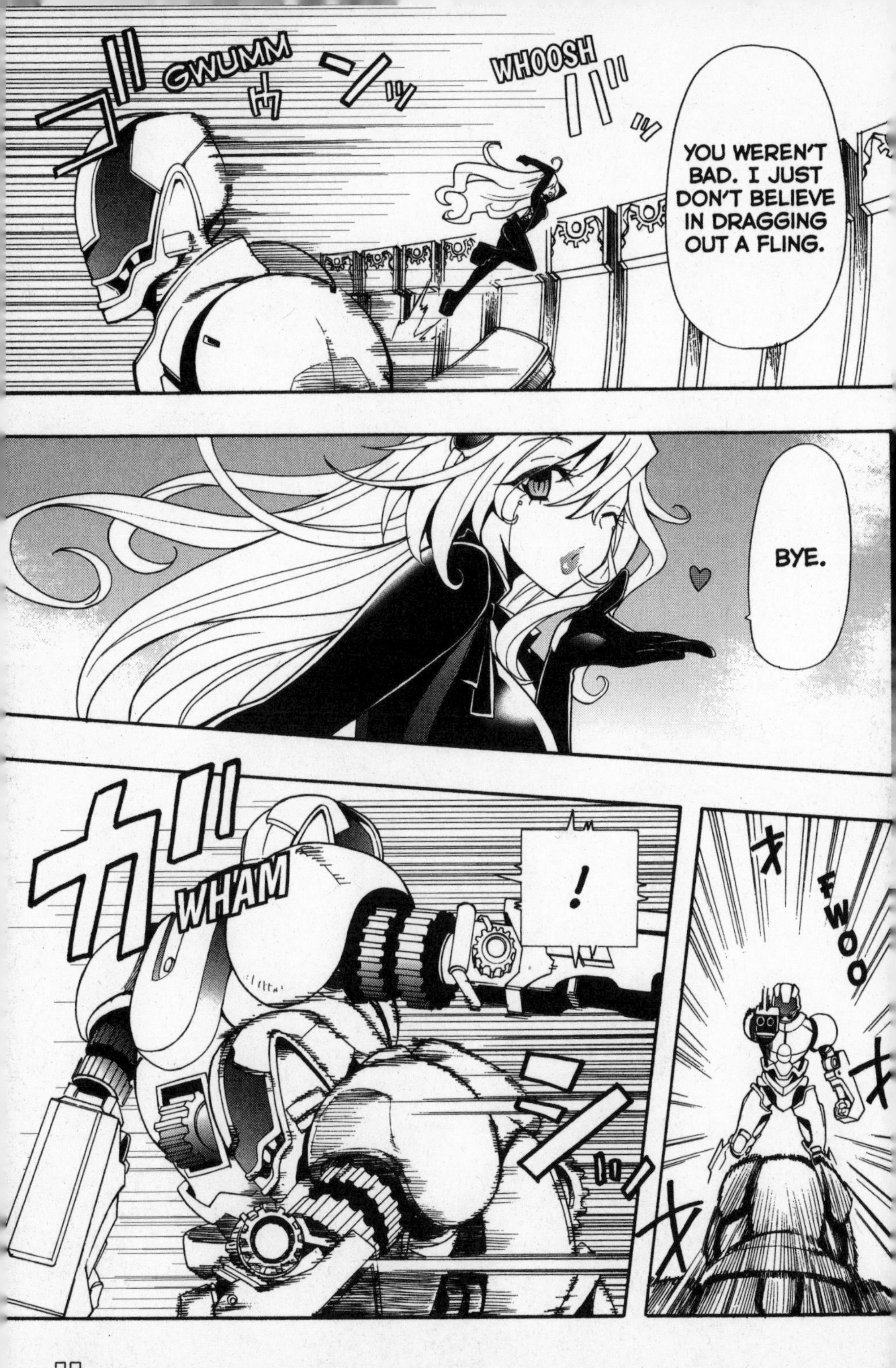
YOU WEREN'T BAD. I JUST DON'T BELIEVE IN DRAGGING OUT A FLING.
WHOOSH
GWUMM
BYE.
FWOO
!
WHAM

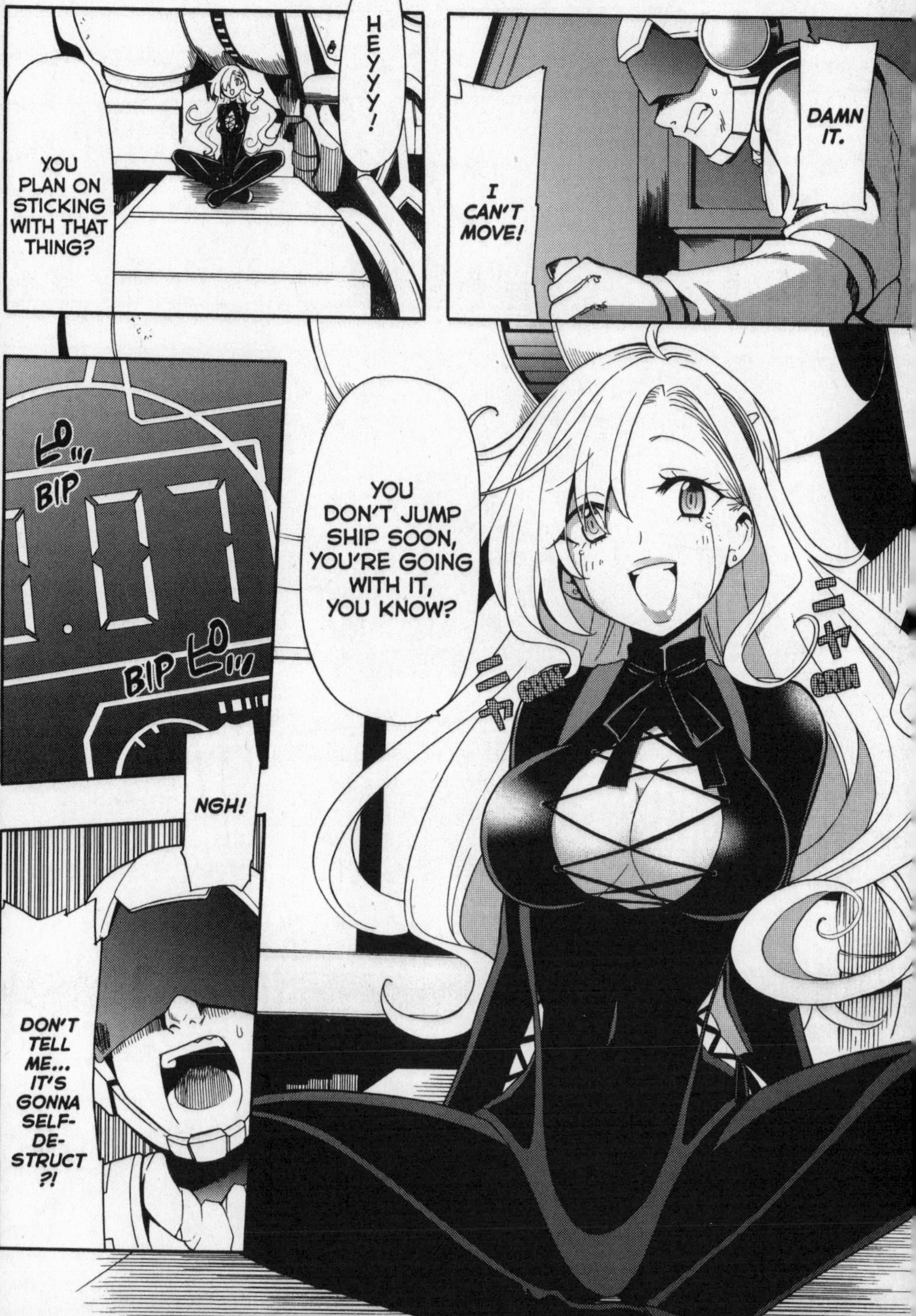
DAMN IT.
I CAN'T MOVE!
HEYYY!
YOU PLAN ON STICKING WITH THAT THING?
YOU DON'T JUMP SHIP SOON, YOU'RE GOING WITH IT, YOU KNOW?
GRIN
GRIN
BIP
BIP
NGH!
DON'T TELL ME... IT'S GONNA SELF-DESTRUCT?!

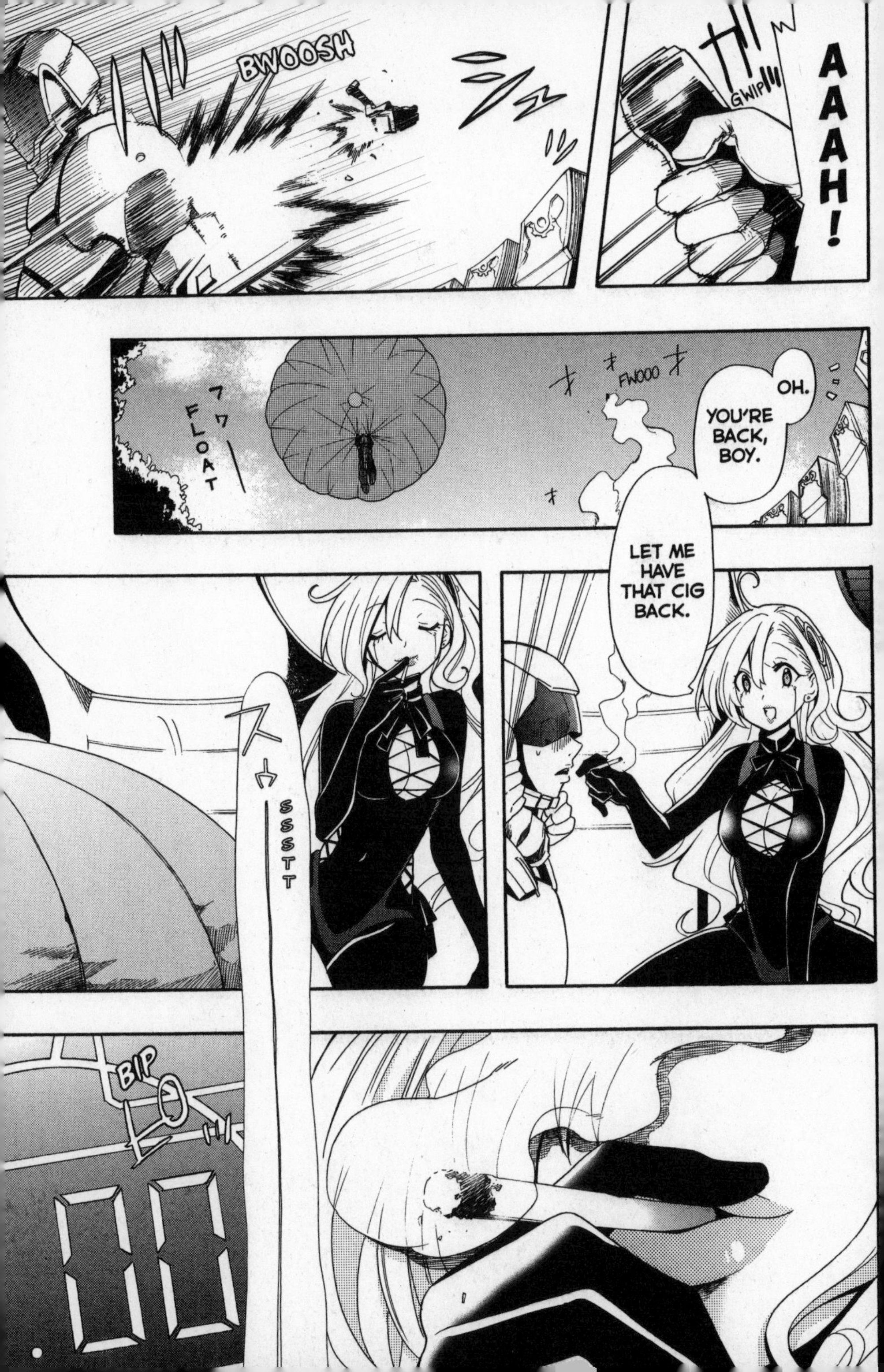
AAAH!
GWIP
BWOOSH
OH.
YOU'RE BACK, BOY.
FWOOO
FLOAT
LET ME HAVE THAT CIG BACK.
SSSTT
BIP

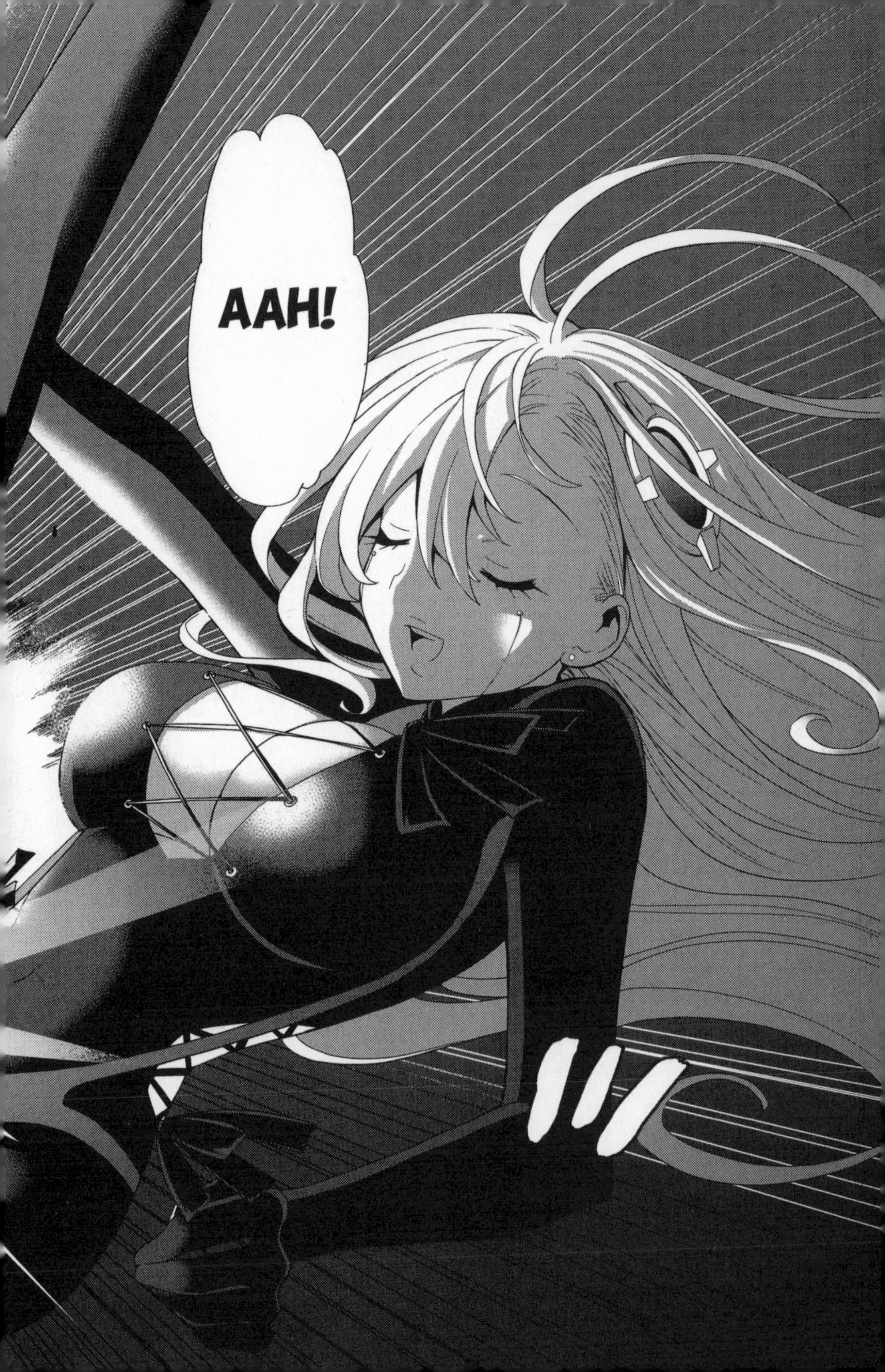
AAH!

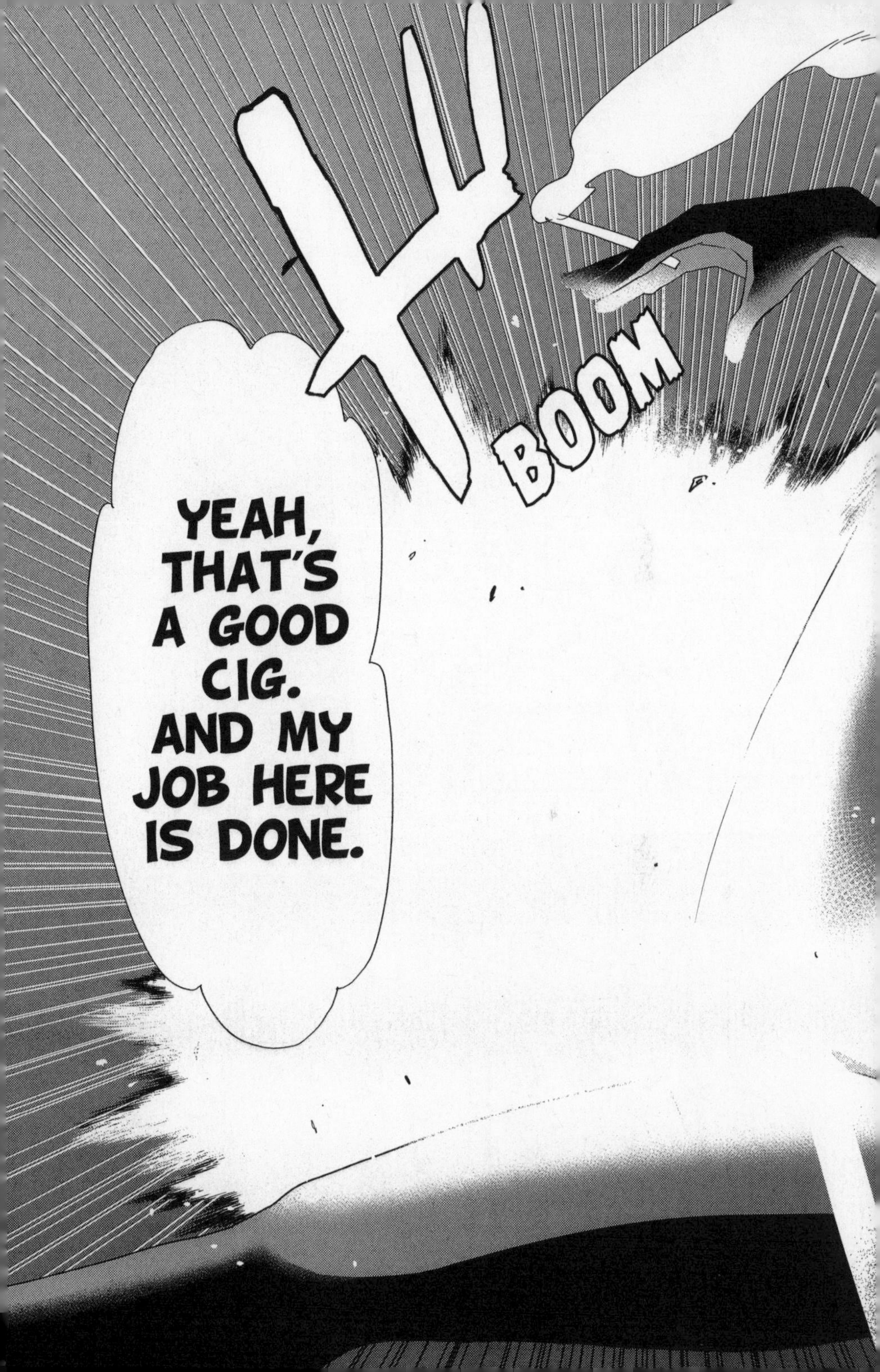
BOOM
YEAH, THAT'S A GOOD CIG. AND MY JOB HERE IS DONE.

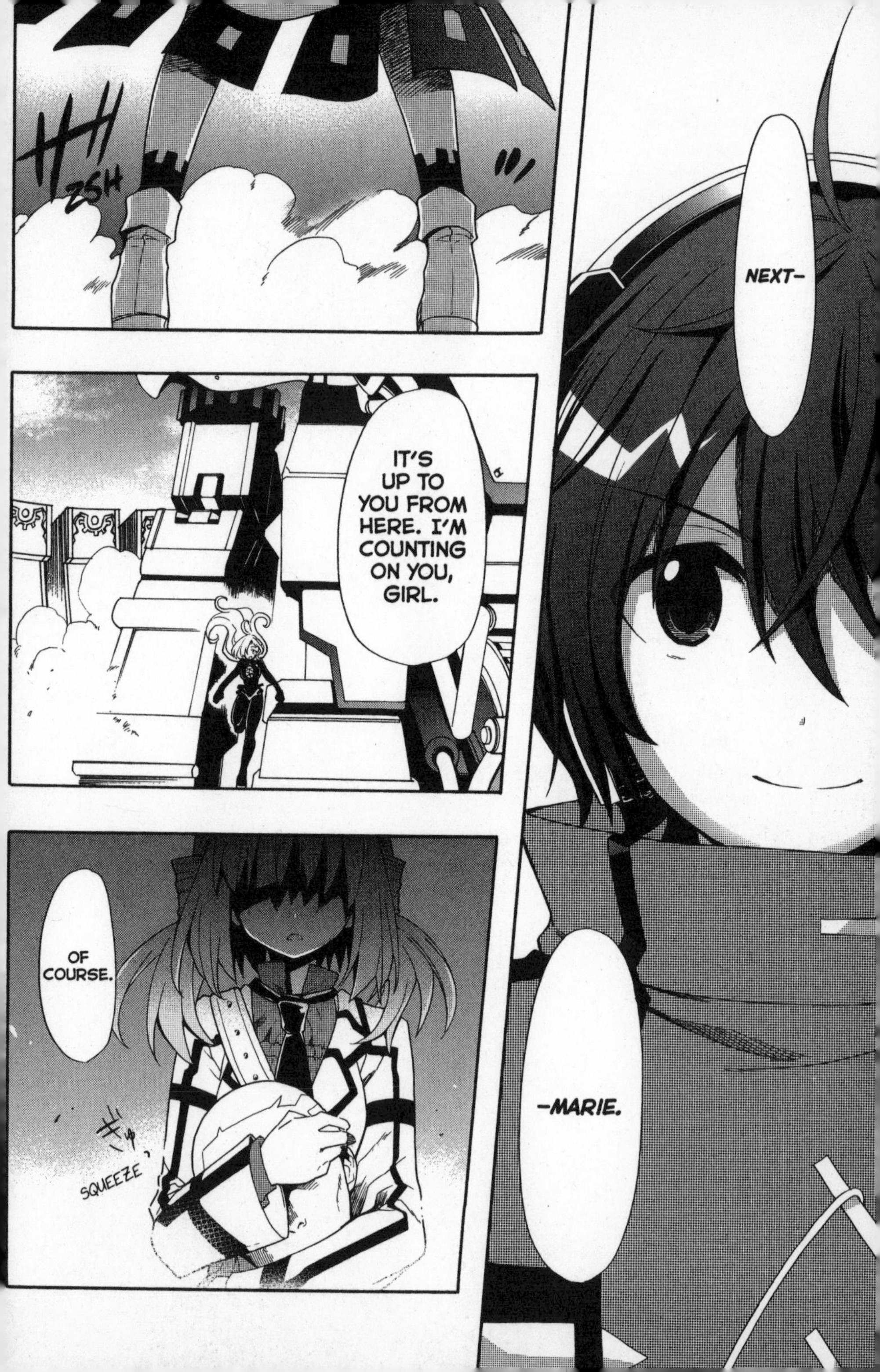
NEXT–
–MARIE.
ZSH
IT'S UP TO YOU FROM HERE. I'M COUNTING ON YOU, GIRL.
OF COURSE.
SQUEEZE

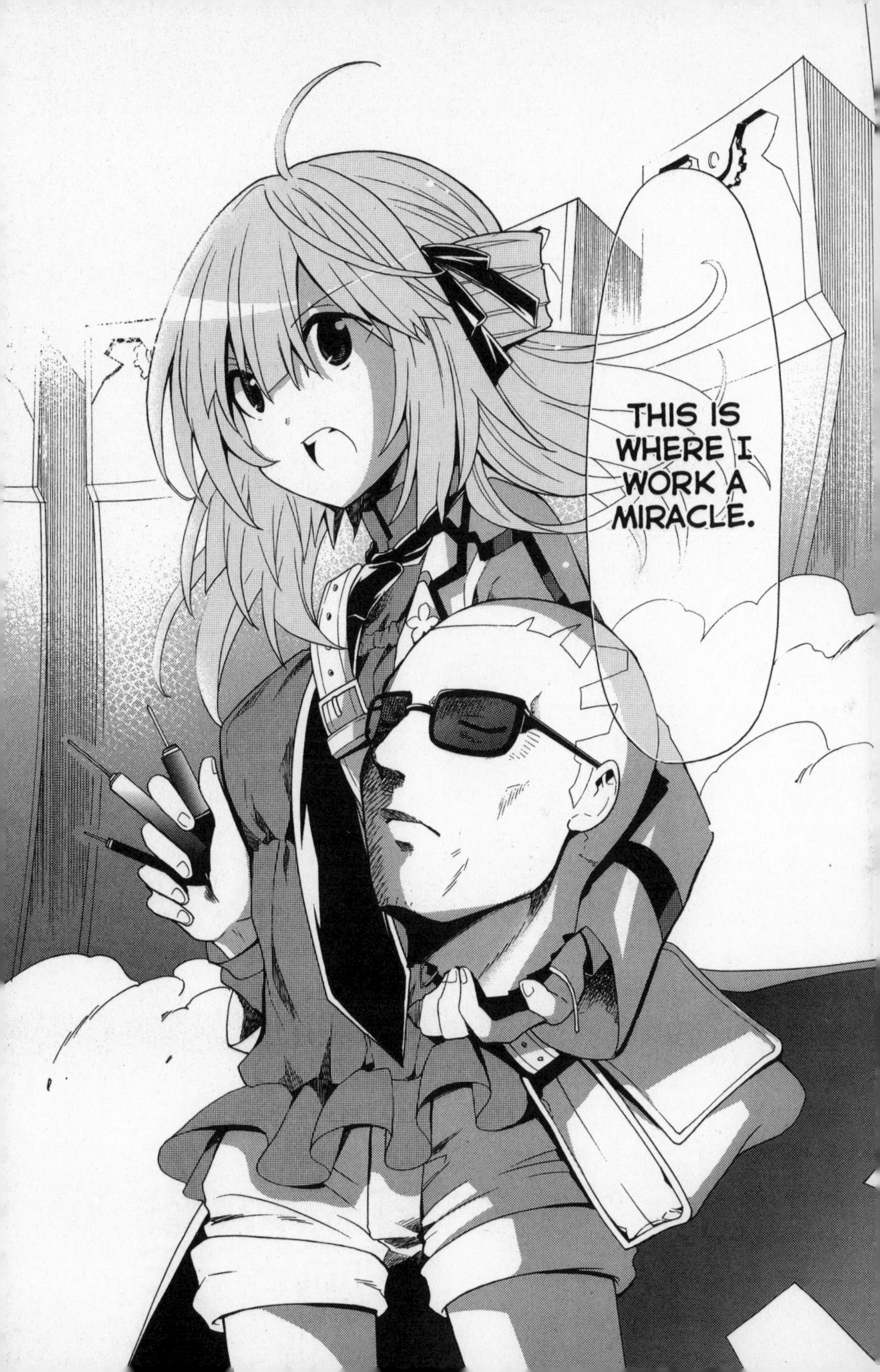
THIS IS WHERE I WORK A MIRACLE.

Clockwork Planet

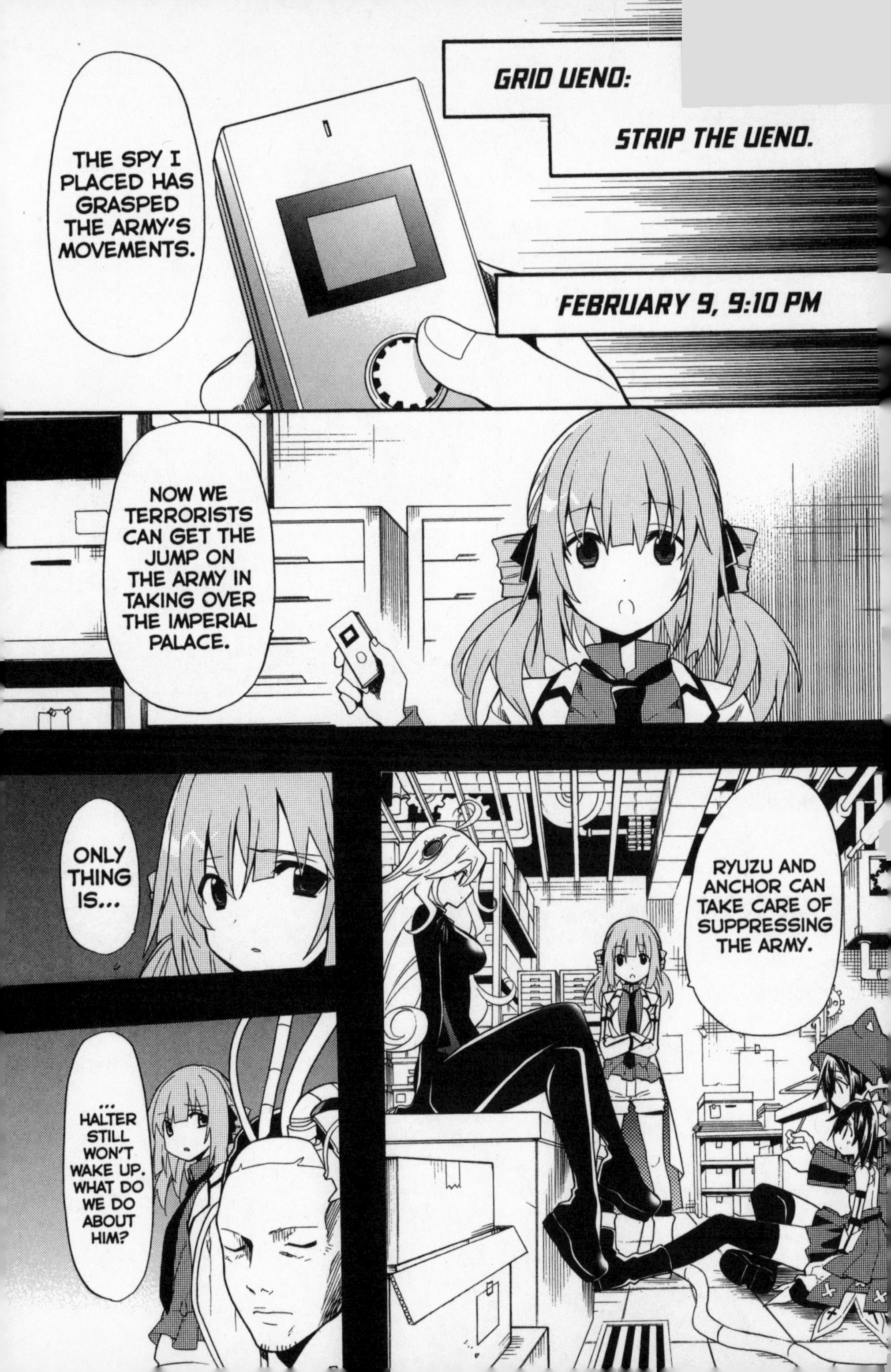
GRID UENO:
STRIP THE UENO.
FEBRUARY 9, 9:10 PM
THE SPY I PLACED HAS GRASPED THE ARMY'S MOVEMENTS.
NOW WE TERRORISTS CAN GET THE JUMP ON THE ARMY IN TAKING OVER THE IMPERIAL PALACE.
RYUZU AND ANCHOR CAN TAKE CARE OF SUPPRESSING THE ARMY.
ONLY THING IS...
...HALTER STILL WON'T WAKE UP. WHAT DO WE DO ABOUT HIM?

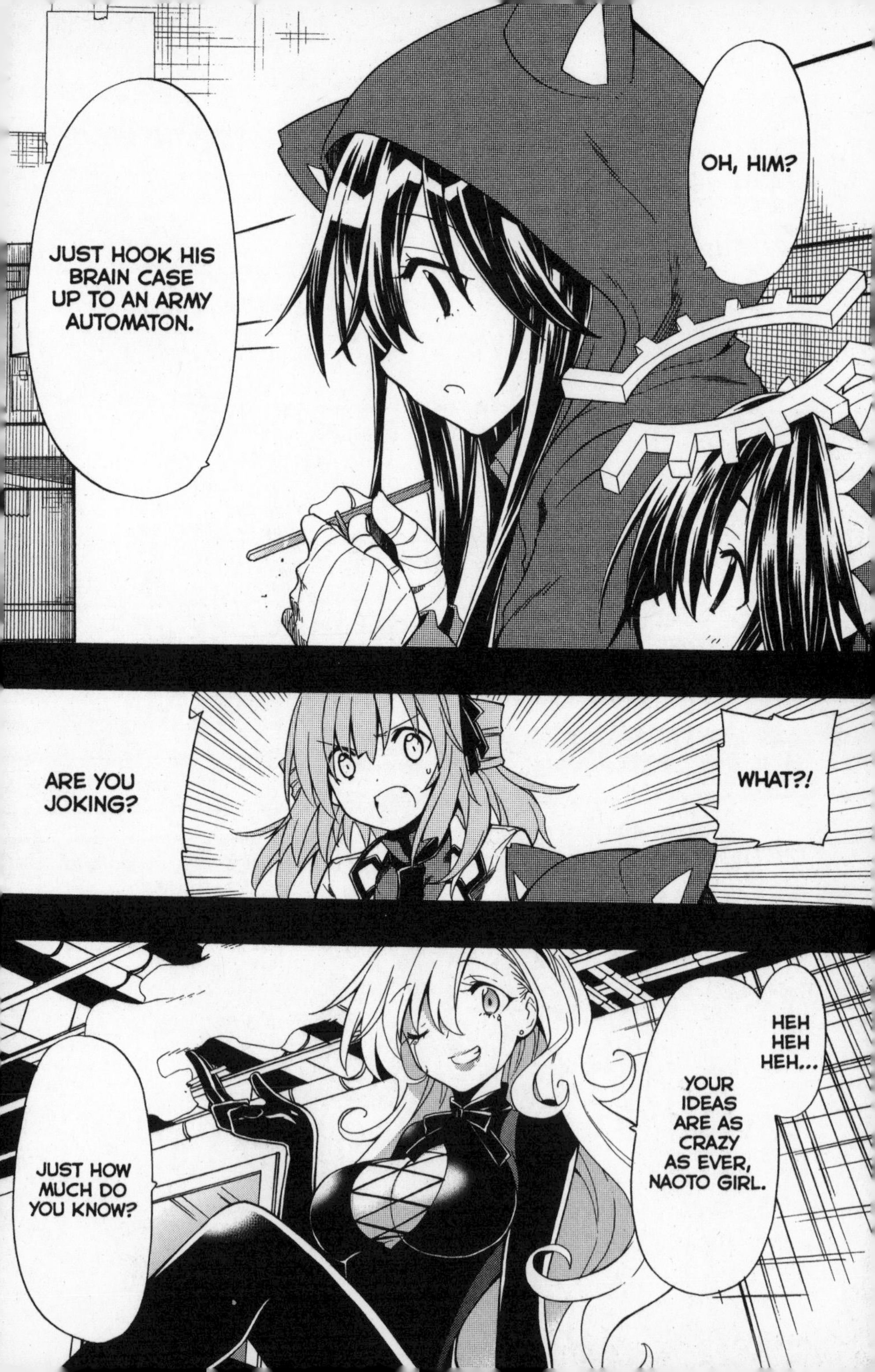
OH, HIM?
JUST HOOK HIS BRAIN CASE UP TO AN ARMY AUTOMATON.
WHAT?!
ARE YOU JOKING?
HEH HEH HEH...
YOUR IDEAS ARE AS CRAZY AS EVER, NAOTO GIRL.
JUST HOW MUCH DO YOU KNOW?

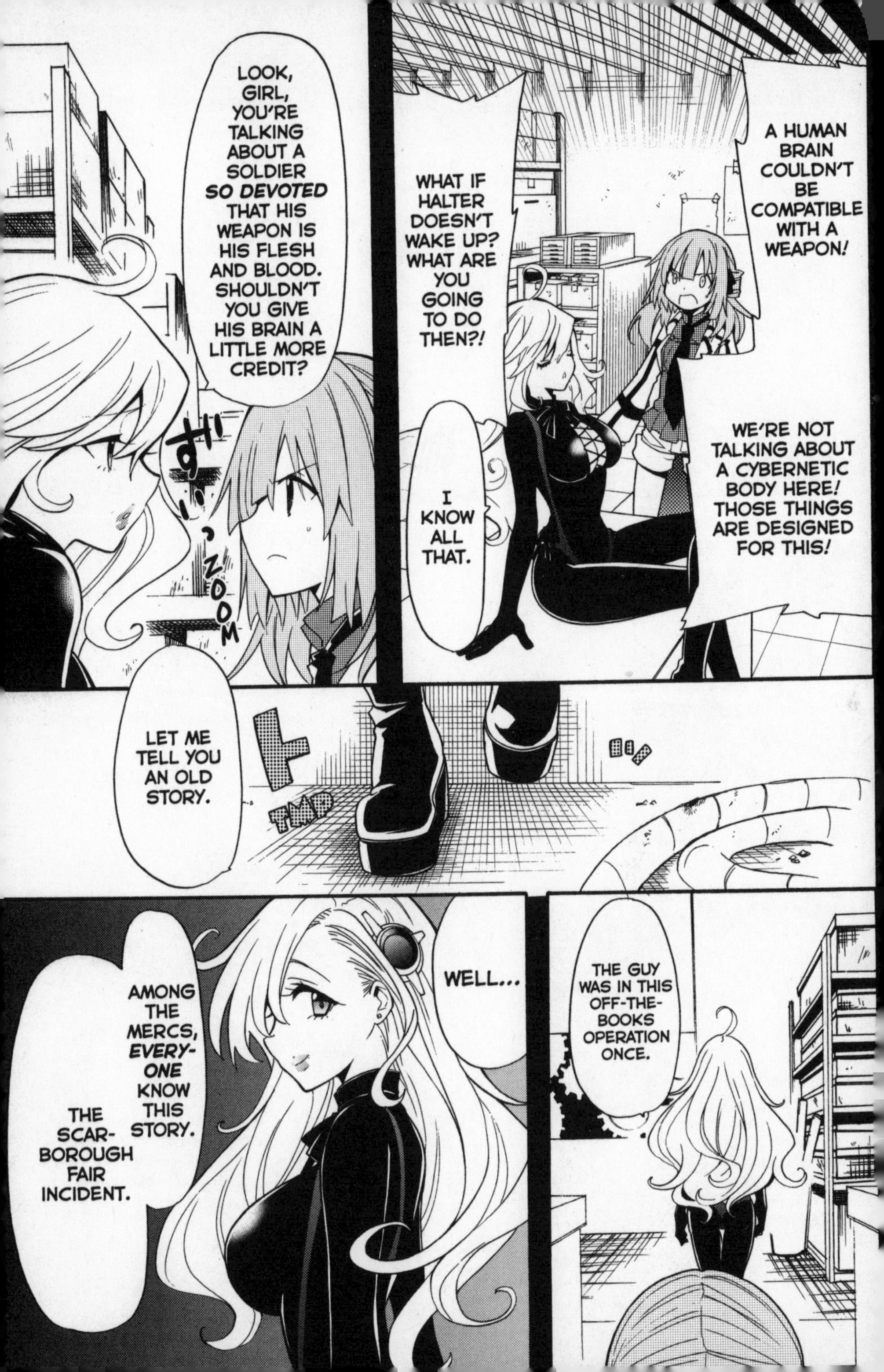
A HUMAN BRAIN COULDN'T BE COMPATIBLE WITH A WEAPON!
WHAT IF HALTER DOESN'T WAKE UP? WHAT ARE YOU GOING TO DO THEN?!
WE'RE NOT TALKING ABOUT A CYBERNETIC BODY HERE! THOSE THINGS ARE DESIGNED FOR THIS!
I KNOW ALL THAT.
LOOK, GIRL, YOU'RE TALKING ABOUT A SOLDIER *SO DEVOTED* THAT HIS WEAPON IS HIS FLESH AND BLOOD. SHOULDN'T YOU GIVE HIS BRAIN A LITTLE MORE CREDIT?
ZOOM
LET ME TELL YOU AN OLD STORY.
TMP
THE GUY WAS IN THIS OFF-THE-BOOKS OPERATION ONCE.
WELL...
AMONG THE MERCS, *EVERY-ONE* KNOW THIS STORY.
THE SCAR-BOROUGH FAIR INCIDENT.

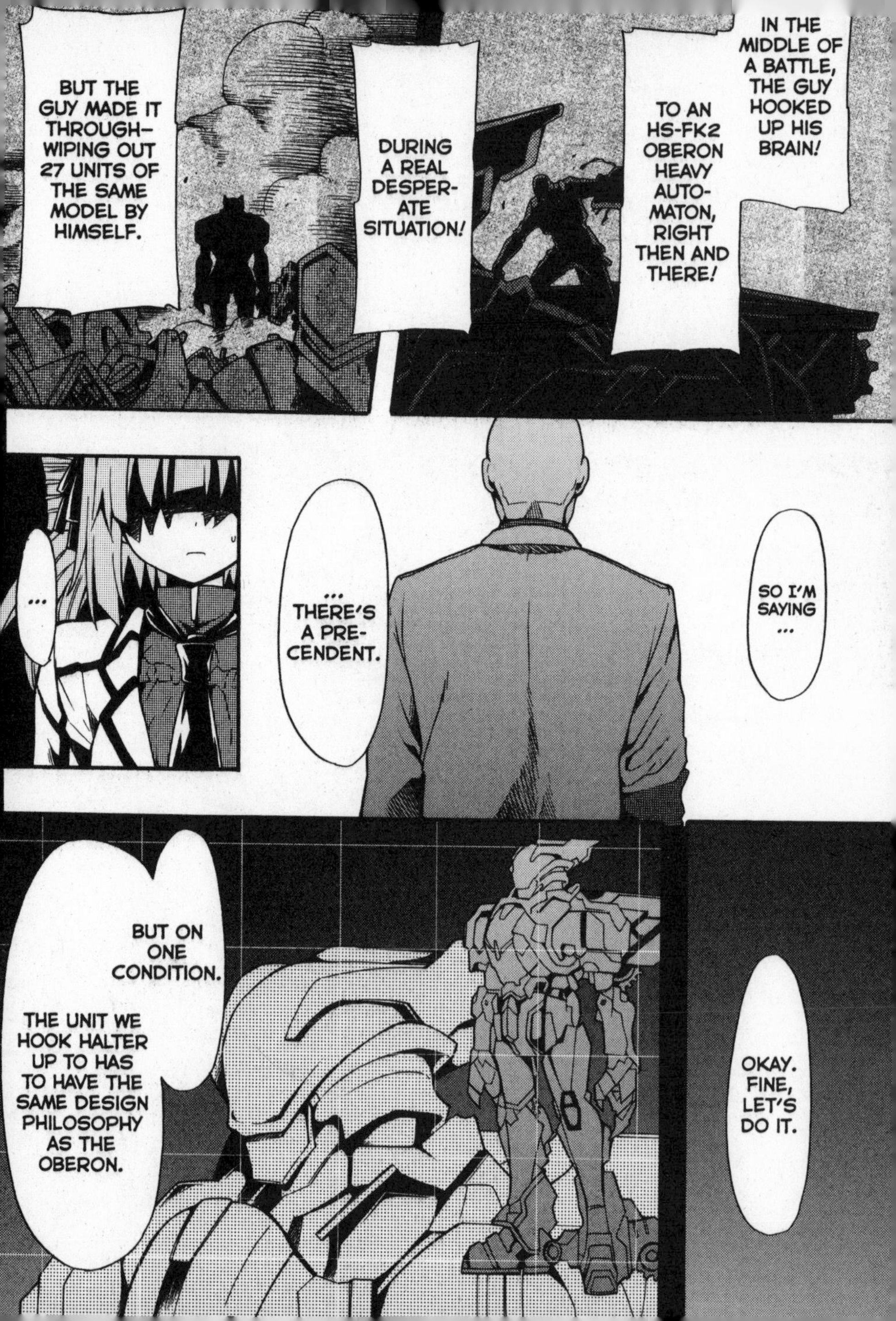
IN THE MIDDLE OF A BATTLE, THE GUY HOOKED UP HIS BRAIN!
TO AN HS-FK2 OBERON HEAVY AUTO-MATON, RIGHT THEN AND THERE!
DURING A REAL DESPER-ATE SITUATION!
BUT THE GUY MADE IT THROUGH— WIPING OUT 27 UNITS OF THE SAME MODEL BY HIMSELF.
SO I'M SAYING ...
... THERE'S A PRE-CENDENT.
...
OKAY. FINE, LET'S DO IT.
BUT ON ONE CONDITION.
THE UNIT WE HOOK HALTER UP TO HAS TO HAVE THE SAME DESIGN PHILOSOPHY AS THE OBERON.

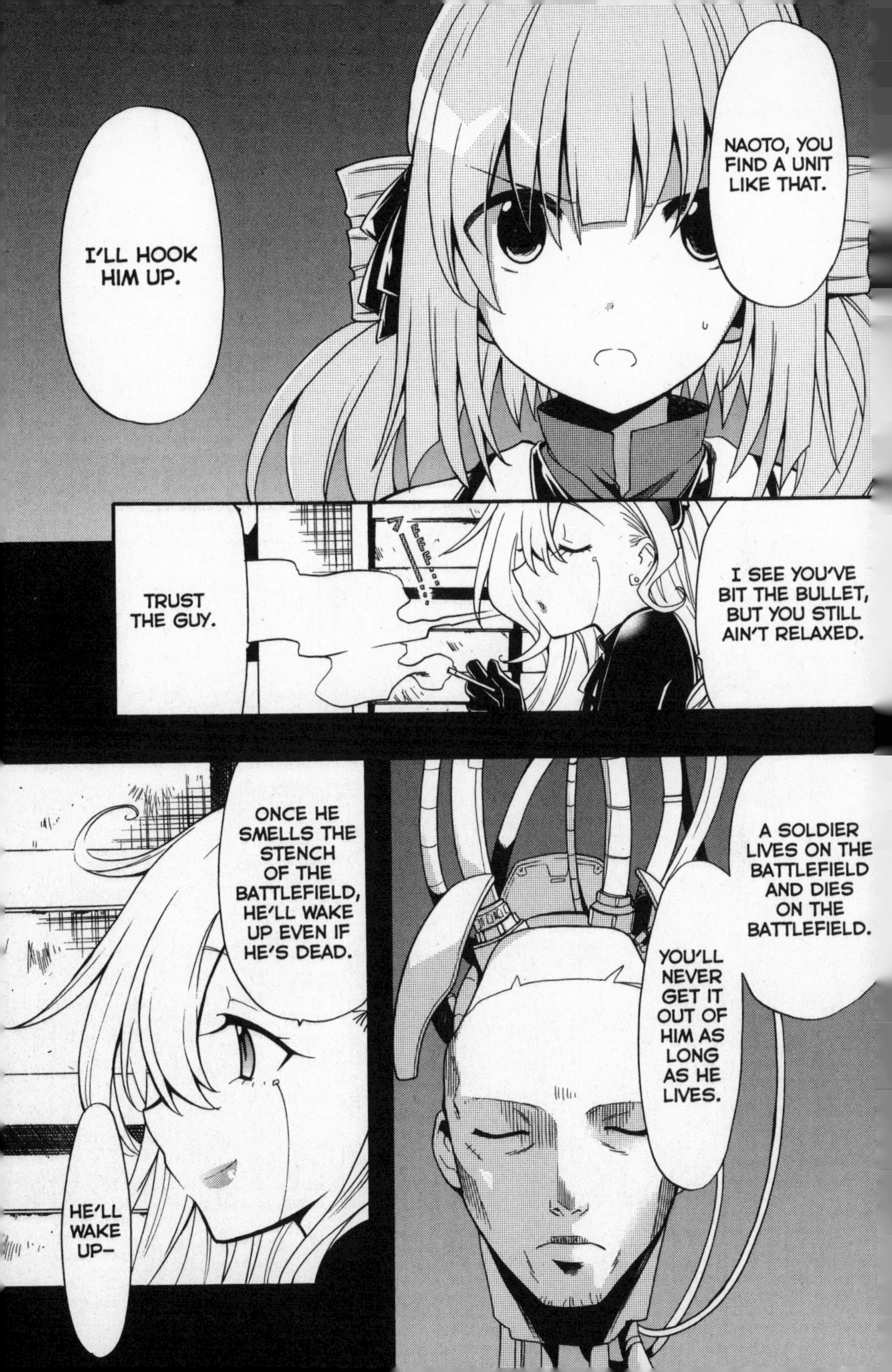
NAOTO, YOU FIND A UNIT LIKE THAT.
I'LL HOOK HIM UP.
I SEE YOU'VE BIT THE BULLET, BUT YOU STILL AIN'T RELAXED.
TRUST THE GUY.
A SOLDIER LIVES ON THE BATTLEFIELD AND DIES ON THE BATTLEFIELD.
YOU'LL NEVER GET IT OUT OF HIM AS LONG AS HE LIVES.
ONCE HE SMELLS THE STENCH OF THE BATTLEFIELD, HE'LL WAKE UP EVEN IF HE'S DEAD.
HE'LL WAKE UP–

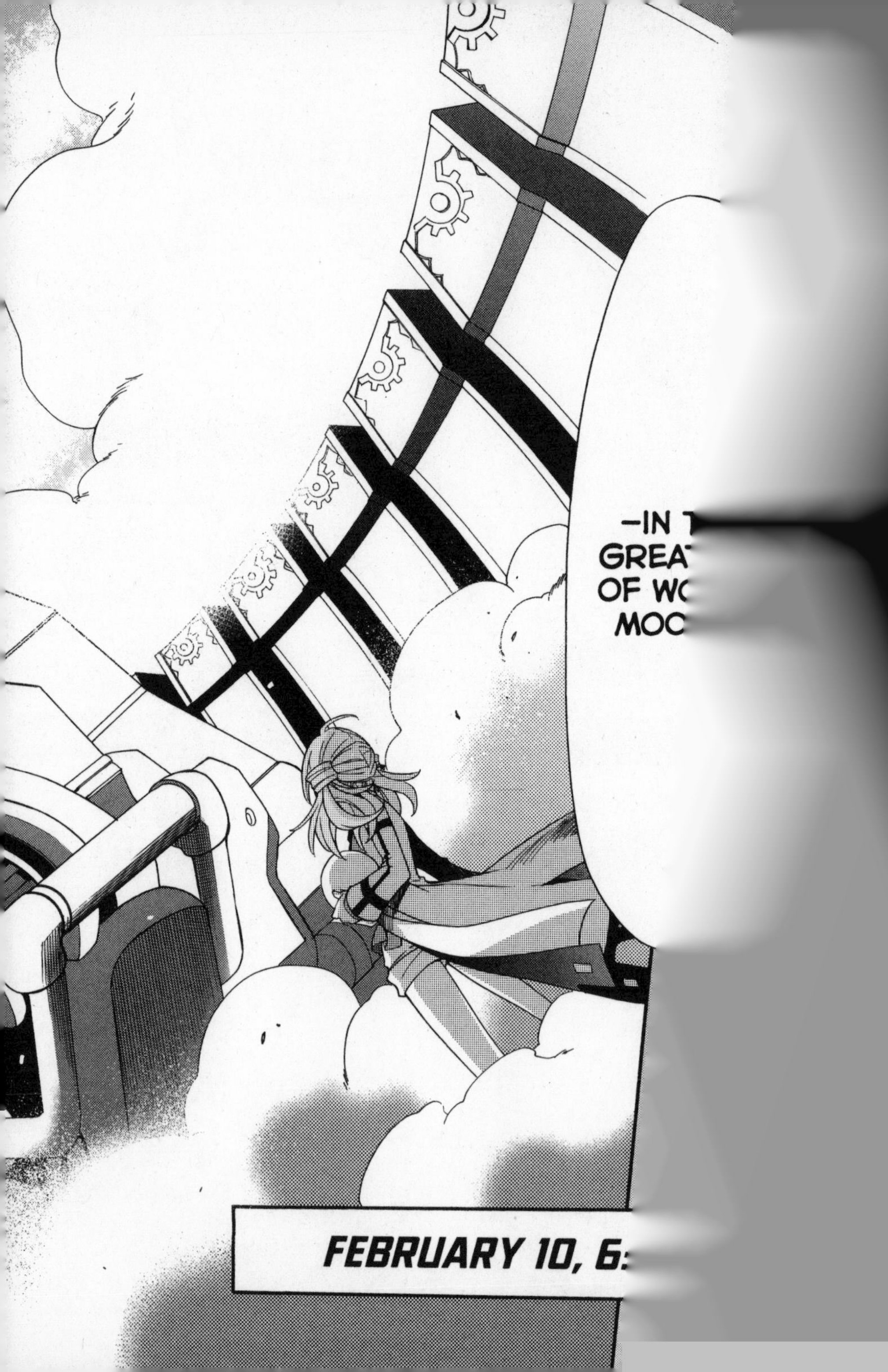

—IN T
GREAT
OF WO
MOO
FEBRUARY 10, 6:

Clock 32: Rise

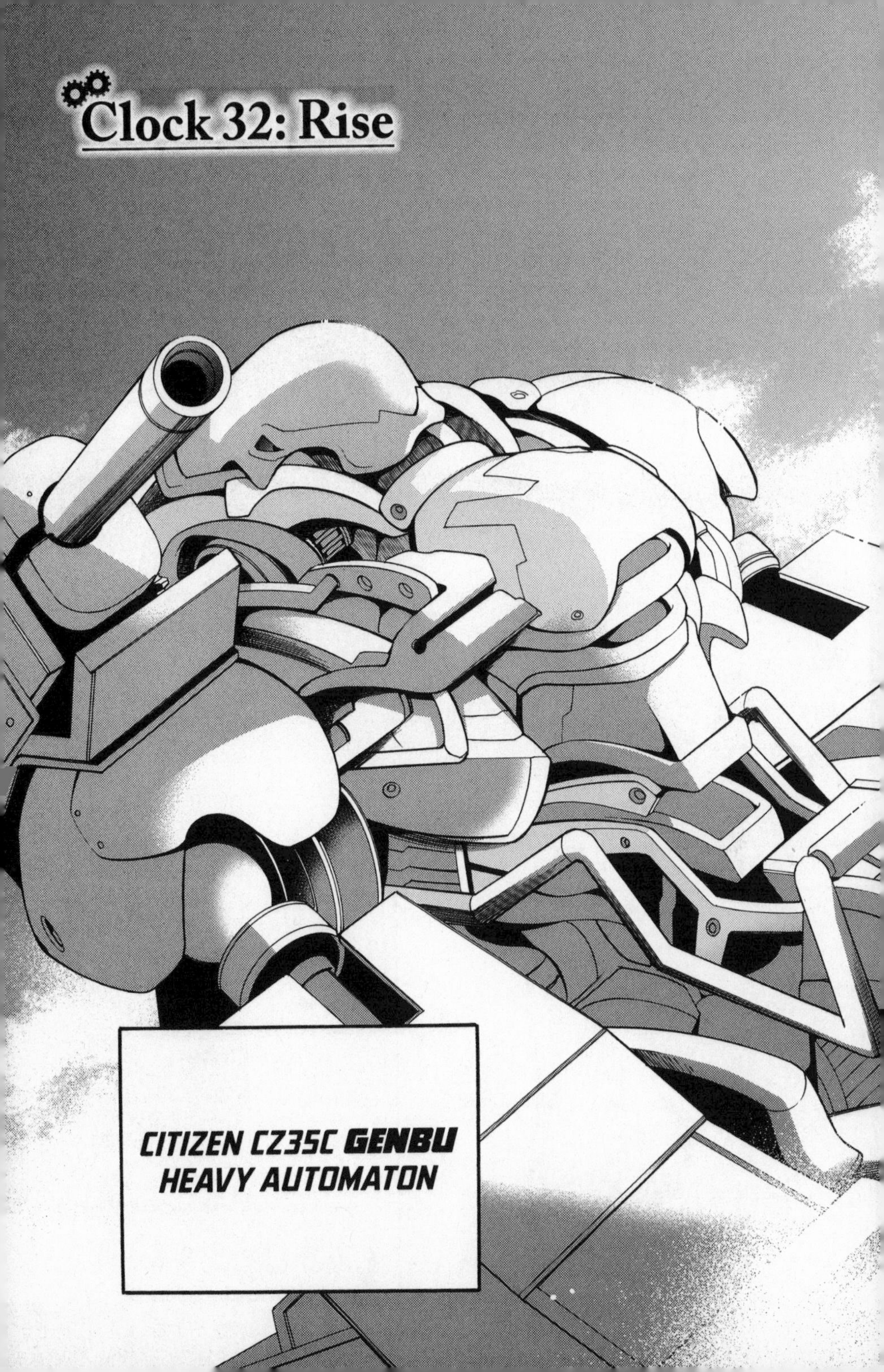
CITIZEN CZ35C GENBU
HEAVY AUTOMATON

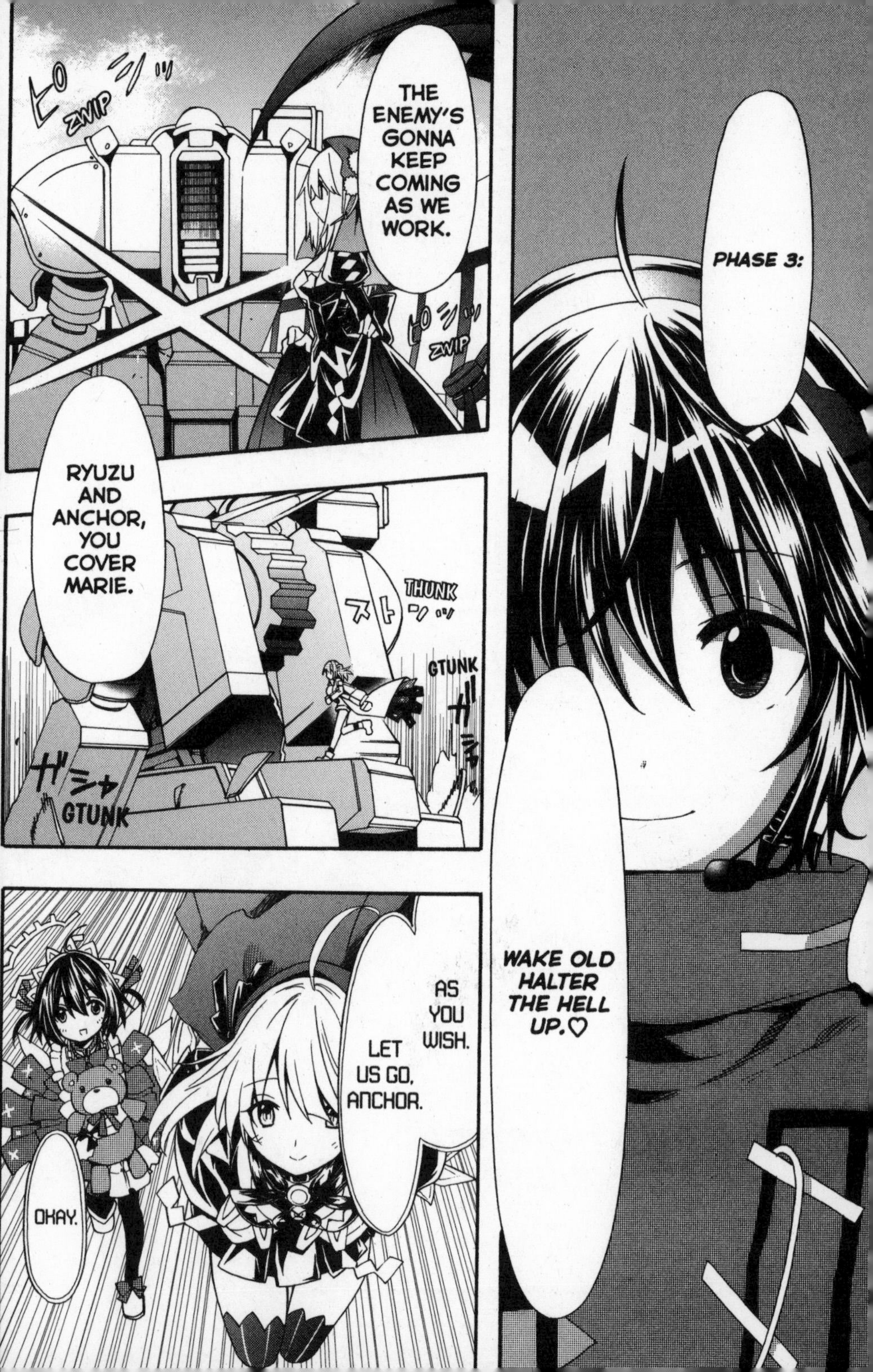
PHASE 3:
WAKE OLD HALTER THE HELL UP.♡
ZWIP
THE ENEMY'S GONNA KEEP COMING AS WE WORK.
ZWIP
RYUZU AND ANCHOR, YOU COVER MARIE.
THUNK
GTUNK
GTUNK
AS YOU WISH.
LET US GO, ANCHOR.
OKAY.

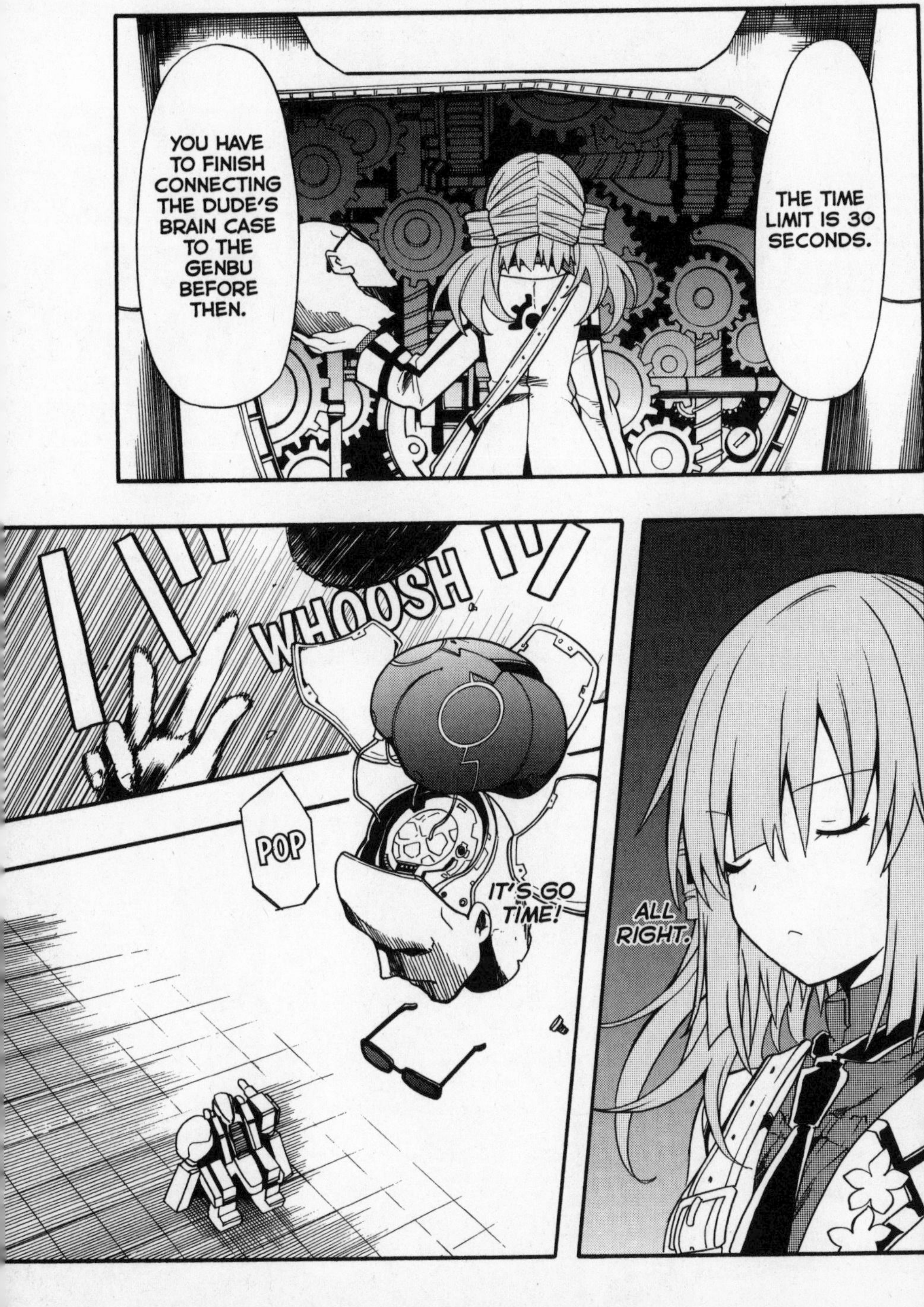
THE TIME LIMIT IS 30 SECONDS.
YOU HAVE TO FINISH CONNECTING THE DUDE'S BRAIN CASE TO THE GENBU BEFORE THEN.
ALL RIGHT.
WHOOSH
POP
IT'S GO TIME!

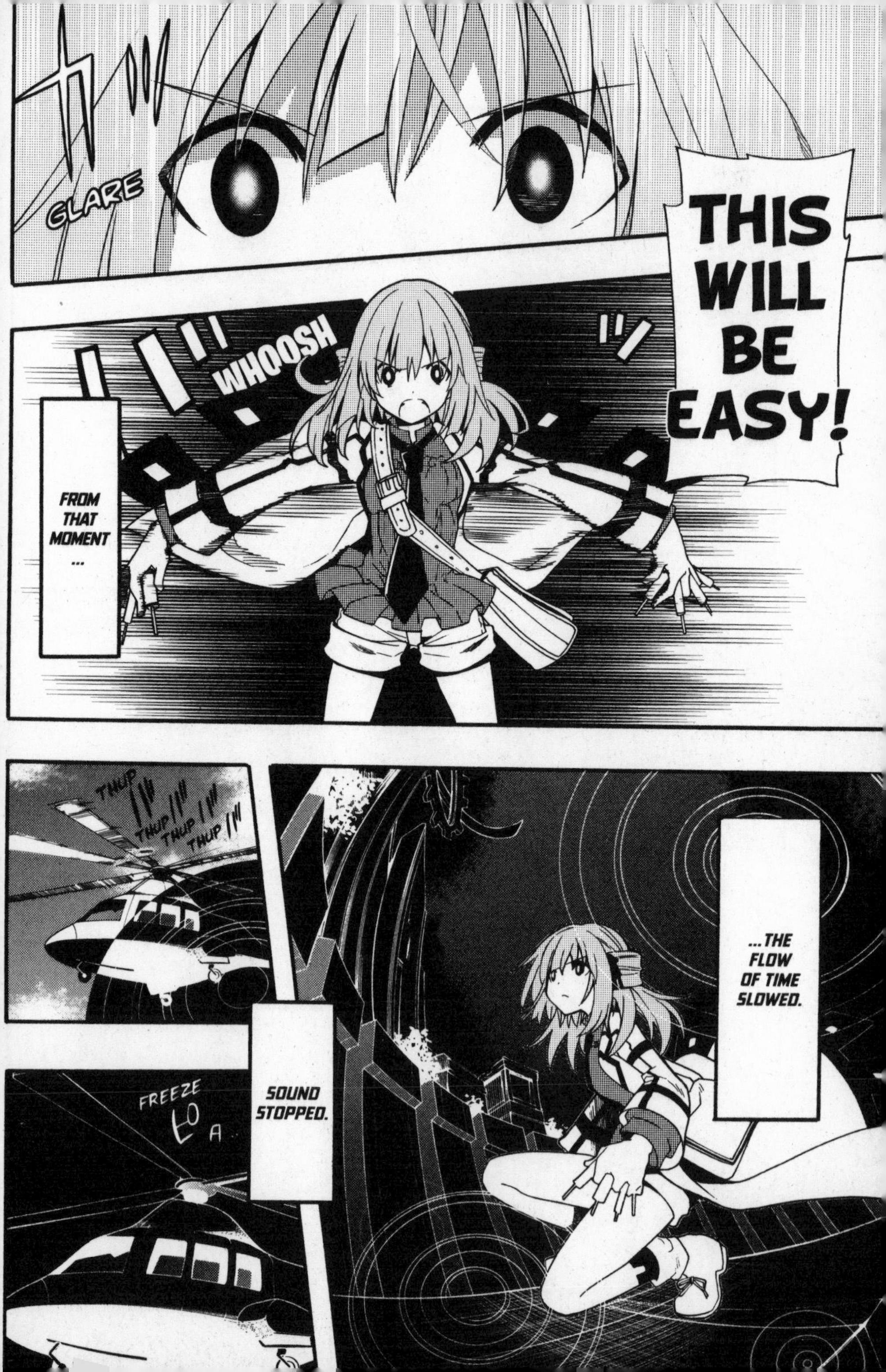
GLARE
THIS WILL BE EASY!
WHOOSH
FROM THAT MOMENT...
...THE FLOW OF TIME SLOWED.
THUP THUP THUP THUP
SOUND STOPPED.
FREEZE

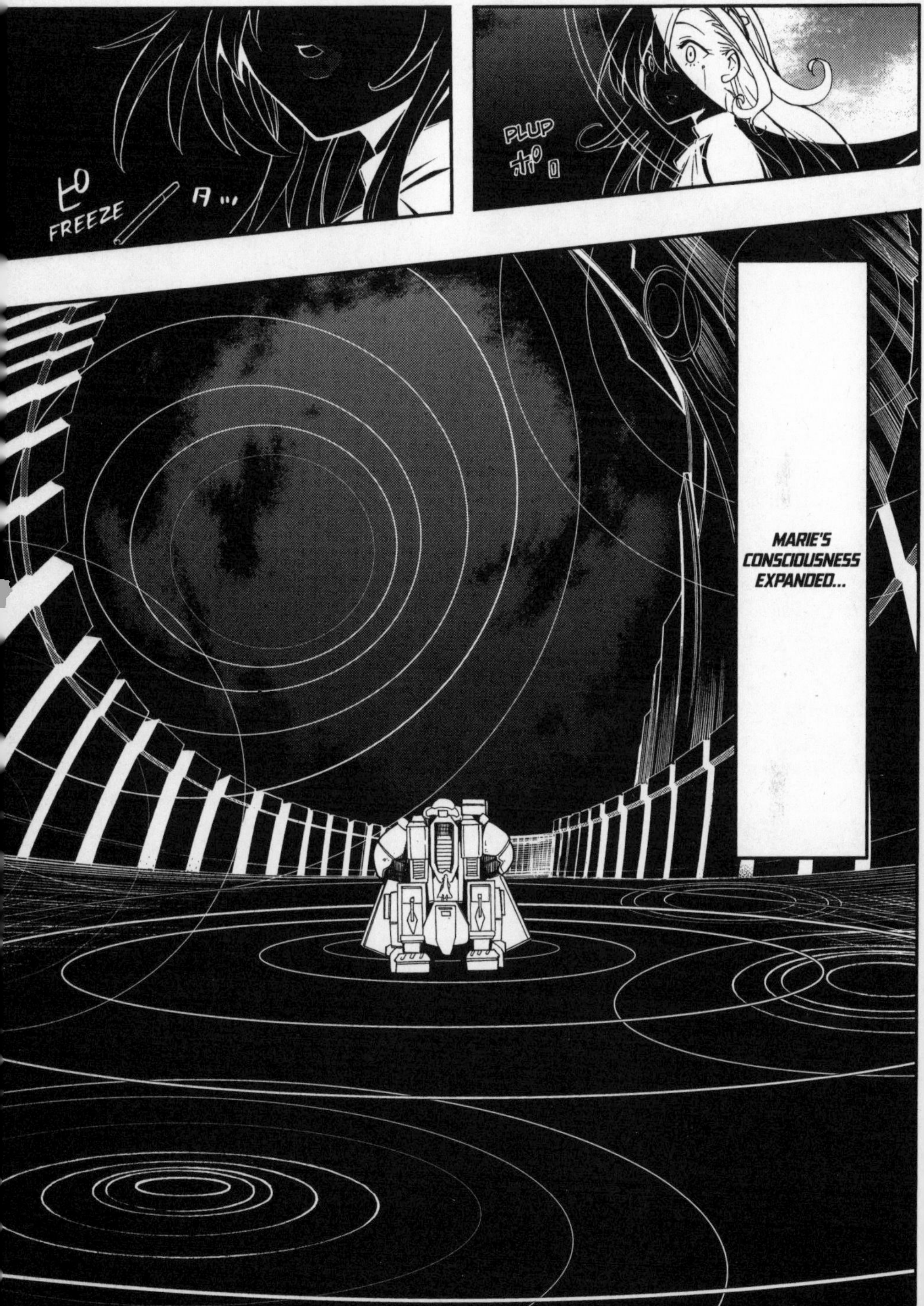
PLUP
ポロ
ピ
FREEZE
タッ
MARIE'S CONSCIOUSNESS EXPANDED...

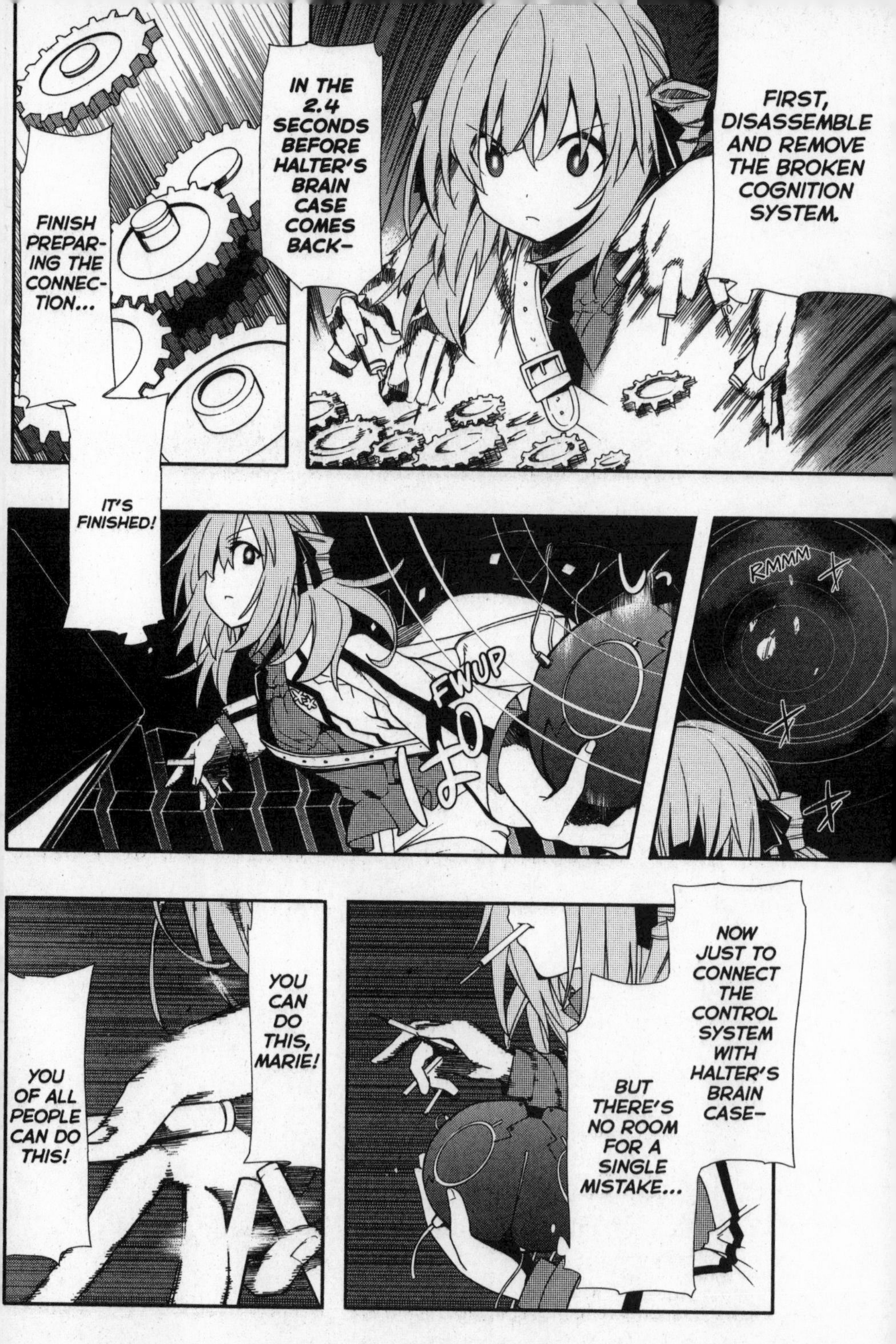
FIRST, DISASSEMBLE AND REMOVE THE BROKEN COGNITION SYSTEM.
IN THE 2.4 SECONDS BEFORE HALTER'S BRAIN CASE COMES BACK–
FINISH PREPARING THE CONNECTION...
RMMM
IT'S FINISHED!
FWUP
NOW JUST TO CONNECT THE CONTROL SYSTEM WITH HALTER'S BRAIN CASE–
BUT THERE'S NO ROOM FOR A SINGLE MISTAKE...
YOU CAN DO THIS, MARIE!
YOU OF ALL PEOPLE CAN DO THIS!

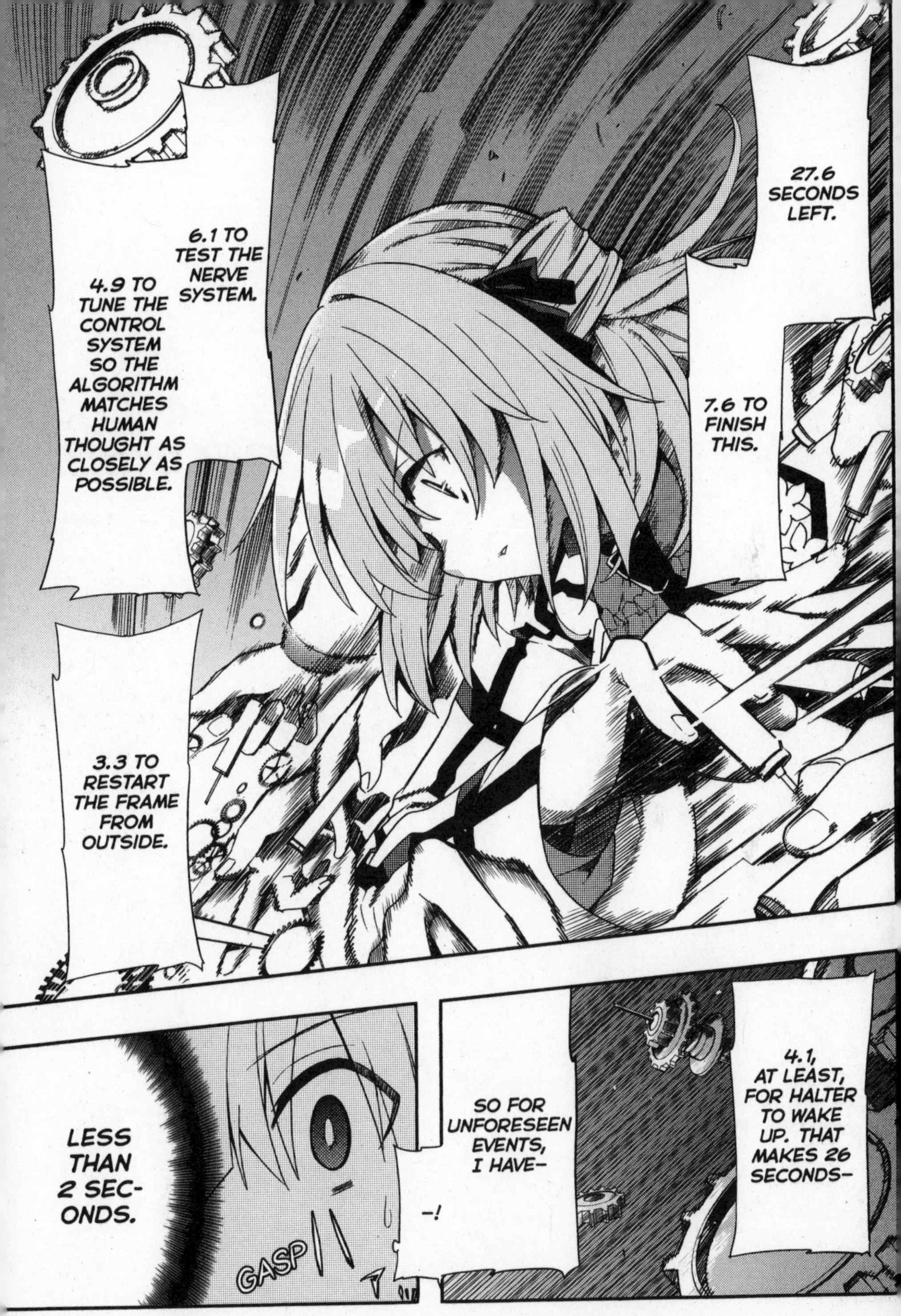
27.6 SECONDS LEFT.
7.6 TO FINISH THIS.
6.1 TO TEST THE NERVE SYSTEM.
4.9 TO TUNE THE CONTROL SYSTEM SO THE ALGORITHM MATCHES HUMAN THOUGHT AS CLOSELY AS POSSIBLE.
3.3 TO RESTART THE FRAME FROM OUTSIDE.
4.1, AT LEAST, FOR HALTER TO WAKE UP. THAT MAKES 26 SECONDS–
SO FOR UNFORESEEN EVENTS, I HAVE–
–!
LESS THAN 2 SEC- ONDS.
GASP

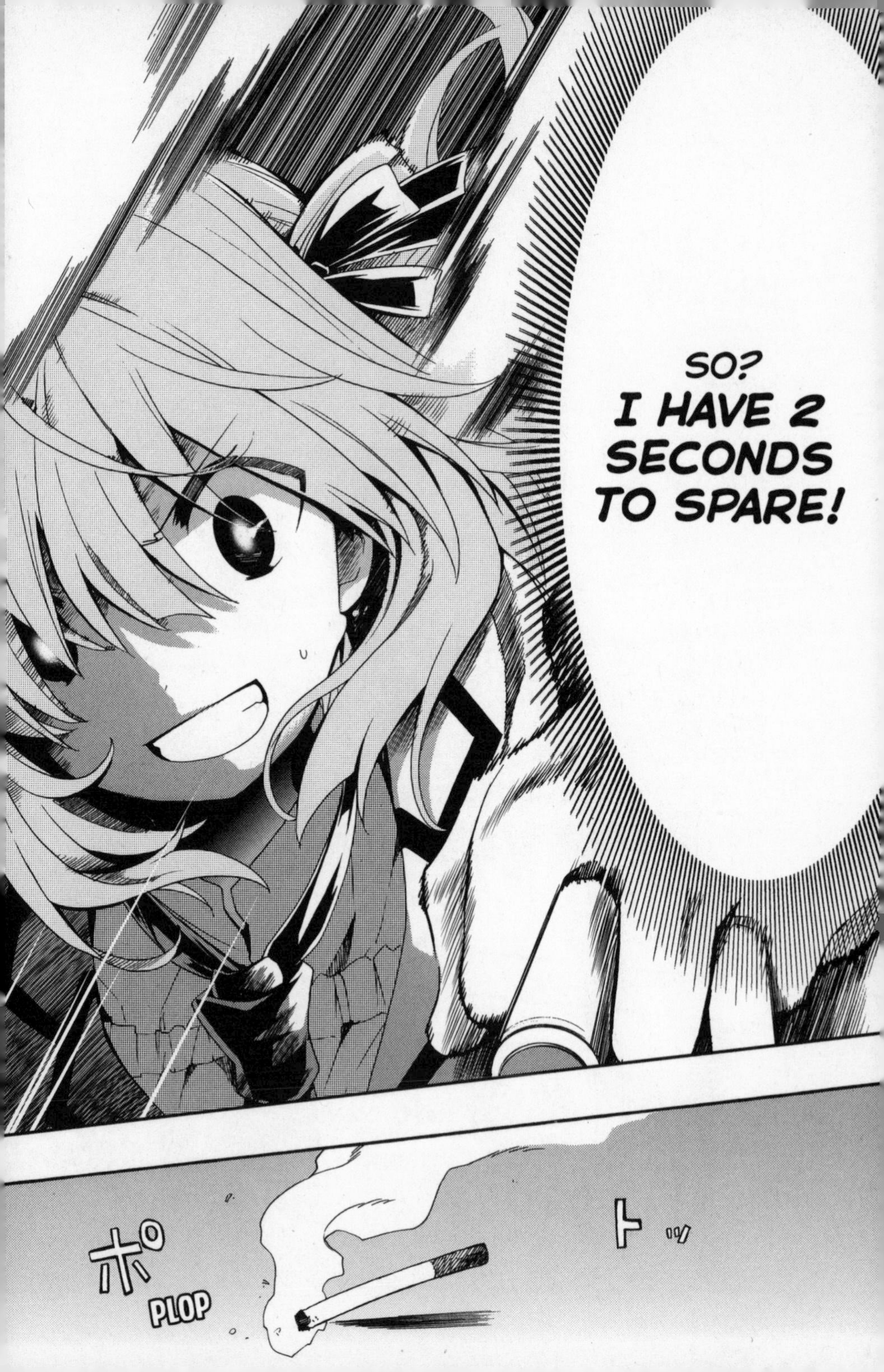
SO?
I HAVE 2 SECONDS TO SPARE!
トッ
ポ
PLOP

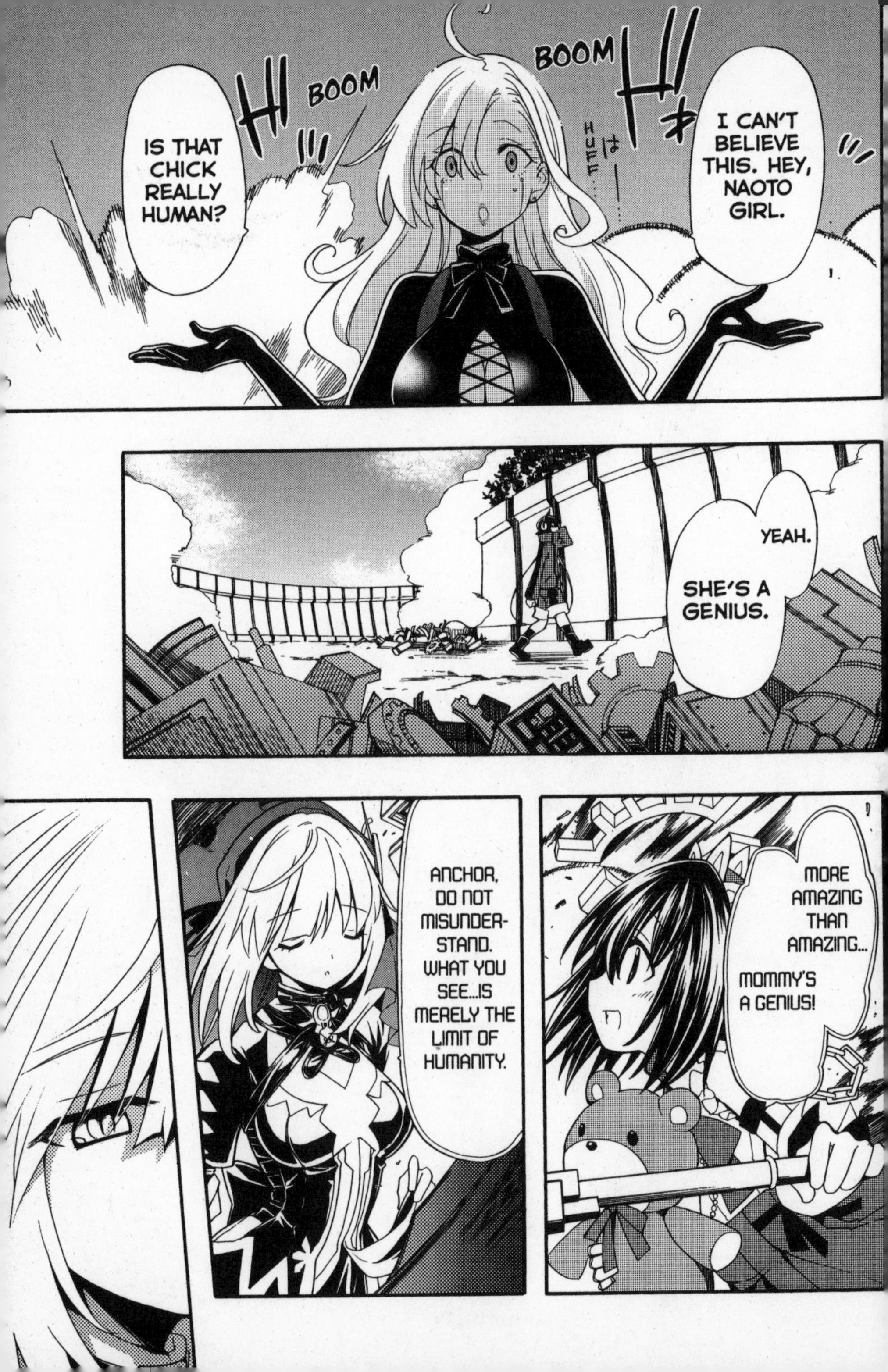
BOOM
I CAN'T BELIEVE THIS. HEY, NAOTO GIRL.
HUFF
BOOM
IS THAT CHICK REALLY HUMAN?
YEAH.
SHE'S A GENIUS.
MORE AMAZING THAN AMAZING...
MOMMY'S A GENIUS!
ANCHOR, DO NOT MISUNDER-STAND. WHAT YOU SEE...IS MERELY THE LIMIT OF HUMANITY.

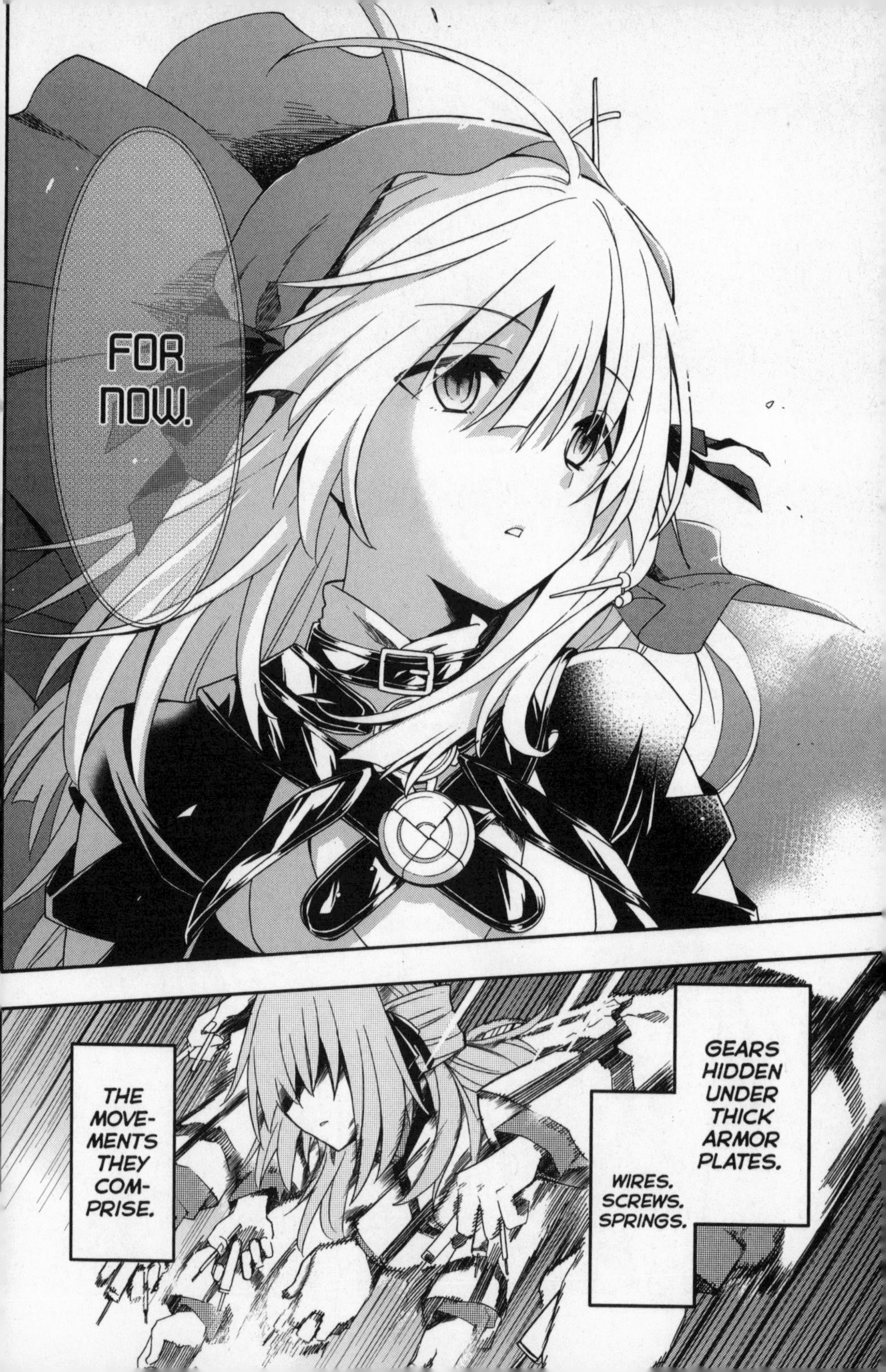
FOR NOW.
GEARS HIDDEN UNDER THICK ARMOR PLATES.
WIRES. SCREWS. SPRINGS.
THE MOVEMENTS THEY COMPRISE.

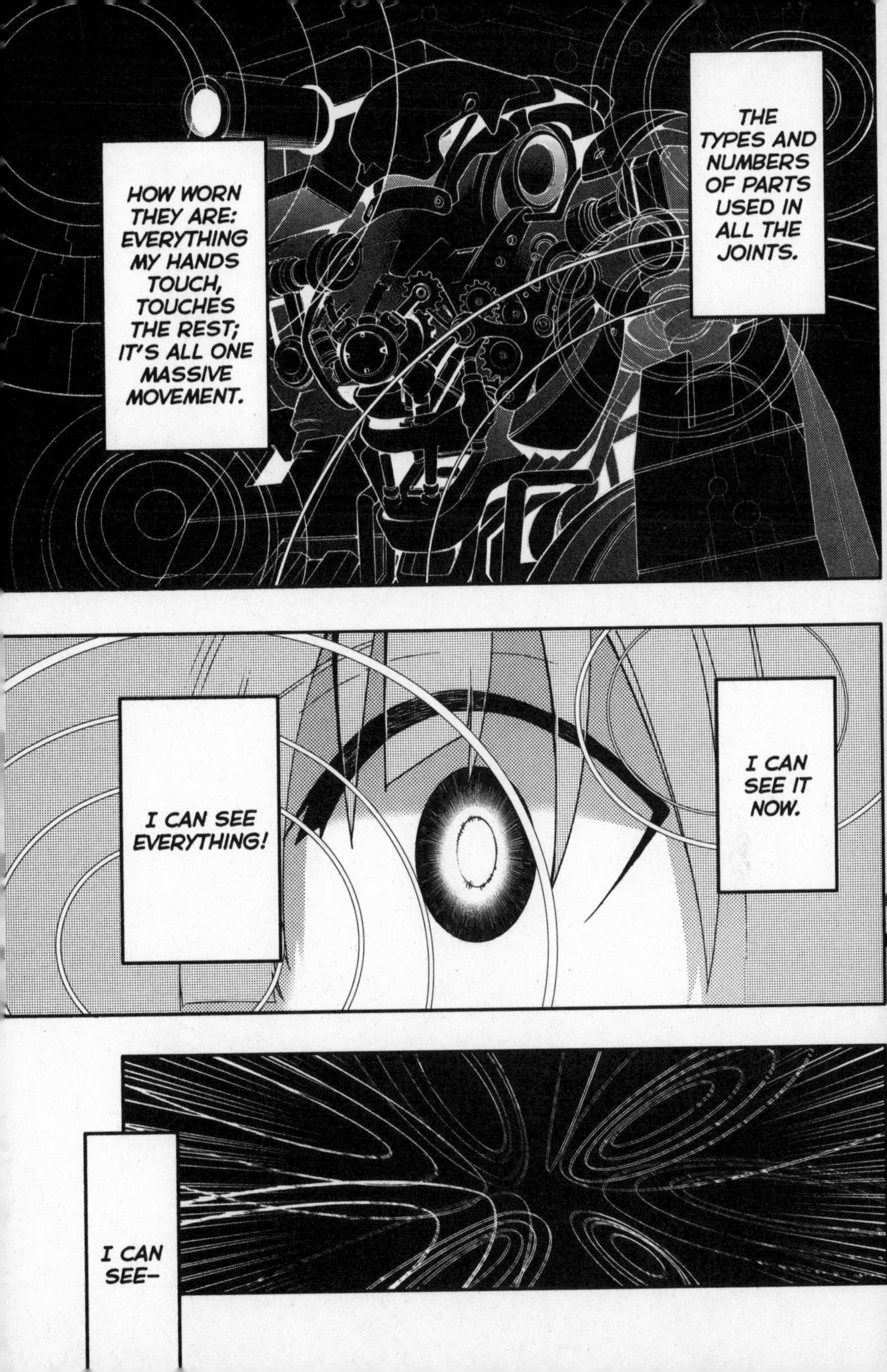
THE TYPES AND NUMBERS OF PARTS USED IN ALL THE JOINTS.
HOW WORN THEY ARE: EVERYTHING MY HANDS TOUCH, TOUCHES THE REST; IT'S ALL ONE MASSIVE MOVEMENT.
I CAN SEE IT NOW.
I CAN SEE EVERYTHING!
I CAN SEE–

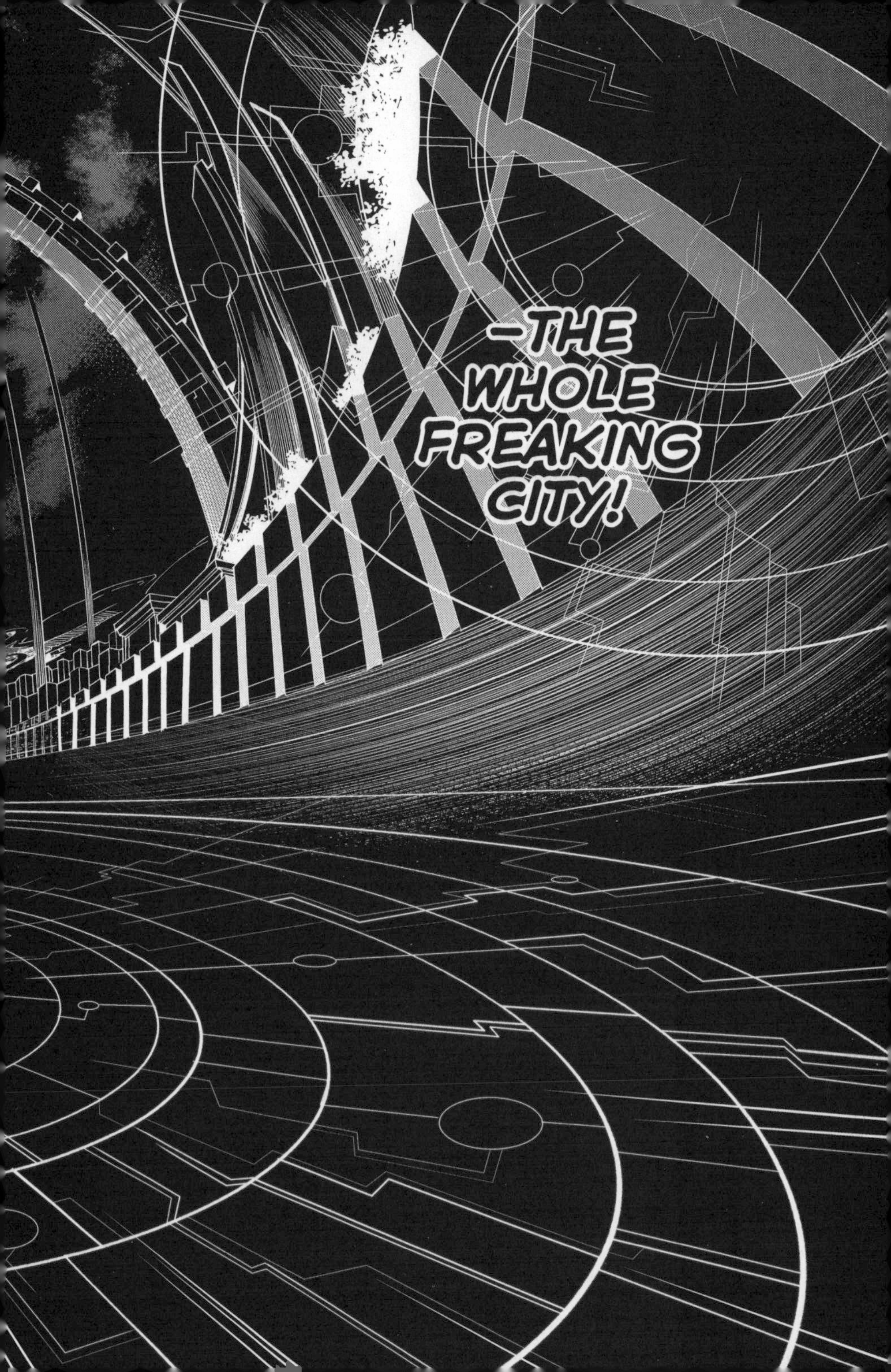
—THE WHOLE FREAKING CITY!

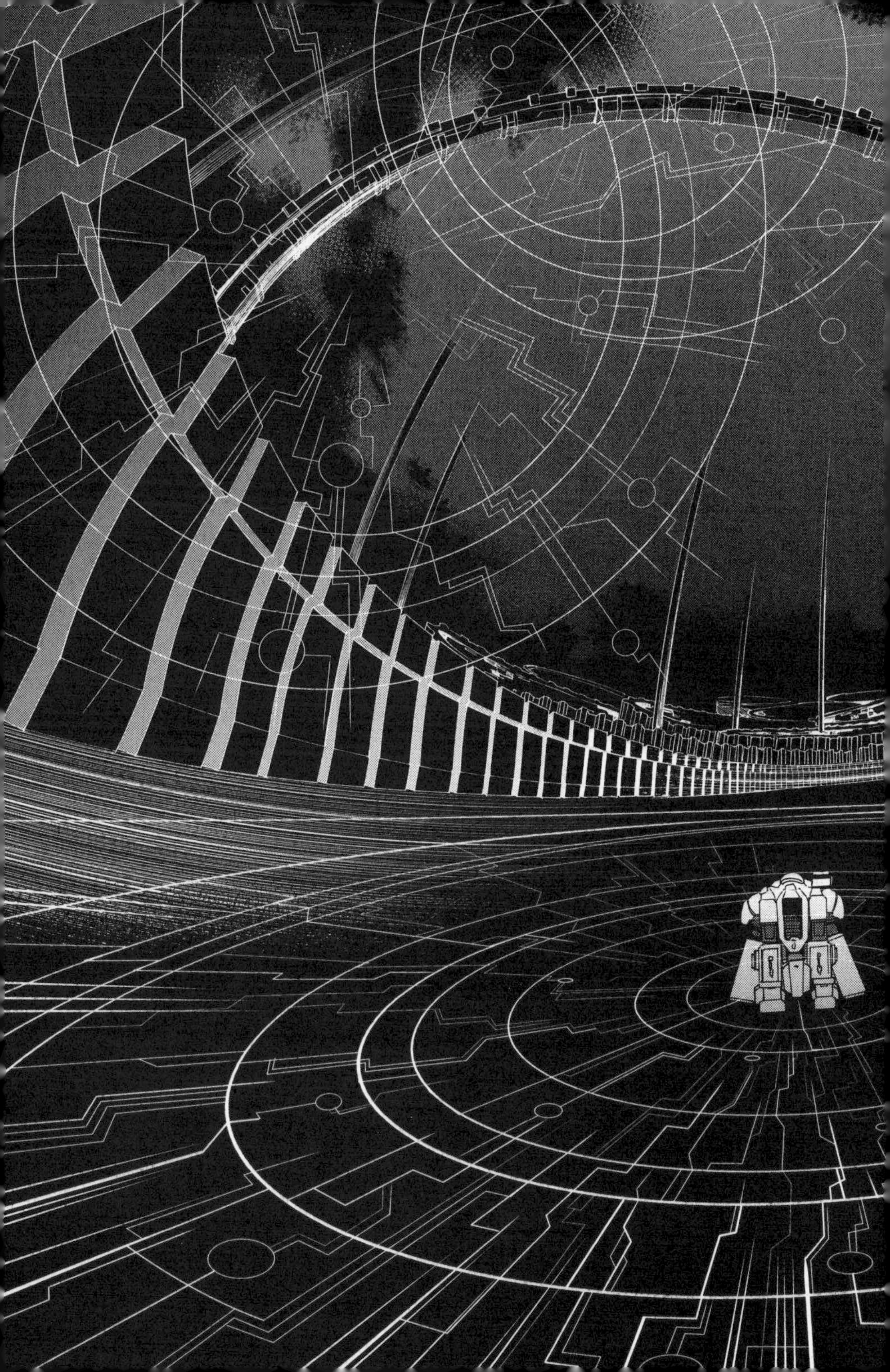

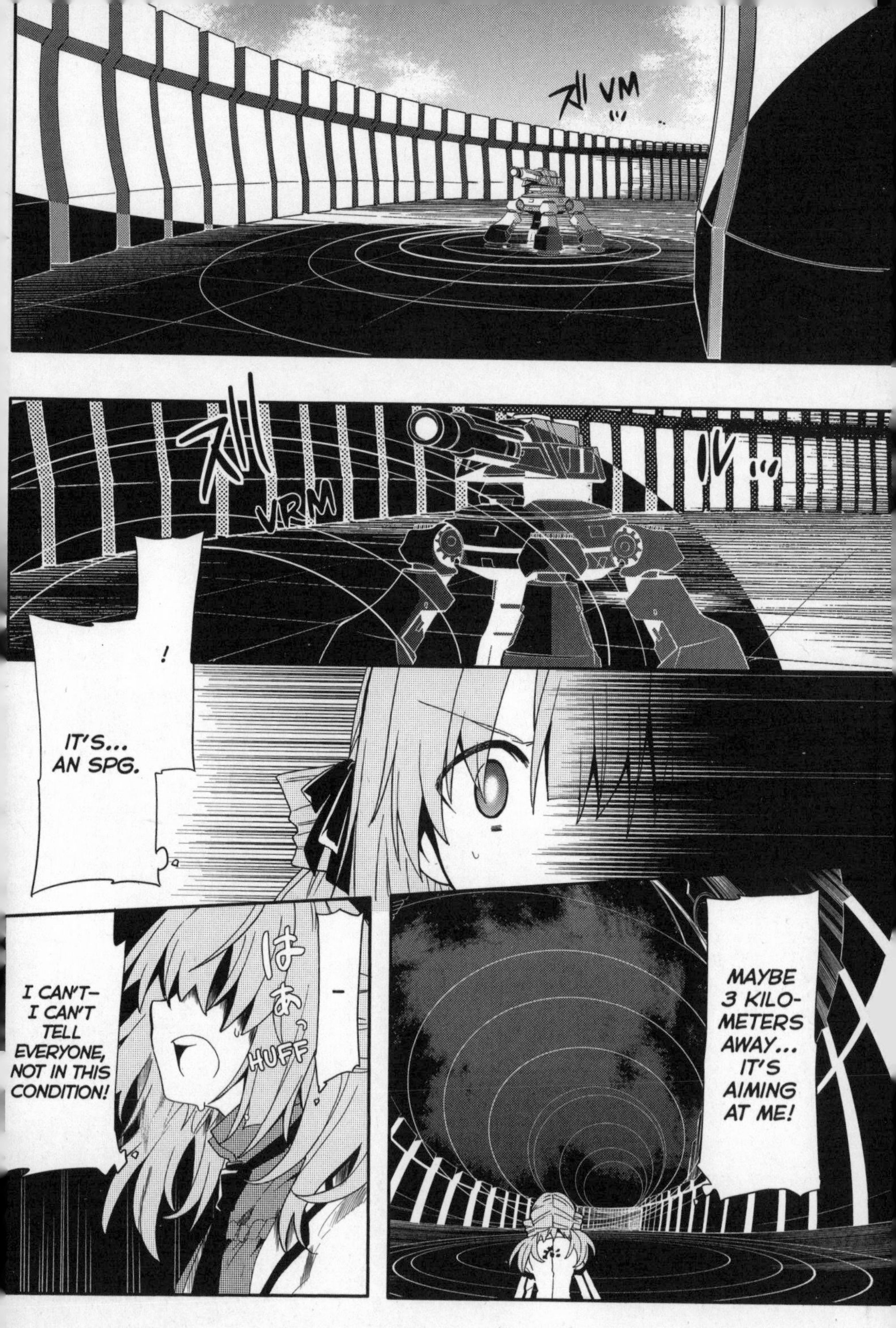
VM
VRM
!
IT'S... AN SPG.
MAYBE 3 KILO-METERS AWAY... IT'S AIMING AT ME!
-
はぁっ
HUFF
I CAN'T— I CAN'T TELL EVERYONE, NOT IN THIS CONDITION!

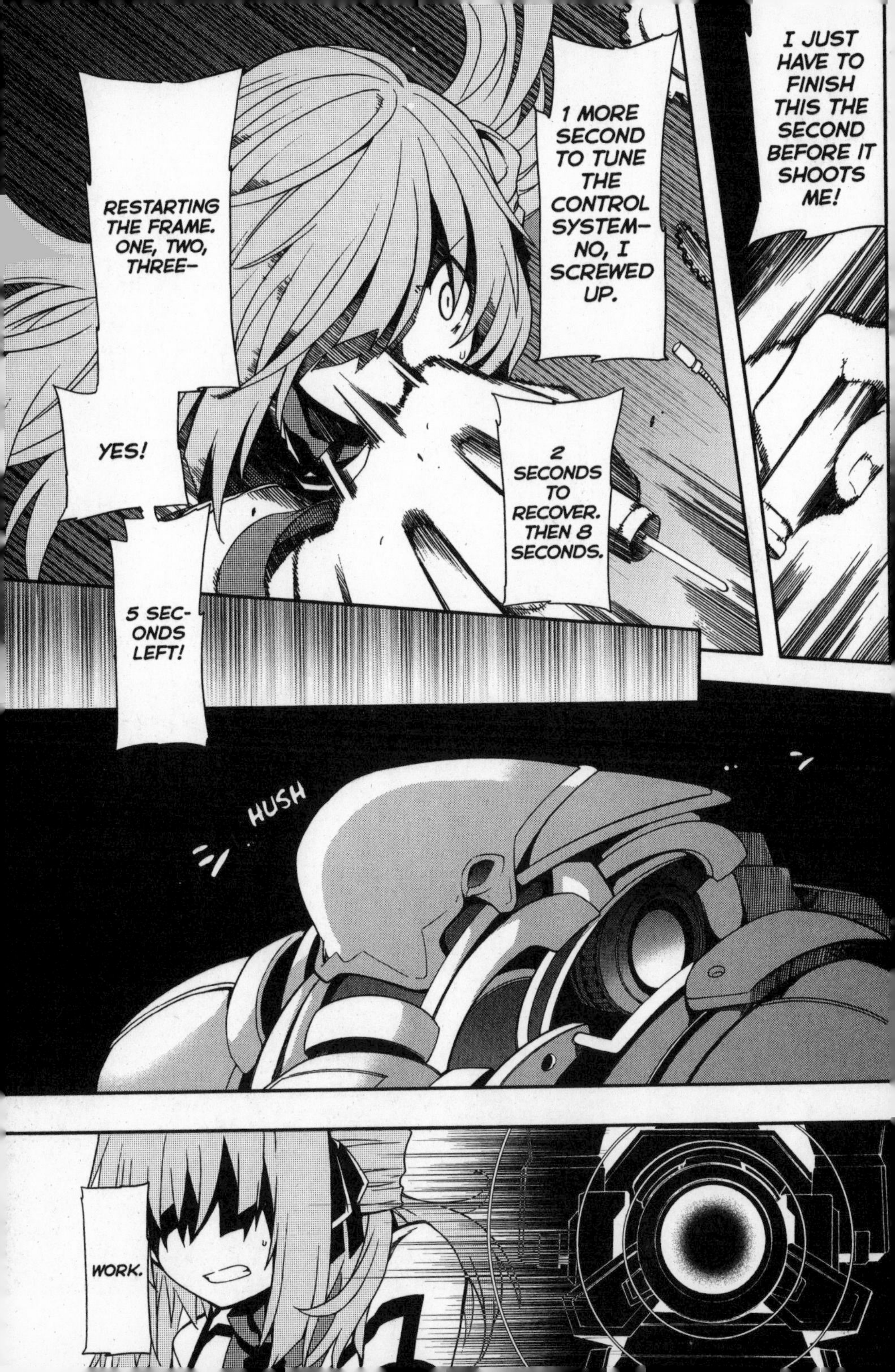
I JUST HAVE TO FINISH THIS THE SECOND BEFORE IT SHOOTS ME!
1 MORE SECOND TO TUNE THE CONTROL SYSTEM—NO, I SCREWED UP.
2 SECONDS TO RECOVER. THEN 8 SECONDS.
RESTARTING THE FRAME. ONE, TWO, THREE—
YES!
5 SEC-ONDS LEFT!
HUSH
WORK.

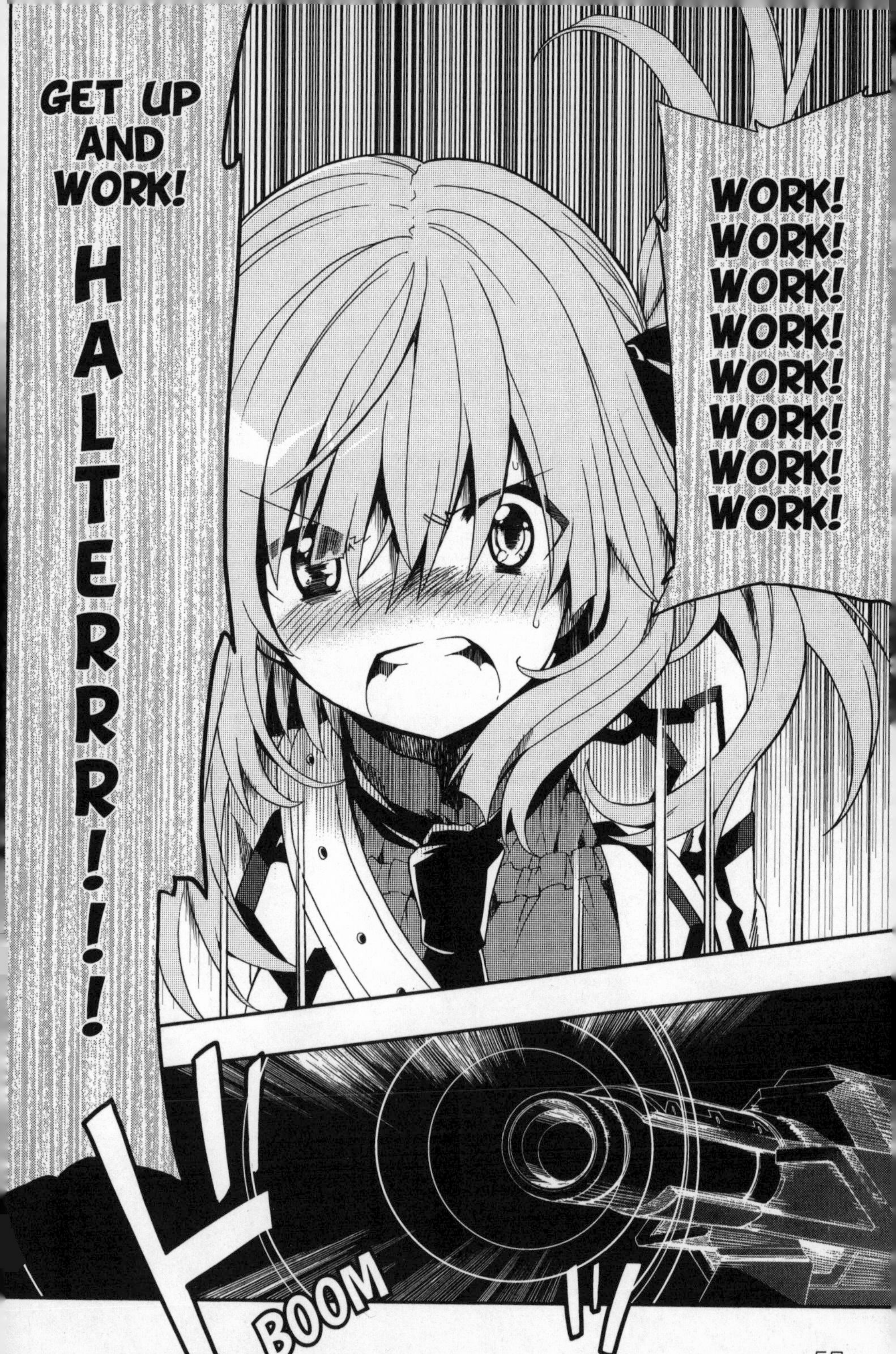
WORK! WORK! WORK! WORK! WORK! WORK! WORK! WORK!
GET UP AND WORK!
HALTERRR!!!
BOOM

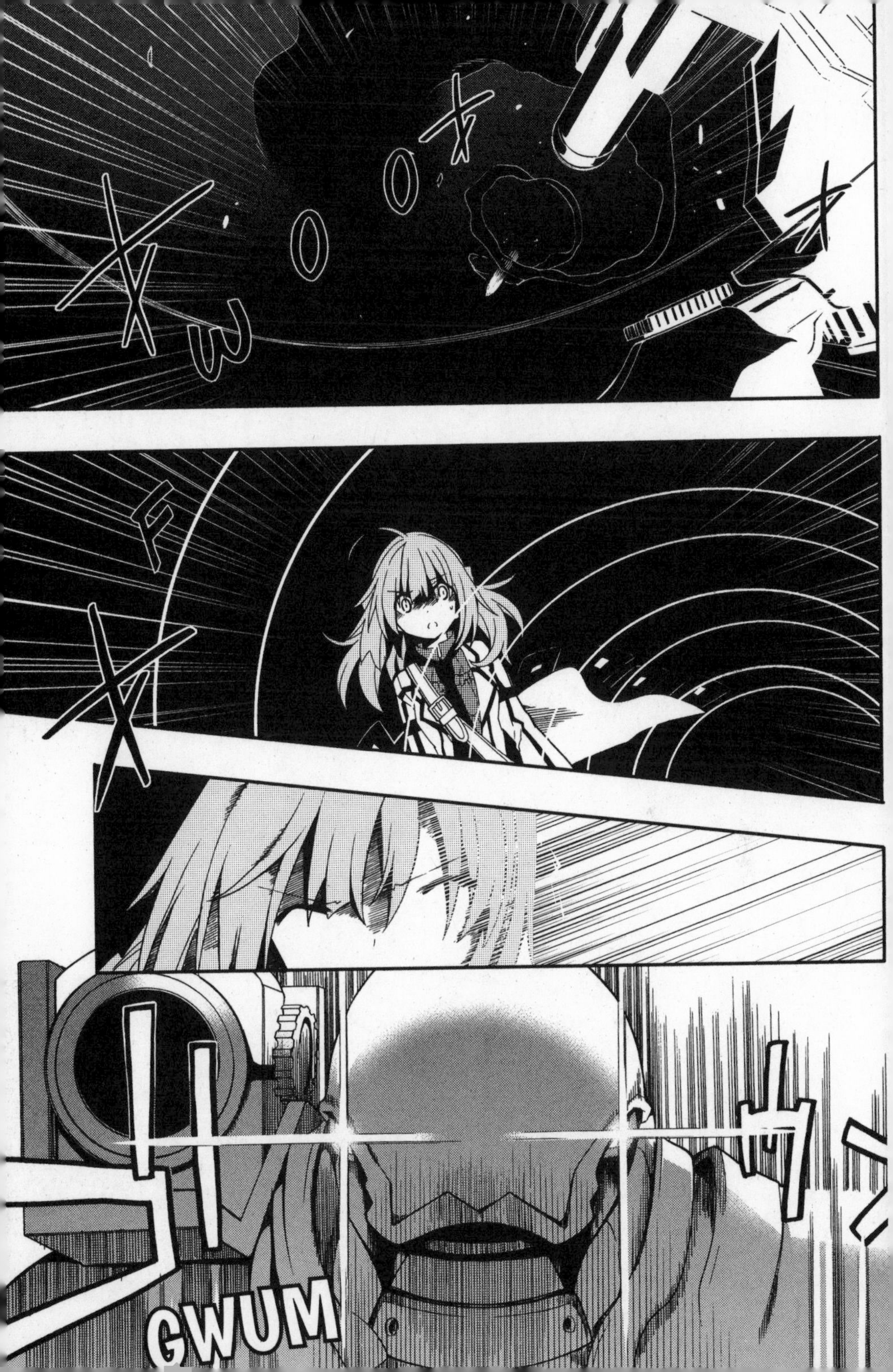
GWUM

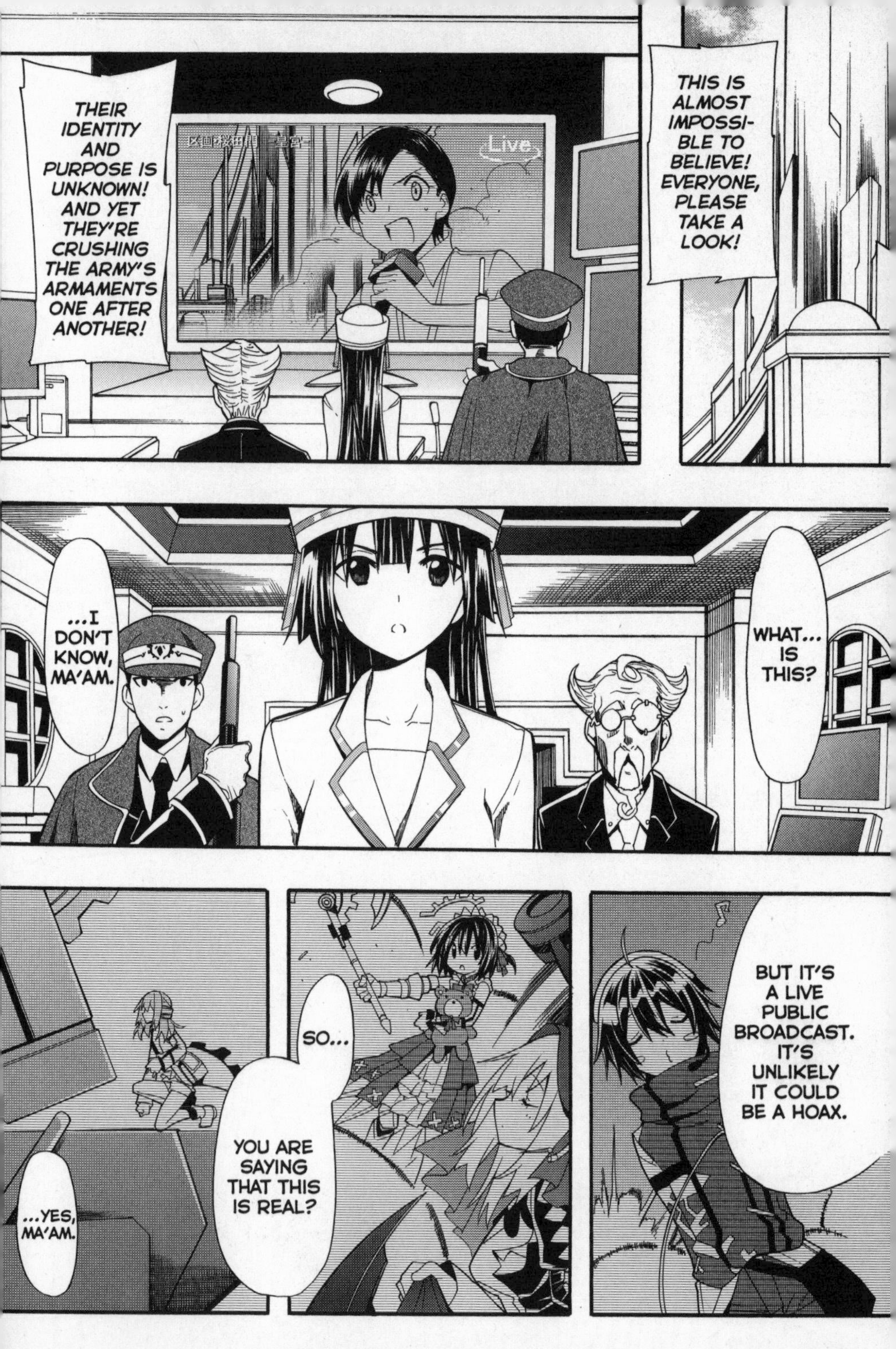
THIS IS ALMOST IMPOSSIBLE TO BELIEVE! EVERYONE, PLEASE TAKE A LOOK!
THEIR IDENTITY AND PURPOSE IS UNKNOWN! AND YET THEY'RE CRUSHING THE ARMY'S ARMAMENTS ONE AFTER ANOTHER!
Live
WHAT... IS THIS?
...I DON'T KNOW, MA'AM.
BUT IT'S A LIVE PUBLIC BROADCAST. IT'S UNLIKELY IT COULD BE A HOAX.
SO...
YOU ARE SAYING THAT THIS IS REAL?
...YES, MA'AM.

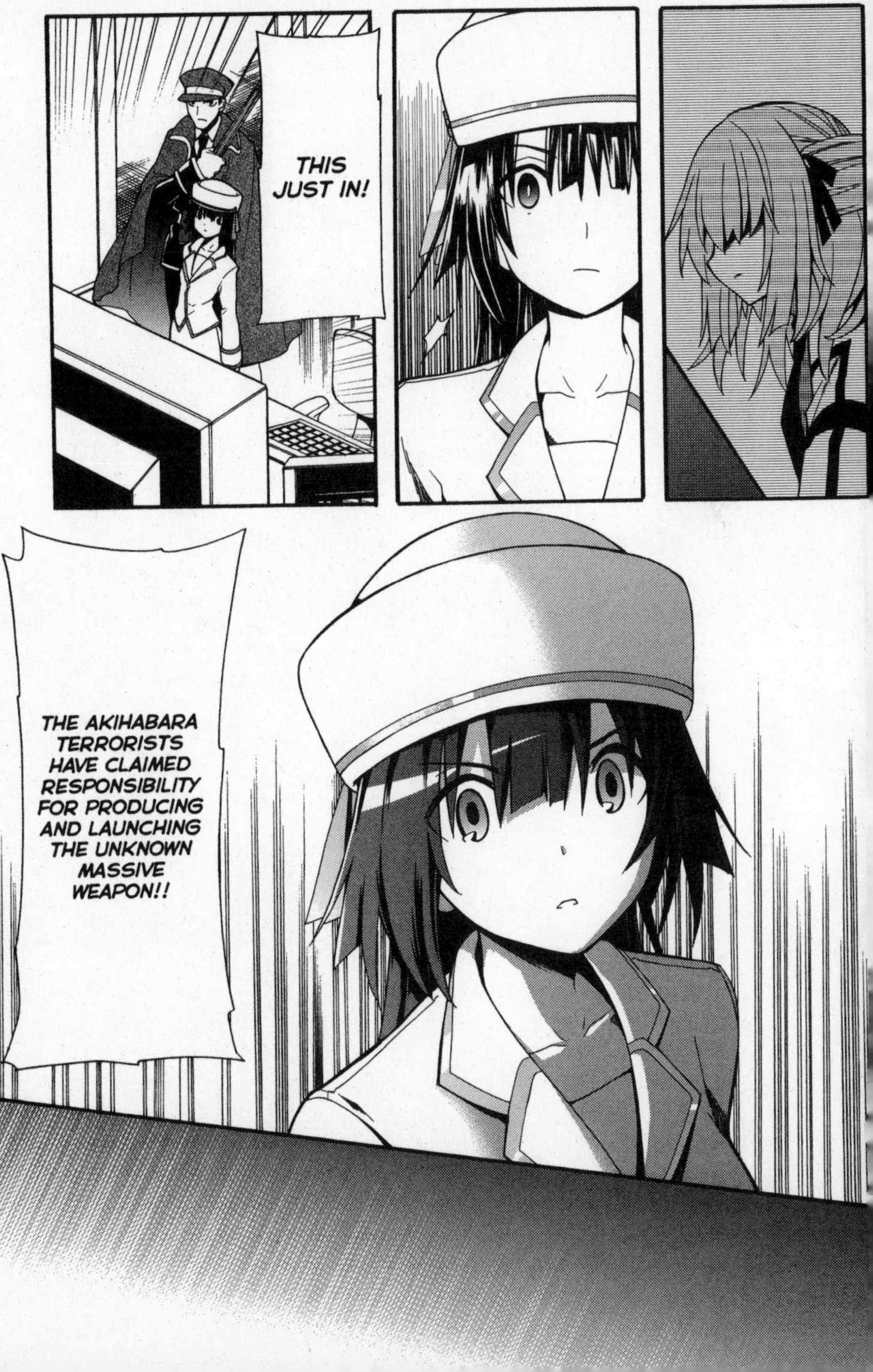
THIS JUST IN!
THE AKIHABARA TERRORISTS HAVE CLAIMED RESPONSIBILITY FOR PRODUCING AND LAUNCHING THE UNKNOWN MASSIVE WEAPON!!

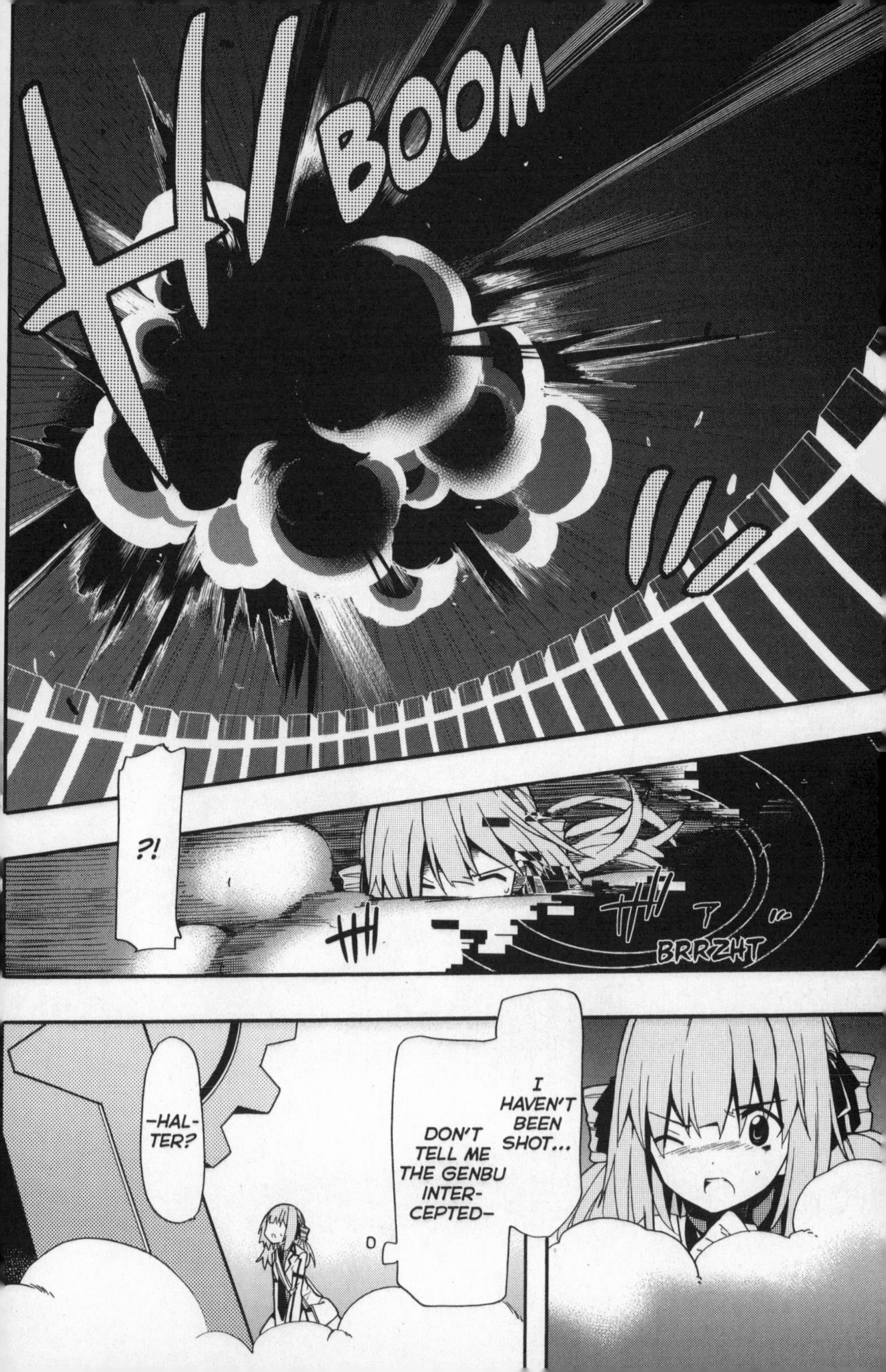
BOOM
?!
BRRZHT
I HAVEN'T BEEN SHOT...
DON'T TELL ME THE GENBU INTERCEPTED–
–HALTER?

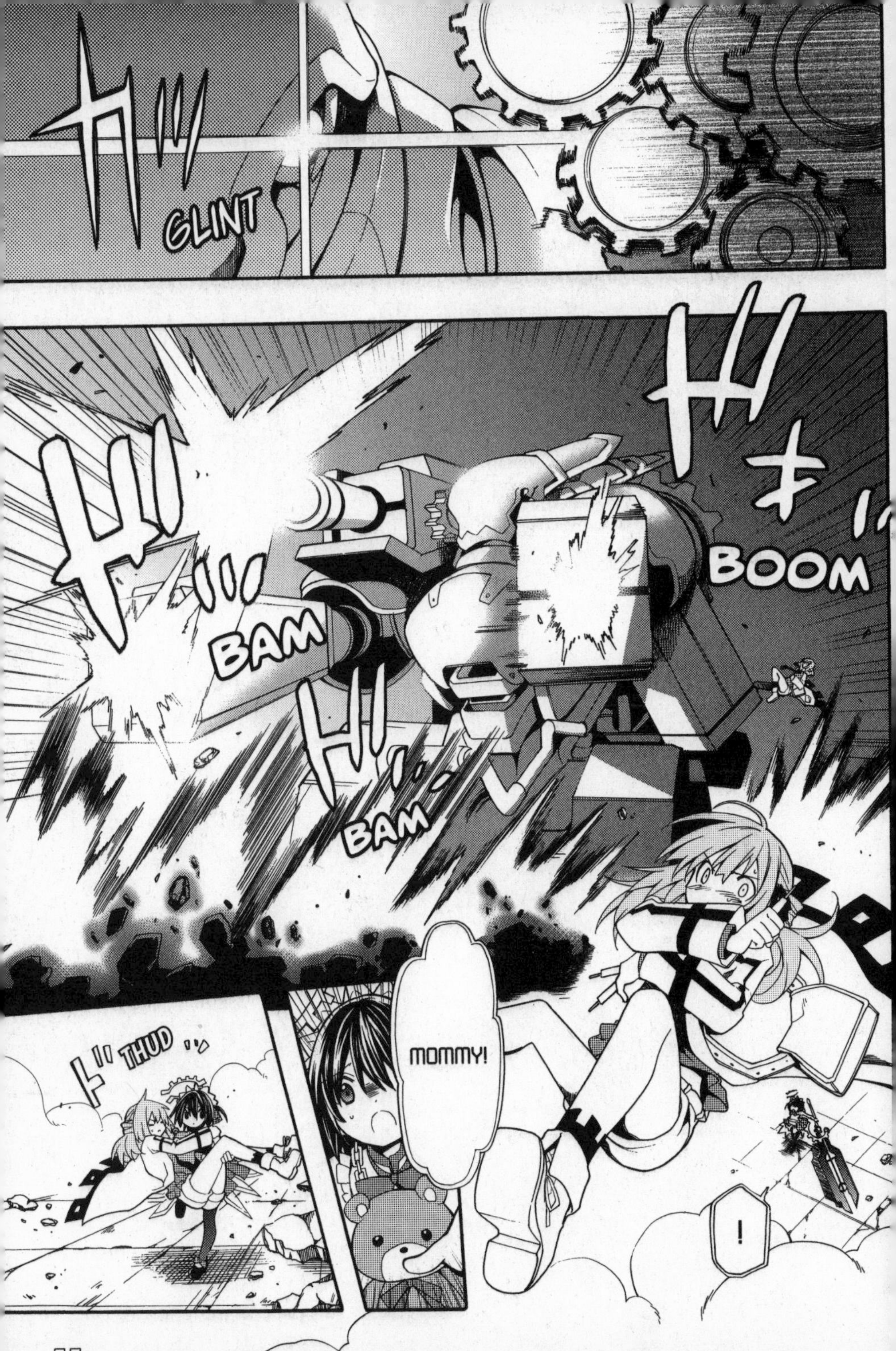
GLINT
BOOM
BAM
BAM
!
MOMMY!
THUD

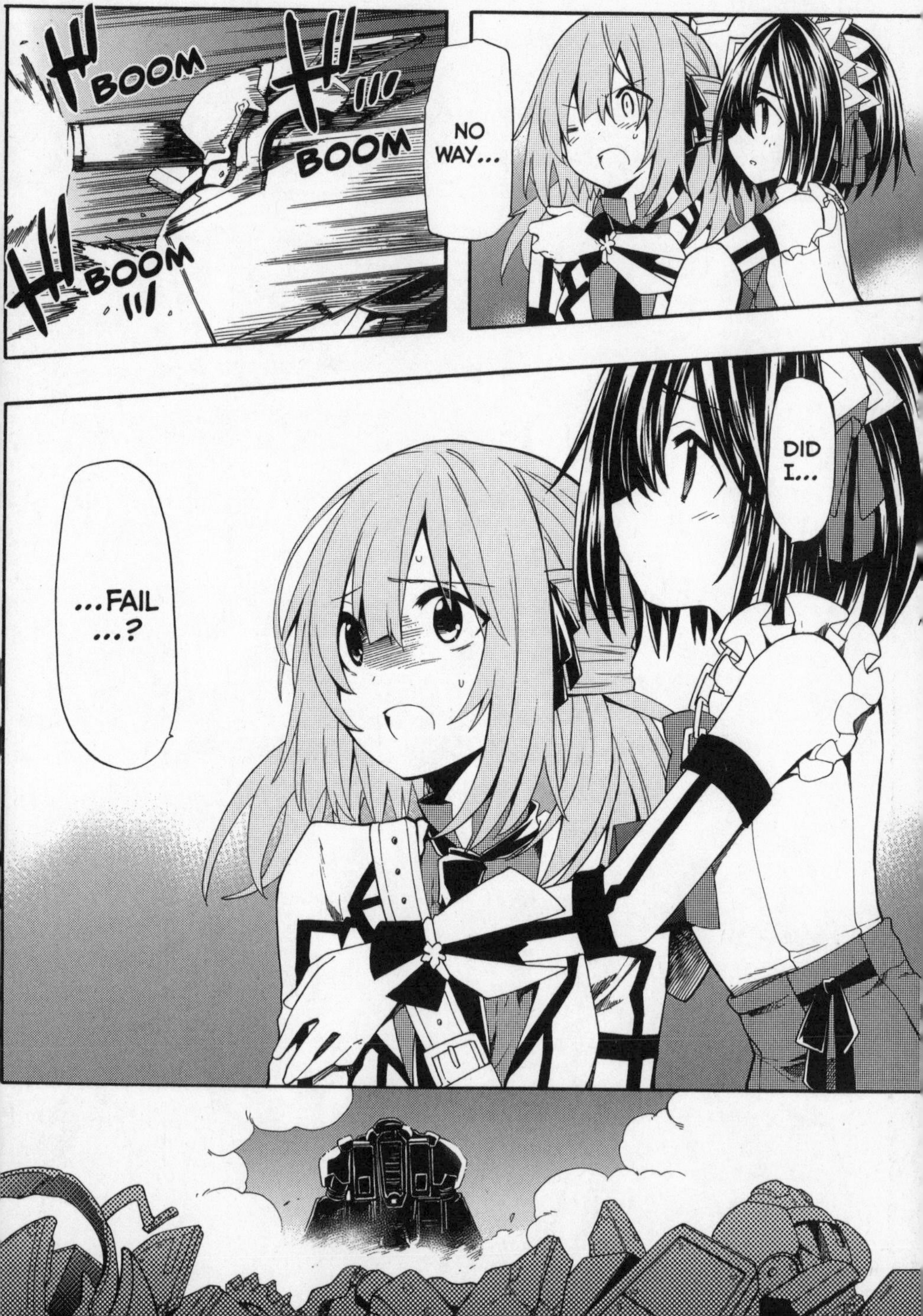
NO WAY...
BOOM
BOOM
BOOM
DID I...
...FAIL ...?

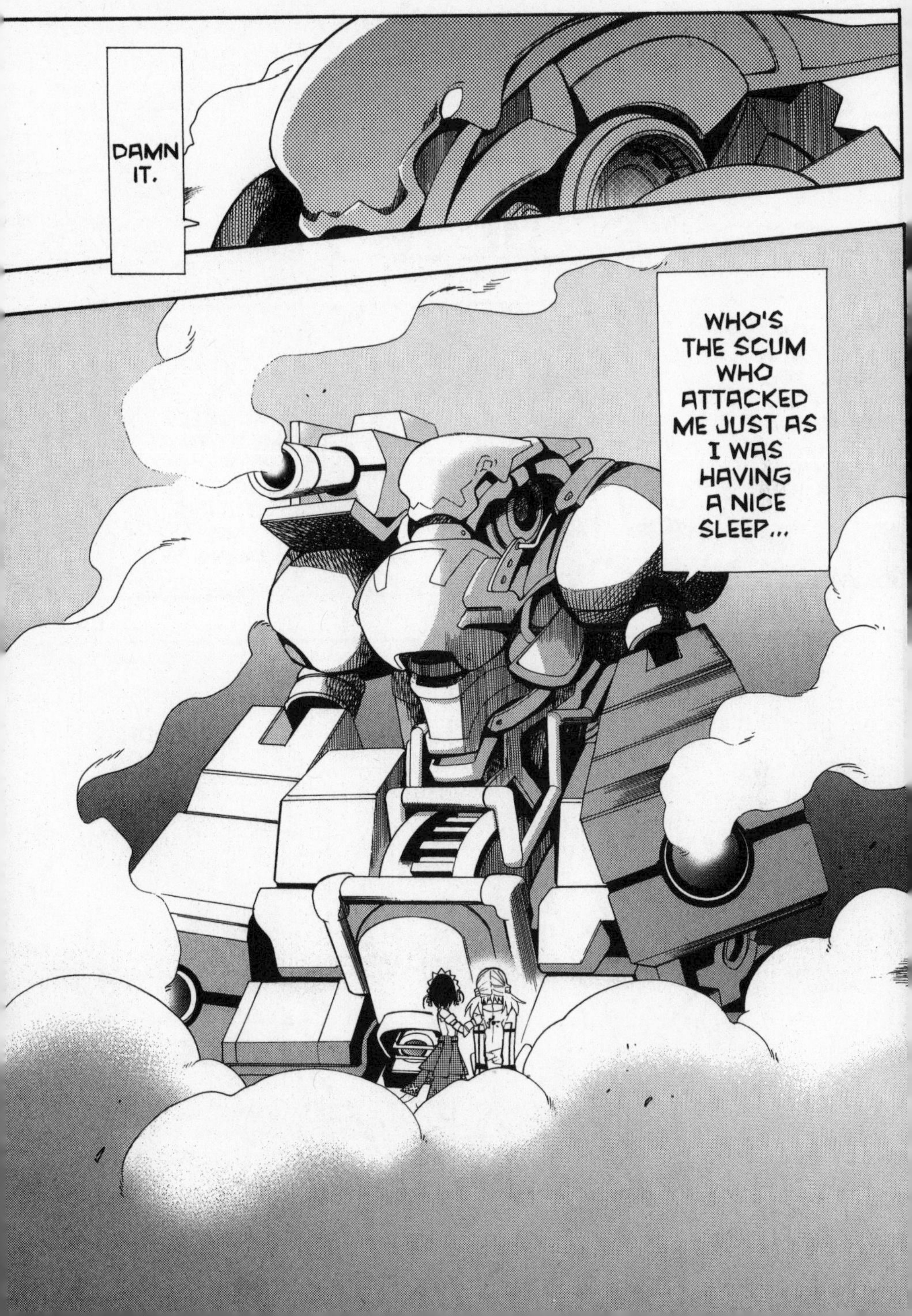
DAMN IT.
WHO'S THE SCUM WHO ATTACKED ME JUST AS I WAS HAVING A NICE SLEEP...

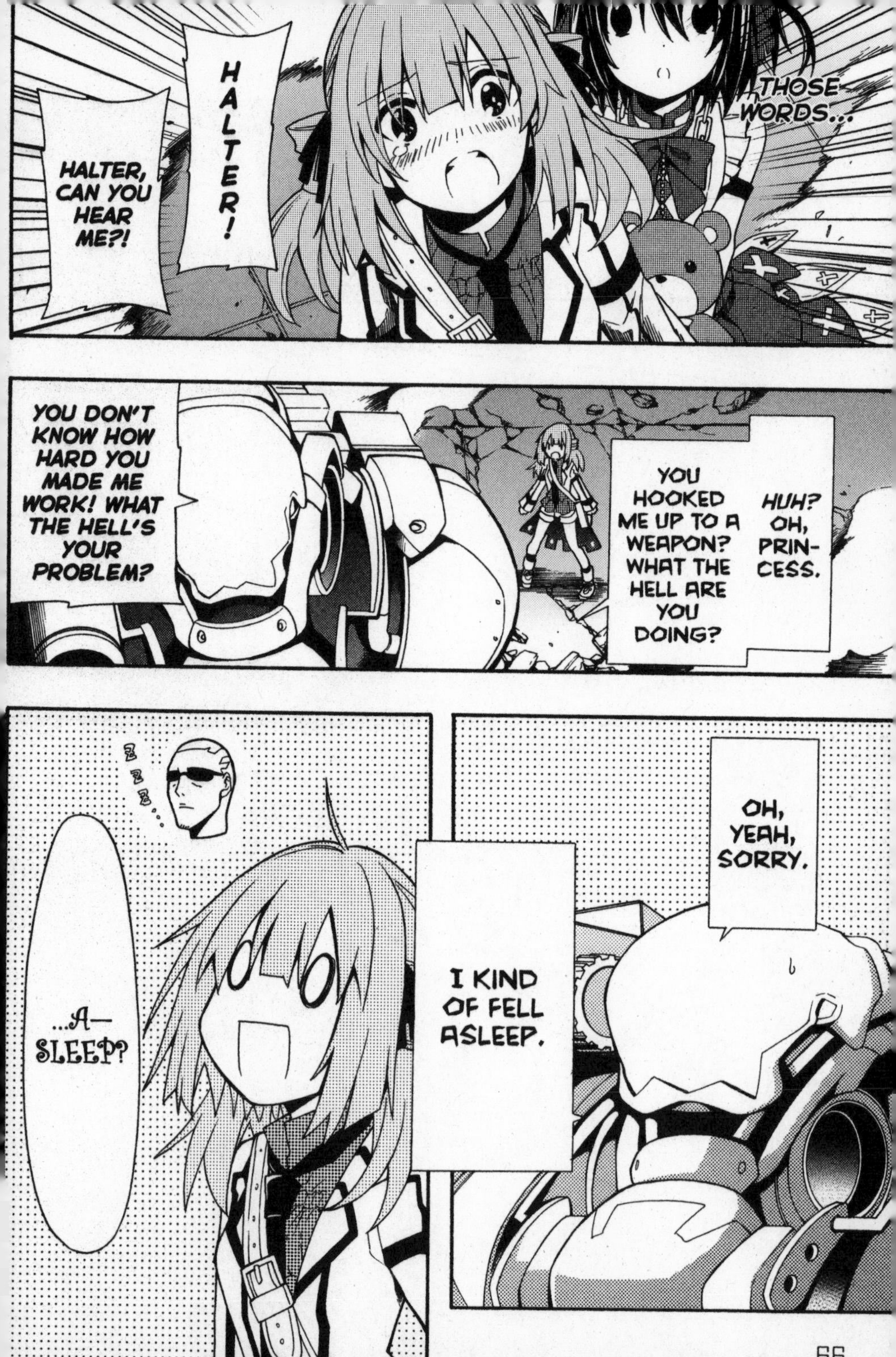
THOSE WORDS...
HALTER!
HALTER, CAN YOU HEAR ME?!
HUH? OH, PRINCESS.
YOU HOOKED ME UP TO A WEAPON? WHAT THE HELL ARE YOU DOING?
YOU DON'T KNOW HOW HARD YOU MADE ME WORK! WHAT THE HELL'S YOUR PROBLEM?
OH, YEAH, SORRY.
I KIND OF FELL ASLEEP.
Z Z Z...
...A— SLEEP?

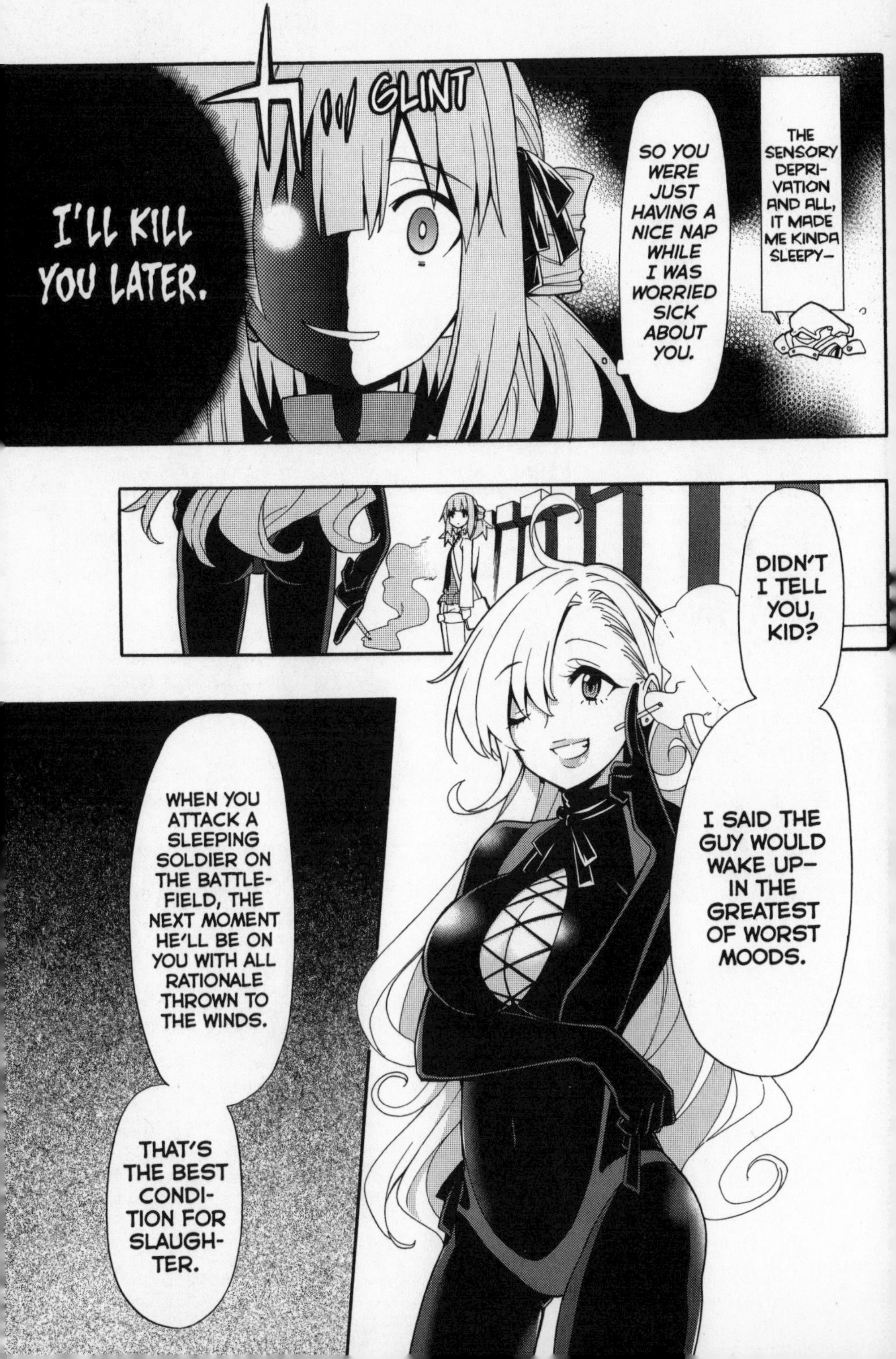
THE SENSORY DEPRIVATION AND ALL, IT MADE ME KINDA SLEEPY—
SO YOU WERE JUST HAVING A NICE NAP WHILE I WAS WORRIED SICK ABOUT YOU.
GLINT
I'LL KILL YOU LATER.
DIDN'T I TELL YOU, KID?
I SAID THE GUY WOULD WAKE UP— IN THE GREATEST OF WORST MOODS.
WHEN YOU ATTACK A SLEEPING SOLDIER ON THE BATTLEFIELD, THE NEXT MOMENT HE'LL BE ON YOU WITH ALL RATIONALE THROWN TO THE WINDS.
THAT'S THE BEST CONDITION FOR SLAUGHTER.

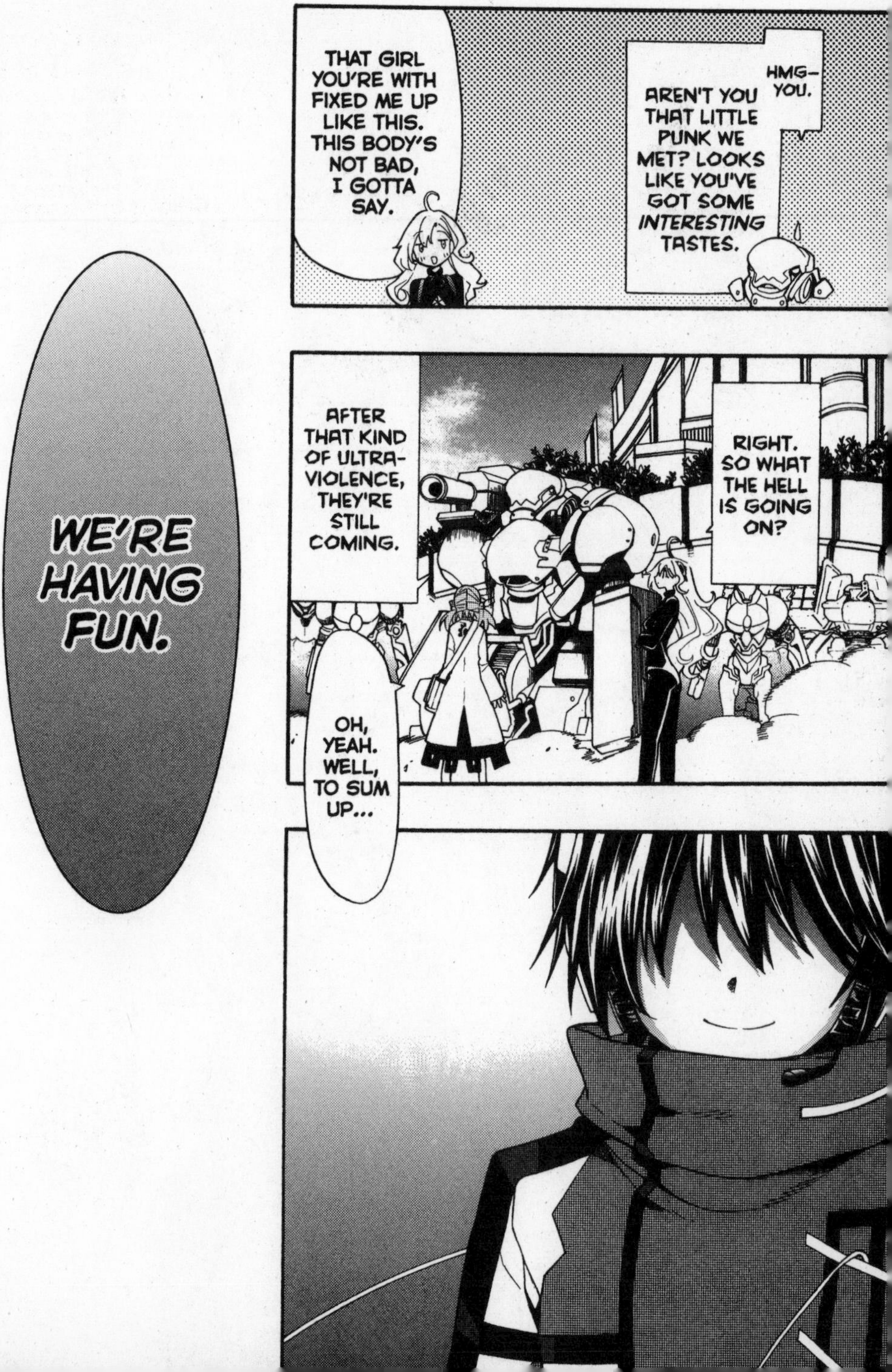
HMG— YOU.
AREN'T YOU THAT LITTLE PUNK WE MET? LOOKS LIKE YOU'VE GOT SOME *INTERESTING* TASTES.
THAT GIRL YOU'RE WITH FIXED ME UP LIKE THIS. THIS BODY'S NOT BAD, I GOTTA SAY.
RIGHT. SO WHAT THE HELL IS GOING ON?
AFTER THAT KIND OF ULTRA-VIOLENCE, THEY'RE STILL COMING.
OH, YEAH. WELL, TO SUM UP...
WE'RE HAVING FUN.

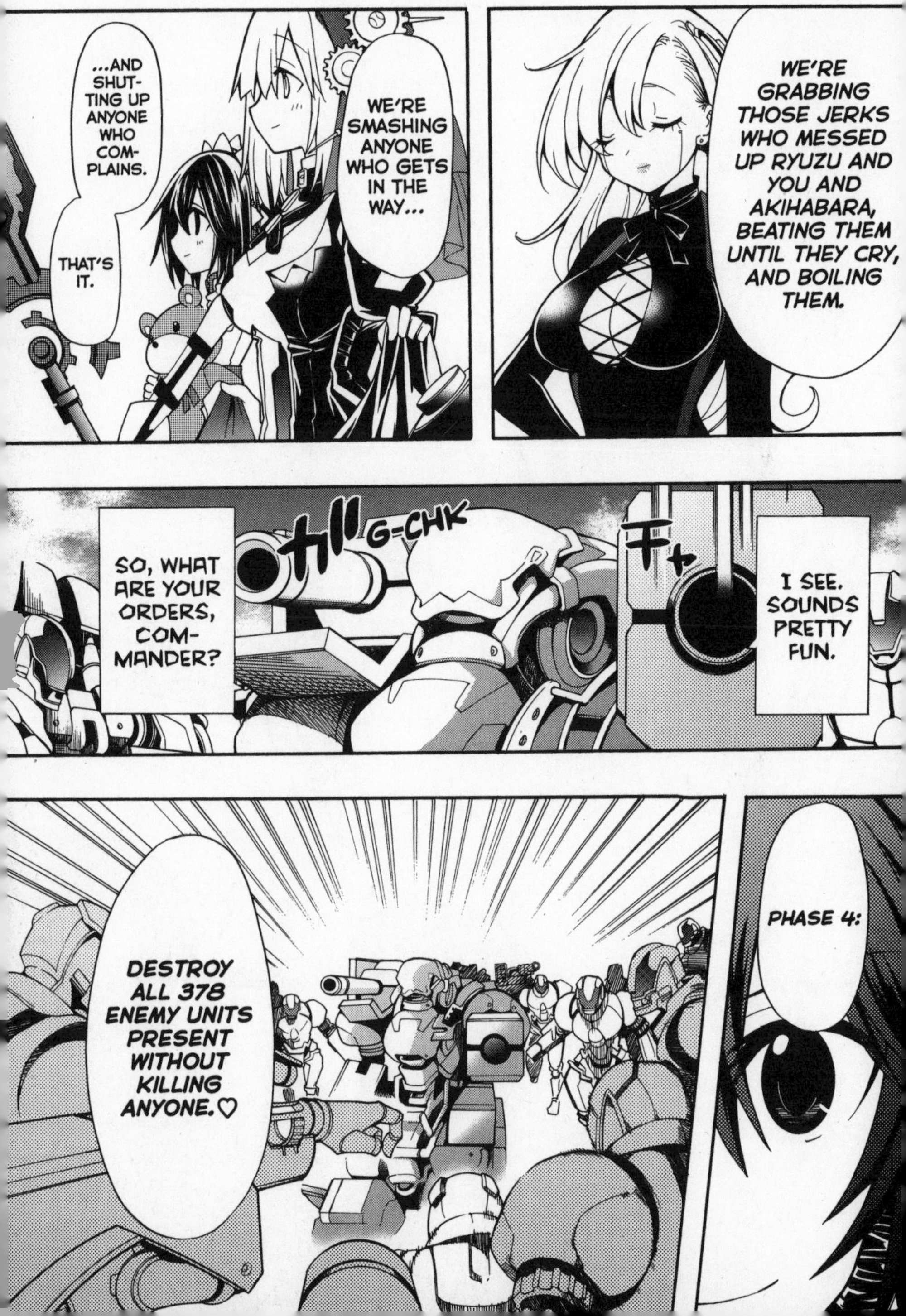
WE'RE GRABBING THOSE JERKS WHO MESSED UP RYUZU AND YOU AND AKIHABARA, BEATING THEM UNTIL THEY CRY, AND BOILING THEM.
WE'RE SMASHING ANYONE WHO GETS IN THE WAY...
...AND SHUTTING UP ANYONE WHO COMPLAINS.
THAT'S IT.
I SEE. SOUNDS PRETTY FUN.
チャ
カリ G-CHK
SO, WHAT ARE YOUR ORDERS, COMMANDER?
PHASE 4:
DESTROY ALL 378 ENEMY UNITS PRESENT WITHOUT KILLING ANYONE.♡

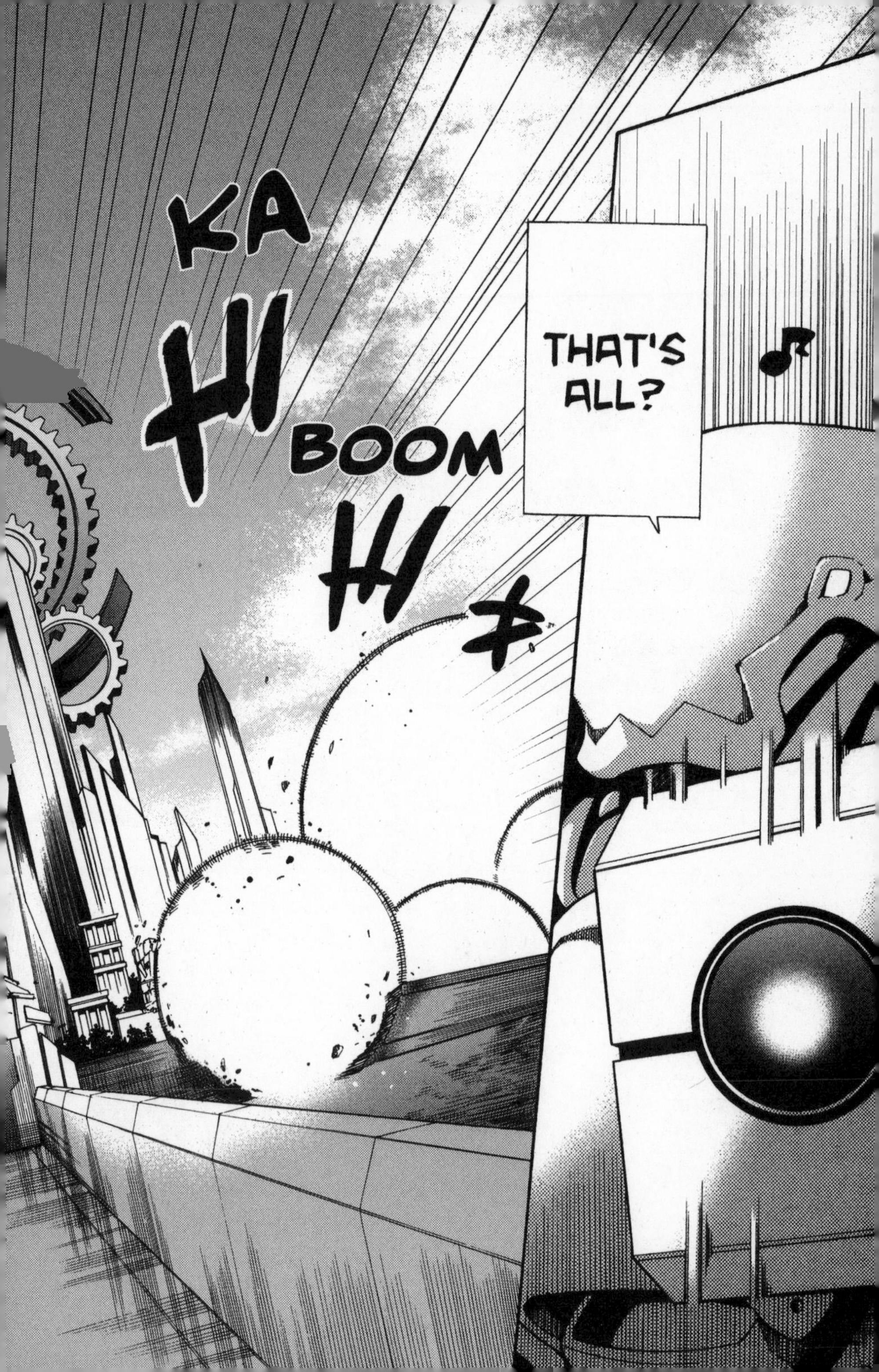
THAT'S ALL?
KA
BOOM

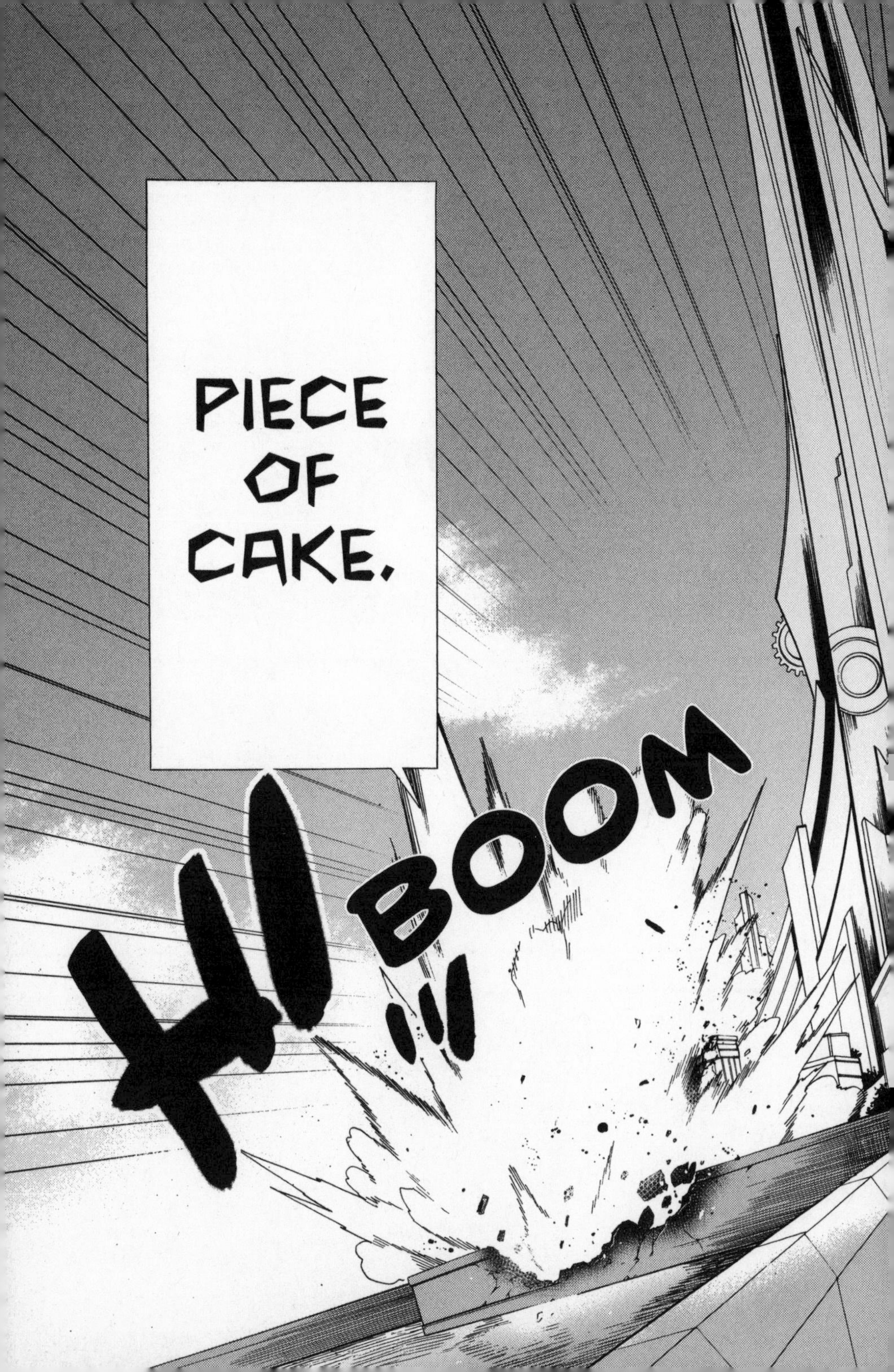

PIECE OF CAKE.
BOOM!!!

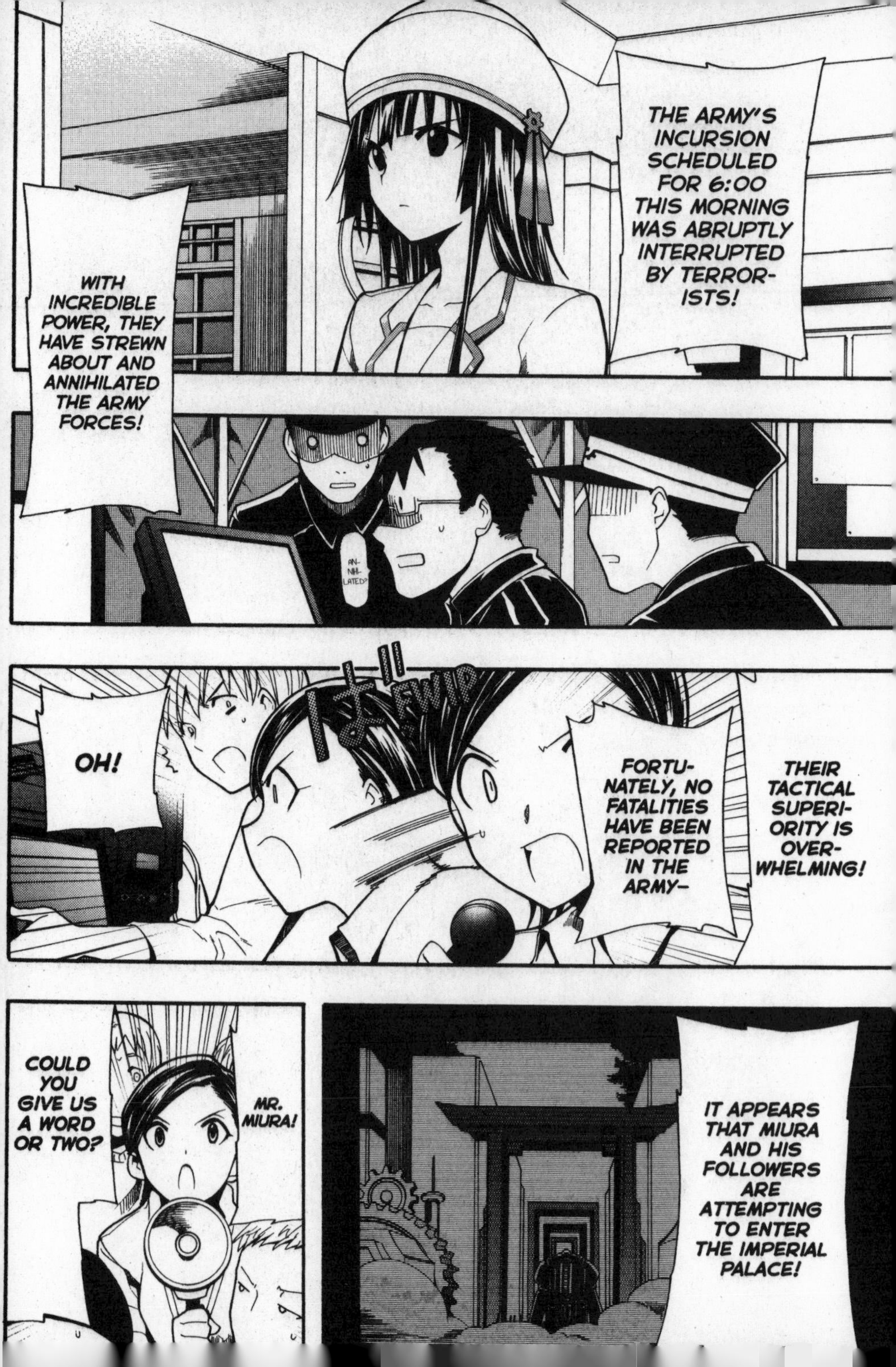
THE ARMY'S INCURSION SCHEDULED FOR 6:00 THIS MORNING WAS ABRUPTLY INTERRUPTED BY TERROR-ISTS!
WITH INCREDIBLE POWER, THEY HAVE STREWN ABOUT AND ANNIHILATED THE ARMY FORCES!
AN-NIHI-LATED?
THEIR TACTICAL SUPERI-ORITY IS OVER-WHELMING!
FORTU-NATELY, NO FATALITIES HAVE BEEN REPORTED IN THE ARMY–
FWIP
OH!
IT APPEARS THAT MIURA AND HIS FOLLOWERS ARE ATTEMPTING TO ENTER THE IMPERIAL PALACE!
MR. MIURA!
COULD YOU GIVE US A WORD OR TWO?

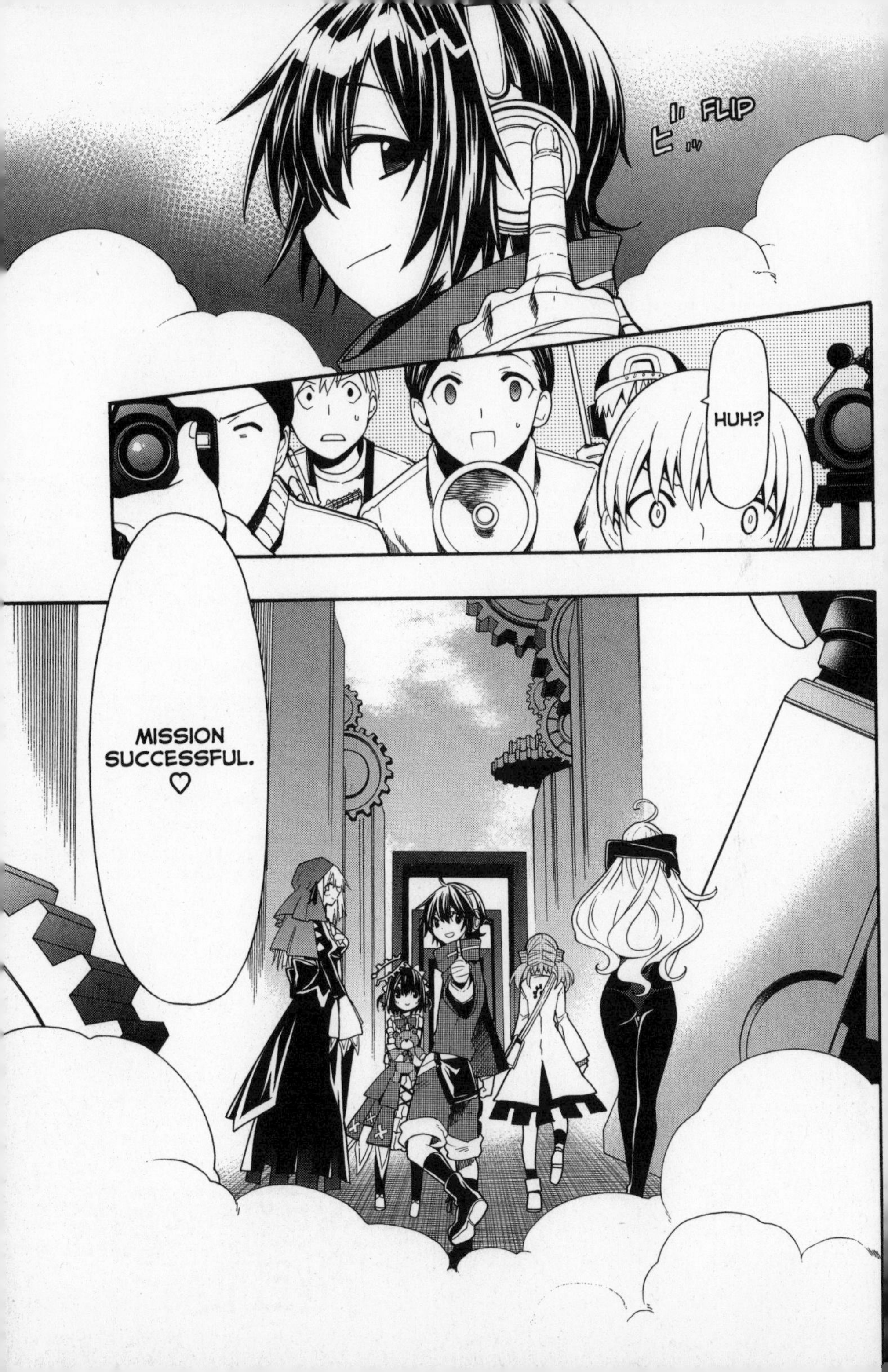
FLIP
HUH?
MISSION SUCCESSFUL. ♡

Clockwork Planet

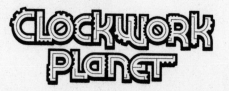

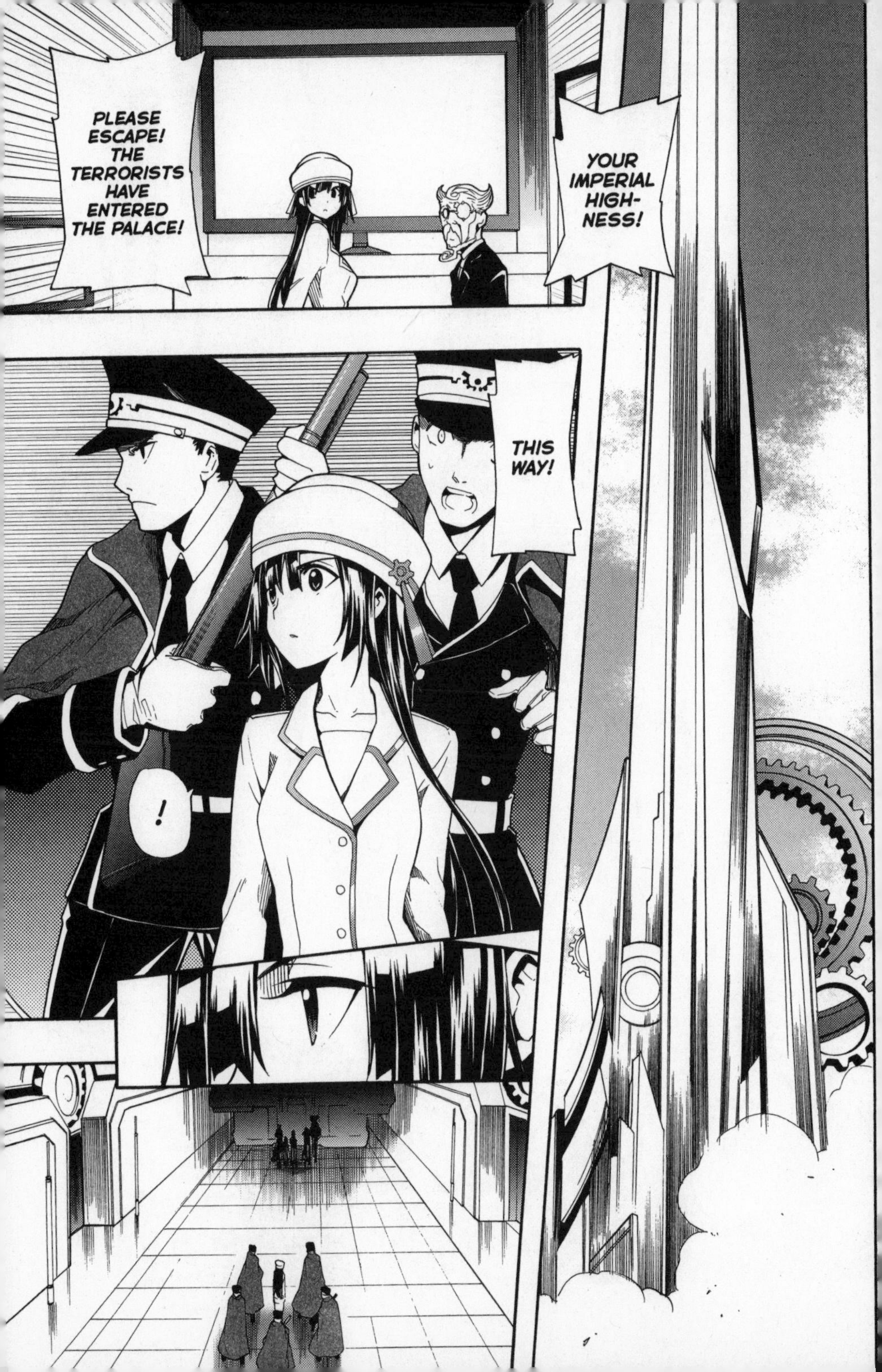
YOUR IMPERIAL HIGH-NESS!
PLEASE ESCAPE! THE TERRORISTS HAVE ENTERED THE PALACE!
THIS WAY!
!

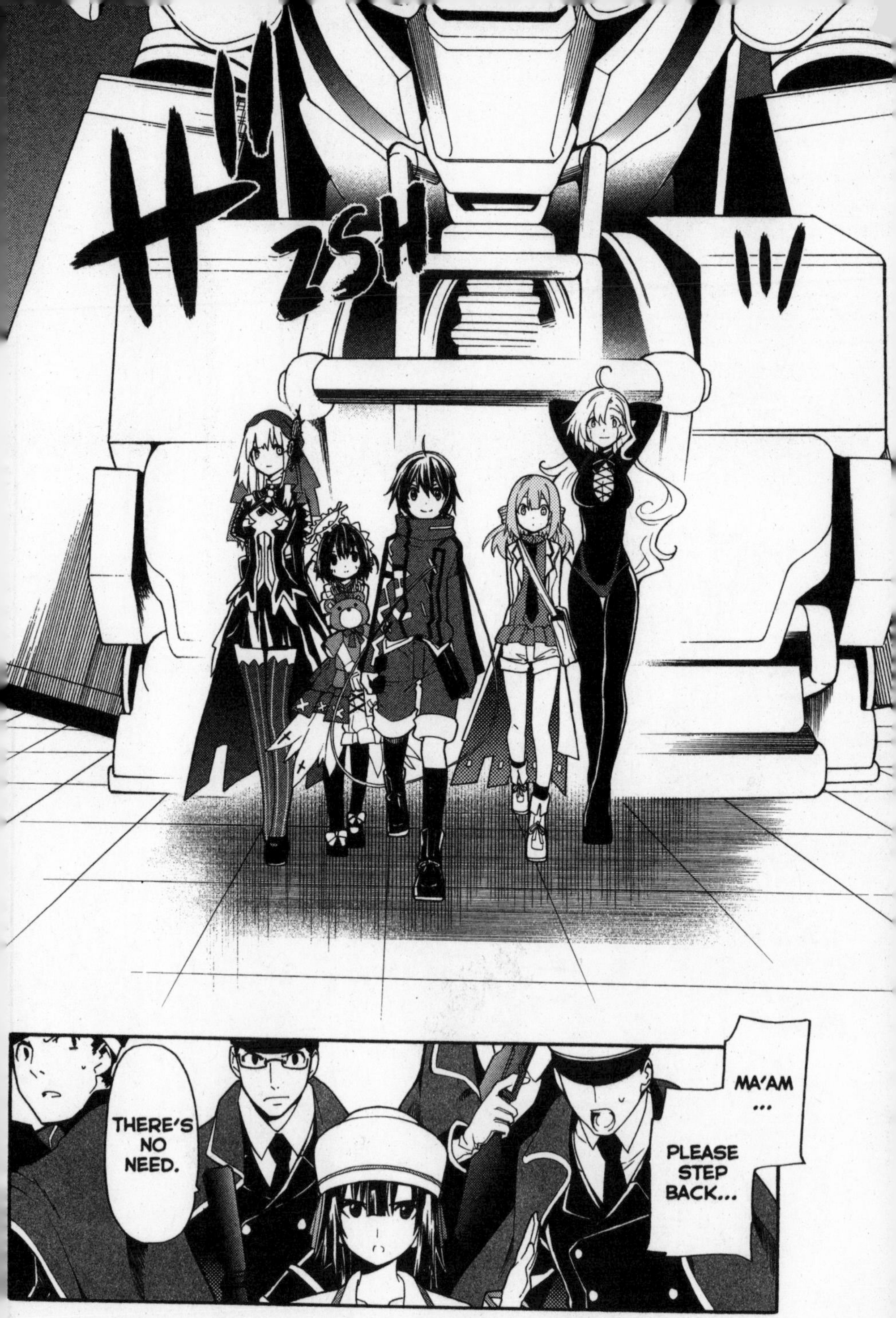
MA'AM ...
PLEASE STEP BACK...
THERE'S NO NEED.

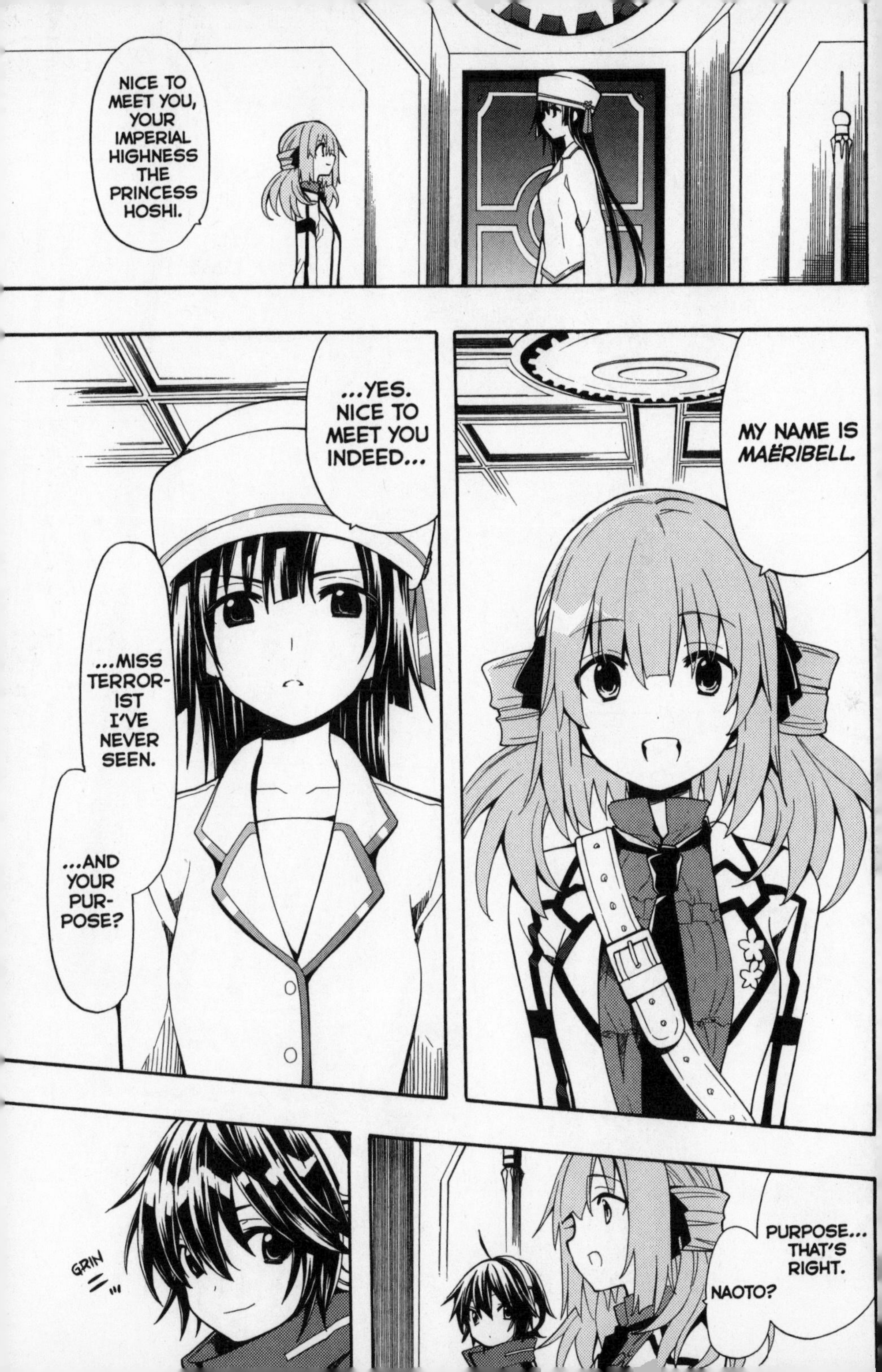
NICE TO MEET YOU, YOUR IMPERIAL HIGHNESS THE PRINCESS HOSHI.
MY NAME IS MAËRIBELL.
...YES. NICE TO MEET YOU INDEED...
...MISS TERRORIST I'VE NEVER SEEN.
...AND YOUR PURPOSE?
PURPOSE... THAT'S RIGHT.
NAOTO?
GRIN

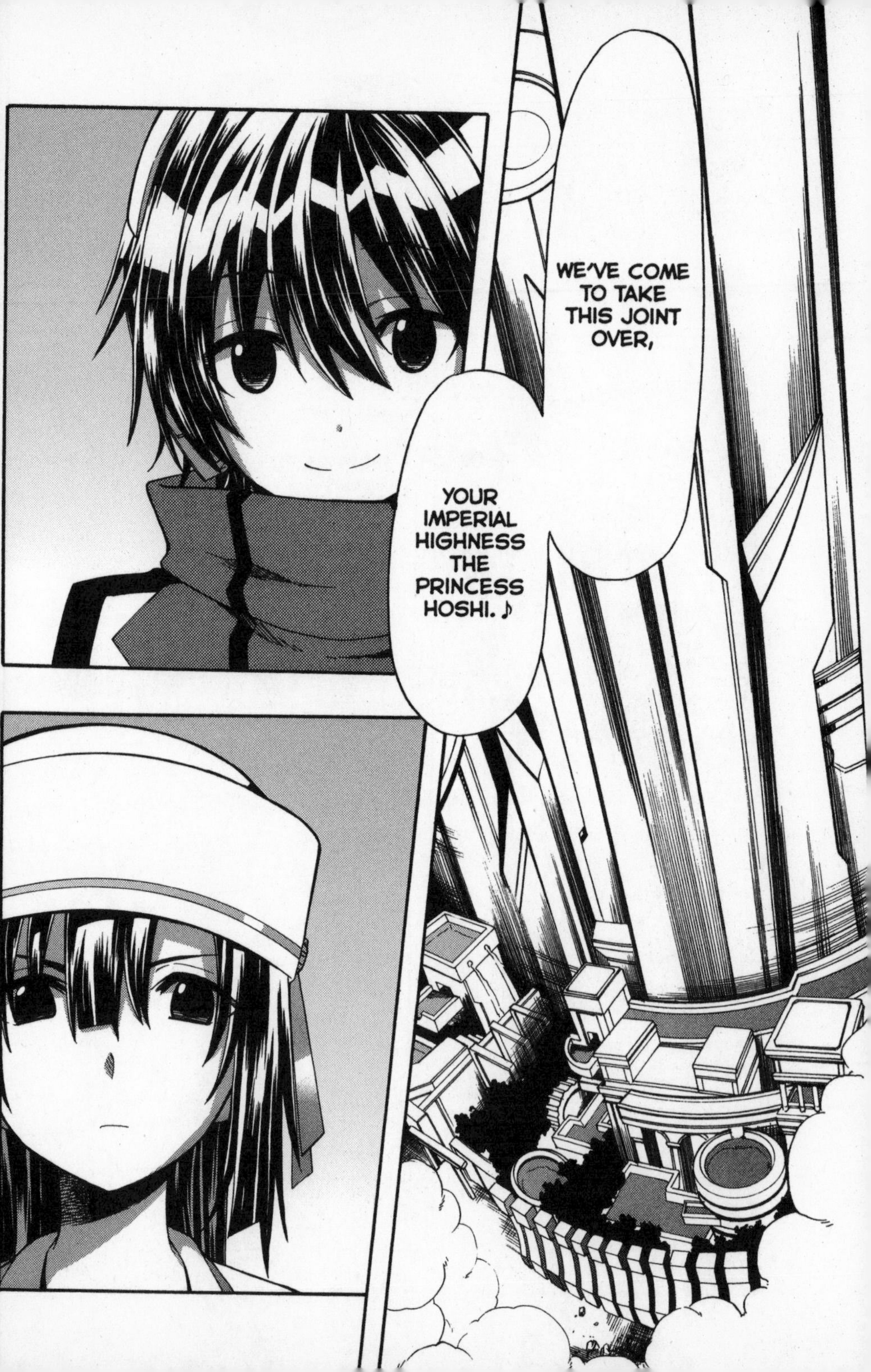
WE'VE COME TO TAKE THIS JOINT OVER,
YOUR IMPERIAL HIGHNESS THE PRINCESS HOSHI. ♪

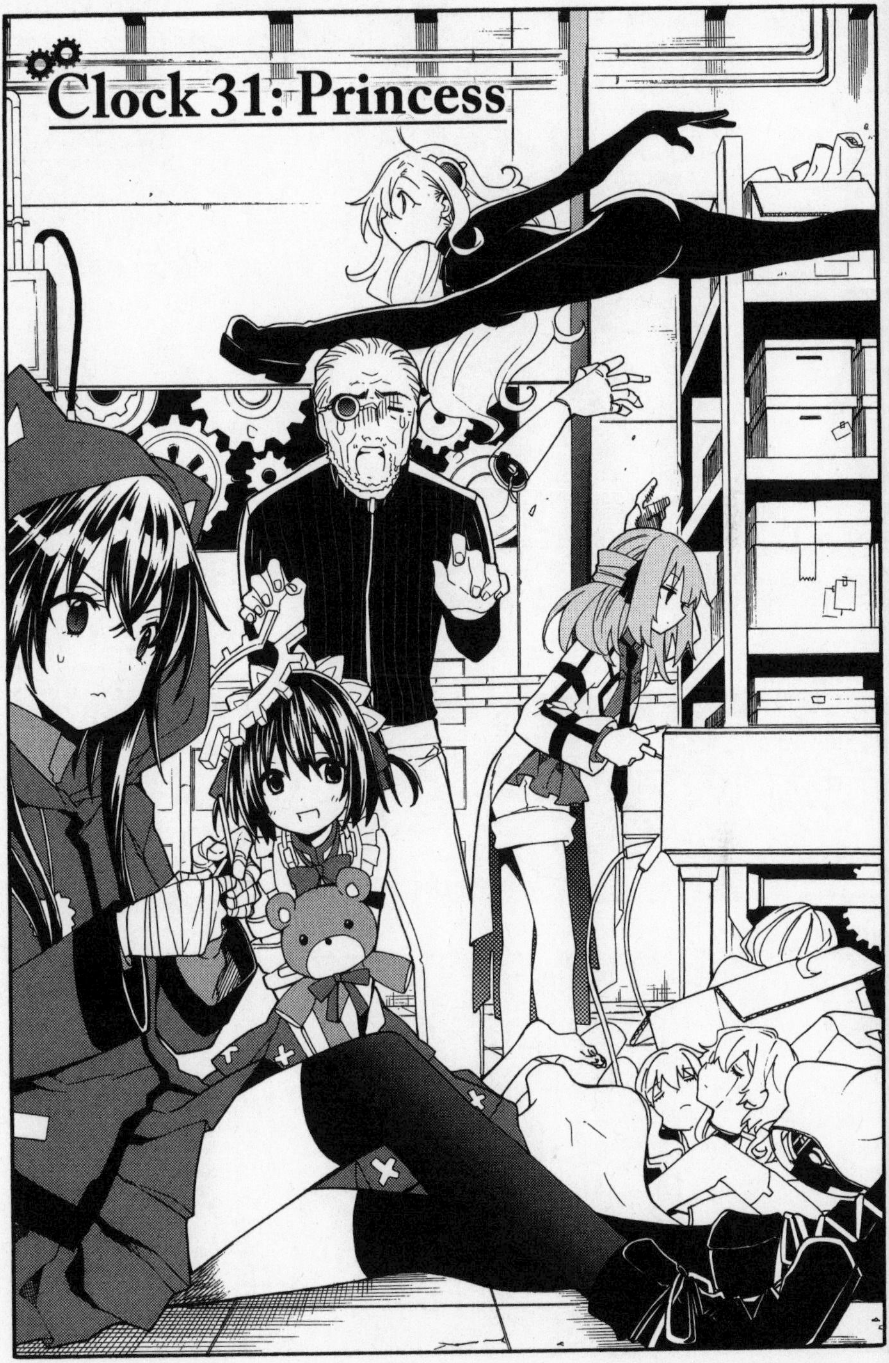
Clock 31: Princess

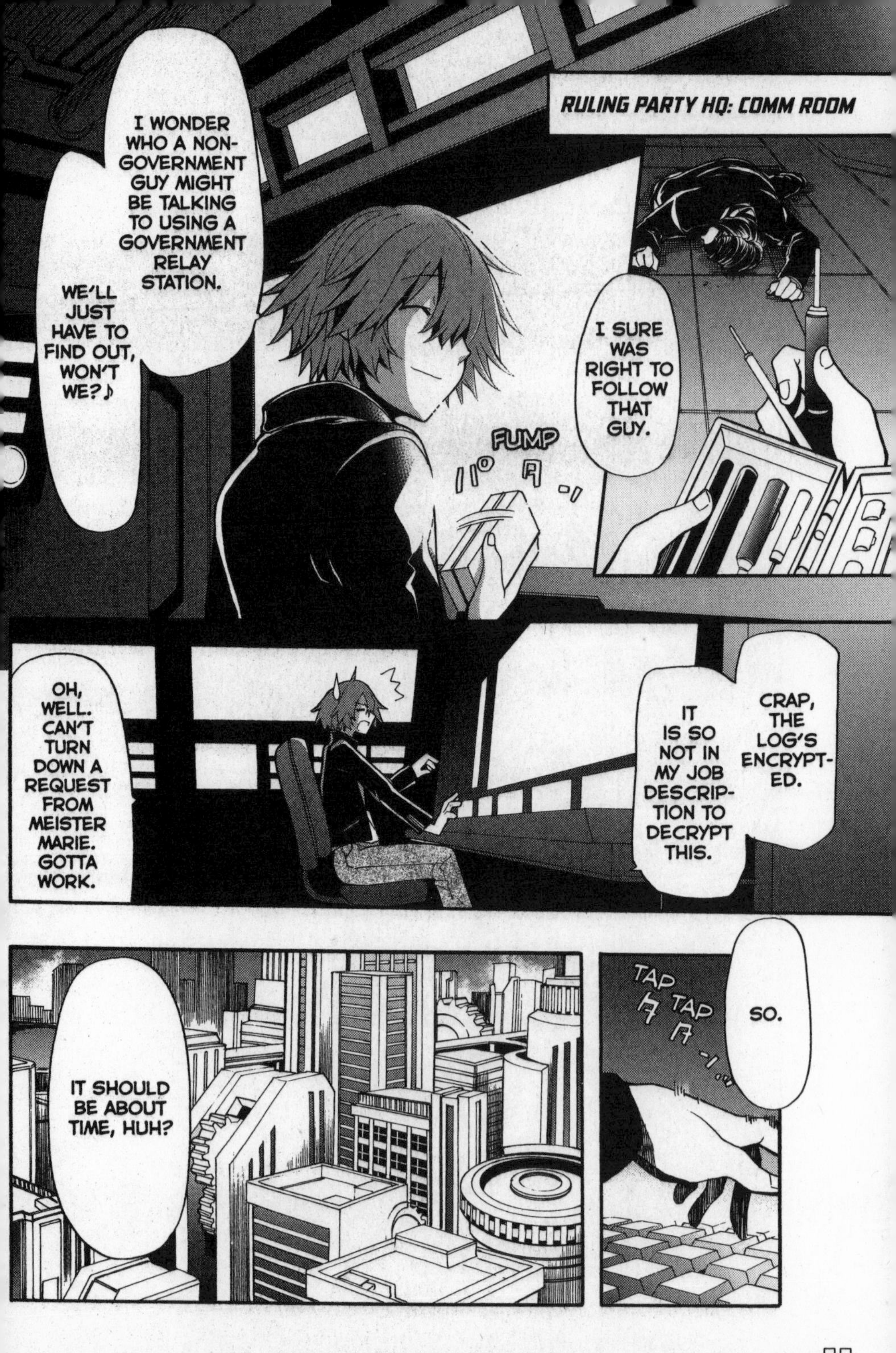
RULING PARTY HQ: COMM ROOM
I SURE WAS RIGHT TO FOLLOW THAT GUY.
FUMP
I WONDER WHO A NON-GOVERNMENT GUY MIGHT BE TALKING TO USING A GOVERNMENT RELAY STATION.
WE'LL JUST HAVE TO FIND OUT, WON'T WE?♪
CRAP, THE LOG'S ENCRYPT-ED.
IT IS SO NOT IN MY JOB DESCRIP-TION TO DECRYPT THIS.
OH, WELL. CAN'T TURN DOWN A REQUEST FROM MEISTER MARIE. GOTTA WORK.
SO.
TAP TAP
IT SHOULD BE ABOUT TIME, HUH?

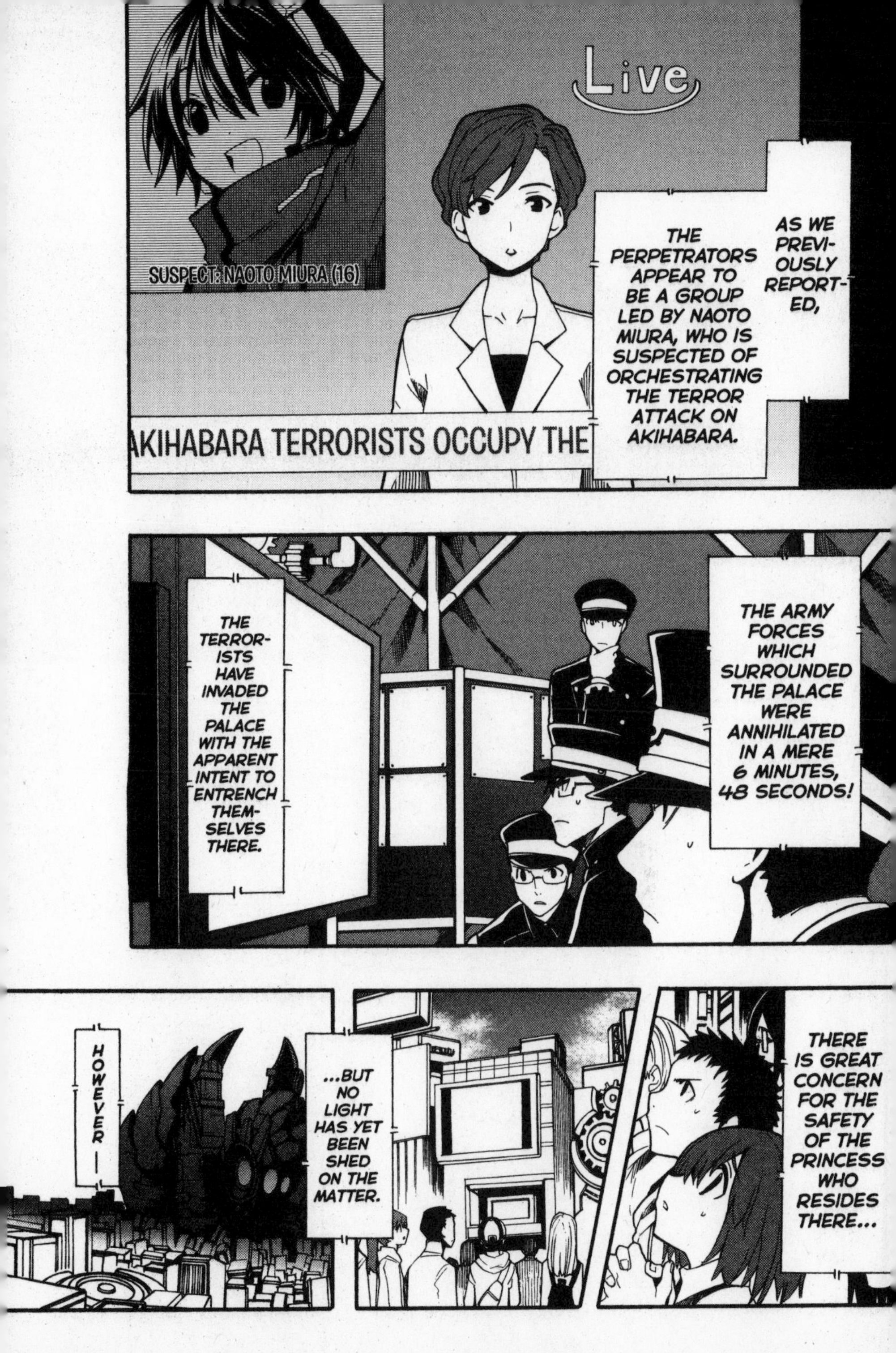
Live
AS WE PREVIOUSLY REPORTED,
THE PERPETRATORS APPEAR TO BE A GROUP LED BY NAOTO MIURA, WHO IS SUSPECTED OF ORCHESTRATING THE TERROR ATTACK ON AKIHABARA.
SUSPECT: NAOTO MIURA (16)
AKIHABARA TERRORISTS OCCUPY THE
THE ARMY FORCES WHICH SURROUNDED THE PALACE WERE ANNIHILATED IN A MERE 6 MINUTES, 48 SECONDS!
THE TERRORISTS HAVE INVADED THE PALACE WITH THE APPARENT INTENT TO ENTRENCH THEMSELVES THERE.
THERE IS GREAT CONCERN FOR THE SAFETY OF THE PRINCESS WHO RESIDES THERE...
...BUT NO LIGHT HAS YET BEEN SHED ON THE MATTER.
HOWEVER—

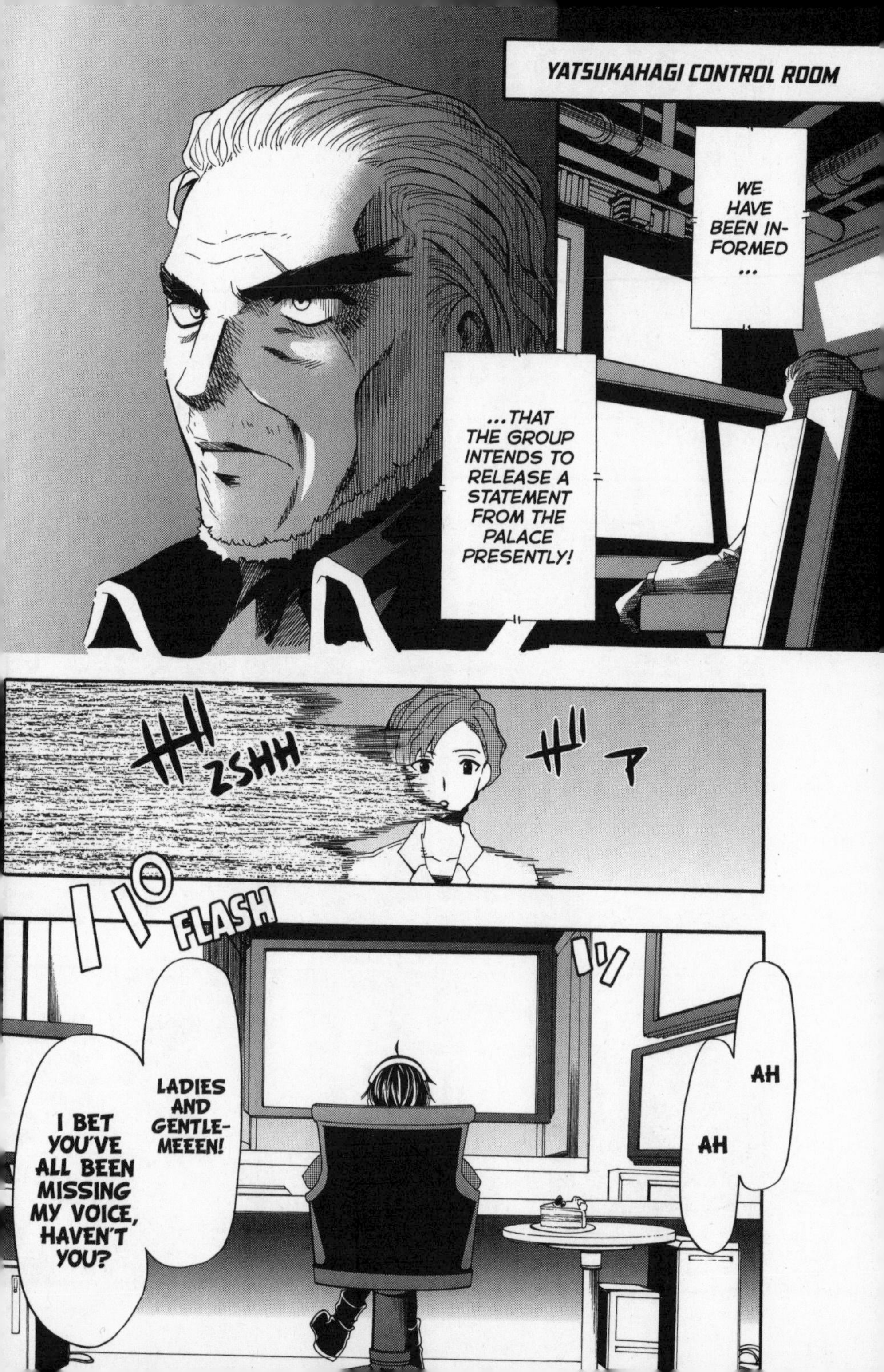
YATSUKAHAGI CONTROL ROOM
WE HAVE BEEN IN-FORMED...
...THAT THE GROUP INTENDS TO RELEASE A STATEMENT FROM THE PALACE PRESENTLY!
ZSHH
FLASH
AH AH
LADIES AND GENTLE-MEEEN!
I BET YOU'VE ALL BEEN MISSING MY VOICE, HAVEN'T YOU?

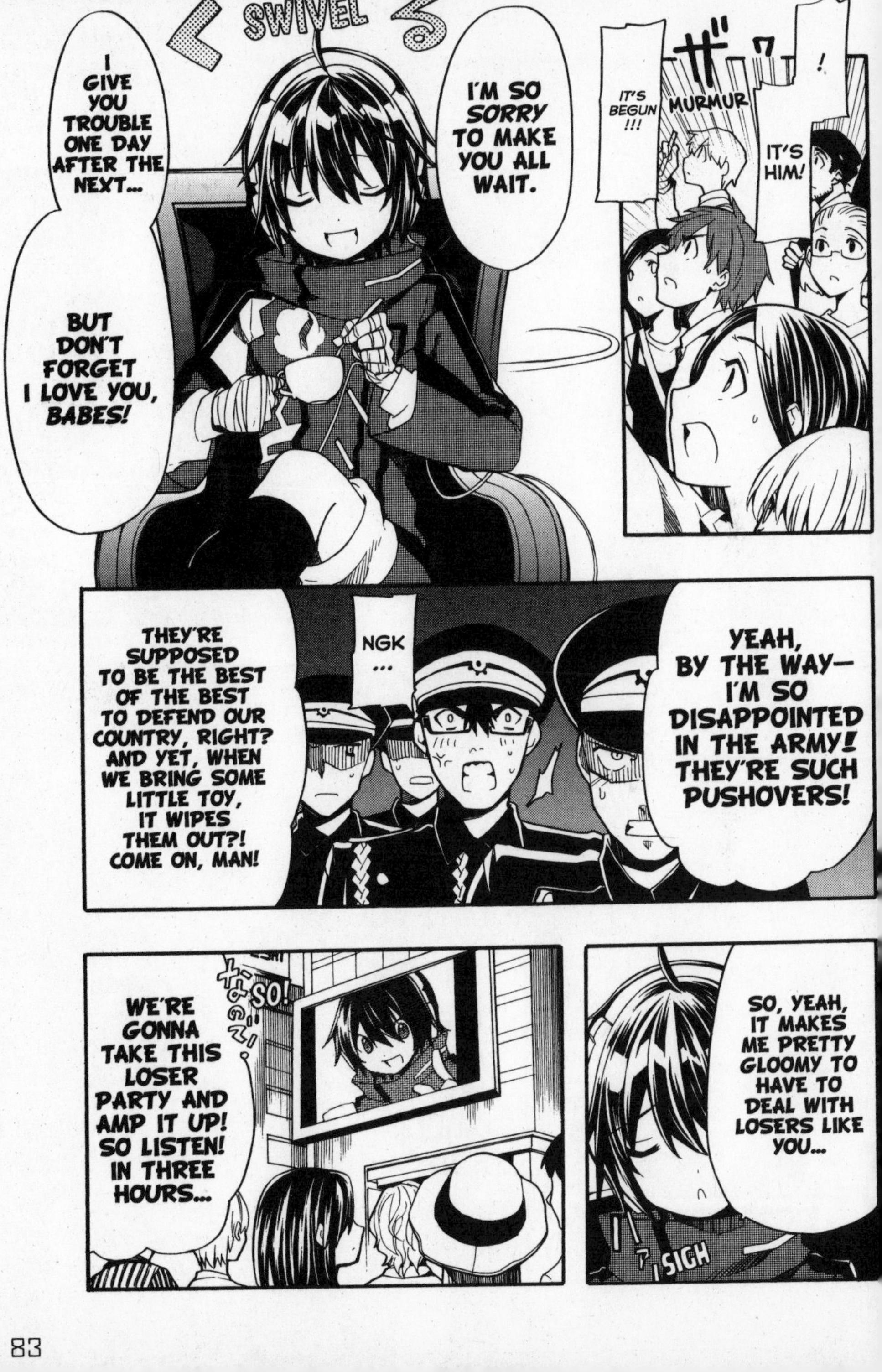

!
IT'S HIM!
ザワ
MURMUR
IT'S BEGUN!!!
SWIVEL
I'M SO SORRY TO MAKE YOU ALL WAIT.
I GIVE YOU TROUBLE ONE DAY AFTER THE NEXT...
BUT DON'T FORGET I LOVE YOU, BABES!
YEAH, BY THE WAY— I'M SO DISAPPOINTED IN THE ARMY! THEY'RE SUCH PUSHOVERS!
NGK...
THEY'RE SUPPOSED TO BE THE BEST OF THE BEST TO DEFEND OUR COUNTRY, RIGHT? AND YET, WHEN WE BRING SOME LITTLE TOY, IT WIPES THEM OUT?! COME ON, MAN!
SO, YEAH, IT MAKES ME PRETTY GLOOMY TO HAVE TO DEAL WITH LOSERS LIKE YOU...
SIGH
SO!
WE'RE GONNA TAKE THIS LOSER PARTY AND AMP IT UP! SO LISTEN! IN THREE HOURS...

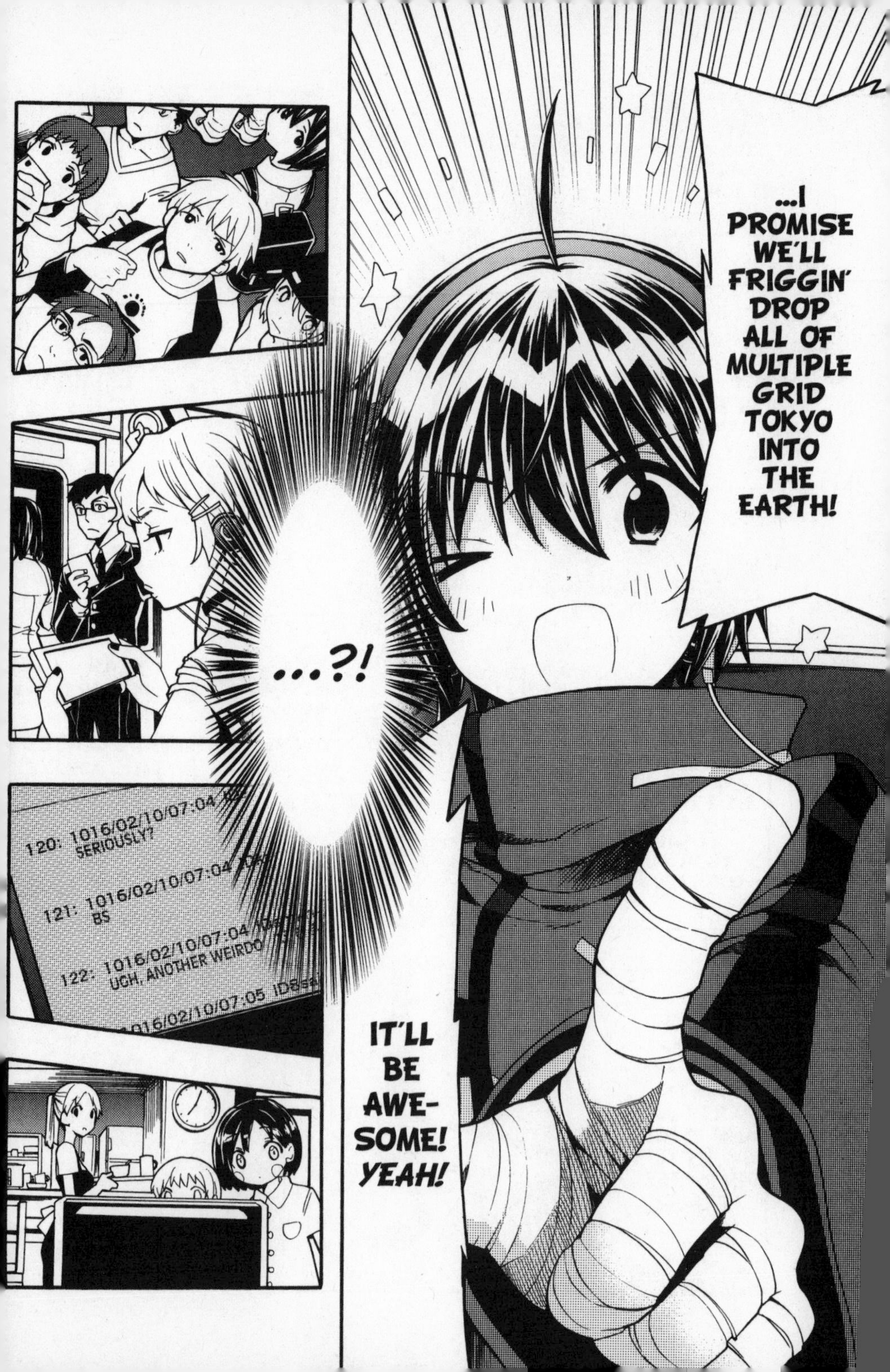
...I PROMISE WE'LL FRIGGIN' DROP ALL OF MULTIPLE GRID TOKYO INTO THE EARTH!
IT'LL BE AWE-SOME! YEAH!
...?!
120: 1016/02/10/07:04
SERIOUSLY?
121: 1016/02/10/07:04
BS
122: 1016/02/10/07:04
UGH, ANOTHER WEIRDO

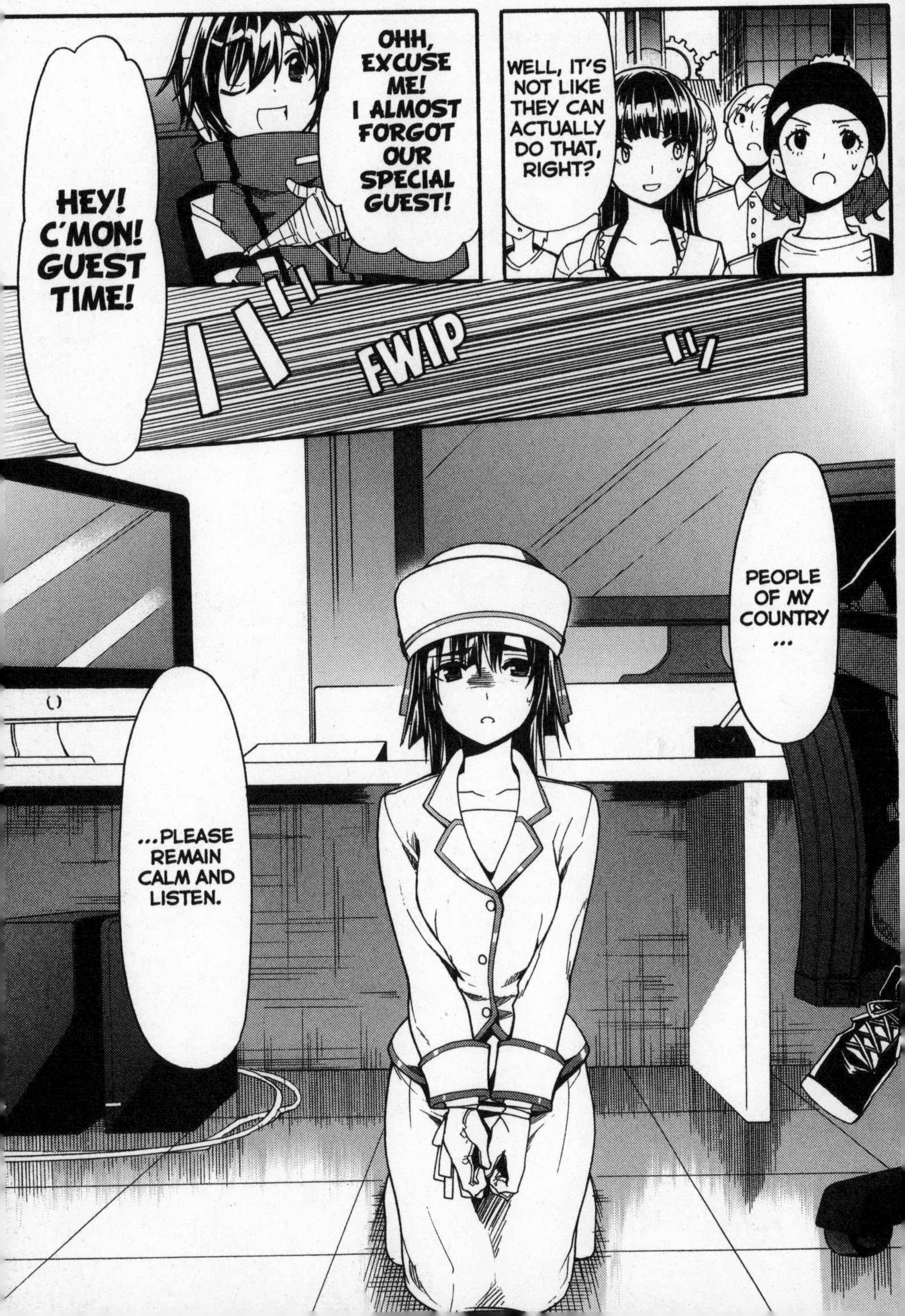
WELL, IT'S NOT LIKE THEY CAN ACTUALLY DO THAT, RIGHT?
OHH, EXCUSE ME! I ALMOST FORGOT OUR SPECIAL GUEST!
HEY! C'MON! GUEST TIME!
FWIP
PEOPLE OF MY COUNTRY...
...PLEASE REMAIN CALM AND LISTEN.

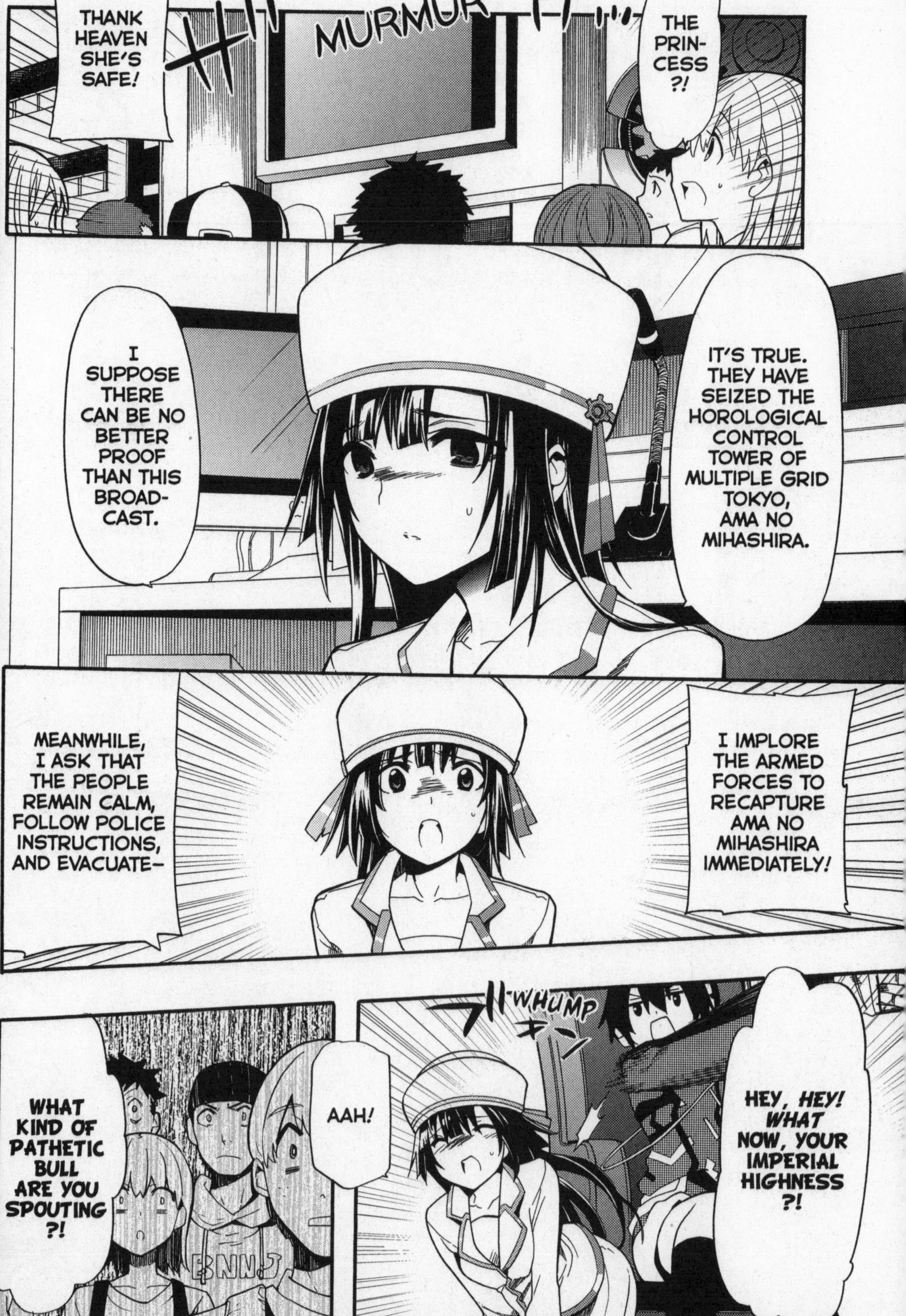
THE PRINCESS?!
MURMUR
THANK HEAVEN SHE'S SAFE!
IT'S TRUE. THEY HAVE SEIZED THE HOROLOGICAL CONTROL TOWER OF MULTIPLE GRID TOKYO, AMA NO MIHASHIRA.
I SUPPOSE THERE CAN BE NO BETTER PROOF THAN THIS BROADCAST.
I IMPLORE THE ARMED FORCES TO RECAPTURE AMA NO MIHASHIRA IMMEDIATELY!
MEANWHILE, I ASK THAT THE PEOPLE REMAIN CALM, FOLLOW POLICE INSTRUCTIONS, AND EVACUATE–
WHUMP
HEY, HEY! WHAT NOW, YOUR IMPERIAL HIGHNESS?!
AAH!
WHAT KIND OF PATHETIC BULL ARE YOU SPOUTING?!

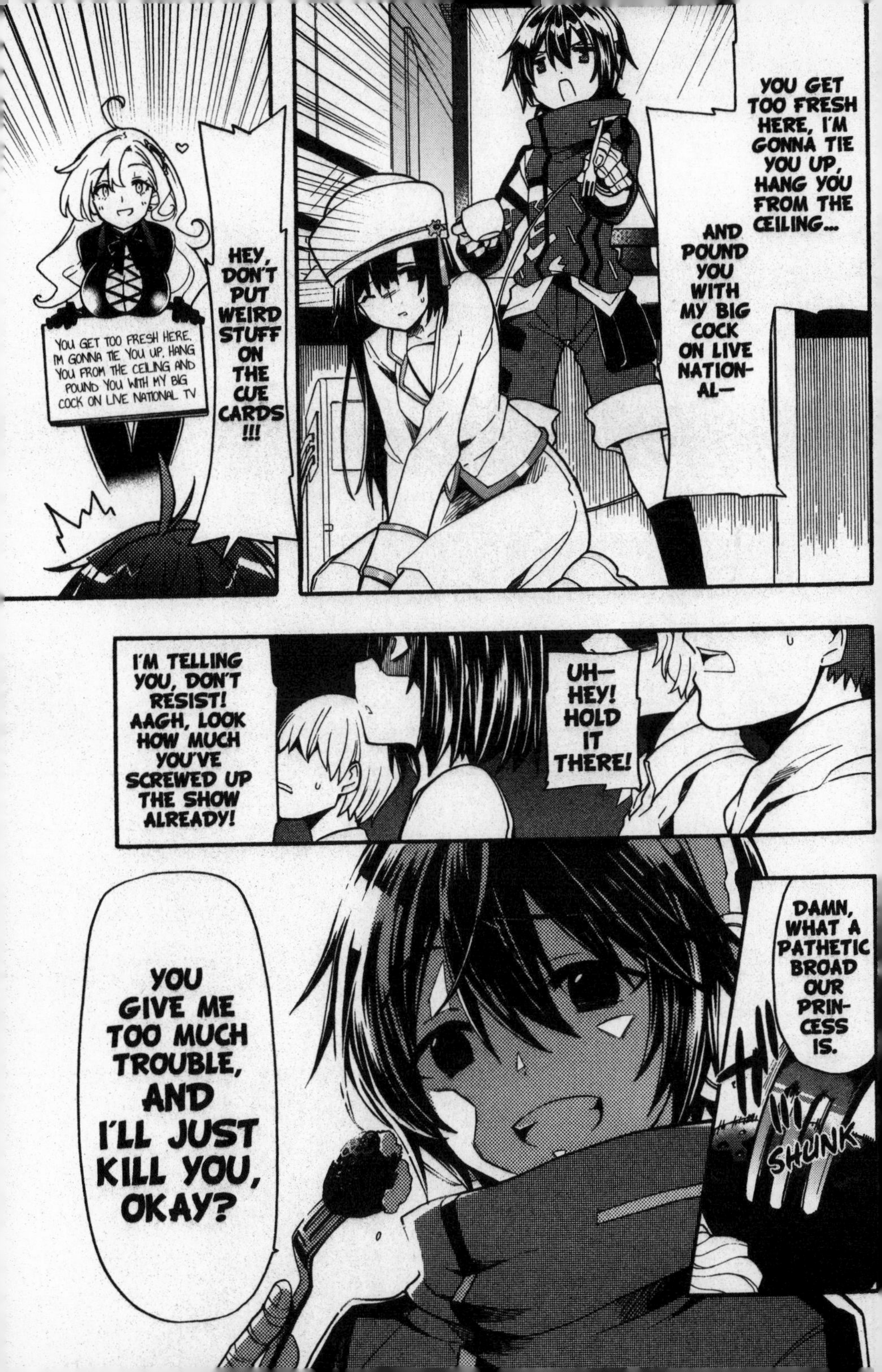
YOU GET TOO FRESH HERE, I'M GONNA TIE YOU UP, HANG YOU FROM THE CEILING...
AND POUND YOU WITH MY BIG COCK ON LIVE NATION-AL—
HEY, DON'T PUT WEIRD STUFF ON THE CUE CARDS!!!
YOU GET TOO FRESH HERE, I'M GONNA TIE YOU UP, HANG YOU FROM THE CEILING AND POUND YOU WITH MY BIG COCK ON LIVE NATIONAL TV
UH— HEY! HOLD IT THERE!
I'M TELLING YOU, DON'T RESIST! AAGH, LOOK HOW MUCH YOU'VE SCREWED UP THE SHOW ALREADY!
DAMN, WHAT A PATHETIC BROAD OUR PRIN-CESS IS.
SHUNK
YOU GIVE ME TOO MUCH TROUBLE, AND I'LL JUST KILL YOU, OKAY?

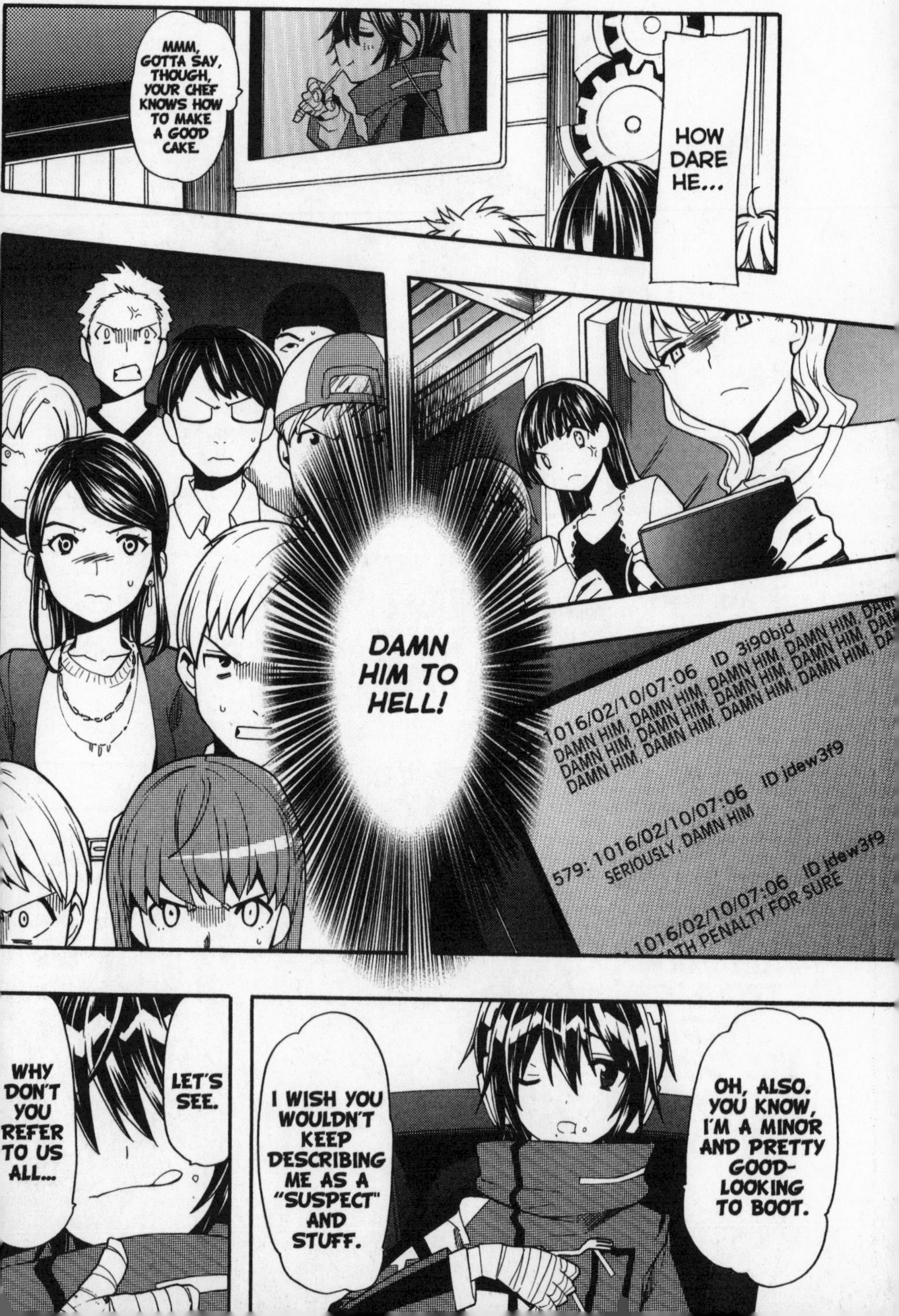
HOW DARE HE...
MMM, GOTTA SAY, THOUGH, YOUR CHEF KNOWS HOW TO MAKE A GOOD CAKE.
ID 3i90bjd
1016/02/10/07:06
DAMN HIM, DAMN HIM,
1016/02/10/07:06 ID jdew3f9
579: 1016/02/10/07:06 ID jdew3f9
SERIOUSLY, DAMN HIM
1016/02/10/07:06
DEATH PENALTY FOR SURE
DAMN HIM TO HELL!
OH, ALSO. YOU KNOW, I'M A MINOR AND PRETTY GOOD-LOOKING TO BOOT.
I WISH YOU WOULDN'T KEEP DESCRIBING ME AS A "SUSPECT" AND STUFF.
LET'S SEE.
WHY DON'T YOU REFER TO US ALL...

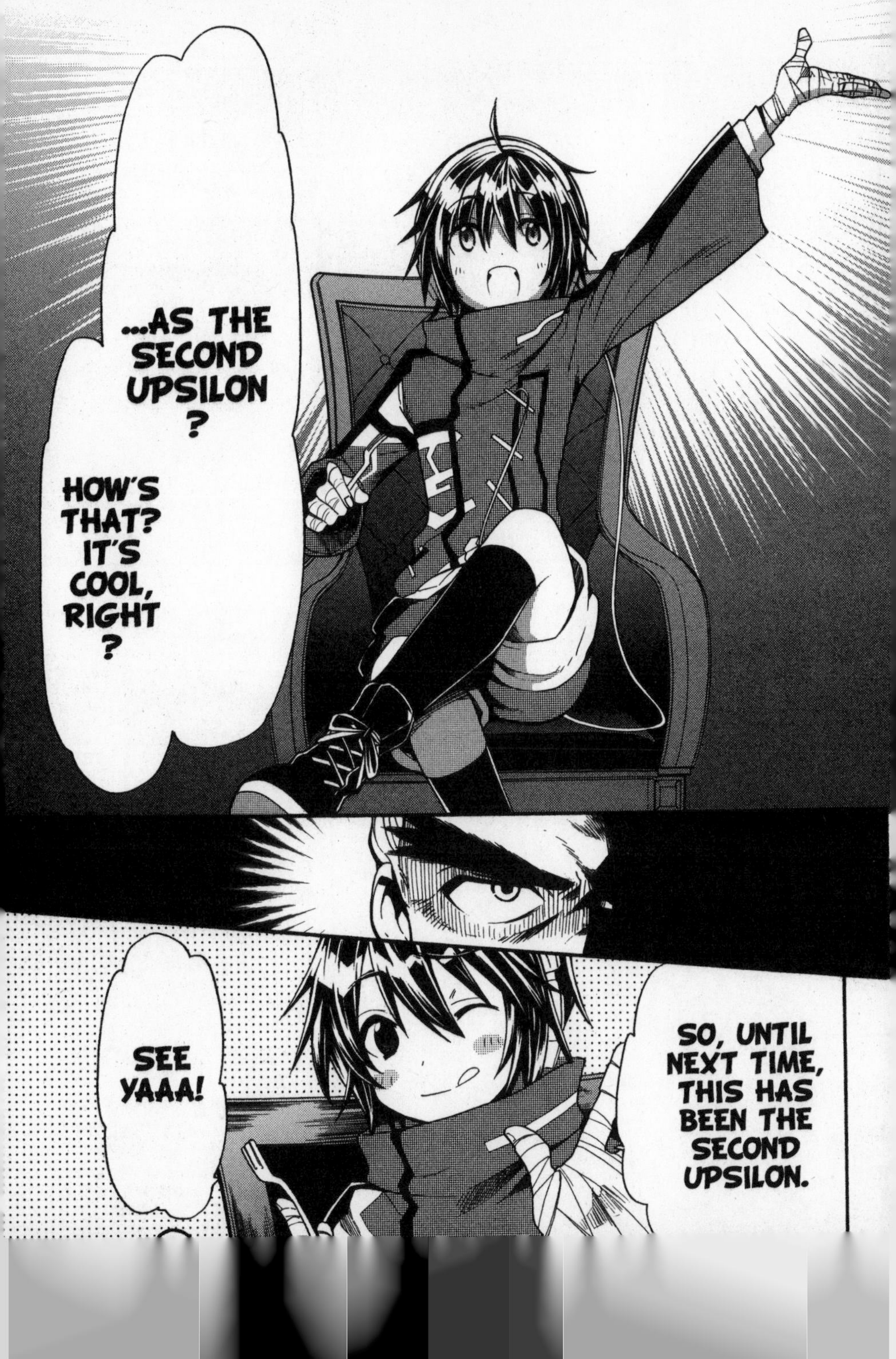
...AS THE SECOND UPSILON?
HOW'S THAT? IT'S COOL, RIGHT?
SO, UNTIL NEXT TIME, THIS HAS BEEN THE SECOND UPSILON.
SEE YAAA!

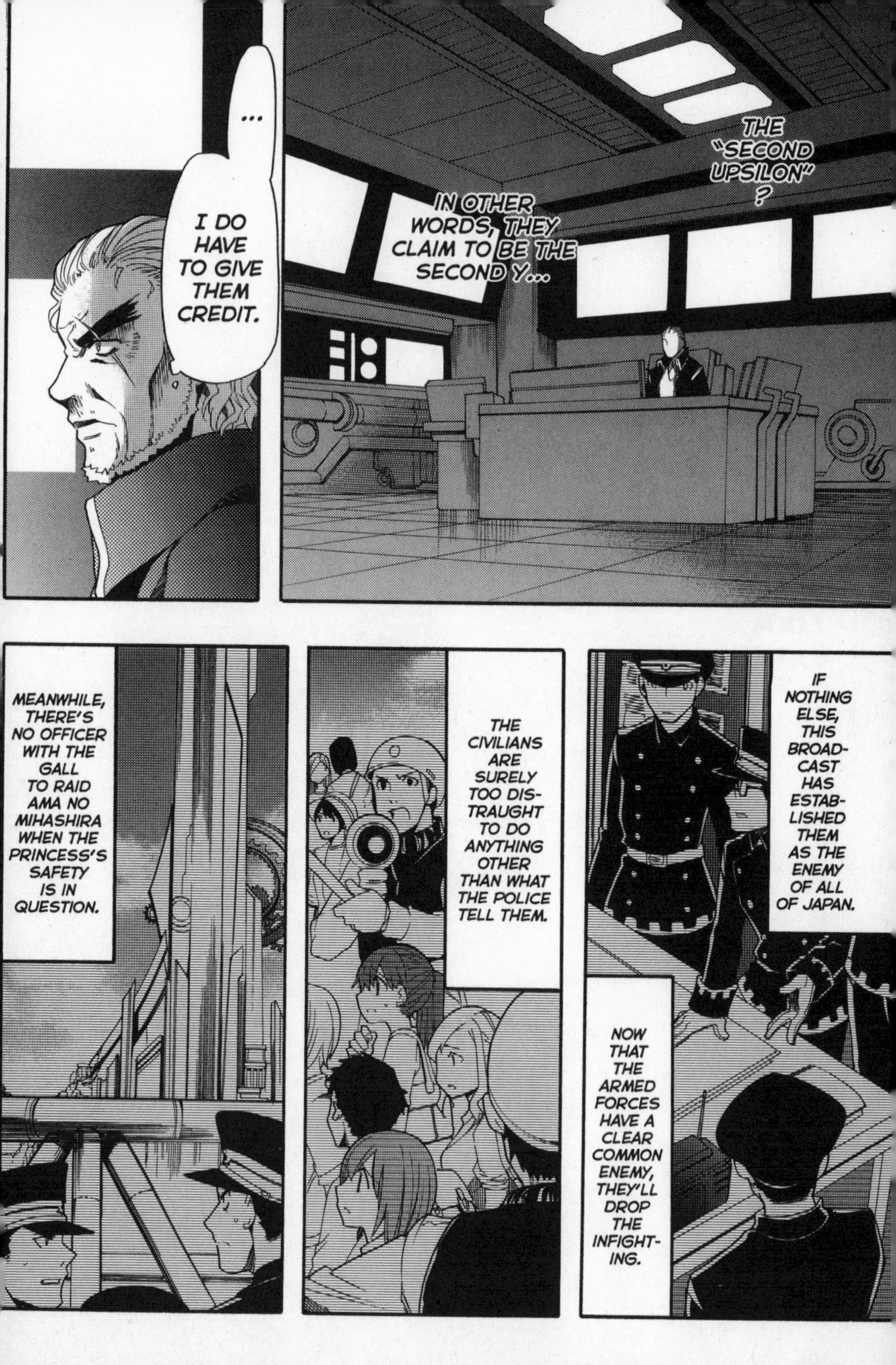
THE "SECOND UPSILON"?
IN OTHER WORDS, THEY CLAIM TO BE THE SECOND Y...
...
I DO HAVE TO GIVE THEM CREDIT.
IF NOTHING ELSE, THIS BROADCAST HAS ESTABLISHED THEM AS THE ENEMY OF ALL OF JAPAN.
NOW THAT THE ARMED FORCES HAVE A CLEAR COMMON ENEMY, THEY'LL DROP THE INFIGHTING.
THE CIVILIANS ARE SURELY TOO DISTRAUGHT TO DO ANYTHING OTHER THAN WHAT THE POLICE TELL THEM.
MEANWHILE, THERE'S NO OFFICER WITH THE GALL TO RAID AMA NO MIHASHIRA WHEN THE PRINCESS'S SAFETY IS IN QUESTION.

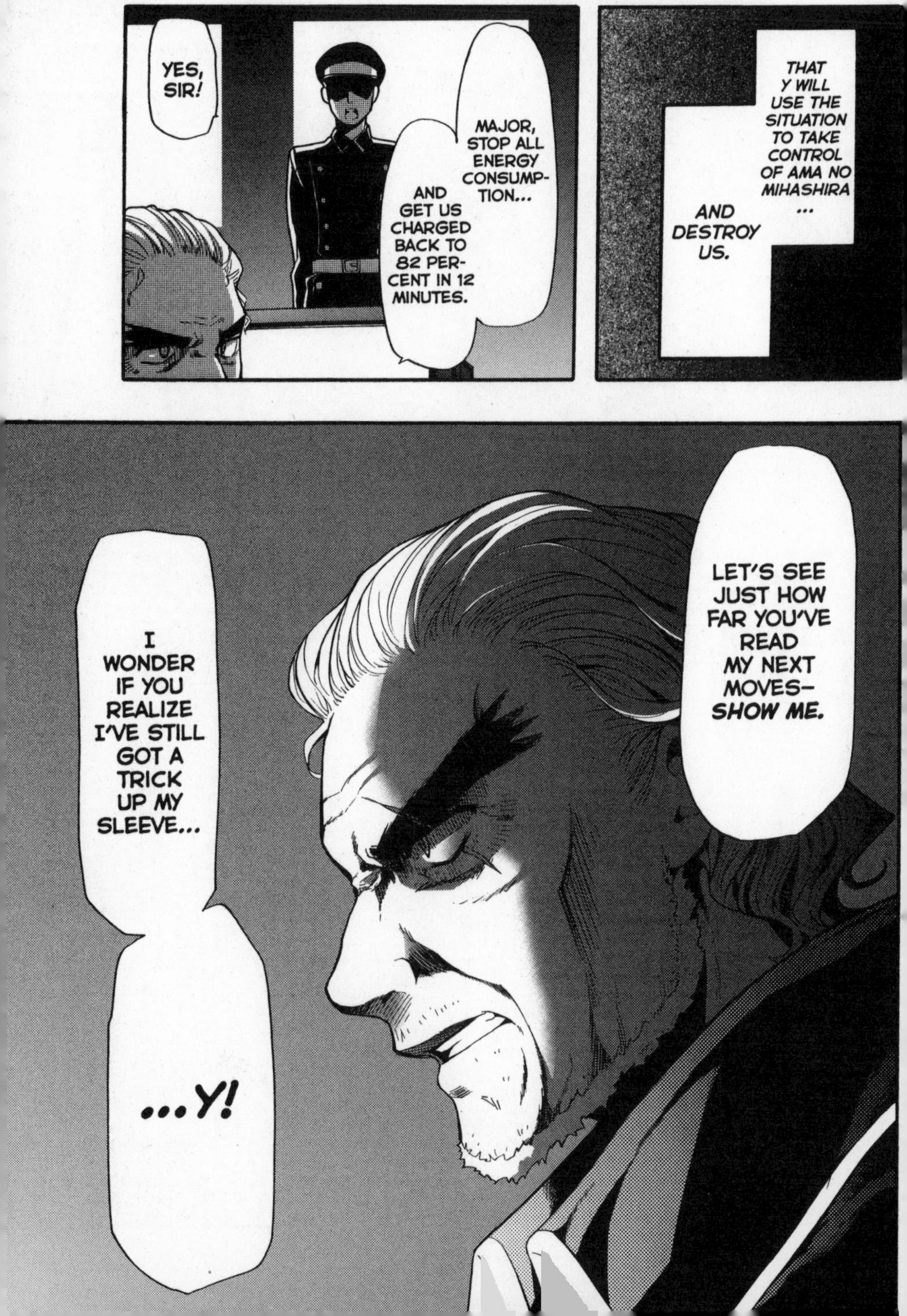
THAT Y WILL USE THE SITUATION TO TAKE CONTROL OF AMA NO MIHASHIRA ...
AND DESTROY US.
MAJOR, STOP ALL ENERGY CONSUMPTION...
AND GET US CHARGED BACK TO 82 PERCENT IN 12 MINUTES.
YES, SIR!
LET'S SEE JUST HOW FAR YOU'VE READ MY NEXT MOVES—*SHOW ME.*
I WONDER IF YOU REALIZE I'VE STILL GOT A TRICK UP MY SLEEVE...
...Y!

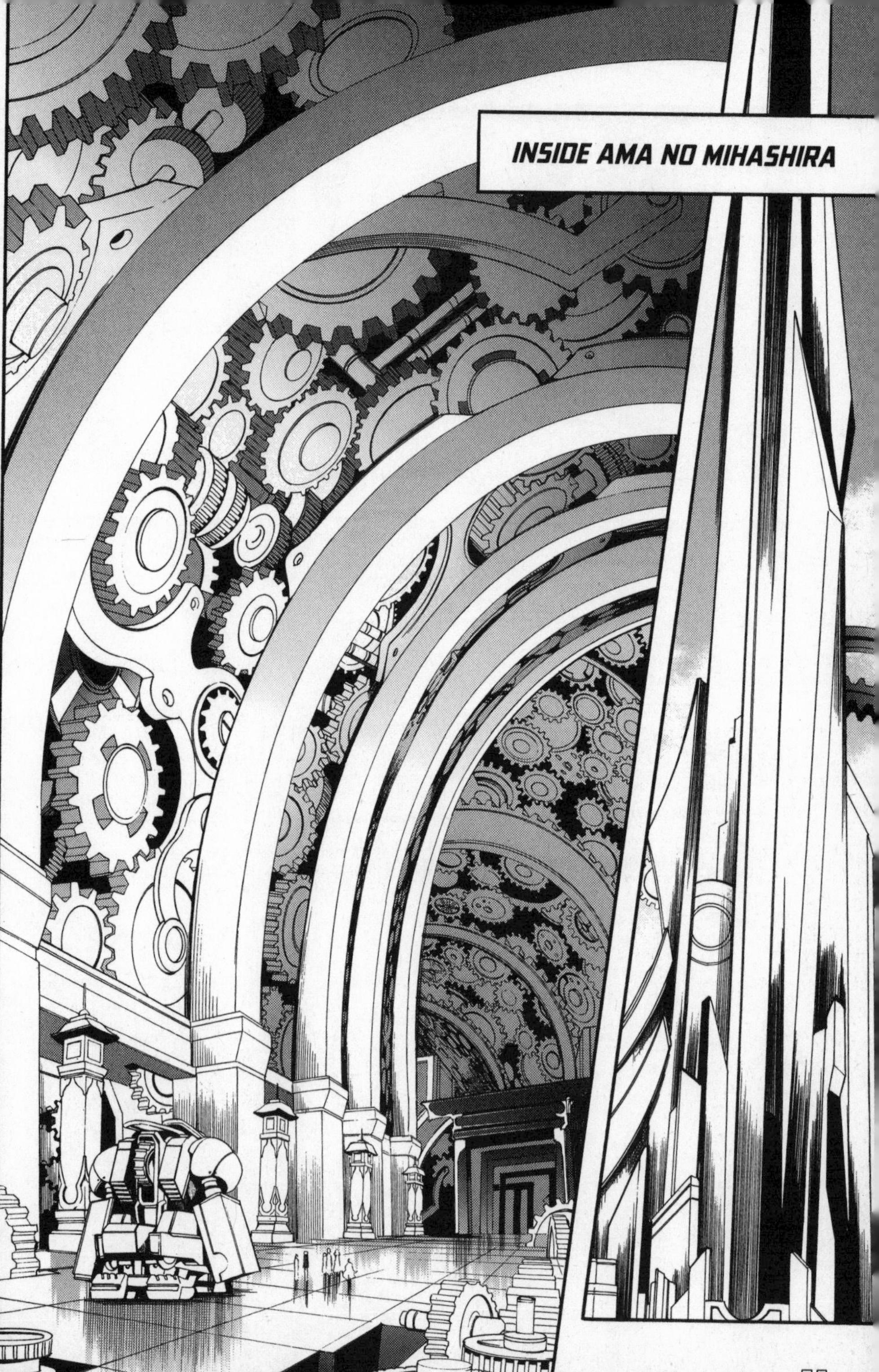
INSIDE AMA NO MIHASHIRA

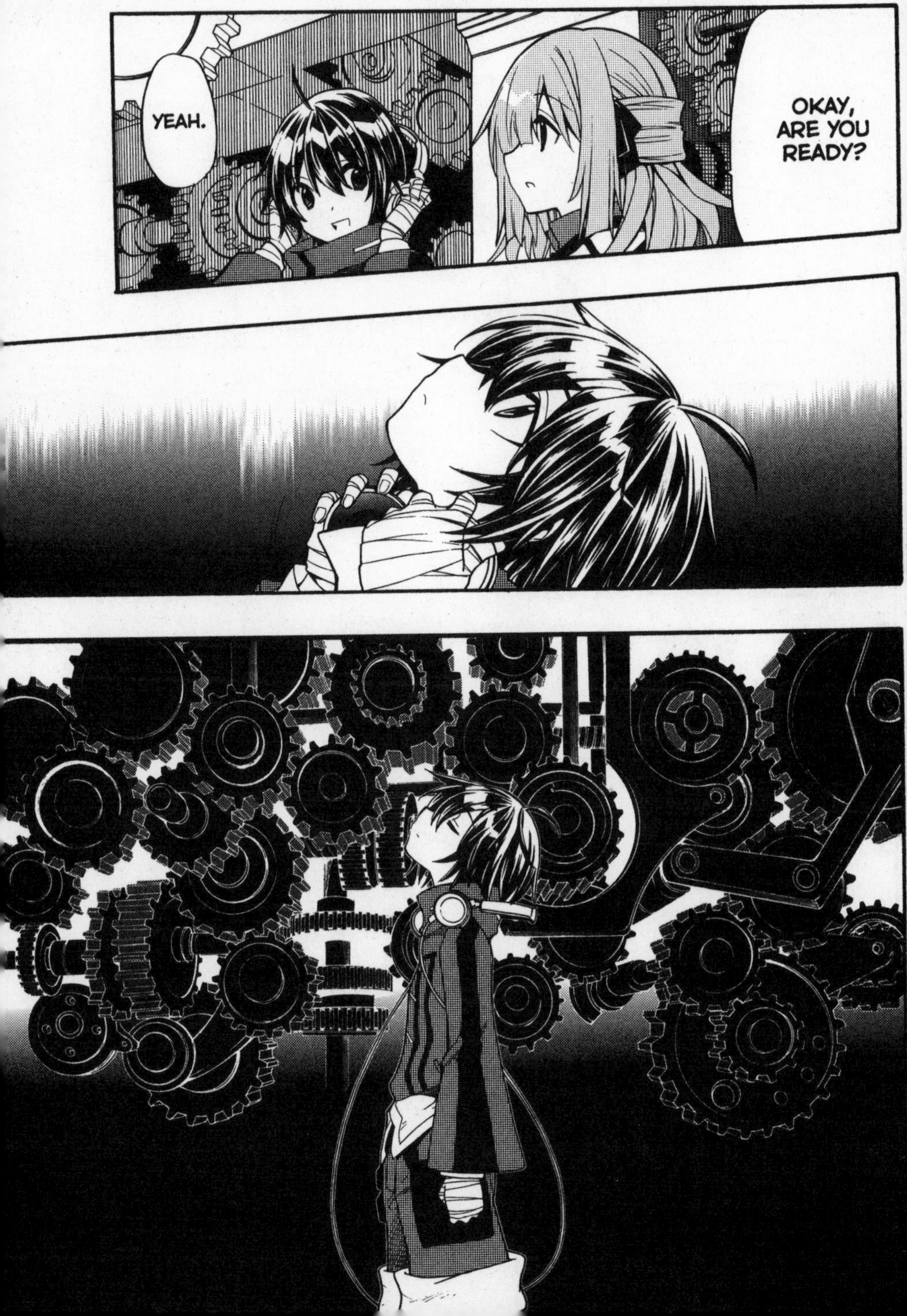
OKAY, ARE YOU READY?
YEAH.

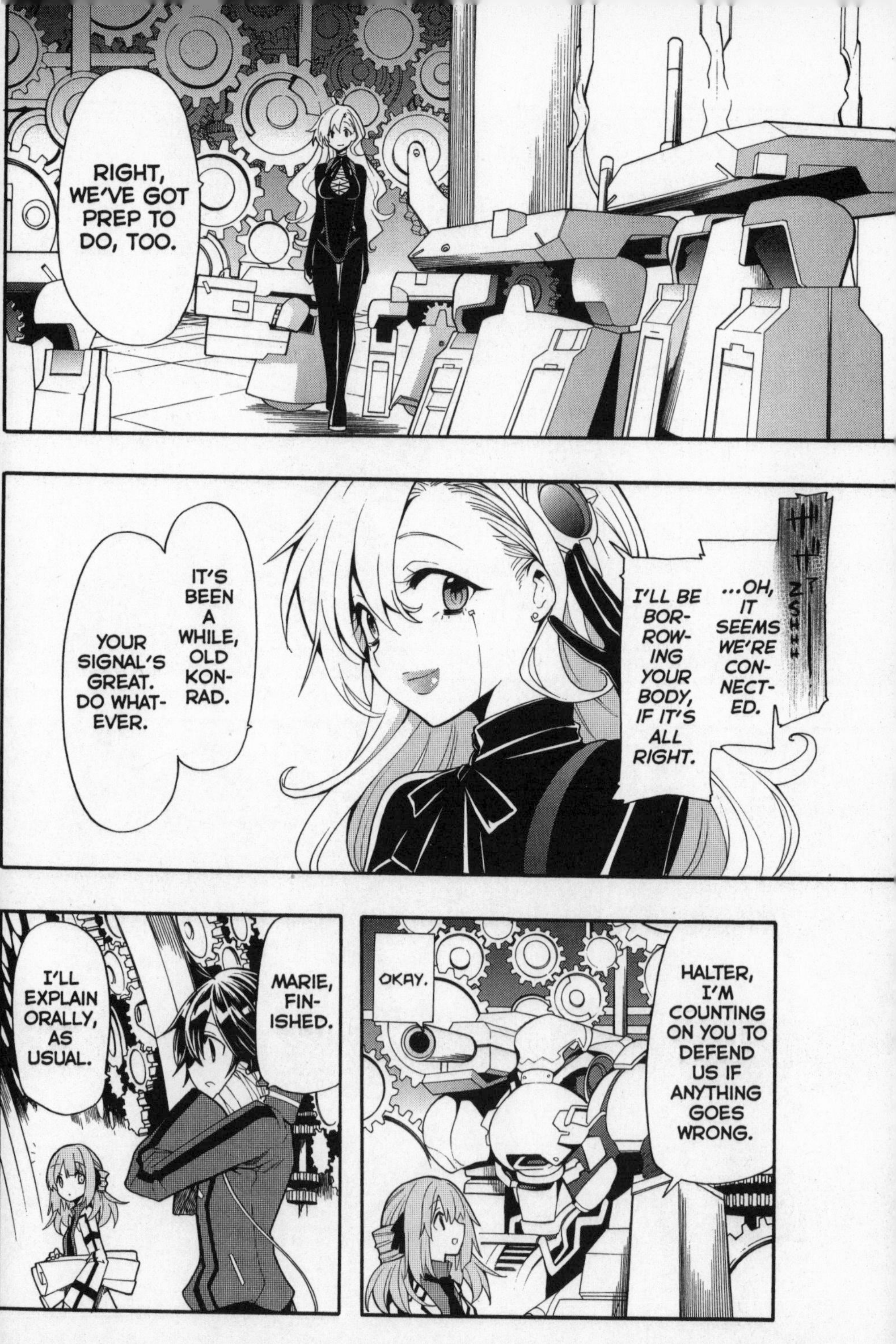
RIGHT, WE'VE GOT PREP TO DO, TOO.
...OH, IT SEEMS WE'RE CON-NECT-ED.
I'LL BE BOR-ROW-ING YOUR BODY, IF IT'S ALL RIGHT.
ZSHHH
IT'S BEEN A WHILE, OLD KON-RAD.
YOUR SIGNAL'S GREAT. DO WHAT-EVER.
HALTER, I'M COUNTING ON YOU TO DEFEND US IF ANYTHING GOES WRONG.
OKAY.
MARIE, FIN-ISHED.
I'LL EXPLAIN ORALLY, AS USUAL.

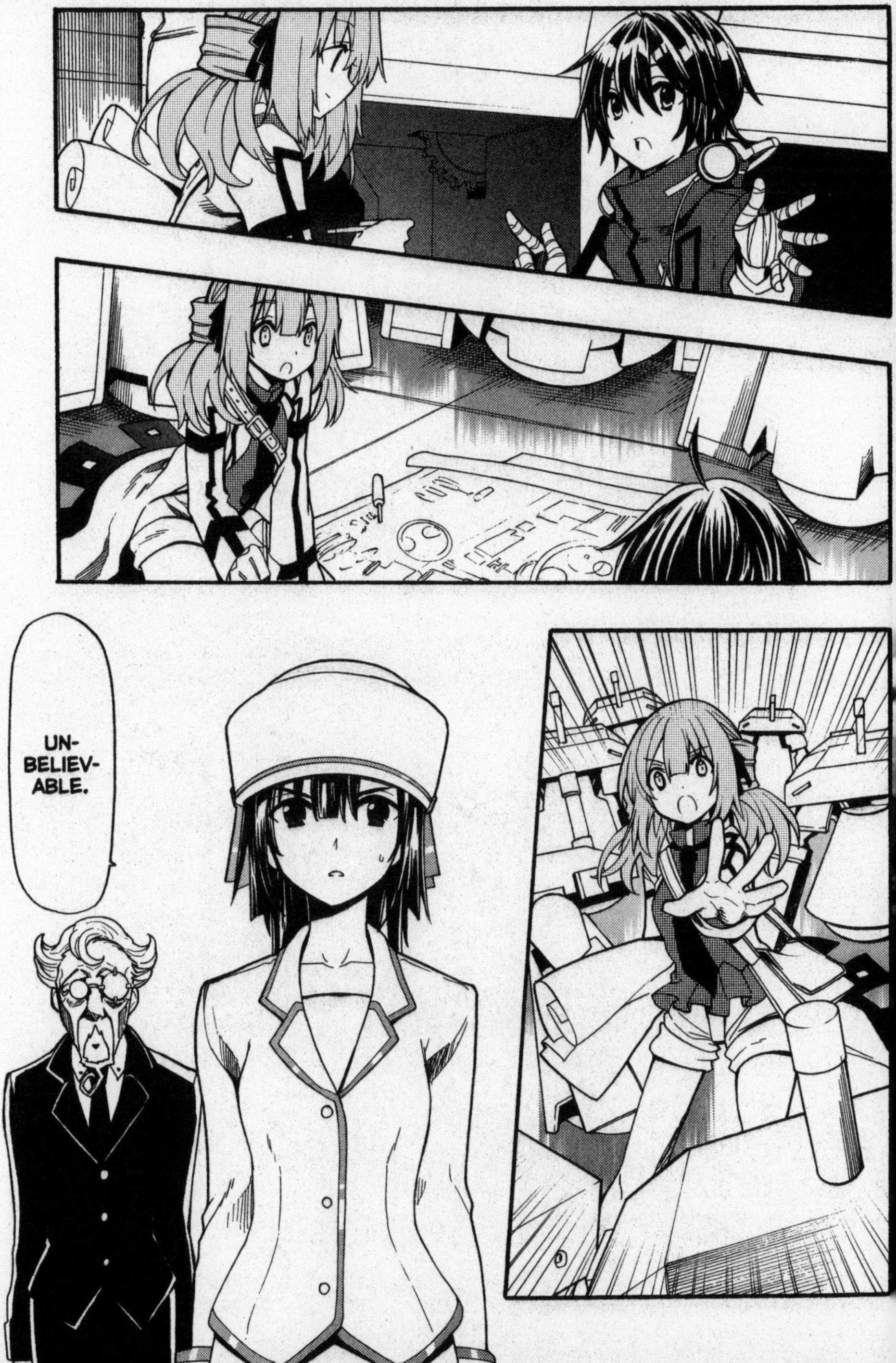
UN-
BELIEV-
ABLE.

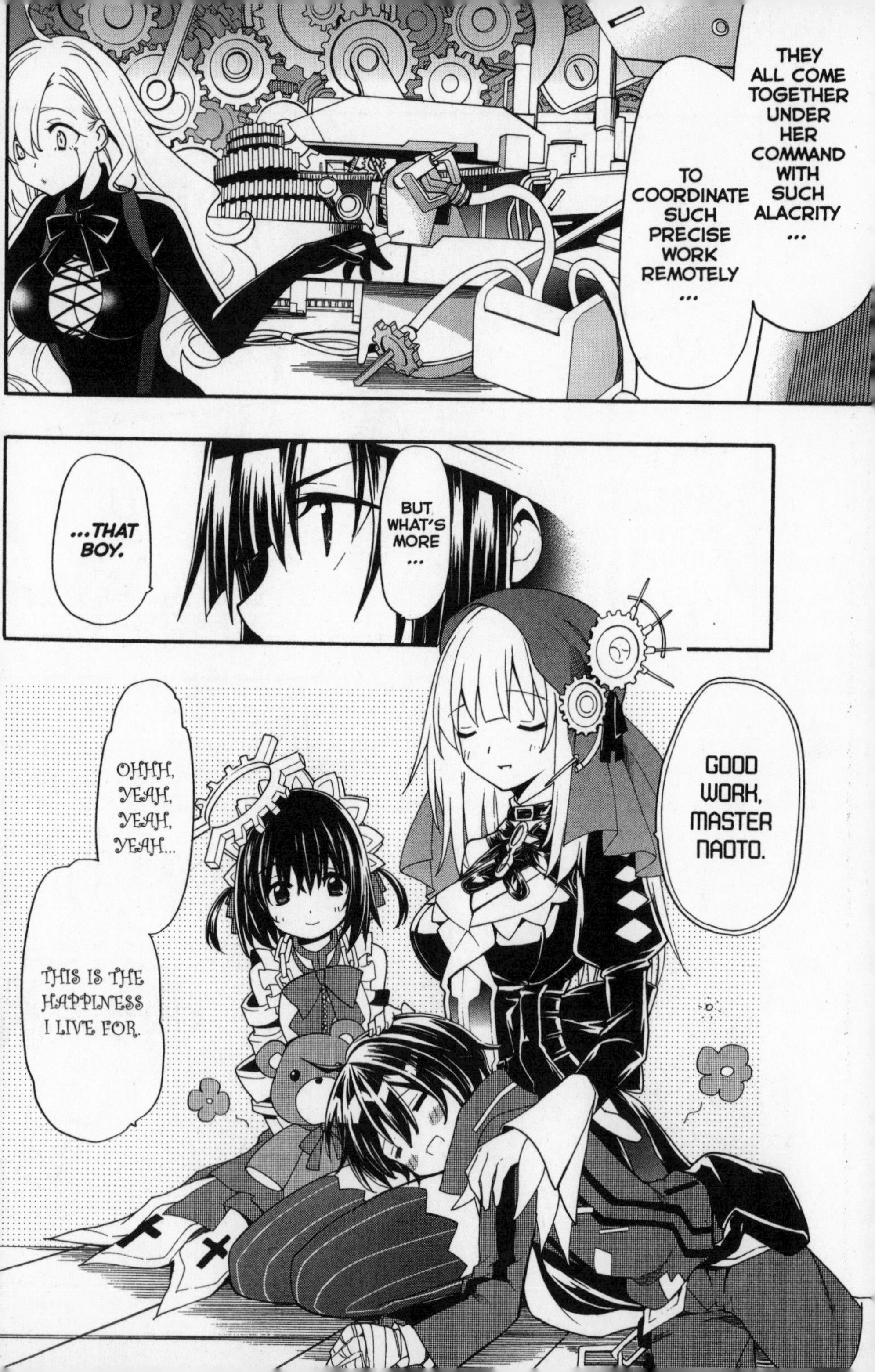
THEY ALL COME TOGETHER UNDER HER COMMAND WITH SUCH ALACRITY...
TO COORDINATE SUCH PRECISE WORK REMOTELY...
BUT WHAT'S MORE...
...THAT BOY.
GOOD WORK, MASTER NAOTO.
OHHH, YEAH, YEAH, YEAH...
THIS IS THE HAPPINESS I LIVE FOR.

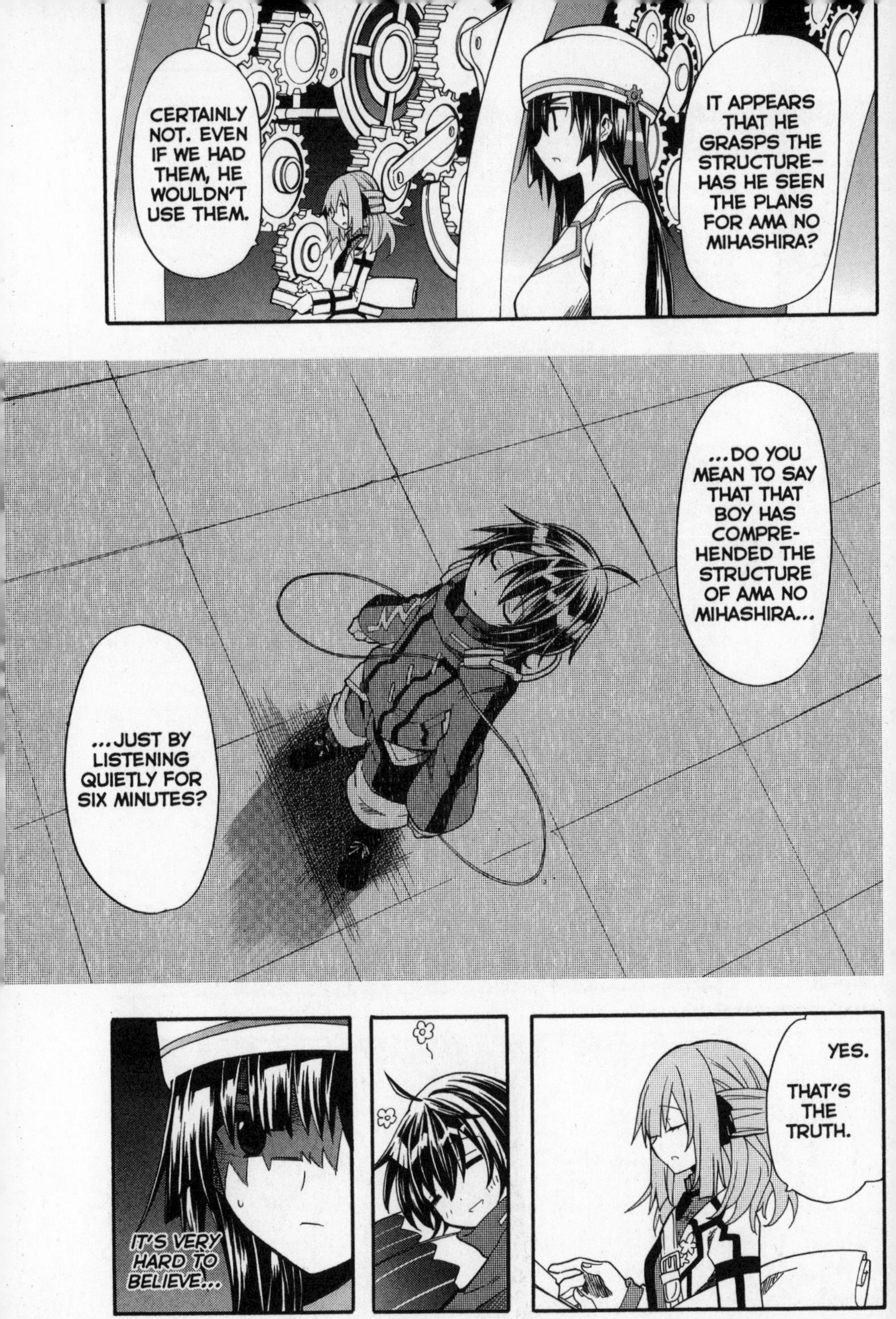
IT APPEARS THAT HE GRASPS THE STRUCTURE—HAS HE SEEN THE PLANS FOR AMA NO MIHASHIRA?
CERTAINLY NOT. EVEN IF WE HAD THEM, HE WOULDN'T USE THEM.
...DO YOU MEAN TO SAY THAT THAT BOY HAS COMPRE-HENDED THE STRUCTURE OF AMA NO MIHASHIRA...
...JUST BY LISTENING QUIETLY FOR SIX MINUTES?
YES.
THAT'S THE TRUTH.
IT'S VERY HARD TO BELIEVE...

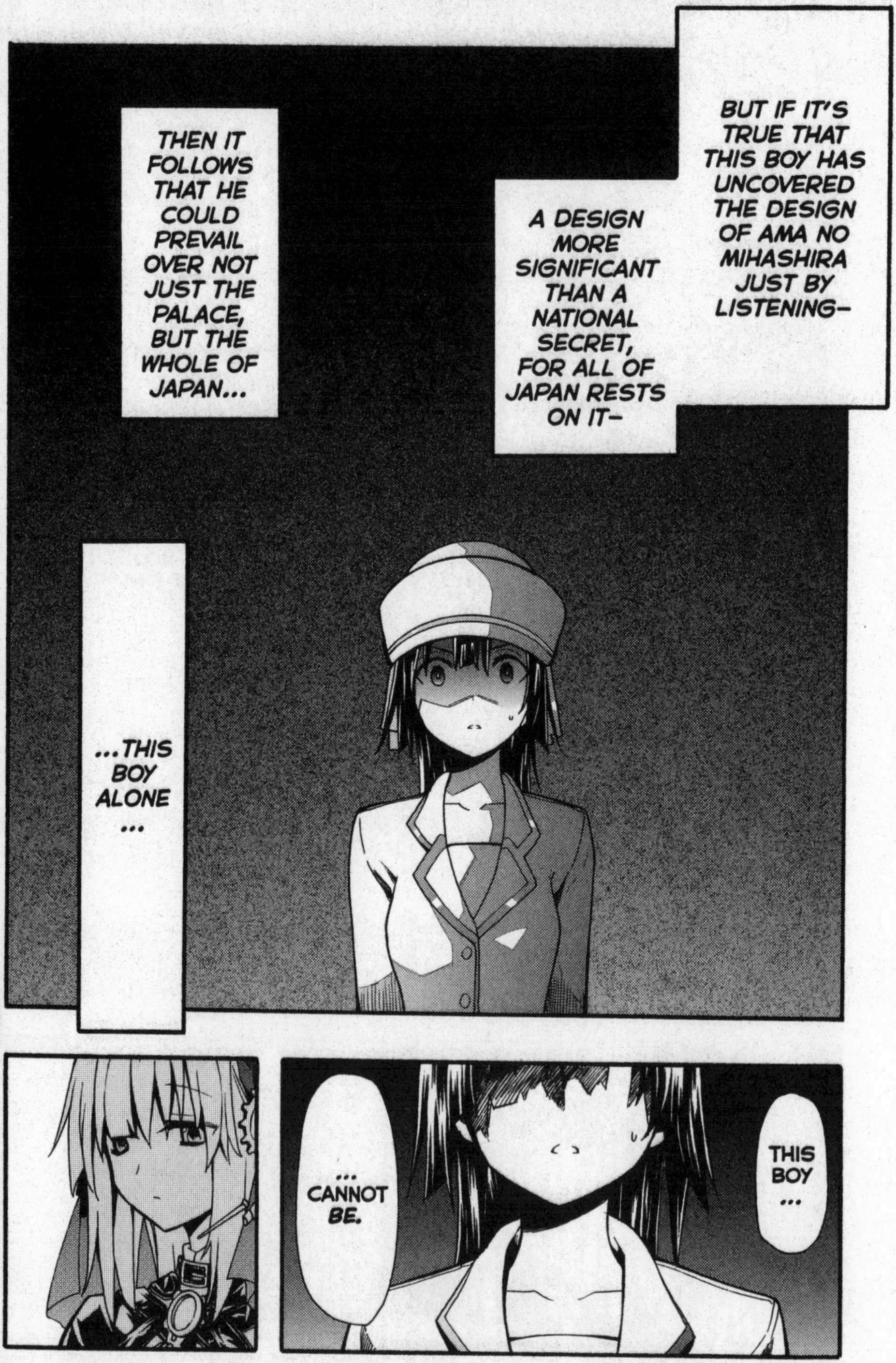
BUT IF IT'S TRUE THAT THIS BOY HAS UNCOVERED THE DESIGN OF AMA NO MIHASHIRA JUST BY LISTENING–
A DESIGN MORE SIGNIFICANT THAN A NATIONAL SECRET, FOR ALL OF JAPAN RESTS ON IT–
THEN IT FOLLOWS THAT HE COULD PREVAIL OVER NOT JUST THE PALACE, BUT THE WHOLE OF JAPAN...
...THIS BOY ALONE ...
THIS BOY ...
... CANNOT BE.

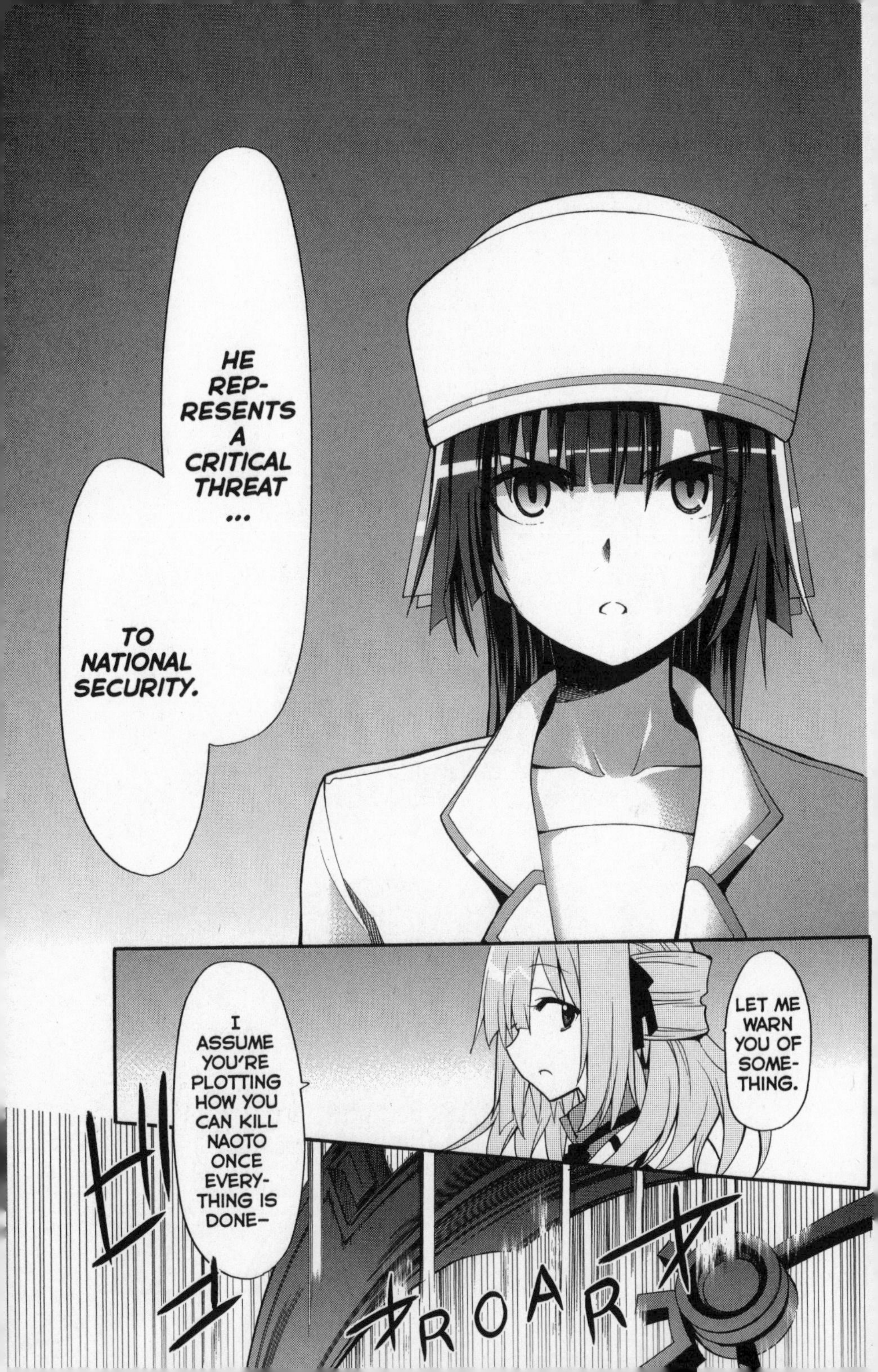
HE REP-RESENTS A CRITICAL THREAT ...
TO NATIONAL SECURITY.
LET ME WARN YOU OF SOME-THING.
I ASSUME YOU'RE PLOTTING HOW YOU CAN KILL NAOTO ONCE EVERY-THING IS DONE–
ROAR

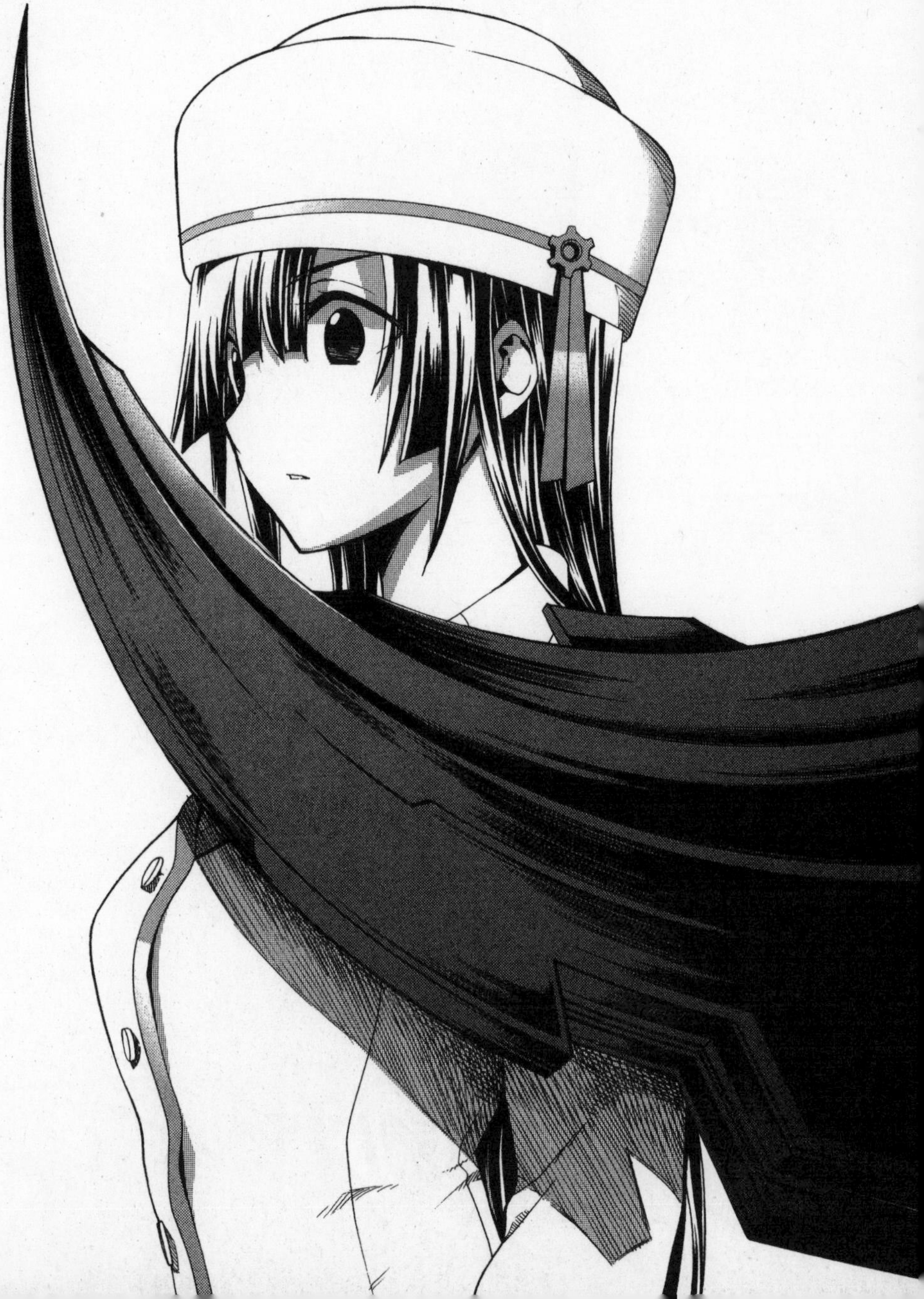

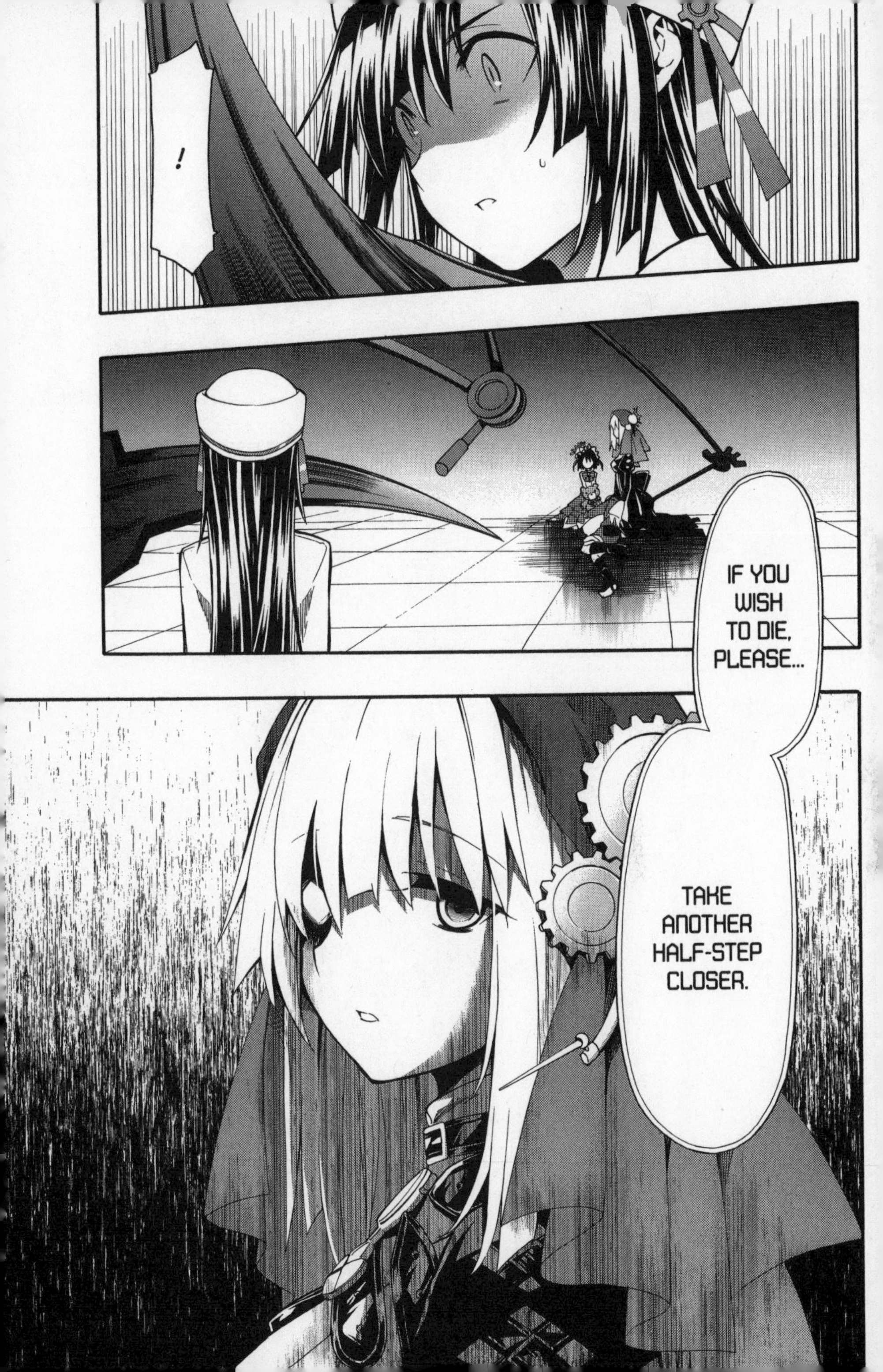
!
IF YOU WISH TO DIE, PLEASE...
TAKE ANOTHER HALF-STEP CLOSER.

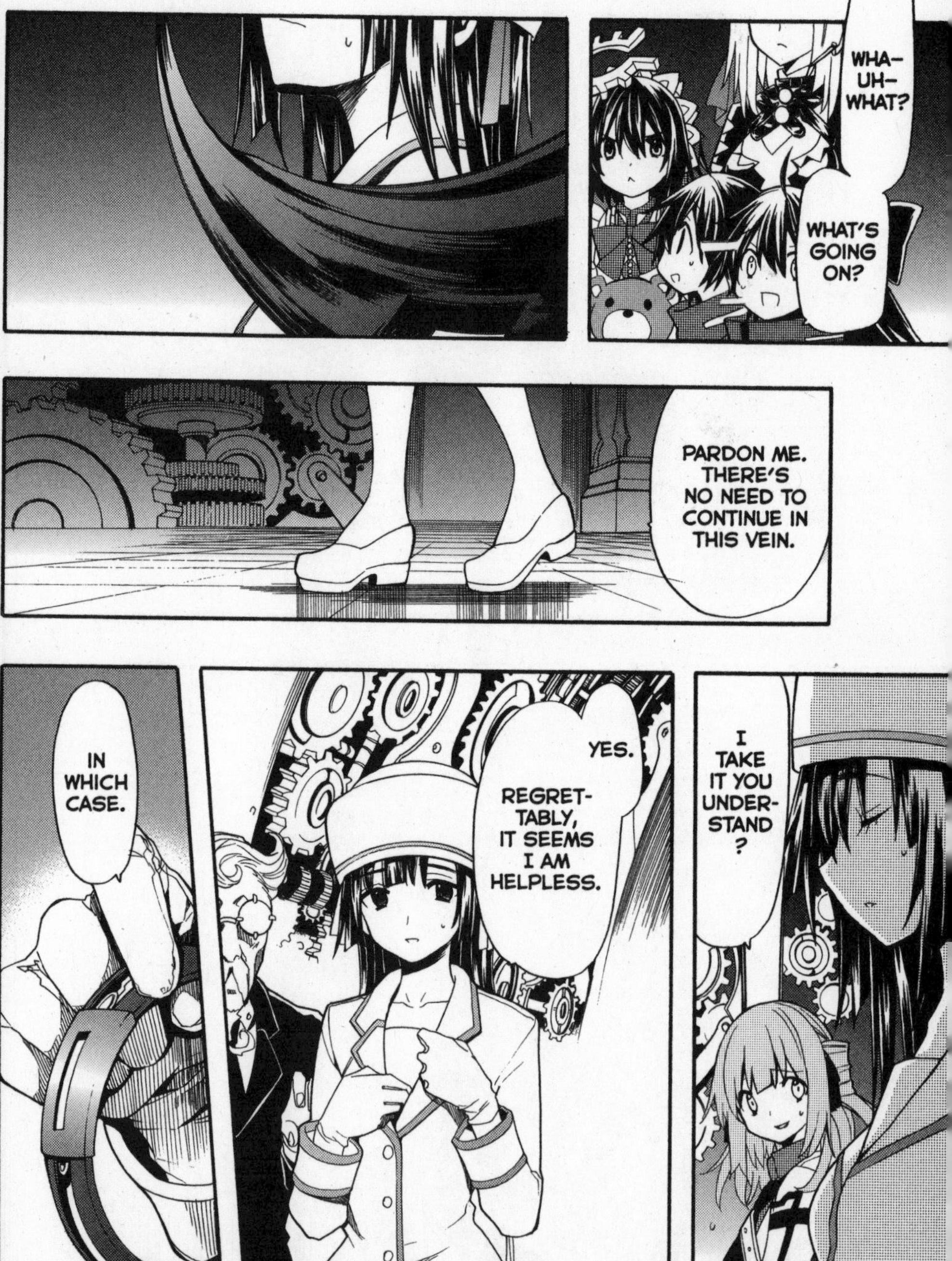
WHA—UH—WHAT?
WHAT'S GOING ON?
PARDON ME. THERE'S NO NEED TO CONTINUE IN THIS VEIN.
I TAKE IT YOU UNDER-STAND?
YES.
REGRET-TABLY, IT SEEMS I AM HELPLESS.
IN WHICH CASE.

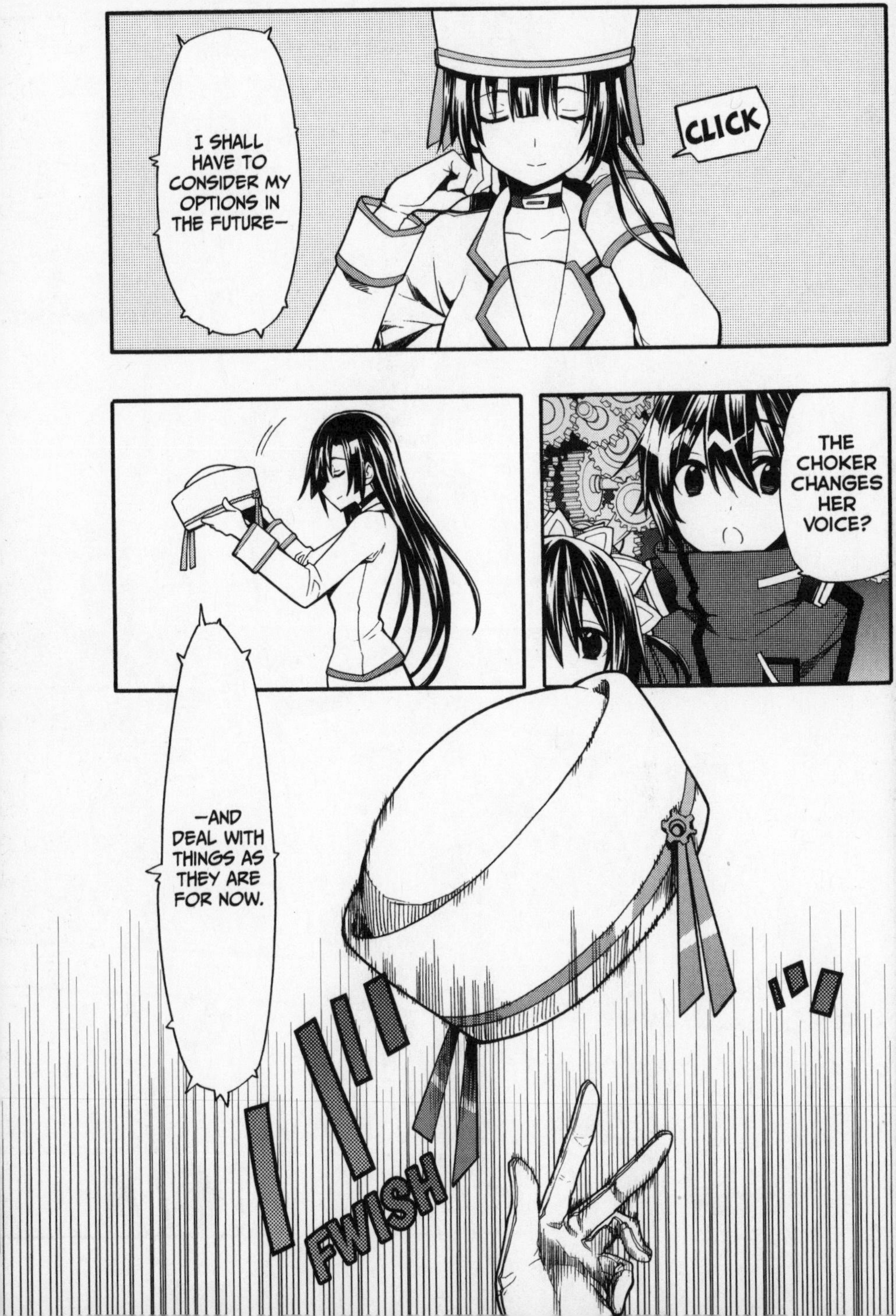
CLICK
I SHALL HAVE TO CONSIDER MY OPTIONS IN THE FUTURE—
THE CHOKER CHANGES HER VOICE?
—AND DEAL WITH THINGS AS THEY ARE FOR NOW.
FWISH

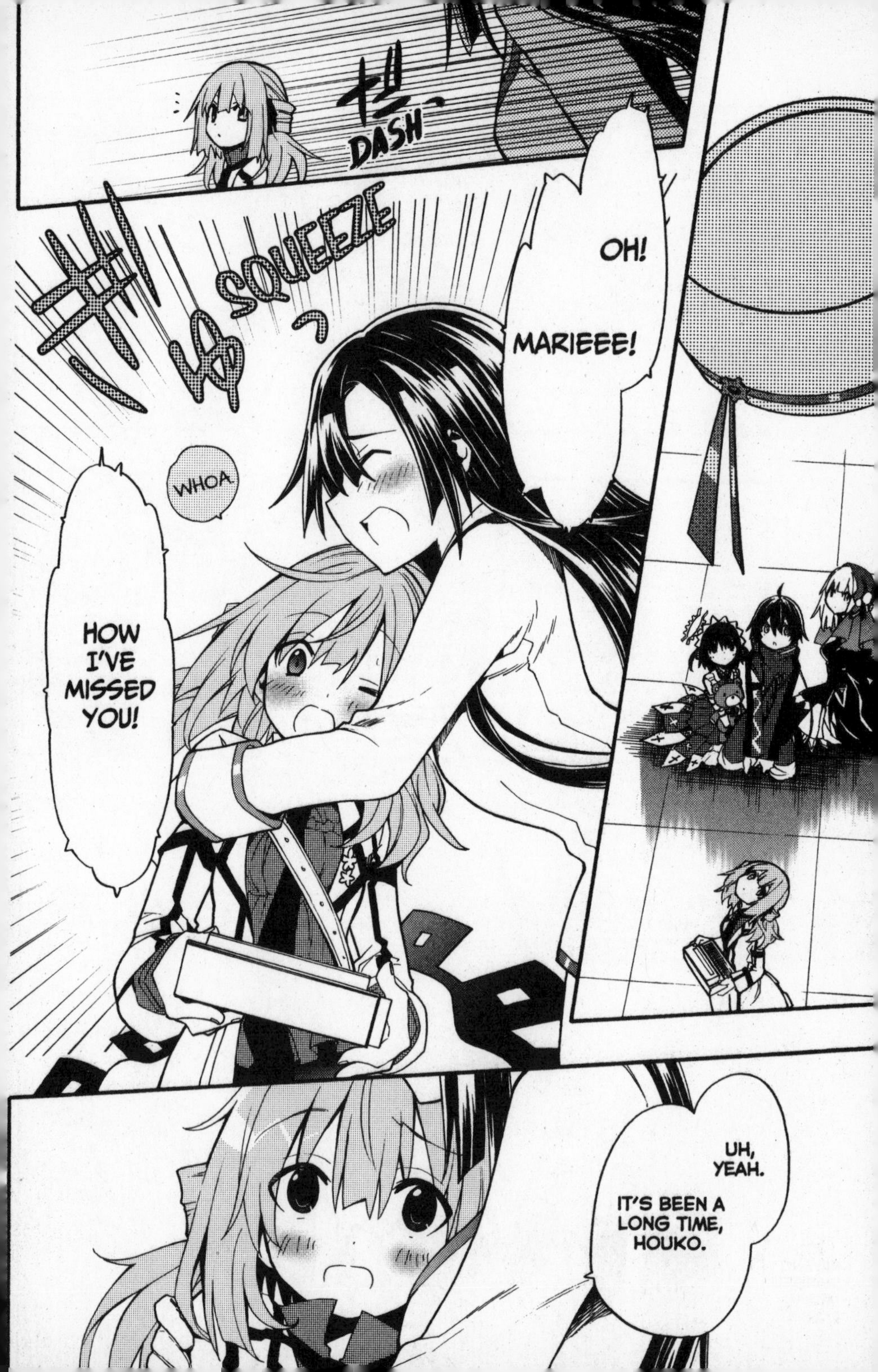
DASH
OH!
MARIEEE!
SQUEEZE
WHOA
HOW I'VE MISSED YOU!
UH, YEAH.
IT'S BEEN A LONG TIME, HOUKO.

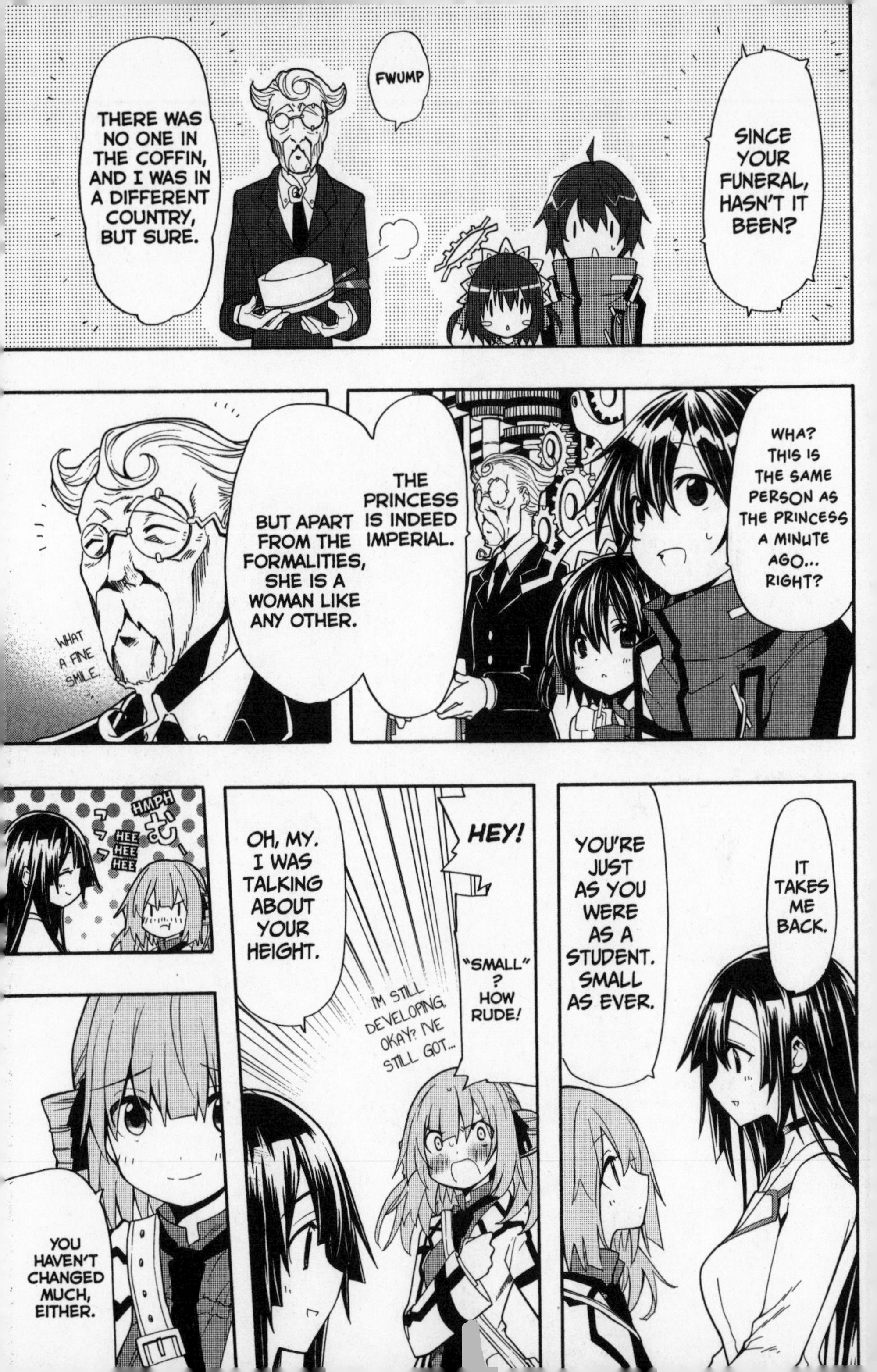
SINCE YOUR FUNERAL, HASN'T IT BEEN?
FWUMP
THERE WAS NO ONE IN THE COFFIN, AND I WAS IN A DIFFERENT COUNTRY, BUT SURE.
WHA? THIS IS THE SAME PERSON AS THE PRINCESS A MINUTE AGO... RIGHT?
THE PRINCESS IS INDEED IMPERIAL.
BUT APART FROM THE FORMALITIES, SHE IS A WOMAN LIKE ANY OTHER.
WHAT A FINE SMILE.
IT TAKES ME BACK.
YOU'RE JUST AS YOU WERE AS A STUDENT. SMALL AS EVER.
HEY!
"SMALL"? HOW RUDE!
I'M STILL DEVELOPING. OKAY? I'VE STILL GOT...
OH, MY. I WAS TALKING ABOUT YOUR HEIGHT.
HMPH
HEE HEE HEE
YOU HAVEN'T CHANGED MUCH, EITHER.

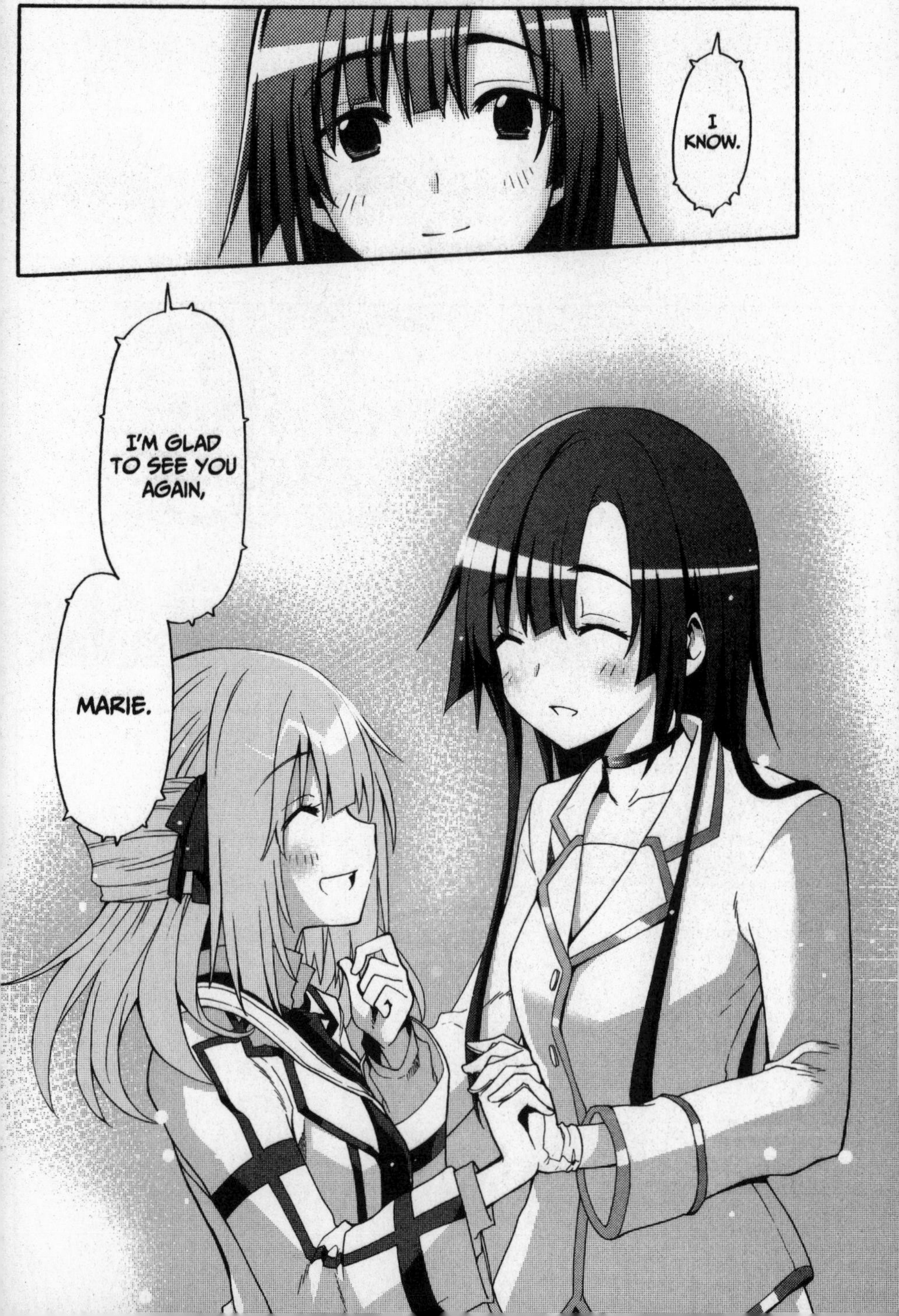
I KNOW.
I'M GLAD TO SEE YOU AGAIN,
MARIE.

Clockwork Planet

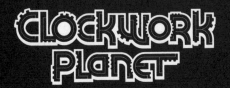

Clockwork Planet

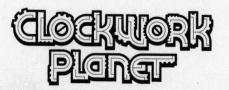

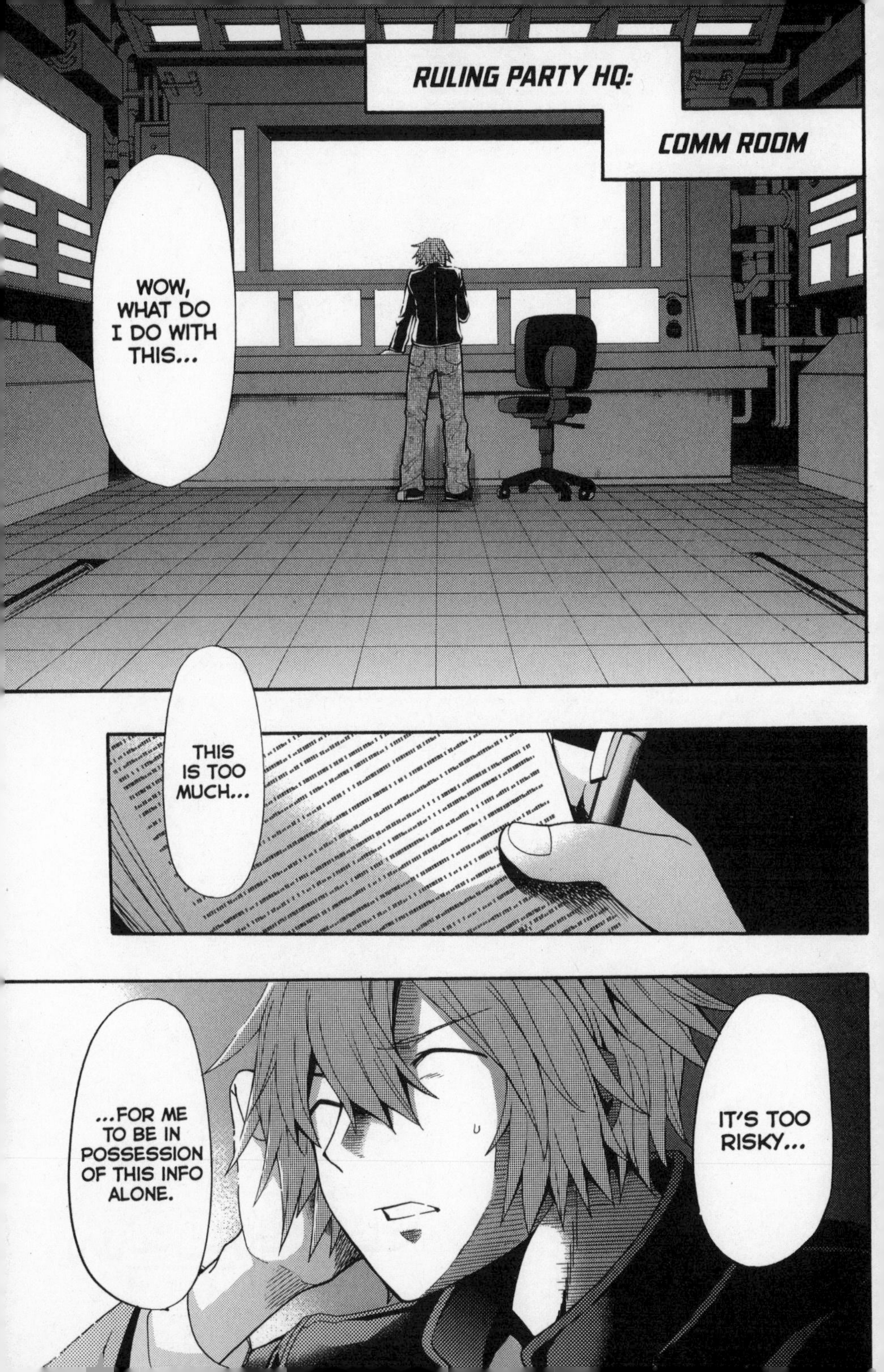
RULING PARTY HQ:
COMM ROOM
WOW, WHAT DO I DO WITH THIS...
THIS IS TOO MUCH...
IT'S TOO RISKY...
...FOR ME TO BE IN POSSESSION OF THIS INFO ALONE.

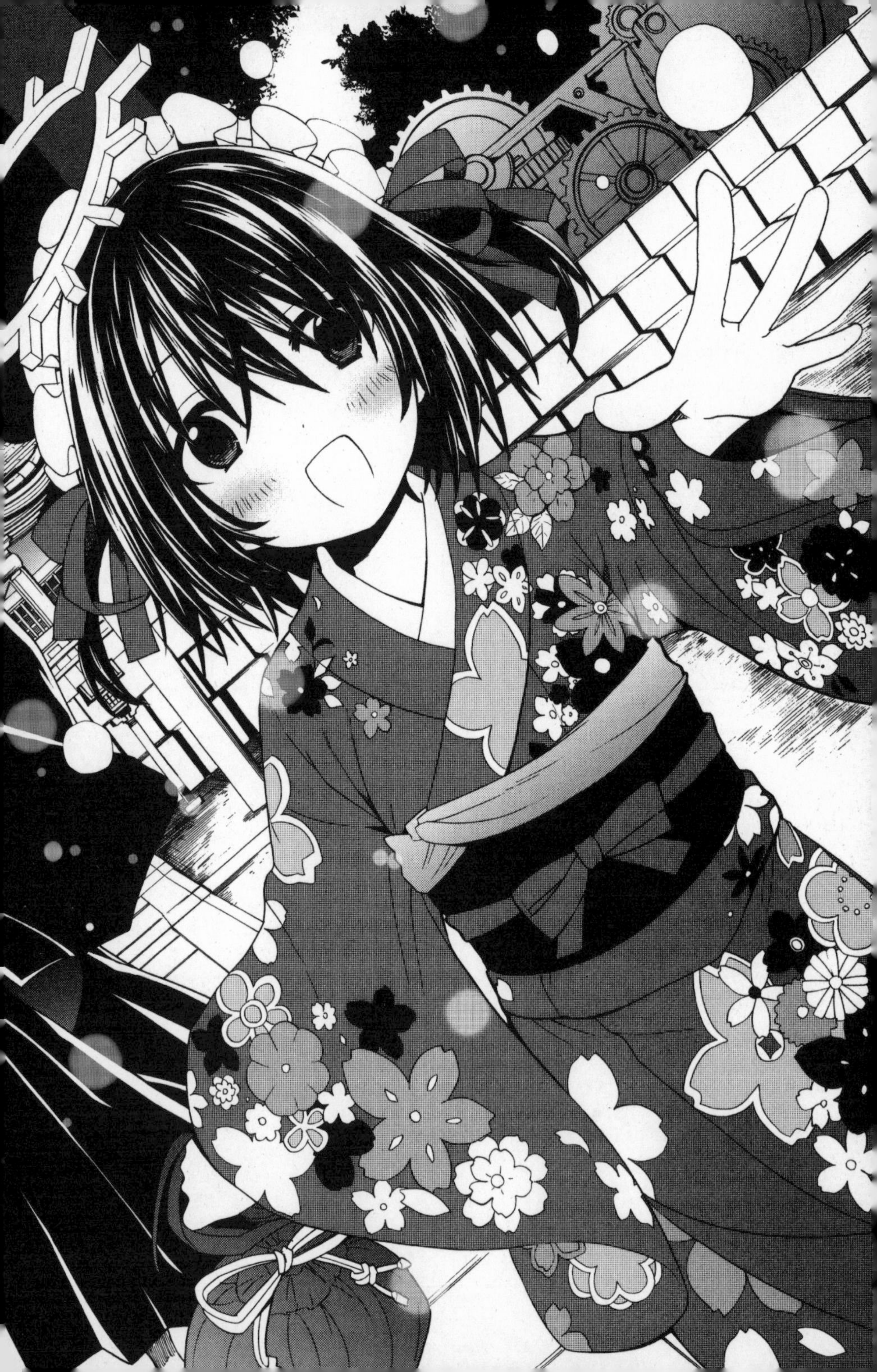

Clock 34: Dear Y!

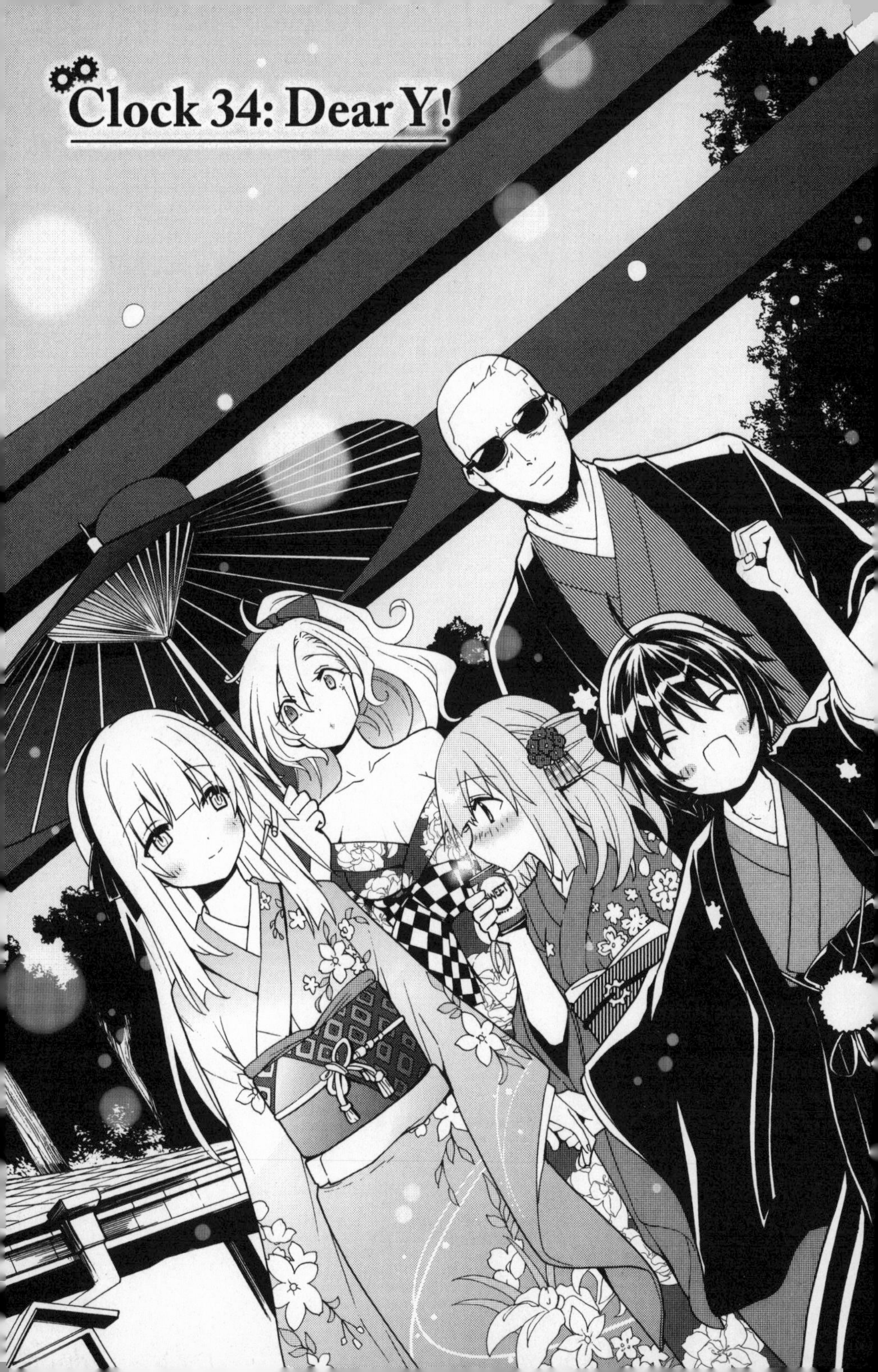

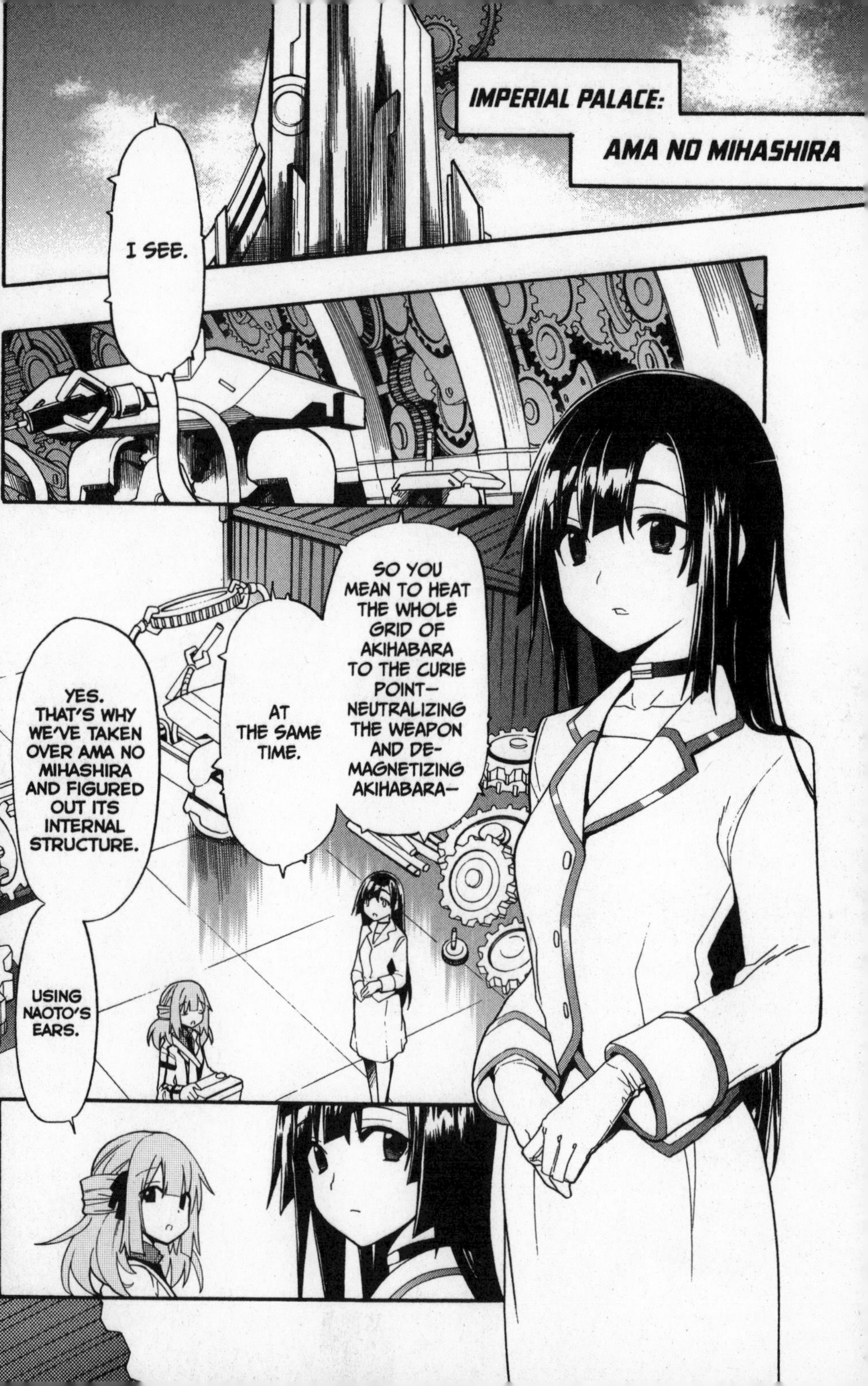
IMPERIAL PALACE:
AMA NO MIHASHIRA
I SEE.
SO YOU MEAN TO HEAT THE WHOLE GRID OF AKIHABARA TO THE CURIE POINT— NEUTRALIZING THE WEAPON AND DE-MAGNETIZING AKIHABARA—
AT THE SAME TIME.
YES. THAT'S WHY WE'VE TAKEN OVER AMA NO MIHASHIRA AND FIGURED OUT ITS INTERNAL STRUCTURE.
USING NAOTO'S EARS.

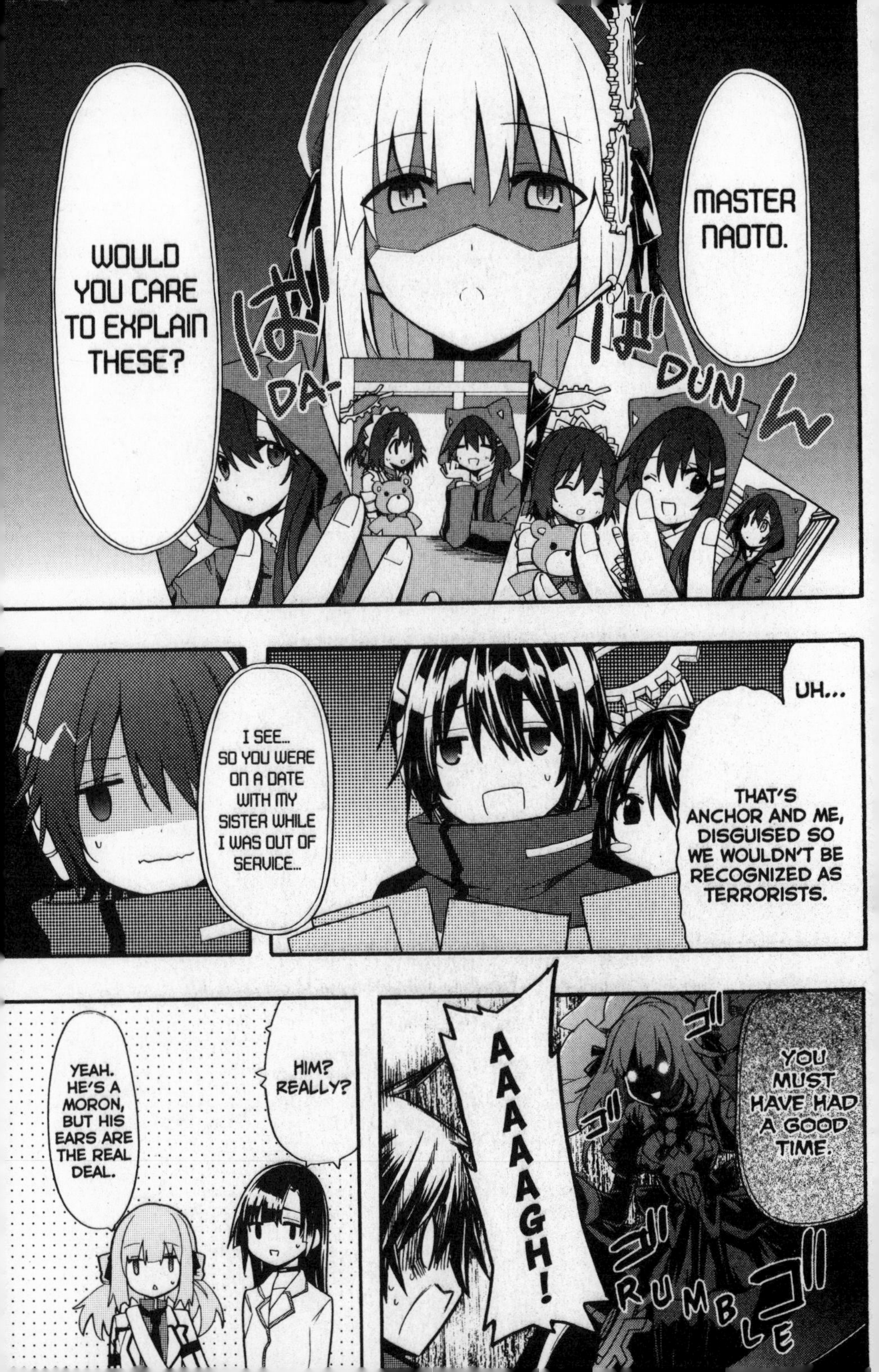
MASTER NAOTO.
WOULD YOU CARE TO EXPLAIN THESE?
DA-DUN
UH...
THAT'S ANCHOR AND ME, DISGUISED SO WE WOULDN'T BE RECOGNIZED AS TERRORISTS.
I SEE... SO YOU WERE ON A DATE WITH MY SISTER WHILE I WAS OUT OF SERVICE...
YOU MUST HAVE HAD A GOOD TIME.
RUMBLE
AAAAAGH!
HIM? REALLY?
YEAH. HE'S A MORON, BUT HIS EARS ARE THE REAL DEAL.

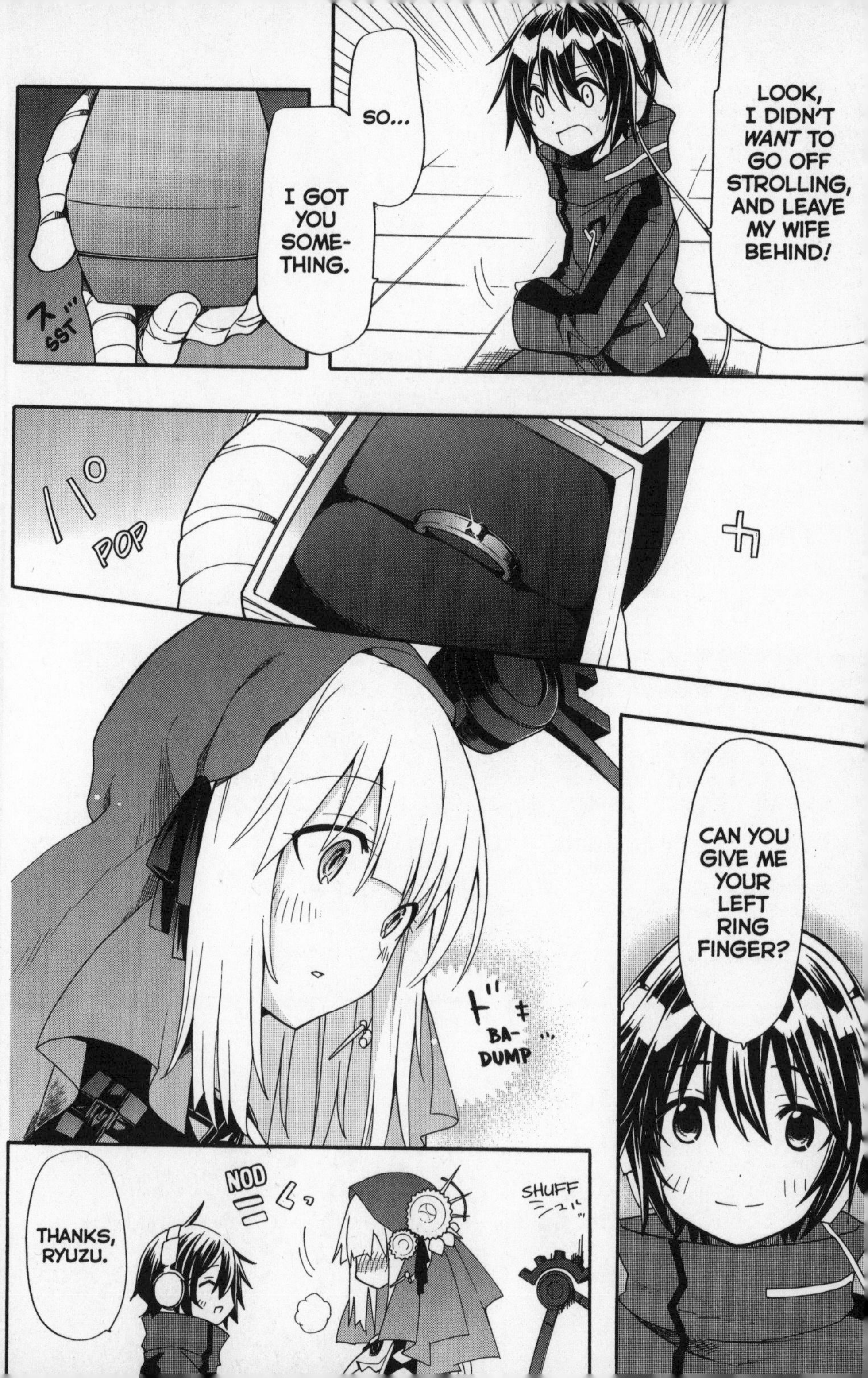
LOOK, I DIDN'T WANT TO GO OFF STROLLING, AND LEAVE MY WIFE BEHIND!
SO...
I GOT YOU SOME-THING.
ス… SST
カ
パ POP
CAN YOU GIVE ME YOUR LEFT RING FINGER?
ドキ BA-DUMP
SHUFF シュル
NOD
THANKS, RYUZU.

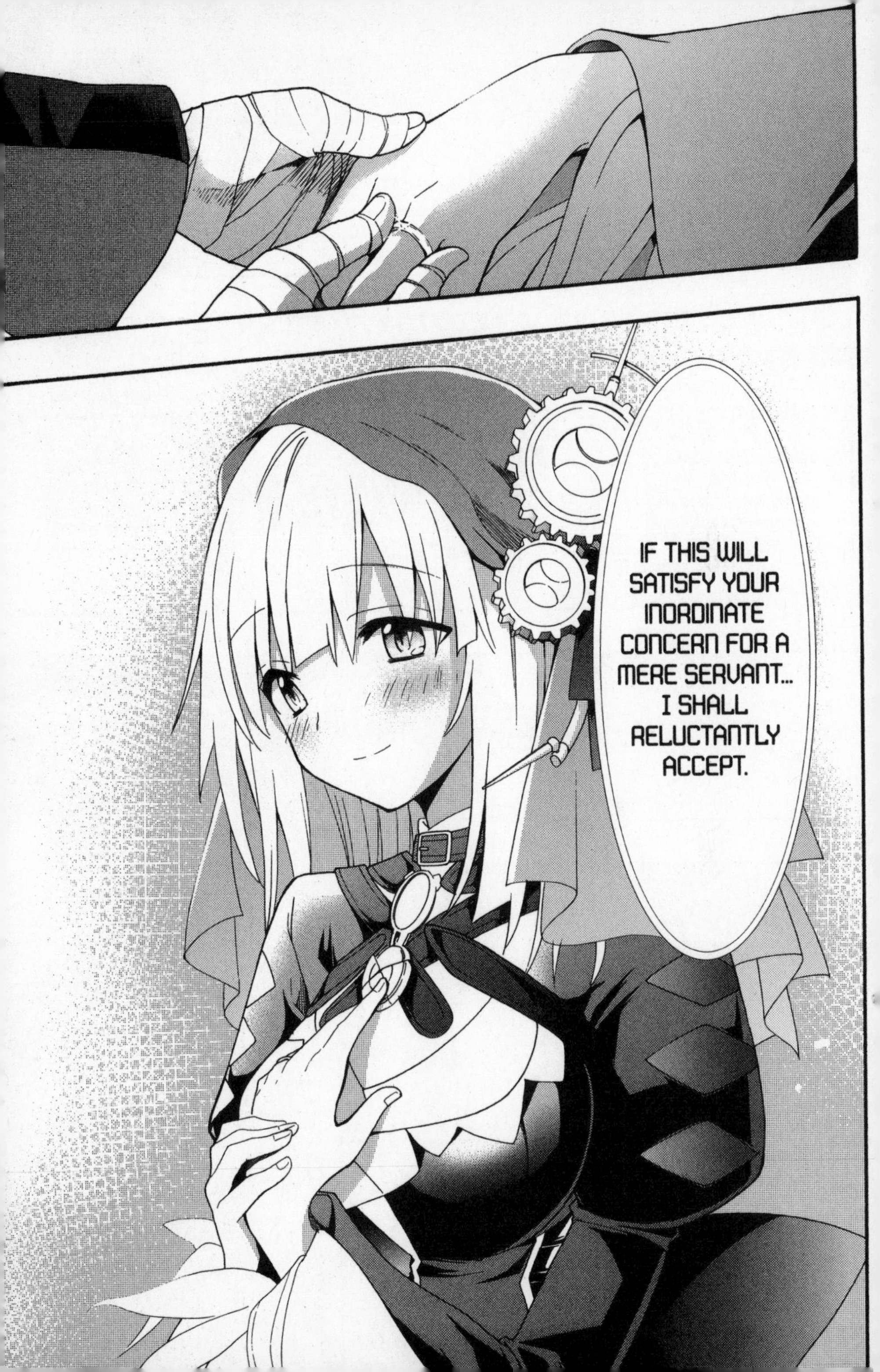
IF THIS WILL SATISFY YOUR INORDINATE CONCERN FOR A MERE SERVANT... I SHALL RELUCTANTLY ACCEPT.

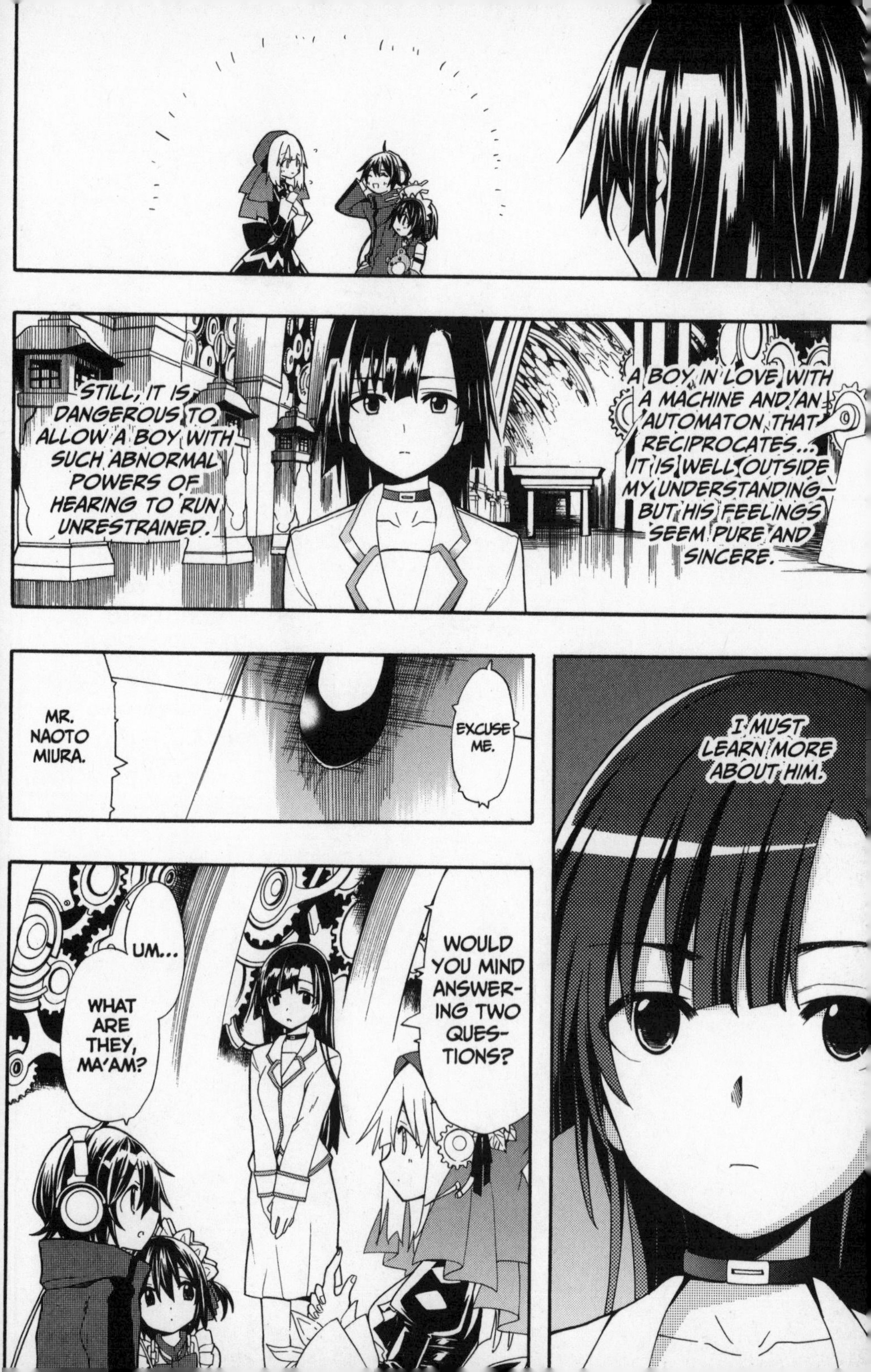
A BOY IN LOVE WITH A MACHINE AND AN AUTOMATON THAT RECIPROCATES... IT IS WELL OUTSIDE MY UNDERSTANDING— BUT HIS FEELINGS SEEM PURE AND SINCERE.
STILL, IT IS DANGEROUS TO ALLOW A BOY WITH SUCH ABNORMAL POWERS OF HEARING TO RUN UNRESTRAINED.
I MUST LEARN MORE ABOUT HIM.
EXCUSE ME.
MR. NAOTO MIURA.
WOULD YOU MIND ANSWERING TWO QUESTIONS?
UM...
WHAT ARE THEY, MA'AM?

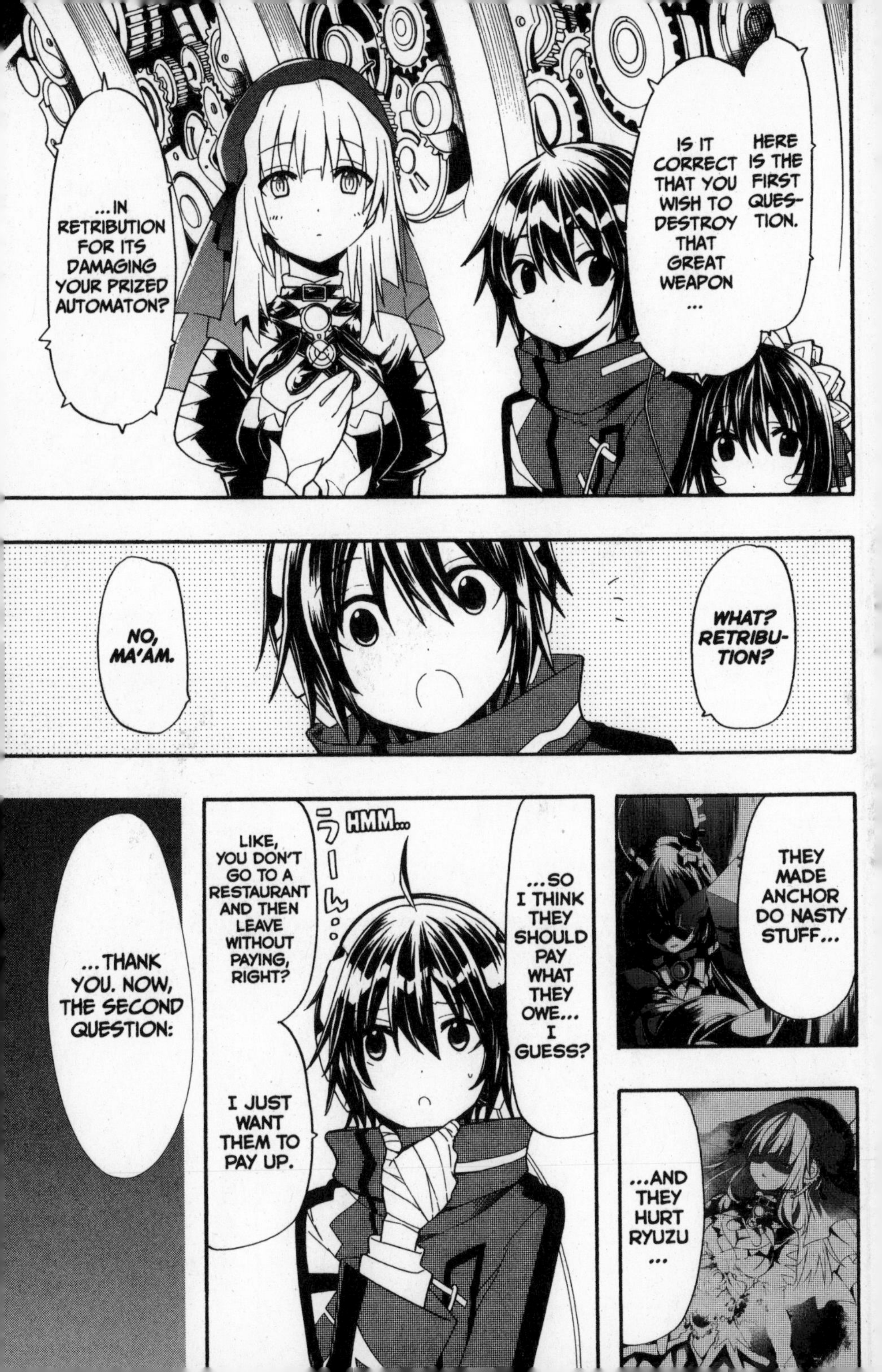

HERE IS THE FIRST QUESTION.
IS IT CORRECT THAT YOU WISH TO DESTROY THAT GREAT WEAPON ...
...IN RETRIBUTION FOR ITS DAMAGING YOUR PRIZED AUTOMATON?
WHAT? RETRIBUTION?
NO, MA'AM.
THEY MADE ANCHOR DO NASTY STUFF...
...AND THEY HURT RYUZU ...
...SO I THINK THEY SHOULD PAY WHAT THEY OWE... I GUESS?
うーん。。
HMM...
LIKE, YOU DON'T GO TO A RESTAURANT AND THEN LEAVE WITHOUT PAYING, RIGHT?
I JUST WANT THEM TO PAY UP.
...THANK YOU. NOW, THE SECOND QUESTION:

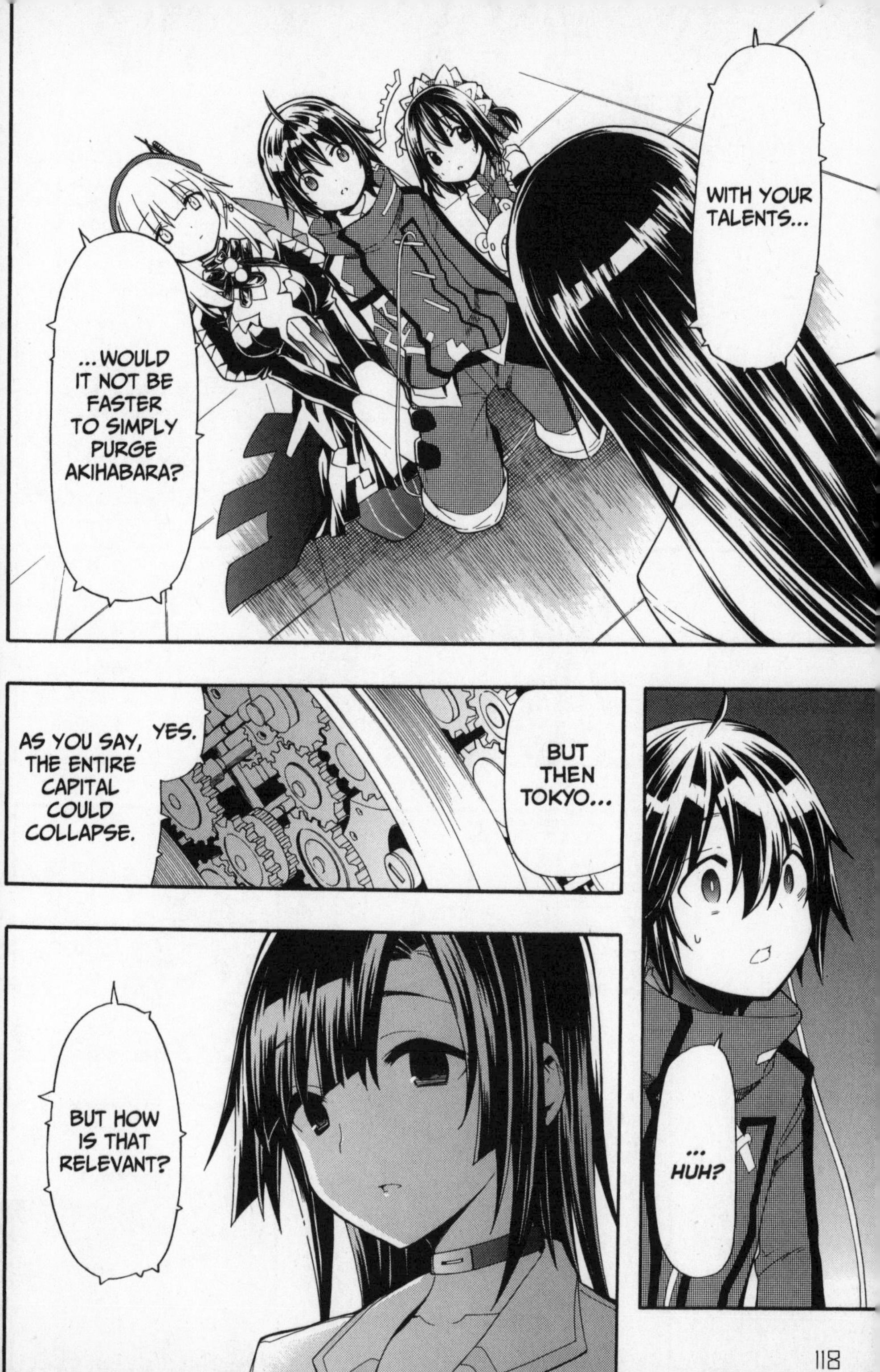
WITH YOUR TALENTS...
...WOULD IT NOT BE FASTER TO SIMPLY PURGE AKIHABARA?
... HUH?
BUT THEN TOKYO...
YES.
AS YOU SAY, THE ENTIRE CAPITAL COULD COLLAPSE.
BUT HOW IS THAT RELEVANT?

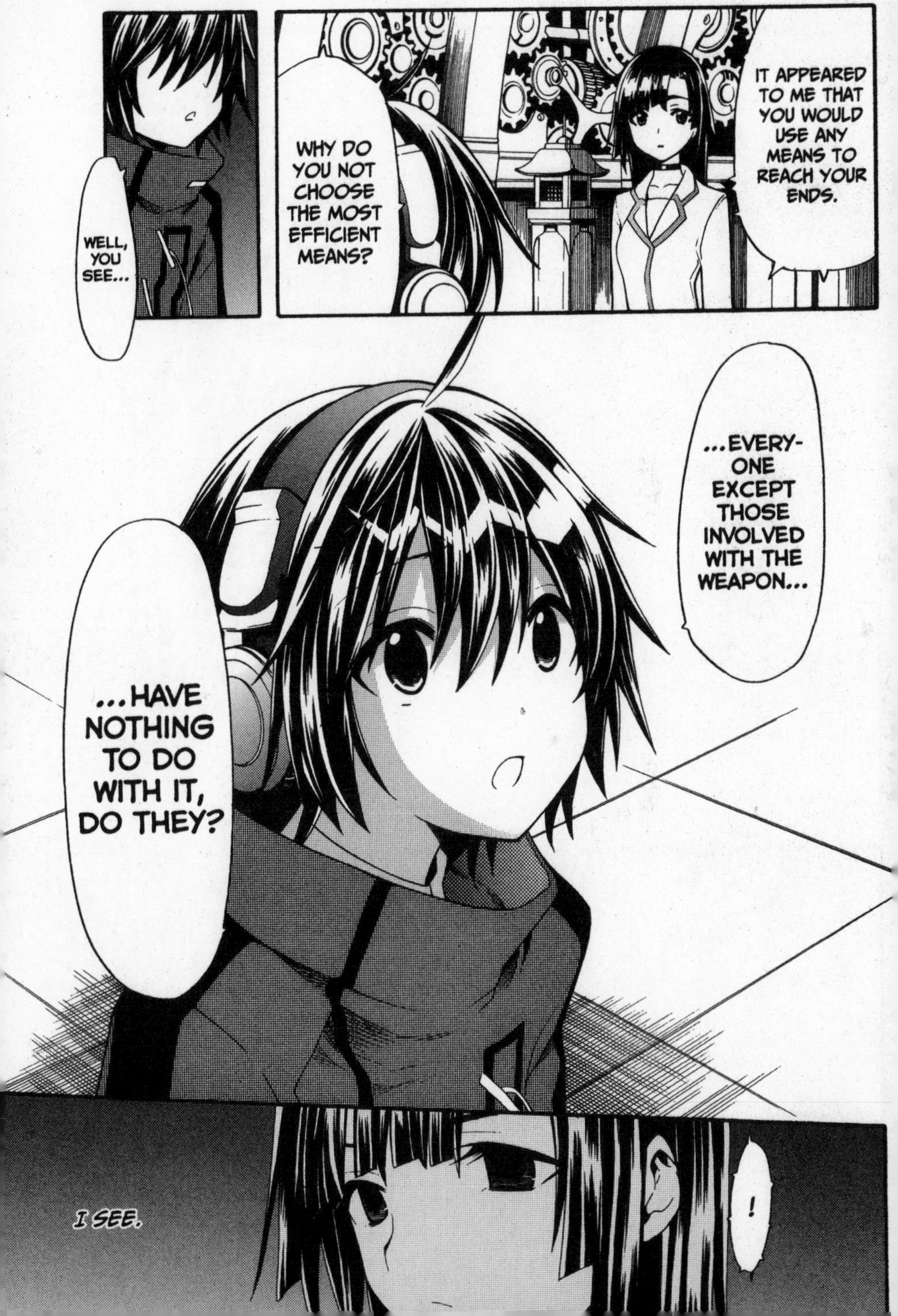
IT APPEARED TO ME THAT YOU WOULD USE ANY MEANS TO REACH YOUR ENDS.
WHY DO YOU NOT CHOOSE THE MOST EFFICIENT MEANS?
WELL, YOU SEE...
...EVERY-ONE EXCEPT THOSE INVOLVED WITH THE WEAPON...
...HAVE NOTHING TO DO WITH IT, DO THEY?
!
I SEE.

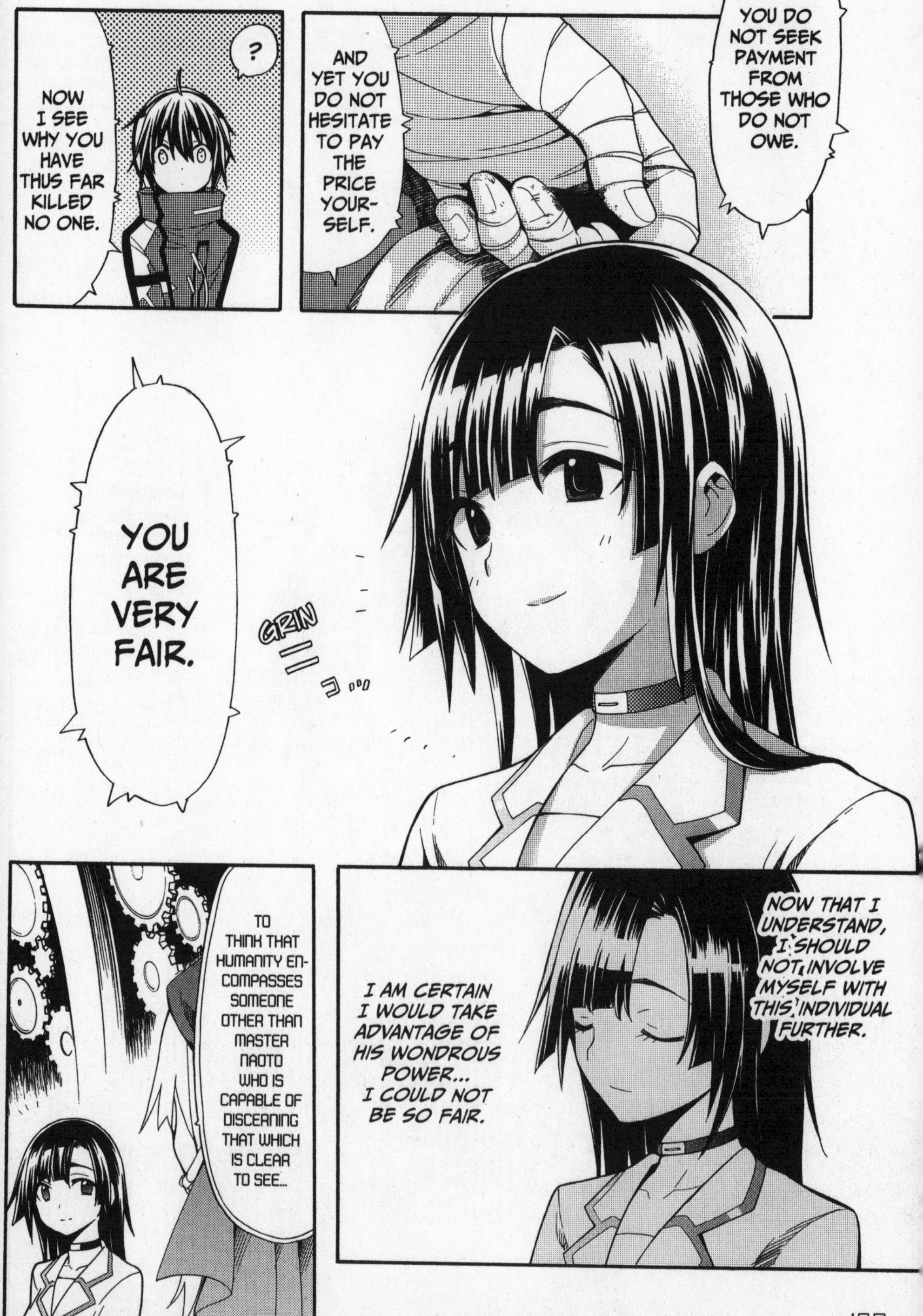
YOU DO NOT SEEK PAYMENT FROM THOSE WHO DO NOT OWE.
AND YET YOU DO NOT HESITATE TO PAY THE PRICE YOURSELF.
?
NOW I SEE WHY YOU HAVE THUS FAR KILLED NO ONE.
YOU ARE VERY FAIR.
GRIN
NOW THAT I UNDERSTAND, I SHOULD NOT INVOLVE MYSELF WITH THIS INDIVIDUAL FURTHER.
I AM CERTAIN I WOULD TAKE ADVANTAGE OF HIS WONDROUS POWER... I COULD NOT BE SO FAIR.
TO THINK THAT HUMANITY ENCOMPASSES SOMEONE OTHER THAN MASTER NAOTO WHO IS CAPABLE OF DISCERNING THAT WHICH IS CLEAR TO SEE...

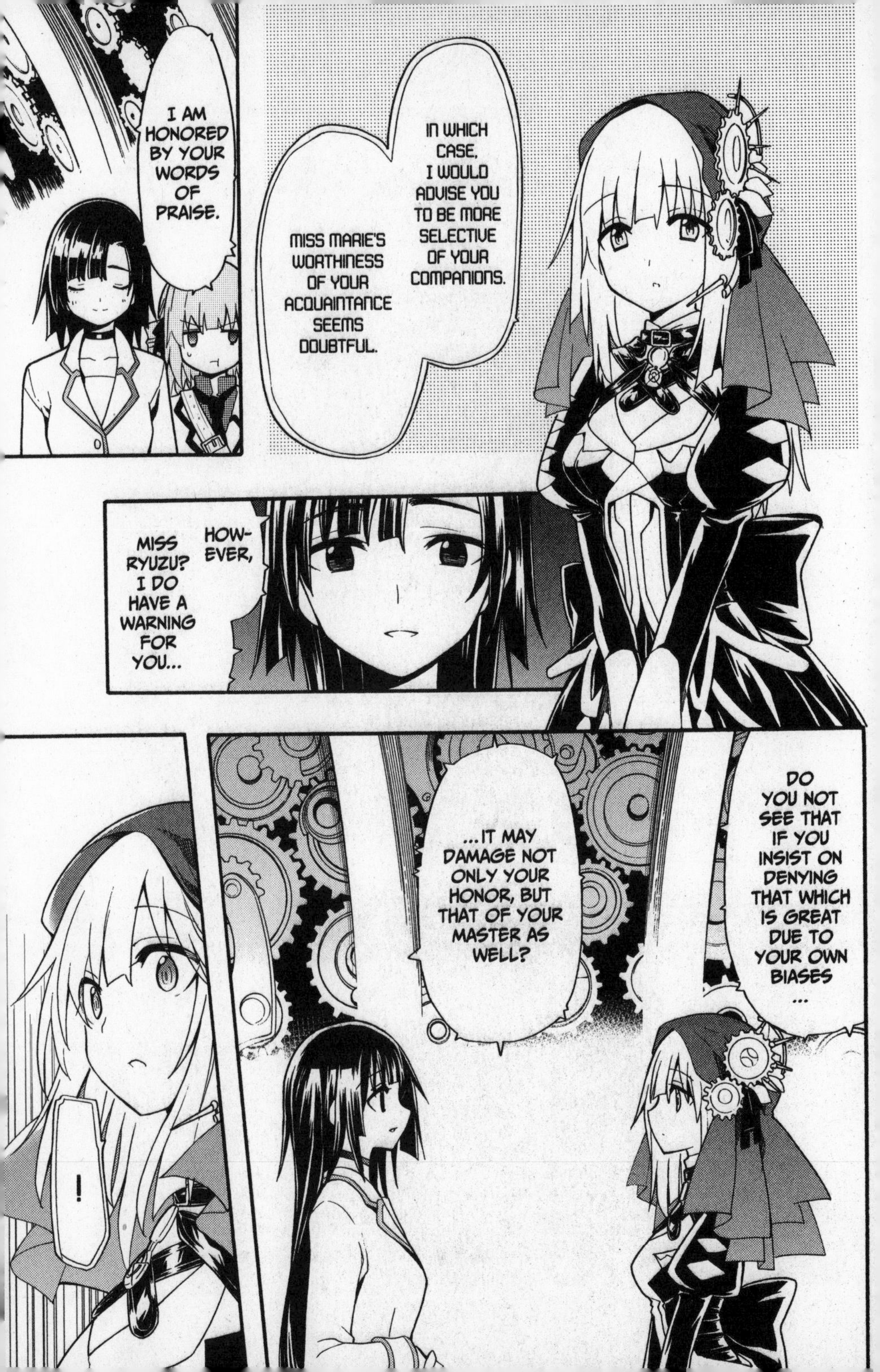
MISS MARIE'S WORTHINESS OF YOUR ACQUAINTANCE SEEMS DOUBTFUL.
IN WHICH CASE, I WOULD ADVISE YOU TO BE MORE SELECTIVE OF YOUR COMPANIONS.
I AM HONORED BY YOUR WORDS OF PRAISE.
HOW-EVER,
MISS RYUZU? I DO HAVE A WARNING FOR YOU...
DO YOU NOT SEE THAT IF YOU INSIST ON DENYING THAT WHICH IS GREAT DUE TO YOUR OWN BIASES ...
...IT MAY DAMAGE NOT ONLY YOUR HONOR, BUT THAT OF YOUR MASTER AS WELL?
!

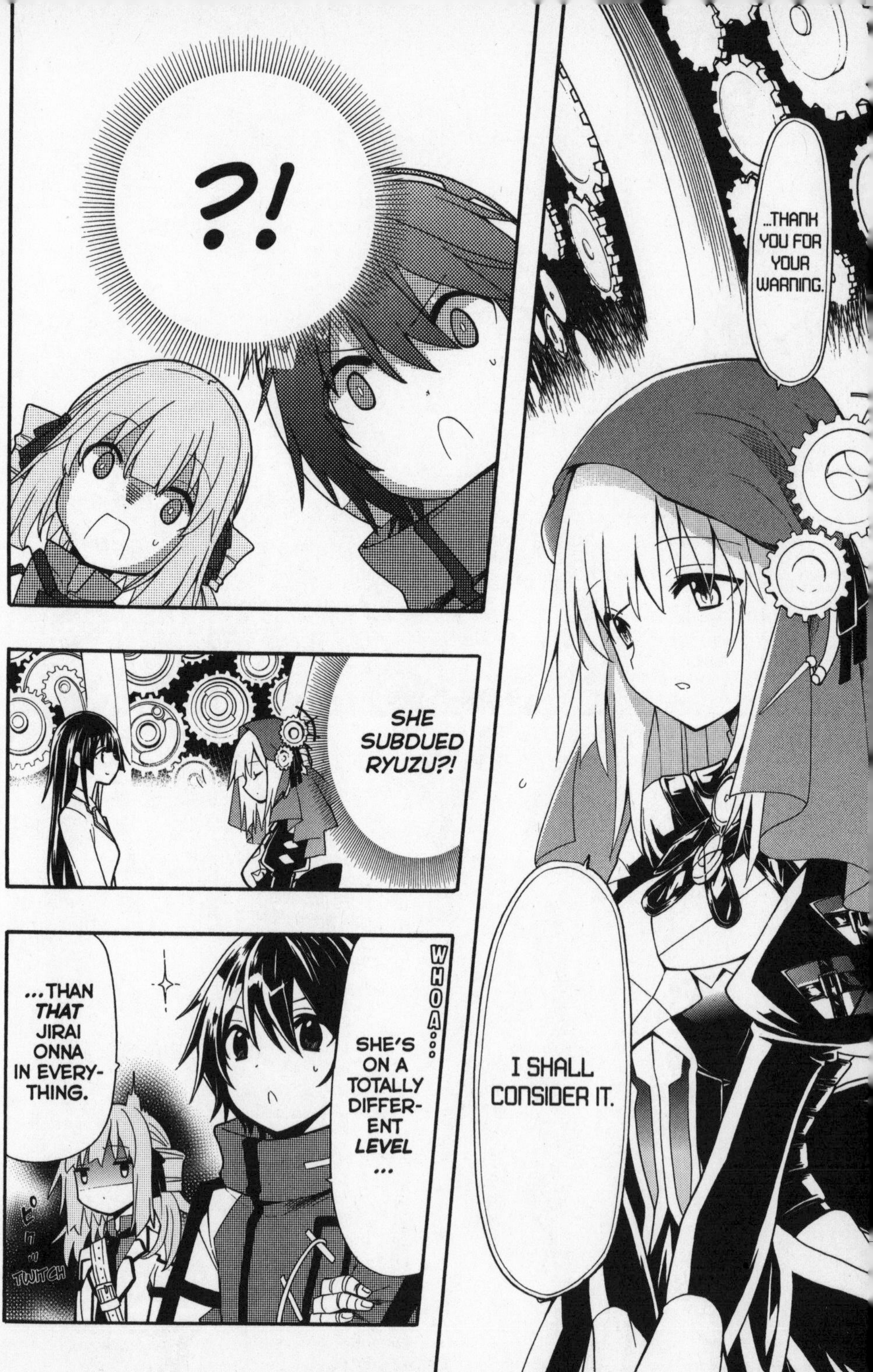
...THANK YOU FOR YOUR WARNING.
I SHALL CONSIDER IT.
?!
SHE SUBDUED RYUZU?!
WHOA...
SHE'S ON A TOTALLY DIFFER-ENT LEVEL...
...THAN THAT JIRAI ONNA IN EVERY-THING.
ピクッ
TWITCH

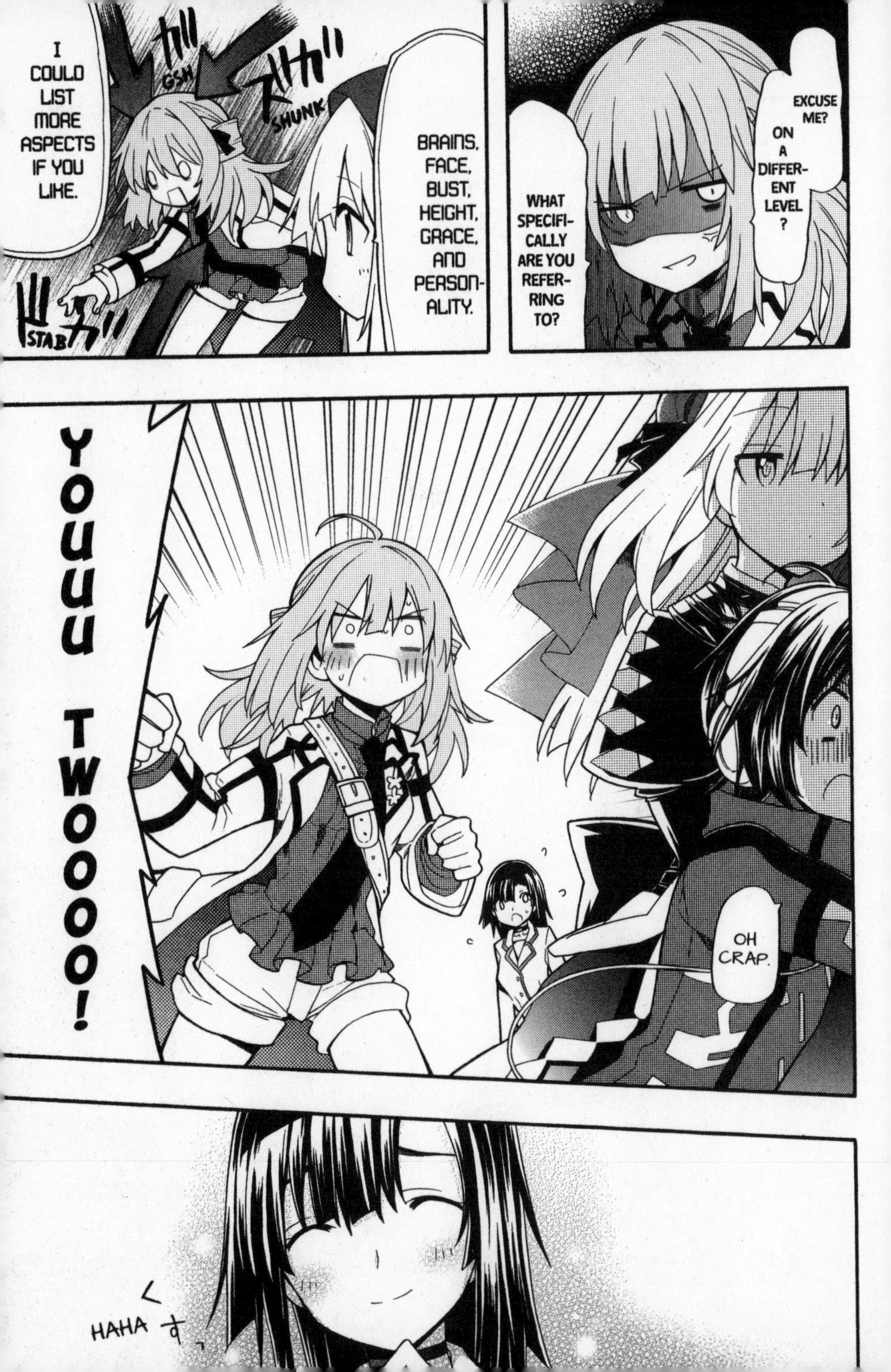
EXCUSE ME? ON A DIFFERENT LEVEL?
WHAT SPECIFICALLY ARE YOU REFERRING TO?
SHUNK
GSH
BRAINS, FACE, BUST, HEIGHT, GRACE, AND PERSONALITY.
I COULD LIST MORE ASPECTS IF YOU LIKE.
STAB
YOUUU TWOOOOO!
OH CRAP.
HAHA

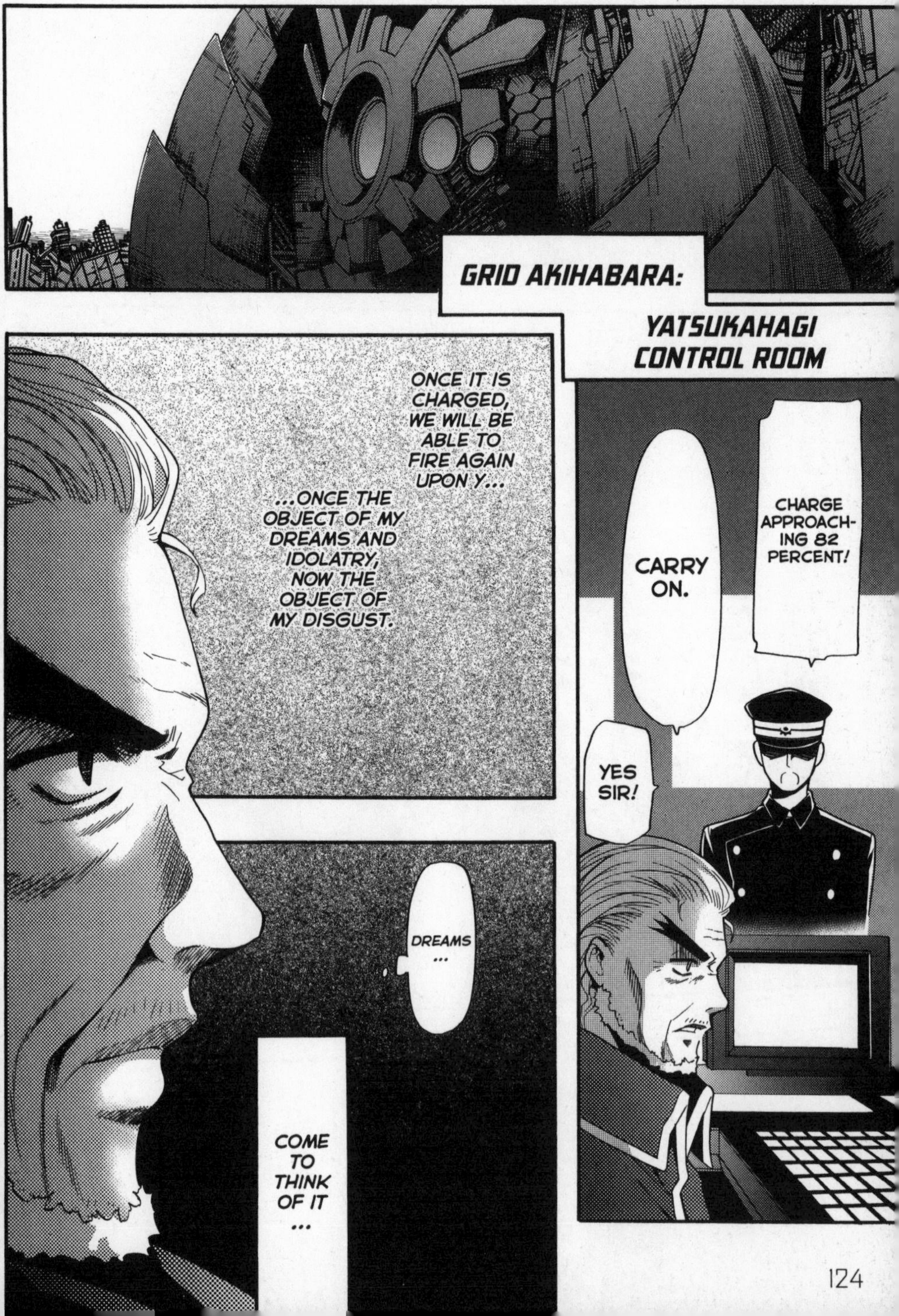
GRID AKIHABARA:
YATSUKAHAGI CONTROL ROOM
CHARGE APPROACHING 82 PERCENT!
CARRY ON.
YES SIR!
ONCE IT IS CHARGED, WE WILL BE ABLE TO FIRE AGAIN UPON Y...
...ONCE THE OBJECT OF MY DREAMS AND IDOLATRY, NOW THE OBJECT OF MY DISGUST.
DREAMS...
COME TO THINK OF IT...

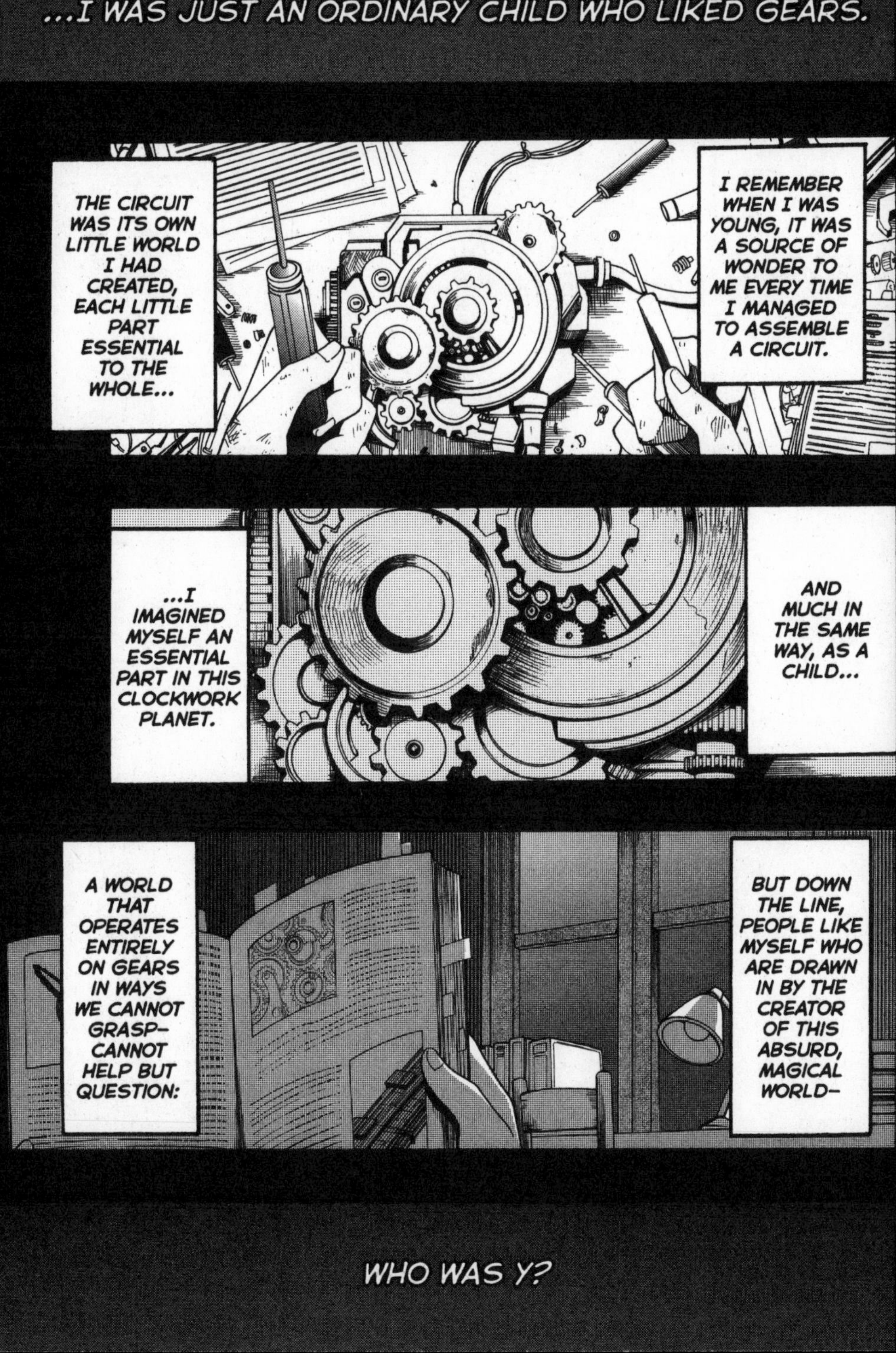
...I WAS JUST AN ORDINARY CHILD WHO LIKED GEARS.
I REMEMBER WHEN I WAS YOUNG, IT WAS A SOURCE OF WONDER TO ME EVERY TIME I MANAGED TO ASSEMBLE A CIRCUIT.
THE CIRCUIT WAS ITS OWN LITTLE WORLD I HAD CREATED, EACH LITTLE PART ESSENTIAL TO THE WHOLE...
AND MUCH IN THE SAME WAY, AS A CHILD...
...I IMAGINED MYSELF AN ESSENTIAL PART IN THIS CLOCKWORK PLANET.
BUT DOWN THE LINE, PEOPLE LIKE MYSELF WHO ARE DRAWN IN BY THE CREATOR OF THIS ABSURD, MAGICAL WORLD–
A WORLD THAT OPERATES ENTIRELY ON GEARS IN WAYS WE CANNOT GRASP– CANNOT HELP BUT QUESTION:
WHO WAS Y?

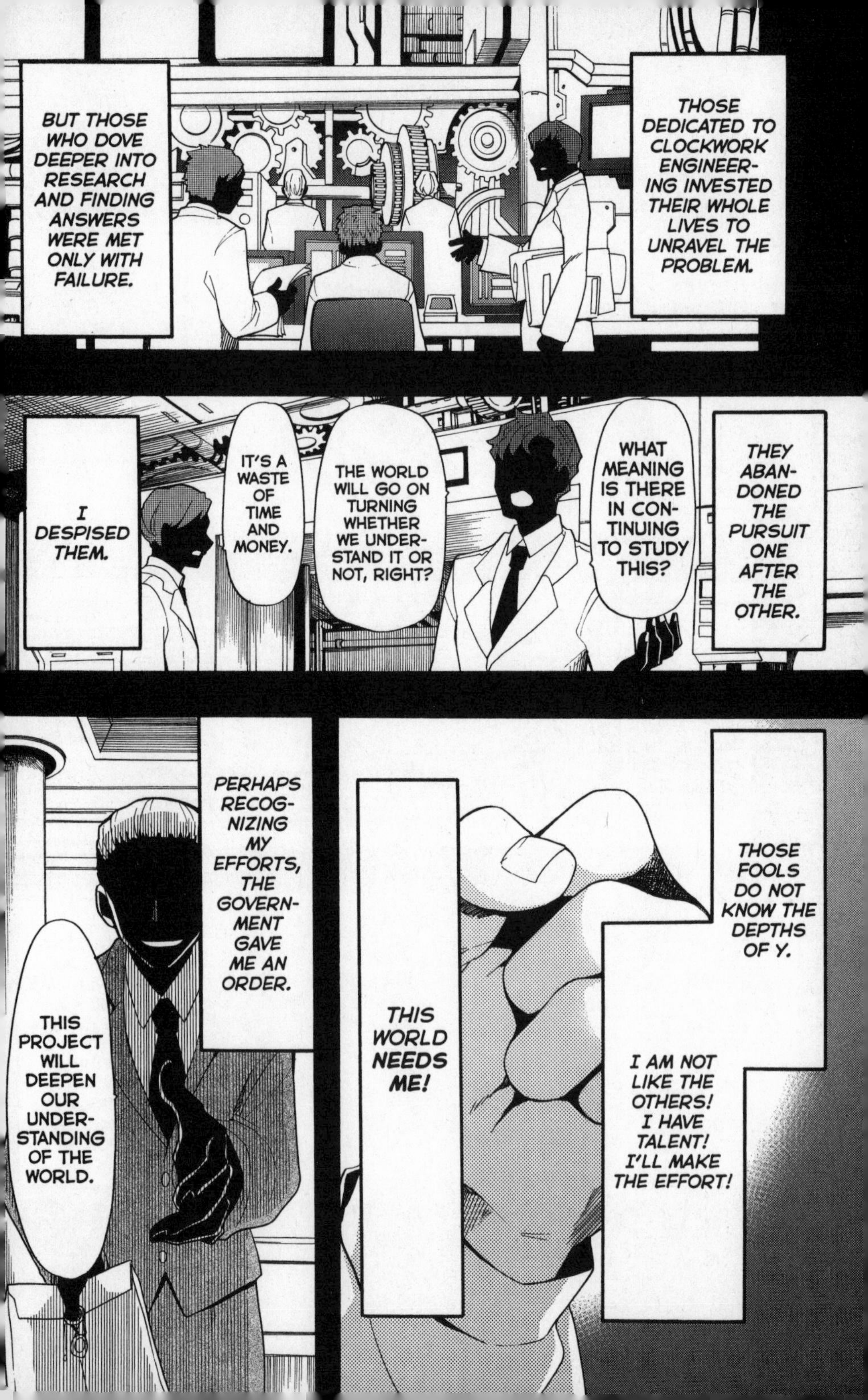
THOSE DEDICATED TO CLOCKWORK ENGINEERING INVESTED THEIR WHOLE LIVES TO UNRAVEL THE PROBLEM.
BUT THOSE WHO DOVE DEEPER INTO RESEARCH AND FINDING ANSWERS WERE MET ONLY WITH FAILURE.
THEY ABANDONED THE PURSUIT ONE AFTER THE OTHER.
WHAT MEANING IS THERE IN CONTINUING TO STUDY THIS?
THE WORLD WILL GO ON TURNING WHETHER WE UNDERSTAND IT OR NOT, RIGHT?
IT'S A WASTE OF TIME AND MONEY.
I DESPISED THEM.
THOSE FOOLS DO NOT KNOW THE DEPTHS OF Y.
I AM NOT LIKE THE OTHERS! I HAVE TALENT! I'LL MAKE THE EFFORT!
THIS WORLD NEEDS ME!
PERHAPS RECOGNIZING MY EFFORTS, THE GOVERNMENT GAVE ME AN ORDER.
THIS PROJECT WILL DEEPEN OUR UNDERSTANDING OF THE WORLD.

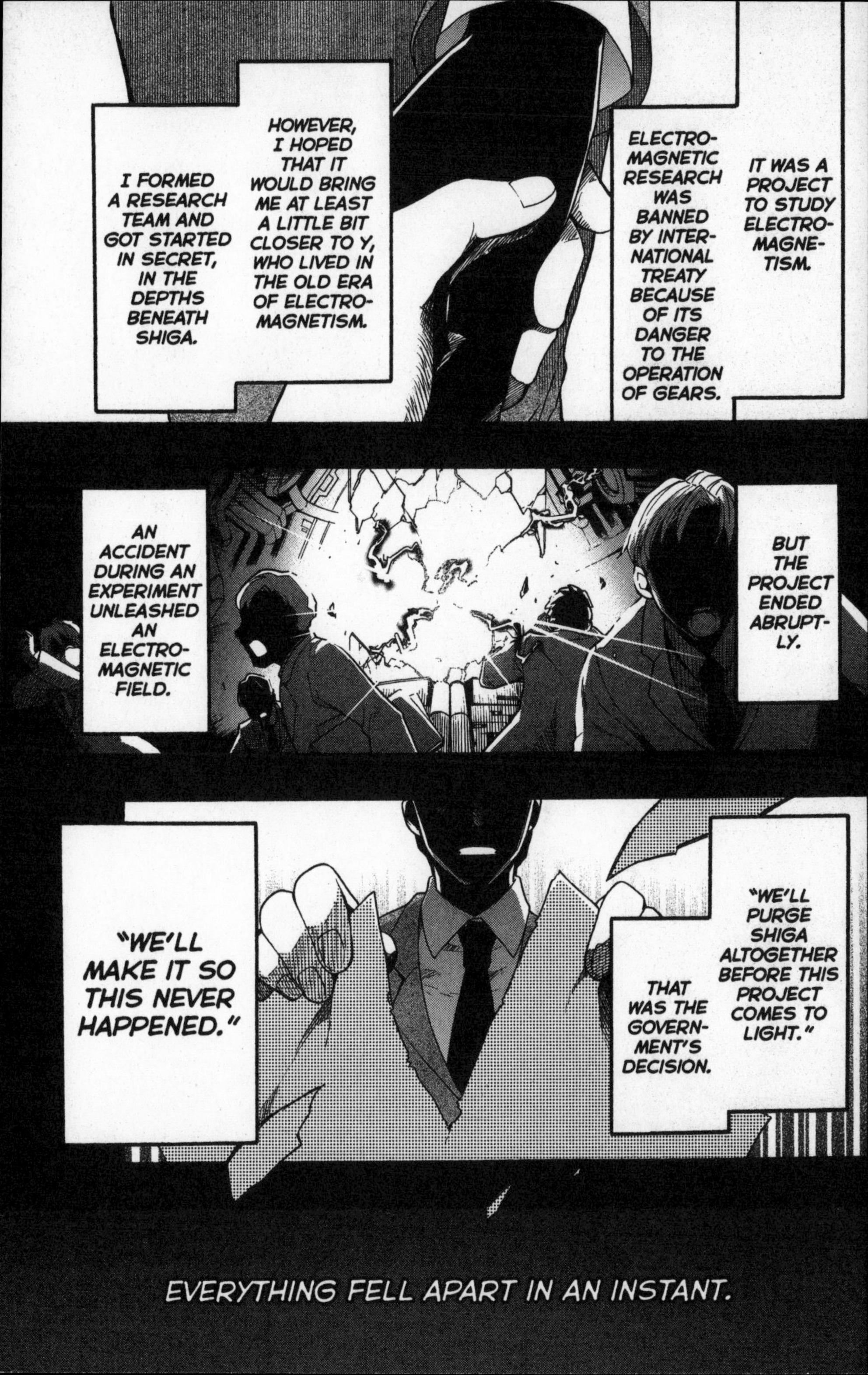
IT WAS A PROJECT TO STUDY ELECTRO-MAGNE-TISM.
ELECTRO-MAGNETIC RESEARCH WAS BANNED BY INTER-NATIONAL TREATY BECAUSE OF ITS DANGER TO THE OPERATION OF GEARS.
HOWEVER, I HOPED THAT IT WOULD BRING ME AT LEAST A LITTLE BIT CLOSER TO Y, WHO LIVED IN THE OLD ERA OF ELECTRO-MAGNETISM.
I FORMED A RESEARCH TEAM AND GOT STARTED IN SECRET, IN THE DEPTHS BENEATH SHIGA.
BUT THE PROJECT ENDED ABRUPT-LY.
AN ACCIDENT DURING AN EXPERIMENT UNLEASHED AN ELECTRO-MAGNETIC FIELD.
"WE'LL PURGE SHIGA ALTOGETHER BEFORE THIS PROJECT COMES TO LIGHT."
THAT WAS THE GOVERN-MENT'S DECISION.
"WE'LL MAKE IT SO THIS NEVER HAPPENED."
EVERYTHING FELL APART IN AN INSTANT.

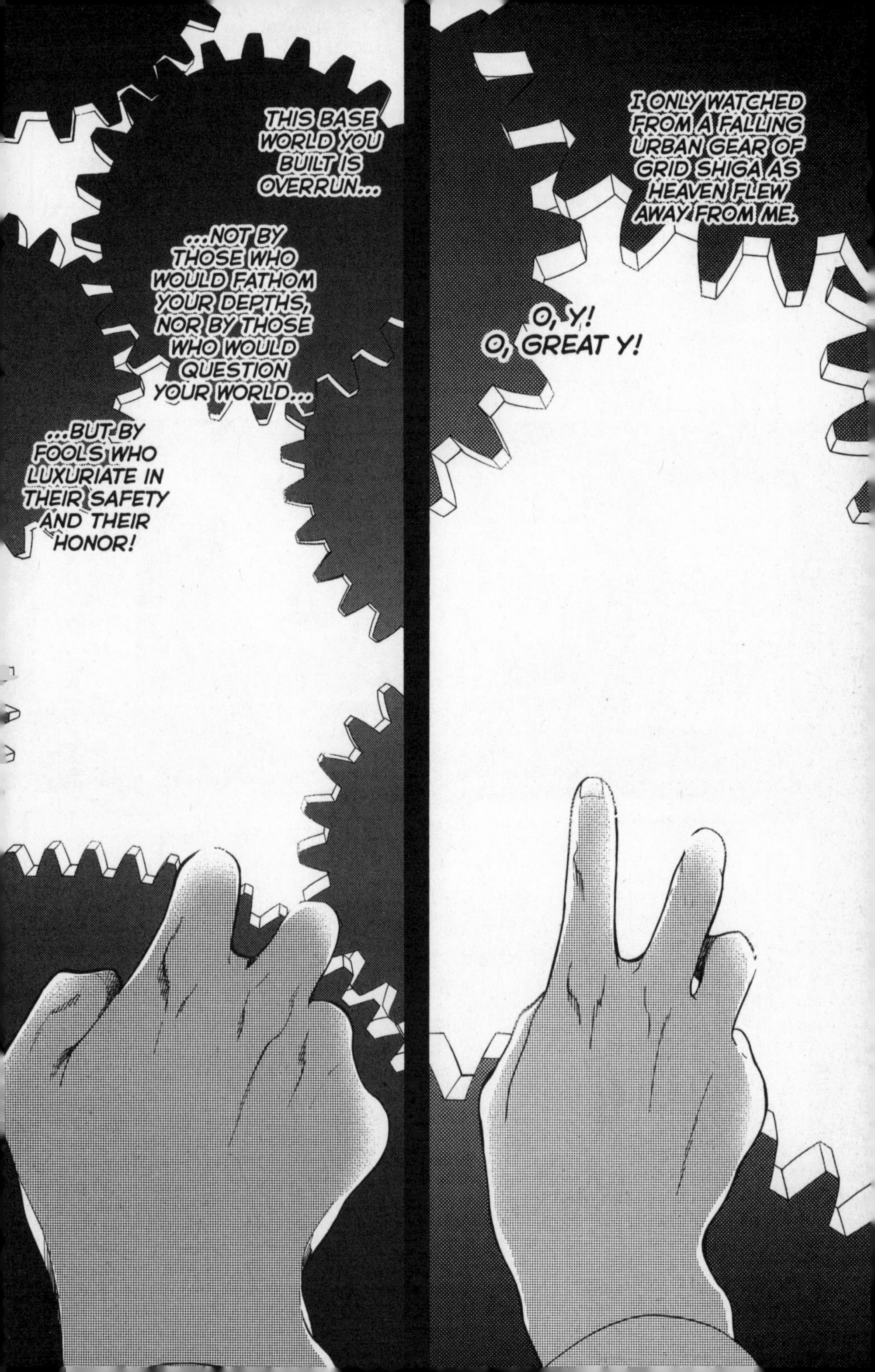
I ONLY WATCHED FROM A FALLING URBAN GEAR OF GRID SHIGA AS HEAVEN FLEW AWAY FROM ME.
O, Y! O, GREAT Y!
THIS BASE WORLD YOU BUILT IS OVERRUN...
...NOT BY THOSE WHO WOULD FATHOM YOUR DEPTHS, NOR BY THOSE WHO WOULD QUESTION YOUR WORLD...
...BUT BY FOOLS WHO LUXURIATE IN THEIR SAFETY AND THEIR HONOR!

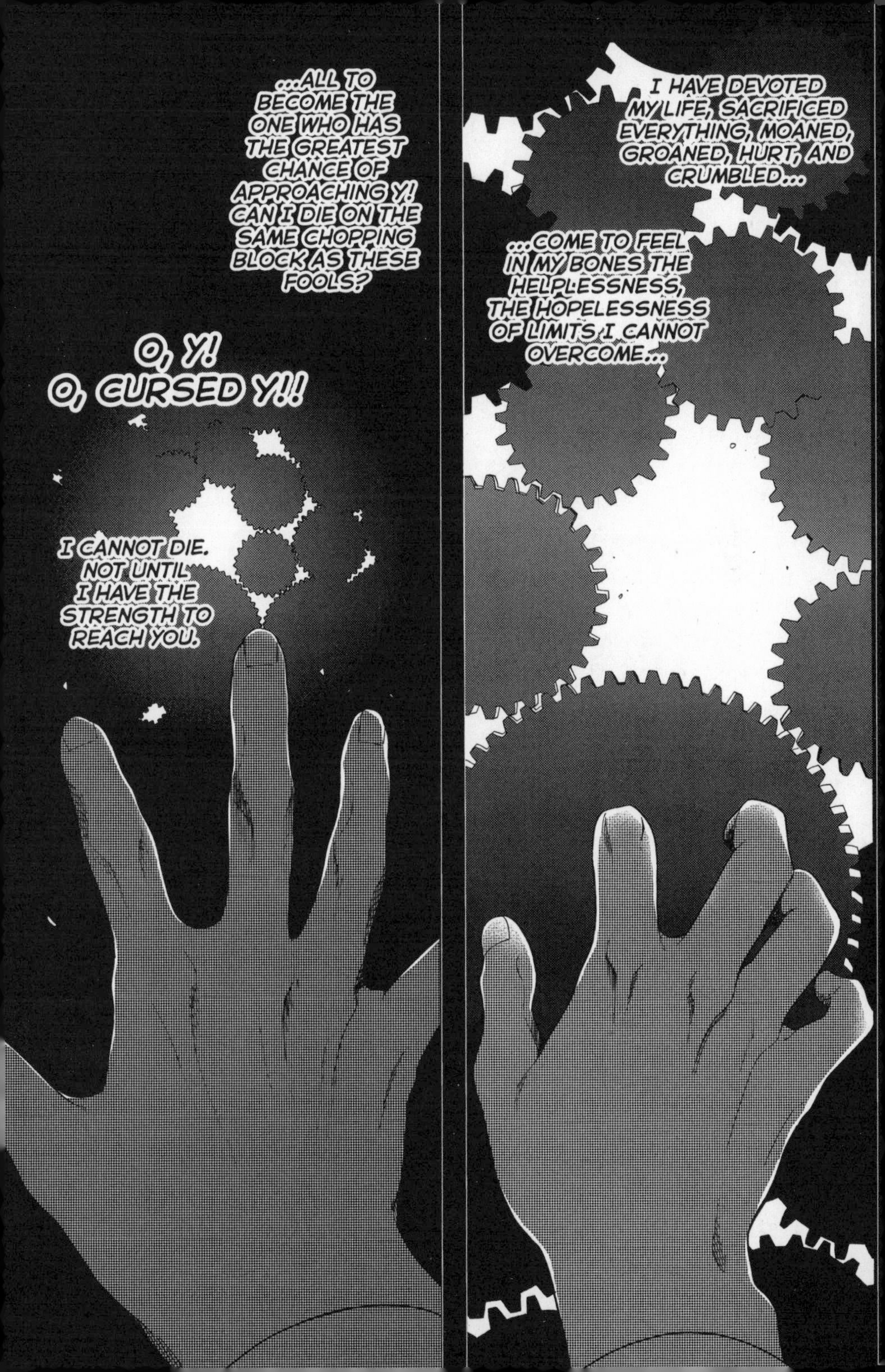
I HAVE DEVOTED MY LIFE, SACRIFICED EVERYTHING, MOANED, GROANED, HURT, AND CRUMBLED...
...COME TO FEEL IN MY BONES THE HELPLESSNESS, THE HOPELESSNESS OF LIMITS I CANNOT OVERCOME...
...ALL TO BECOME THE ONE WHO HAS THE GREATEST CHANCE OF APPROACHING Y! CAN I DIE ON THE SAME CHOPPING BLOCK AS THESE FOOLS?
O, Y! O, CURSED Y!!
I CANNOT DIE. NOT UNTIL I HAVE THE STRENGTH TO REACH YOU.

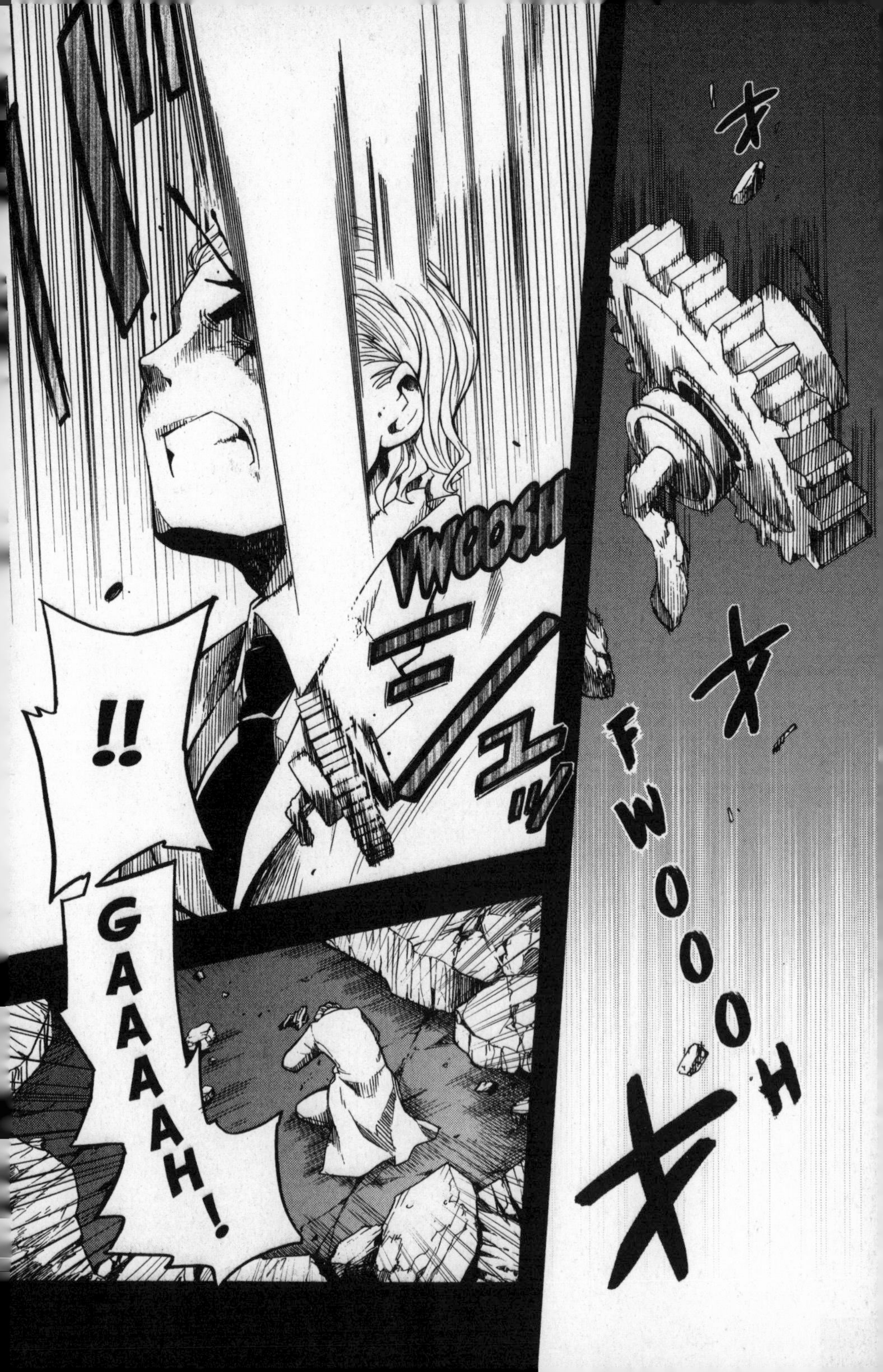
FWOOOH
VWOOSH
!!
GAAAAH!

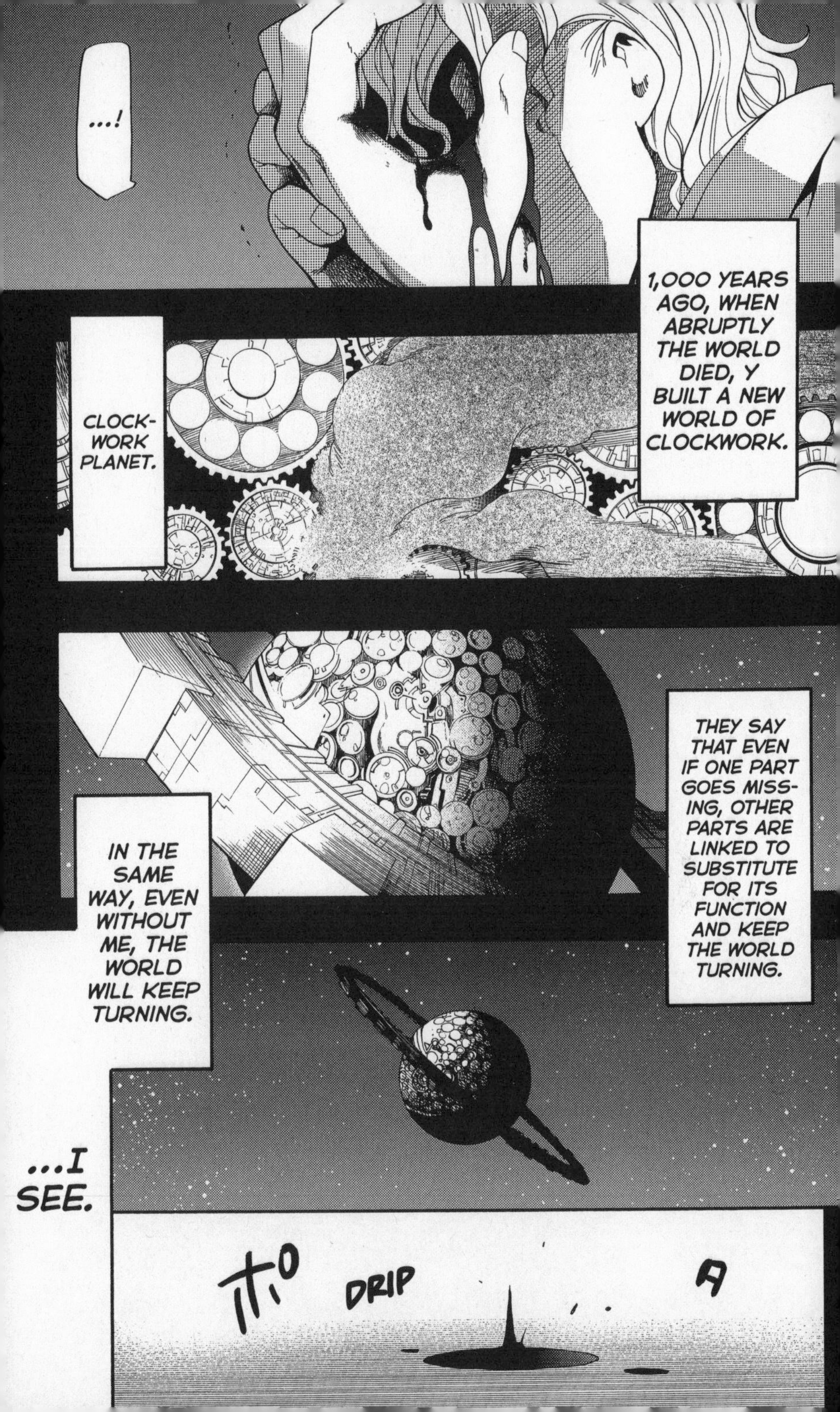
...!
1,000 YEARS AGO, WHEN ABRUPTLY THE WORLD DIED, Y BUILT A NEW WORLD OF CLOCKWORK.
CLOCK-WORK PLANET.
THEY SAY THAT EVEN IF ONE PART GOES MISS-ING, OTHER PARTS ARE LINKED TO SUBSTITUTE FOR ITS FUNCTION AND KEEP THE WORLD TURNING.
IN THE SAME WAY, EVEN WITHOUT ME, THE WORLD WILL KEEP TURNING.
...I SEE.
DRIP

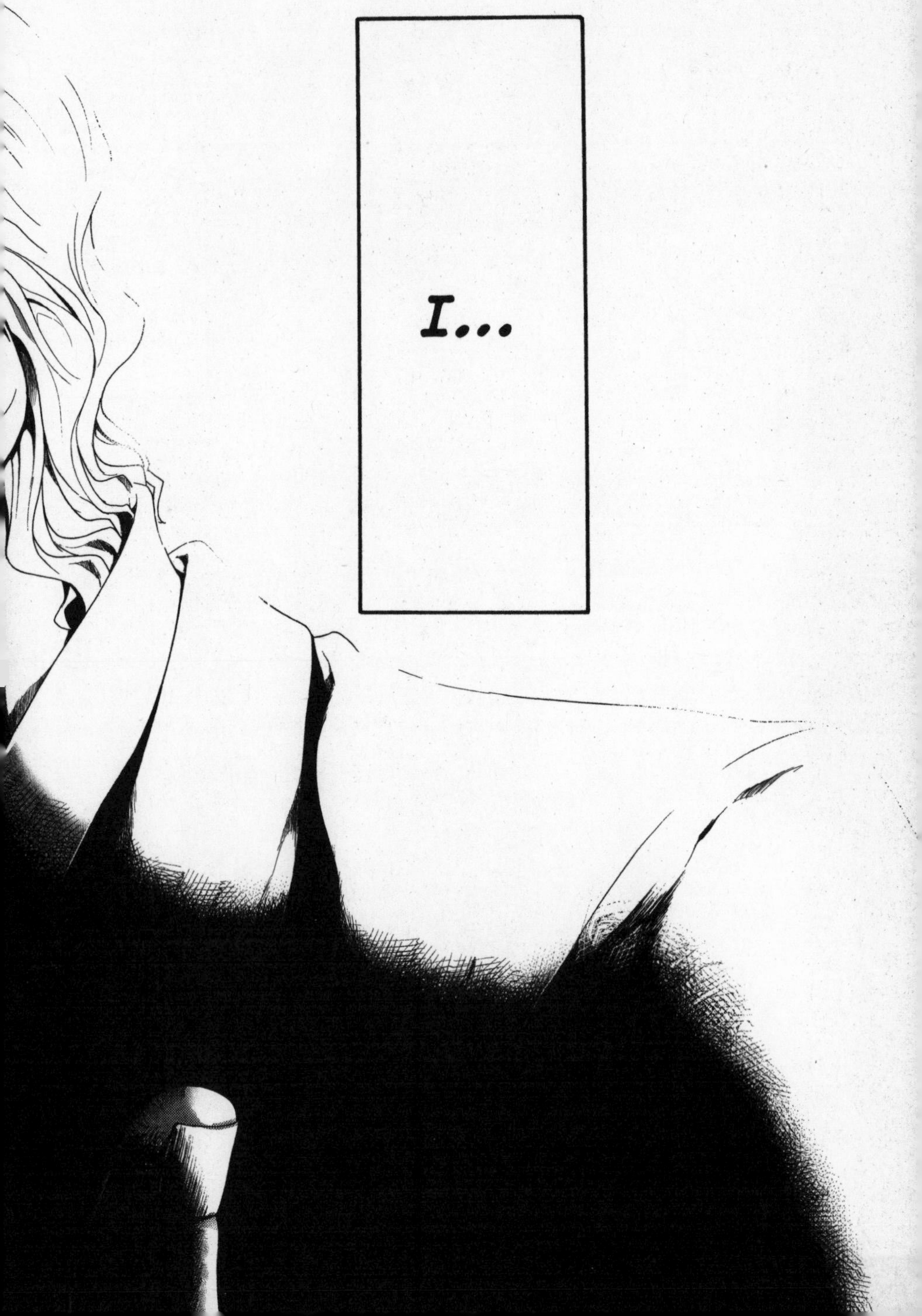
I...

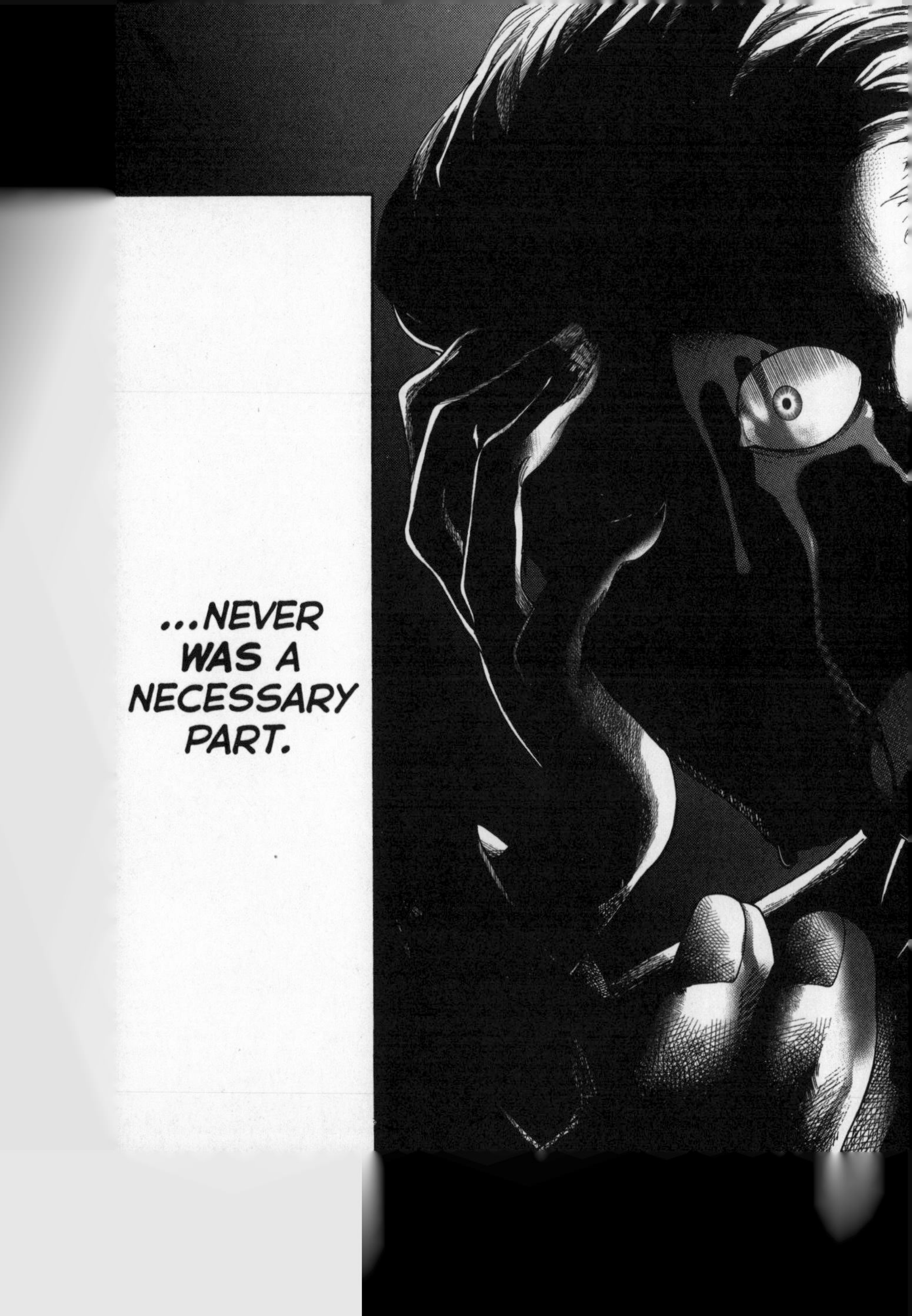
...NEVER WAS A NECESSARY PART.

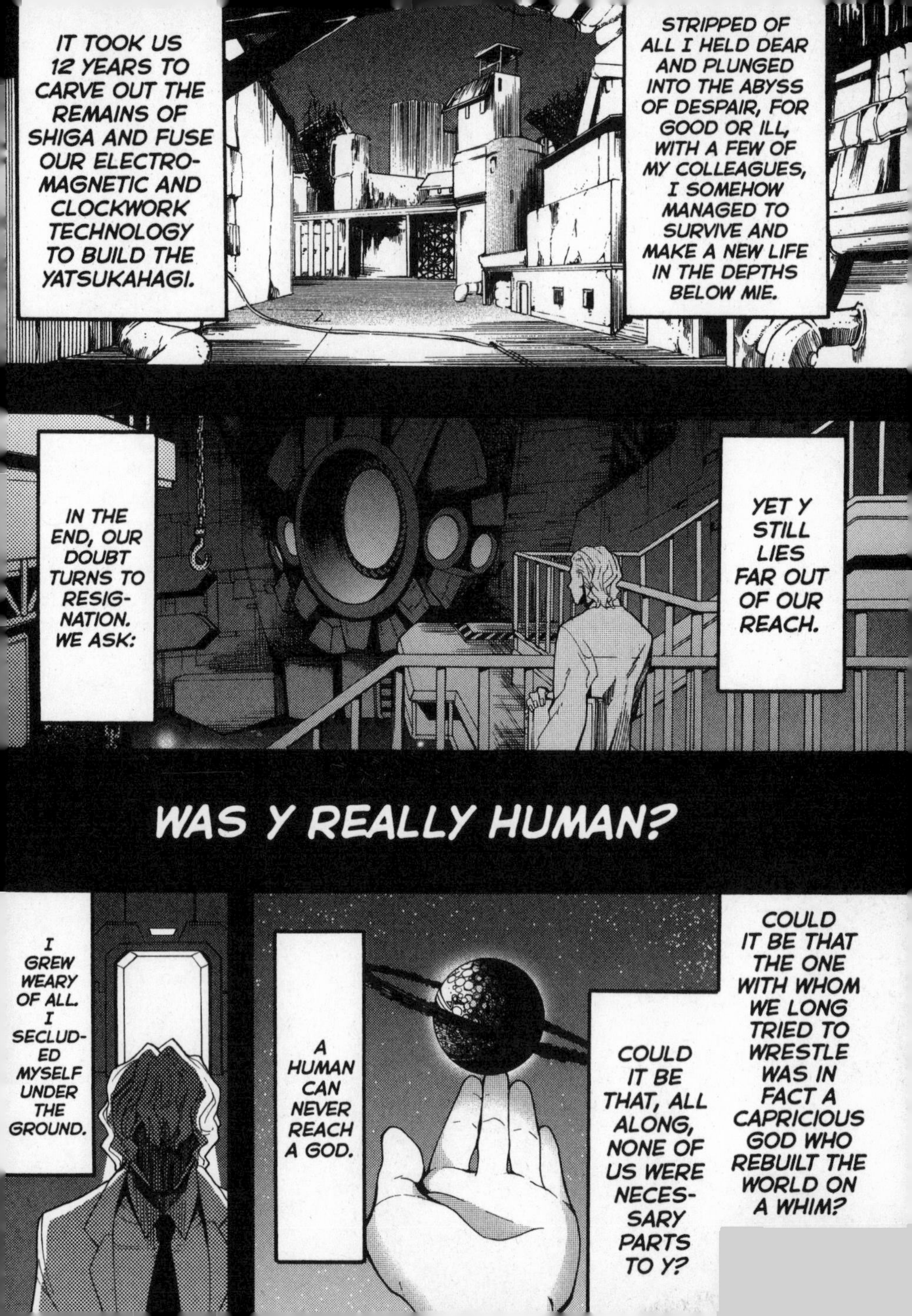
STRIPPED OF ALL I HELD DEAR AND PLUNGED INTO THE ABYSS OF DESPAIR, FOR GOOD OR ILL, WITH A FEW OF MY COLLEAGUES, I SOMEHOW MANAGED TO SURVIVE AND MAKE A NEW LIFE IN THE DEPTHS BELOW MIE.
IT TOOK US 12 YEARS TO CARVE OUT THE REMAINS OF SHIGA AND FUSE OUR ELECTRO-MAGNETIC AND CLOCKWORK TECHNOLOGY TO BUILD THE YATSUKAHAGI.
YET Y STILL LIES FAR OUT OF OUR REACH.
IN THE END, OUR DOUBT TURNS TO RESIG-NATION. WE ASK:
WAS Y REALLY HUMAN?
COULD IT BE THAT THE ONE WITH WHOM WE LONG TRIED TO WRESTLE WAS IN FACT A CAPRICIOUS GOD WHO REBUILT THE WORLD ON A WHIM?
COULD IT BE THAT, ALL ALONG, NONE OF US WERE NECES-SARY PARTS TO Y?
A HUMAN CAN NEVER REACH A GOD.
I GREW WEARY OF ALL. I SECLUD-ED MYSELF UNDER THE GROUND.

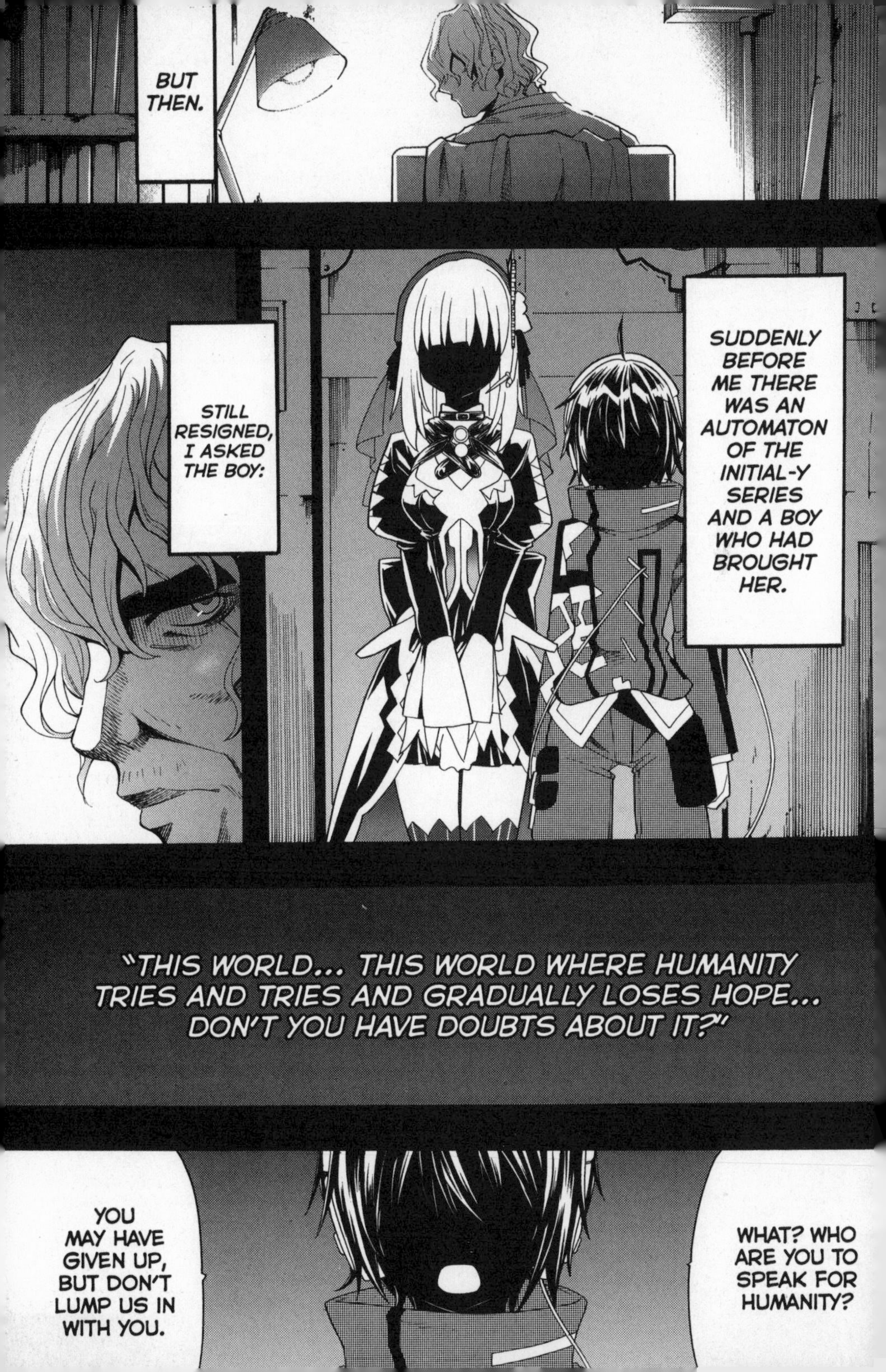
BUT THEN.
SUDDENLY BEFORE ME THERE WAS AN AUTOMATON OF THE INITIAL-Y SERIES AND A BOY WHO HAD BROUGHT HER.
STILL RESIGNED, I ASKED THE BOY:
"THIS WORLD... THIS WORLD WHERE HUMANITY TRIES AND TRIES AND GRADUALLY LOSES HOPE... DON'T YOU HAVE DOUBTS ABOUT IT?"
WHAT? WHO ARE YOU TO SPEAK FOR HUMANITY?
YOU MAY HAVE GIVEN UP, BUT DON'T LUMP US IN WITH YOU.

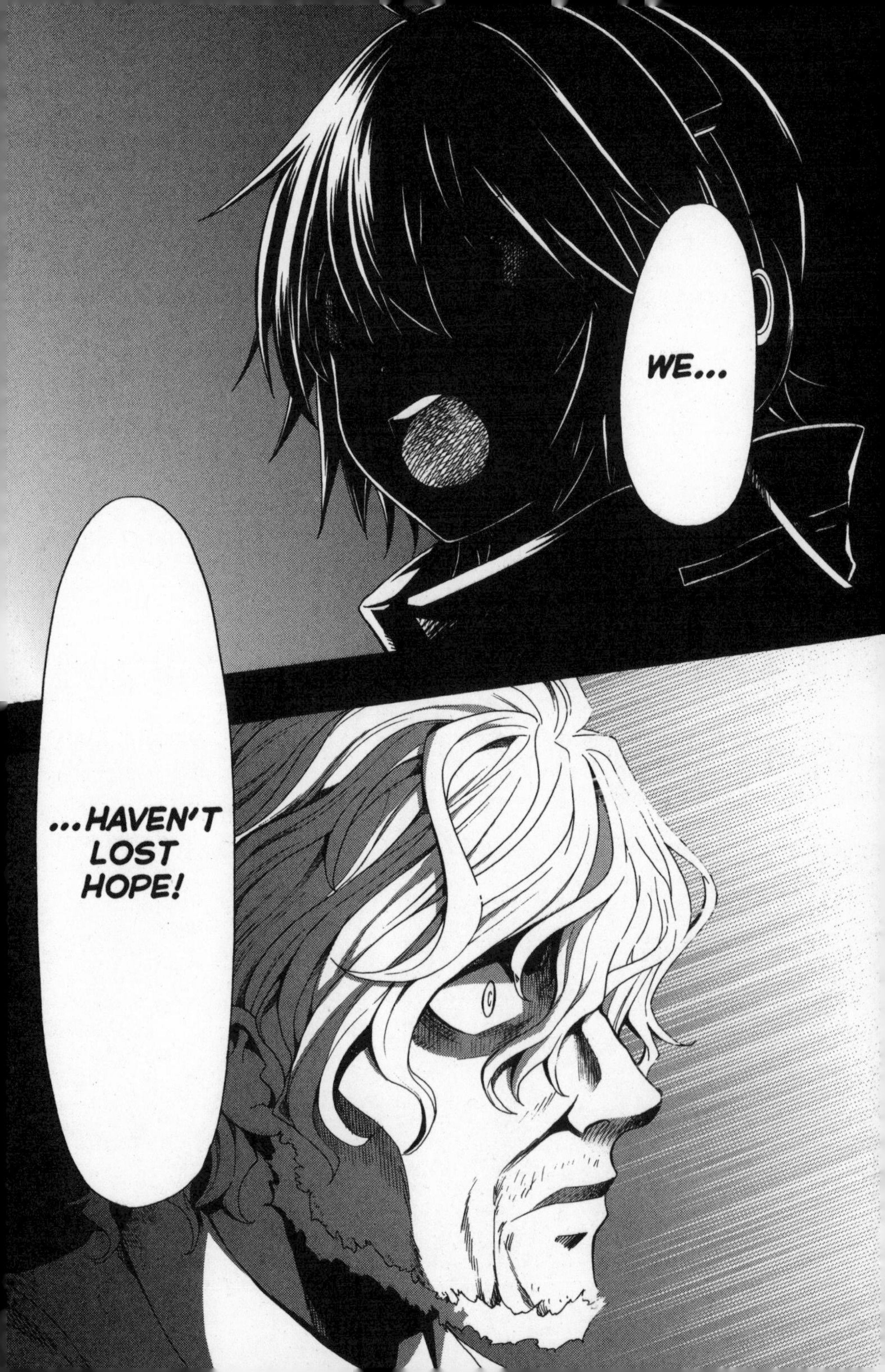
WE...
...HAVEN'T LOST HOPE!

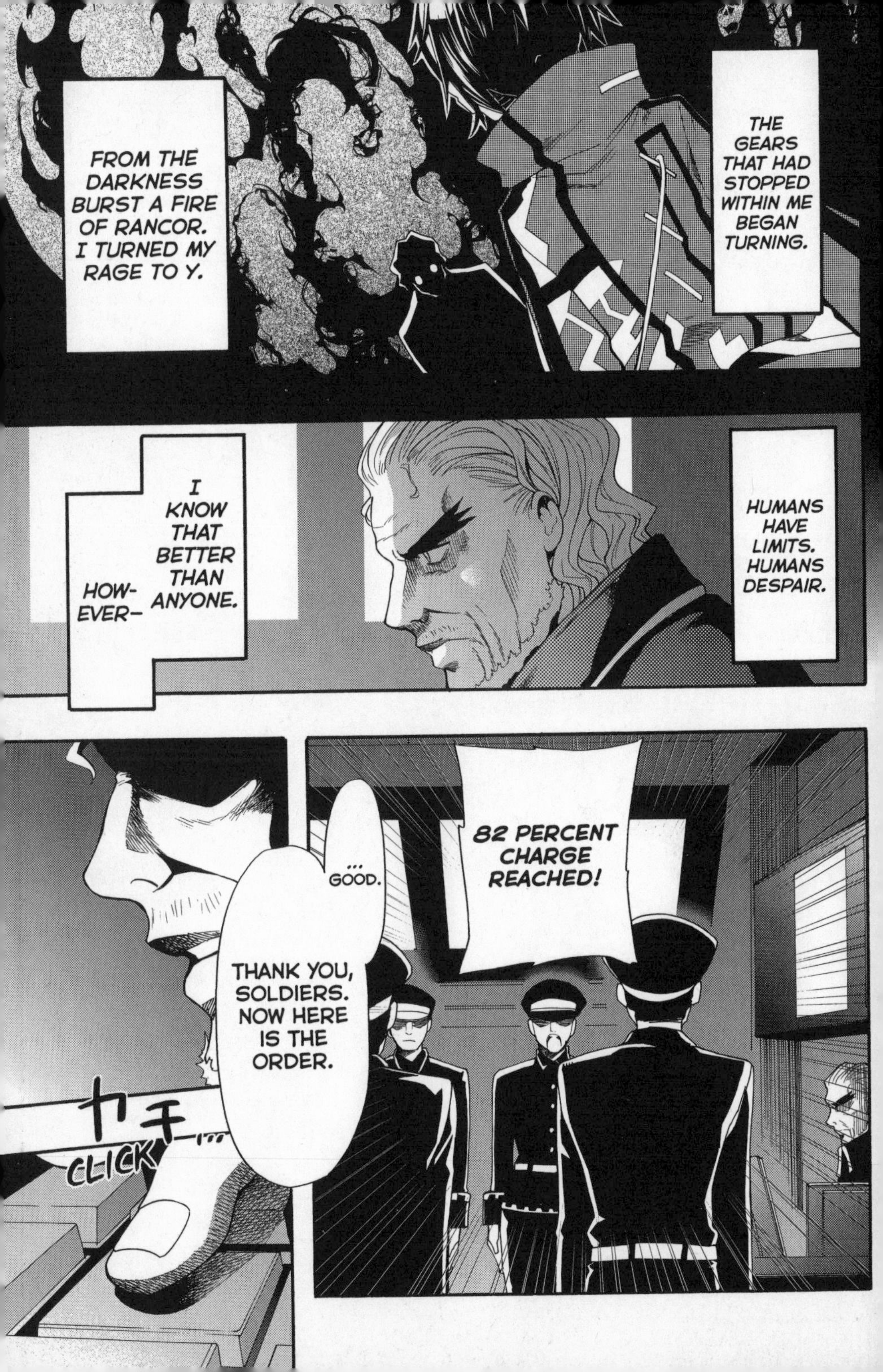
THE GEARS THAT HAD STOPPED WITHIN ME BEGAN TURNING.
FROM THE DARKNESS BURST A FIRE OF RANCOR. I TURNED MY RAGE TO Y.
HUMANS HAVE LIMITS. HUMANS DESPAIR.
I KNOW THAT BETTER THAN ANYONE.
HOW-EVER–
82 PERCENT CHARGE REACHED!
...GOOD.
THANK YOU, SOLDIERS. NOW HERE IS THE ORDER.
カチ…
CLICK

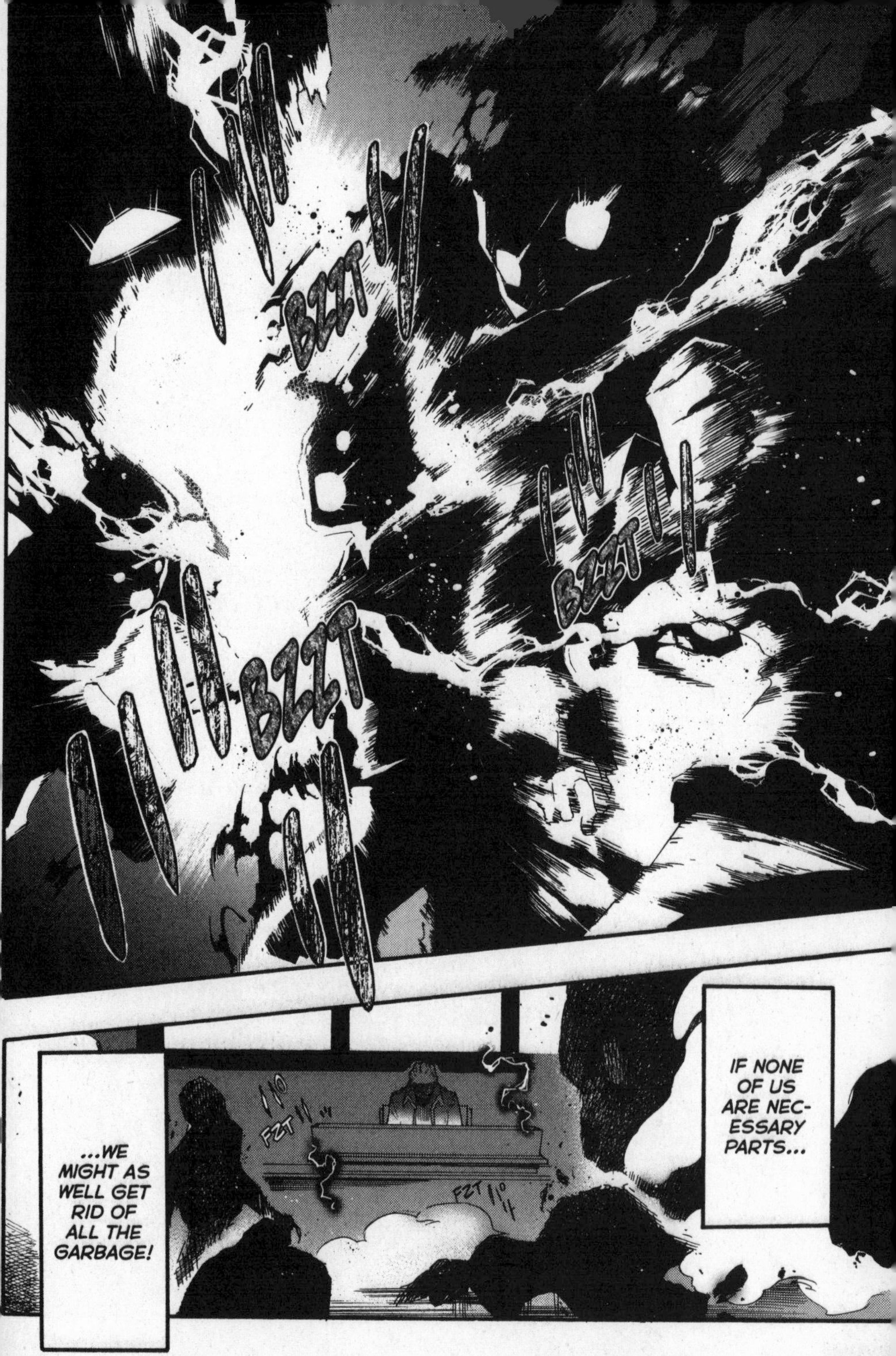
BZZT
BZZT
BZZT
IF NONE OF US ARE NEC-ESSARY PARTS...
FZT
FZT
...WE MIGHT AS WELL GET RID OF ALL THE GARBAGE!

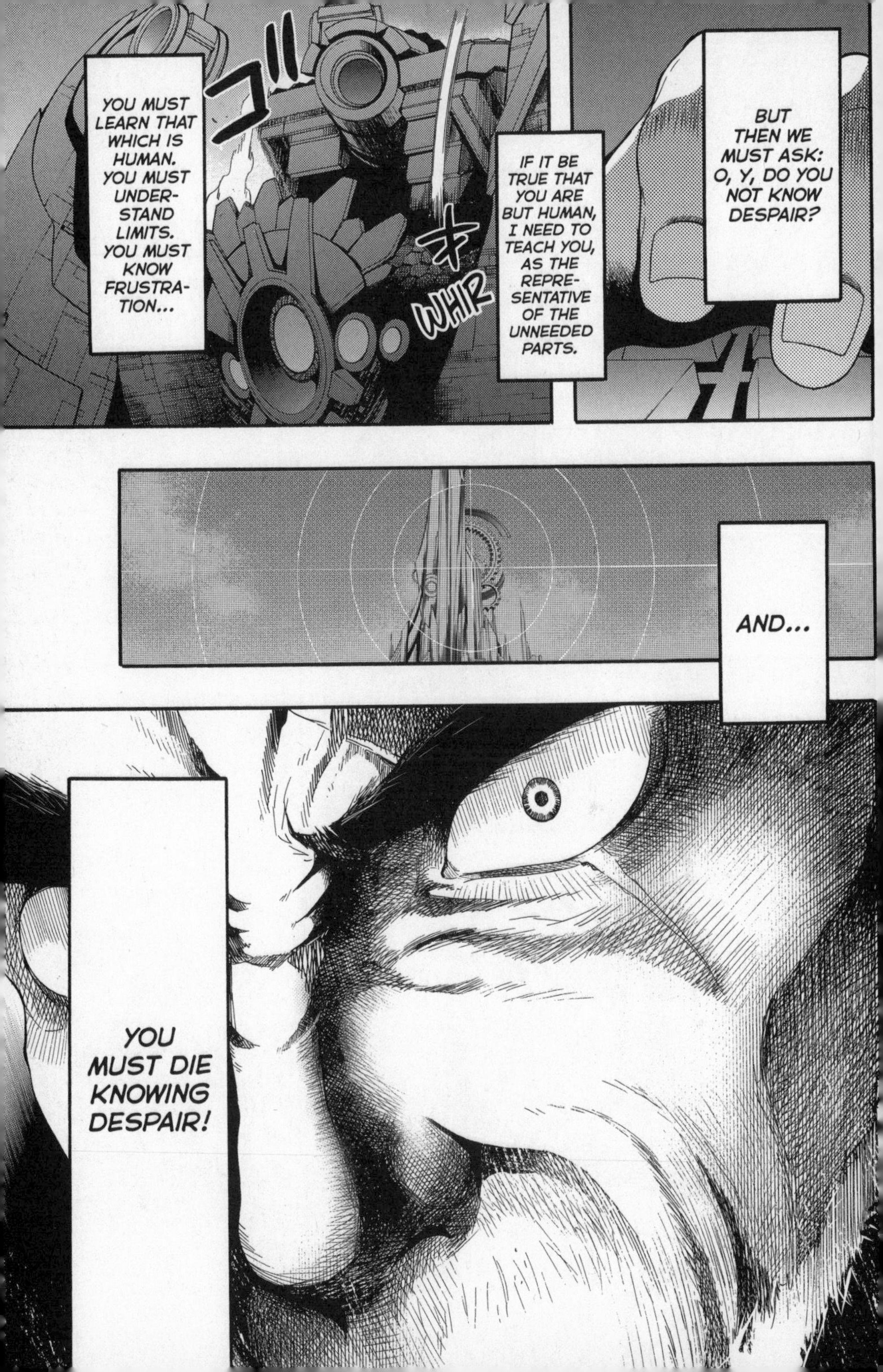
BUT THEN WE MUST ASK: O, Y, DO YOU NOT KNOW DESPAIR?
IF IT BE TRUE THAT YOU ARE BUT HUMAN, I NEED TO TEACH YOU, AS THE REPRESENTATIVE OF THE UNNEEDED PARTS.
YOU MUST LEARN THAT WHICH IS HUMAN. YOU MUST UNDERSTAND LIMITS. YOU MUST KNOW FRUSTRATION...
WHR
AND...
YOU MUST DIE KNOWING DESPAIR!

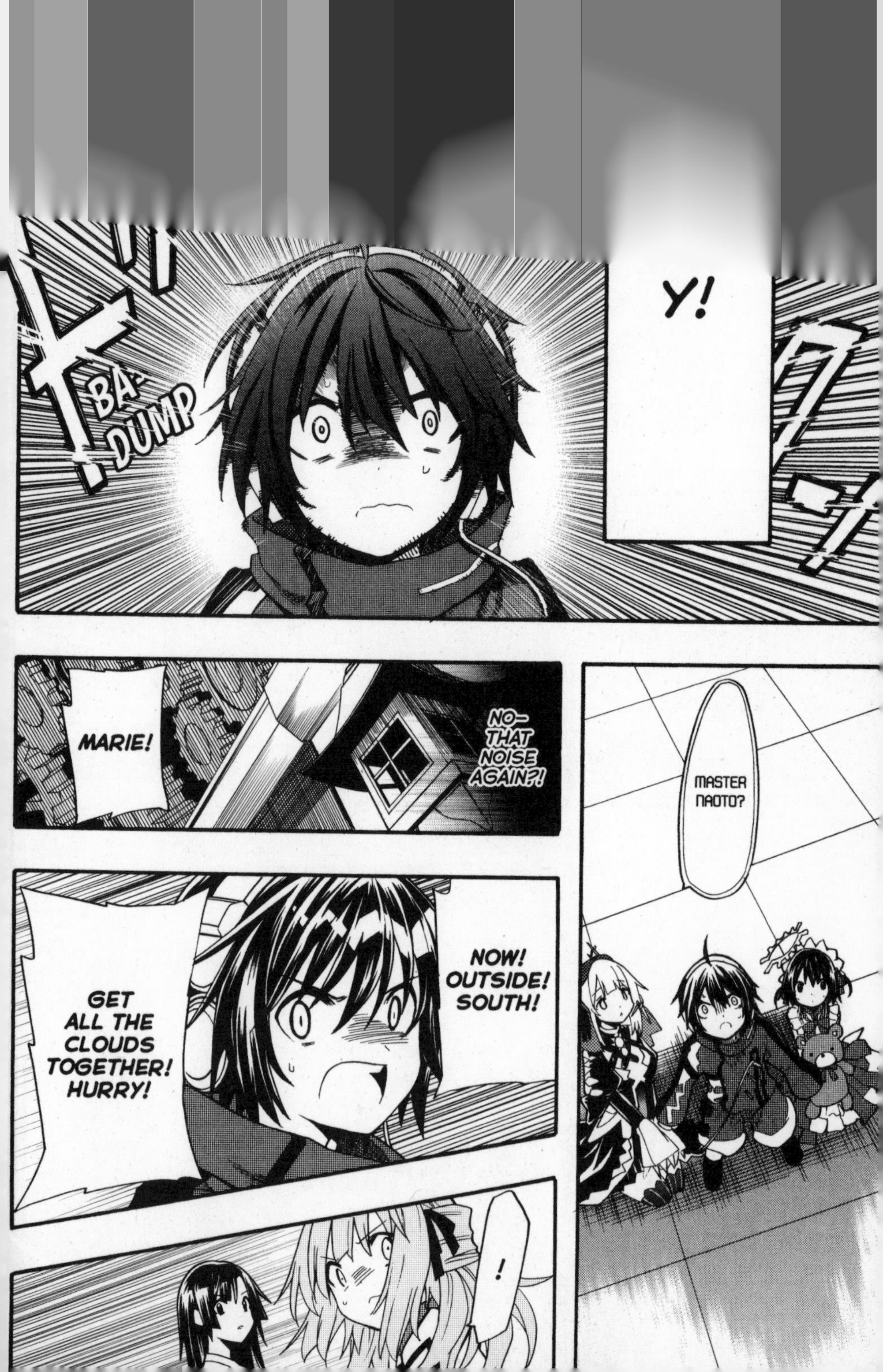
Y!
BA-DUMP
MASTER NAOTO?
NO— THAT NOISE AGAIN?!
MARIE!
NOW! OUTSIDE! SOUTH!
GET ALL THE CLOUDS TOGETHER! HURRY!
!

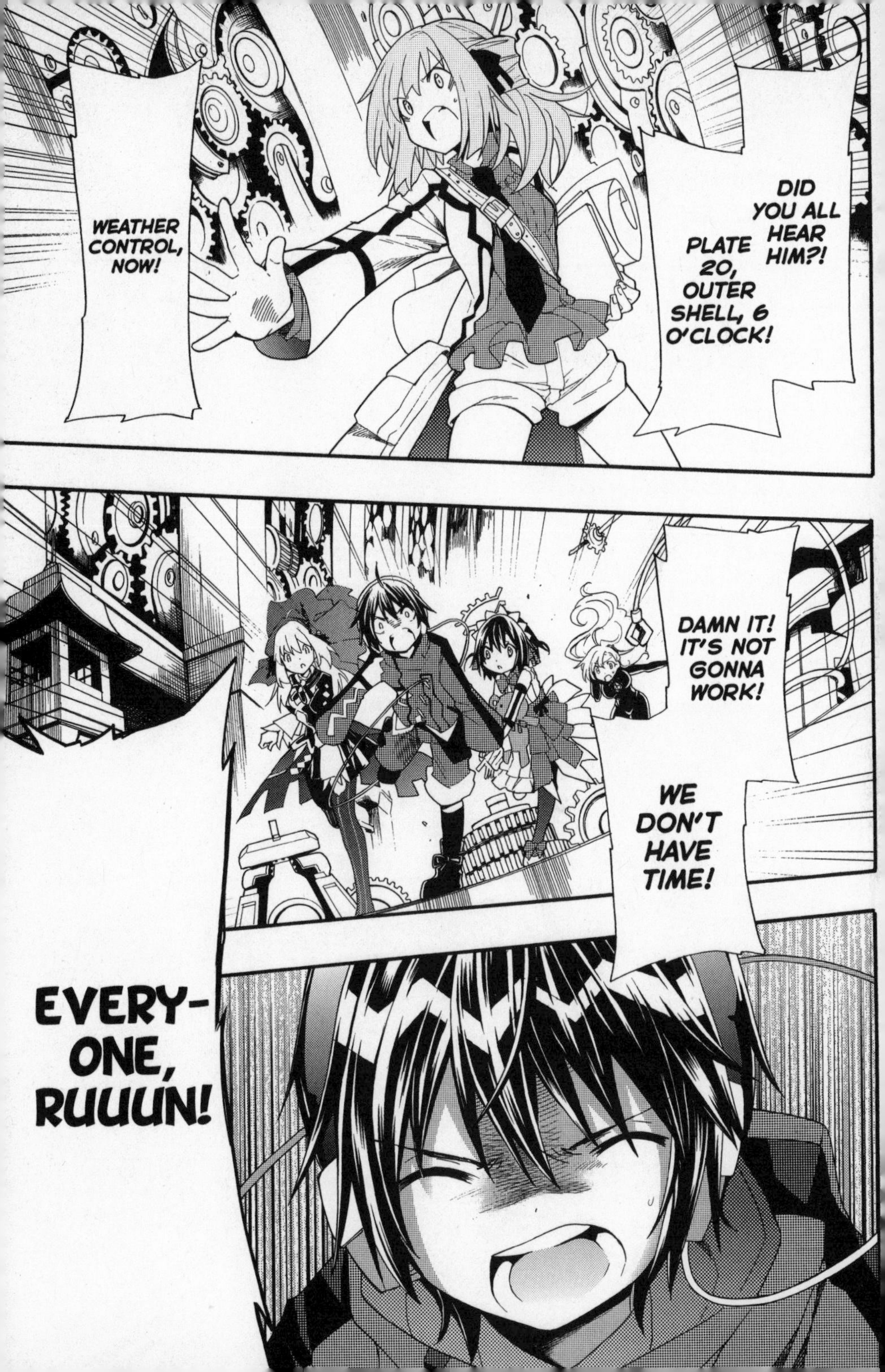
DID YOU ALL HEAR HIM?! PLATE 20, OUTER SHELL, 6 O'CLOCK!
WEATHER CONTROL, NOW!
DAMN IT! IT'S NOT GONNA WORK!
WE DON'T HAVE TIME!
EVERY-ONE, RUUUN!

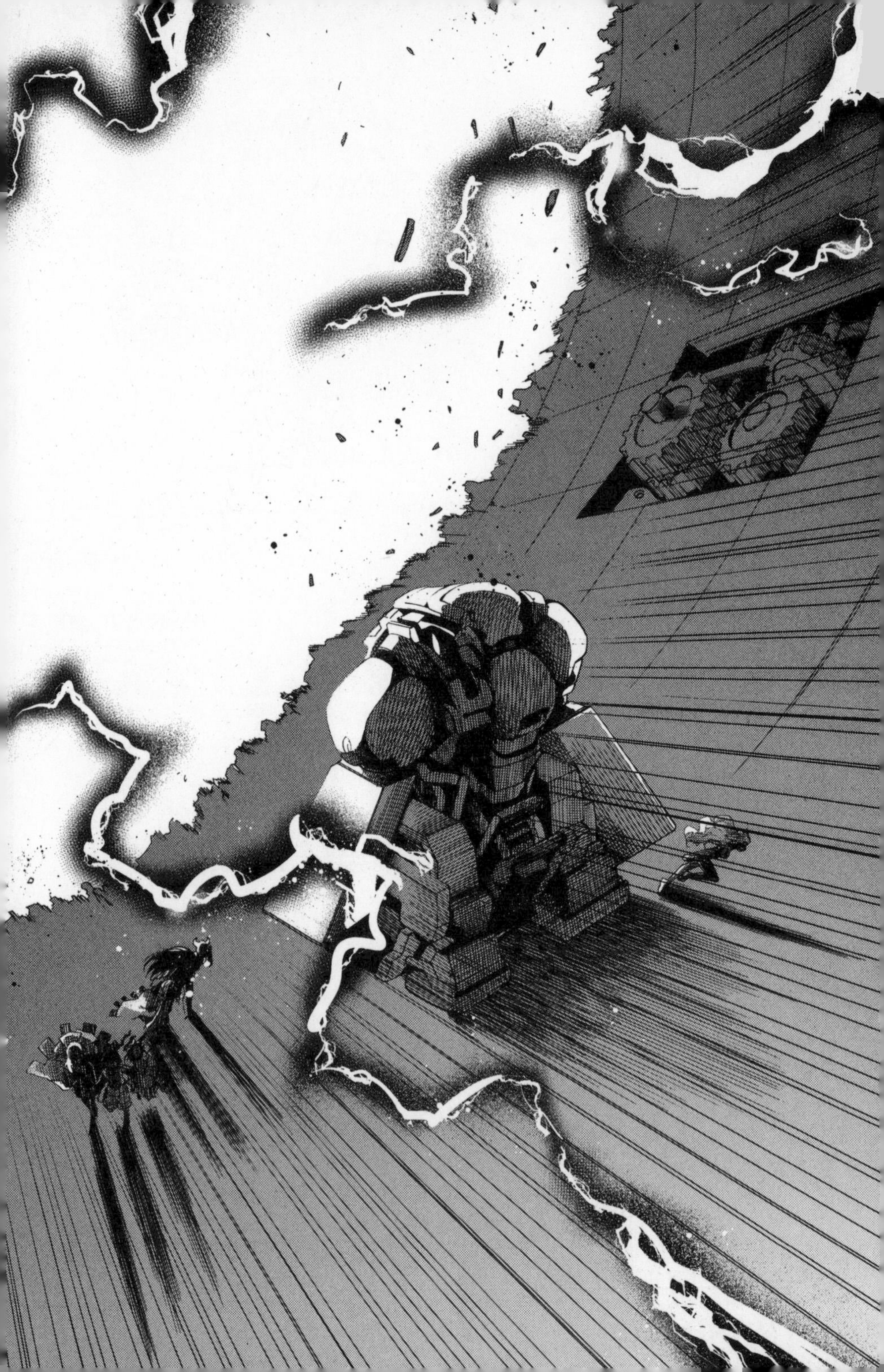

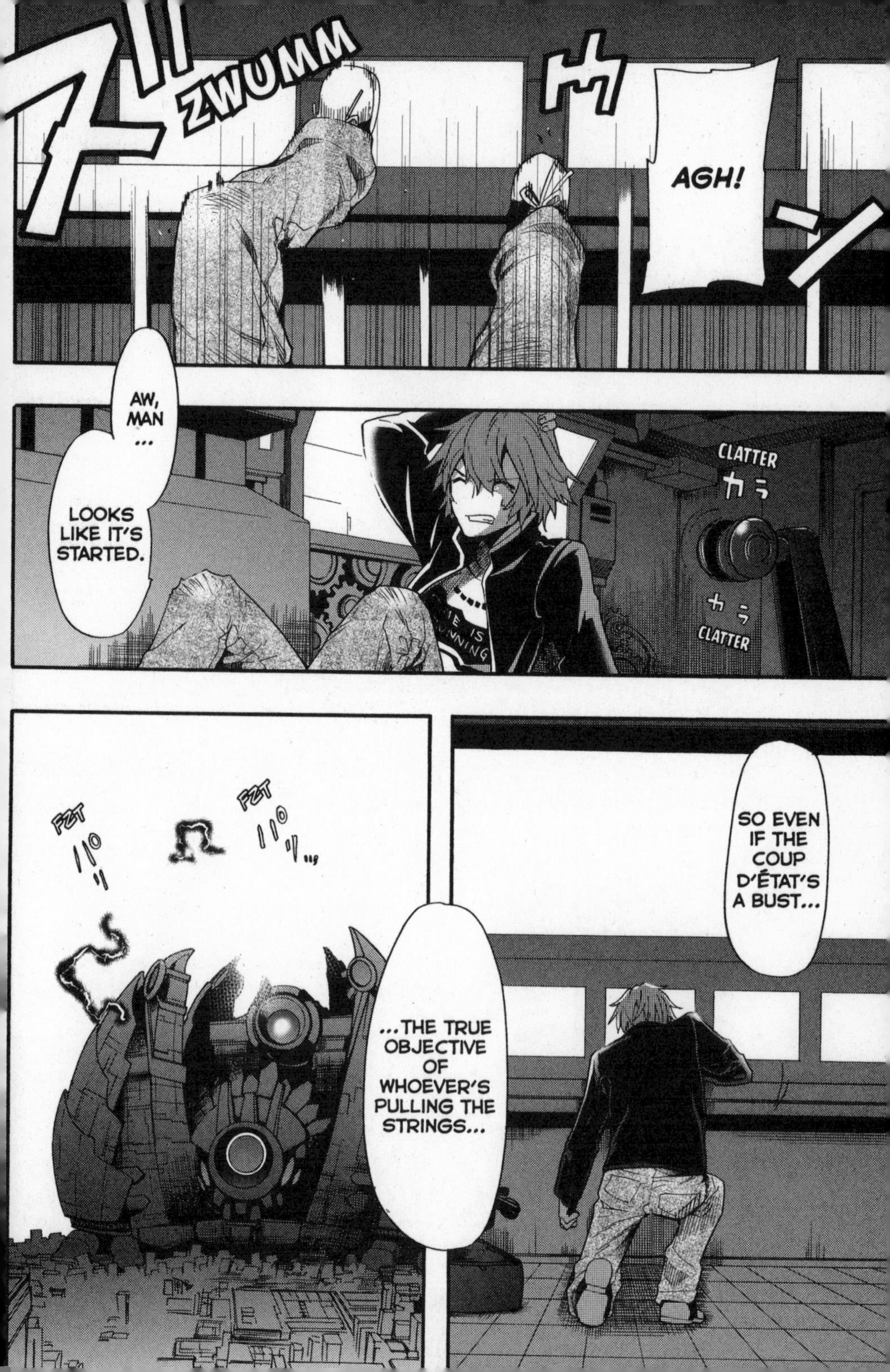
ZWUMM
AGH!
AW, MAN...
LOOKS LIKE IT'S STARTED.
CLATTER
CLATTER
SO EVEN IF THE COUP D'ÉTAT'S A BUST...
...THE TRUE OBJECTIVE OF WHOEVER'S PULLING THE STRINGS...
FZT
FZT

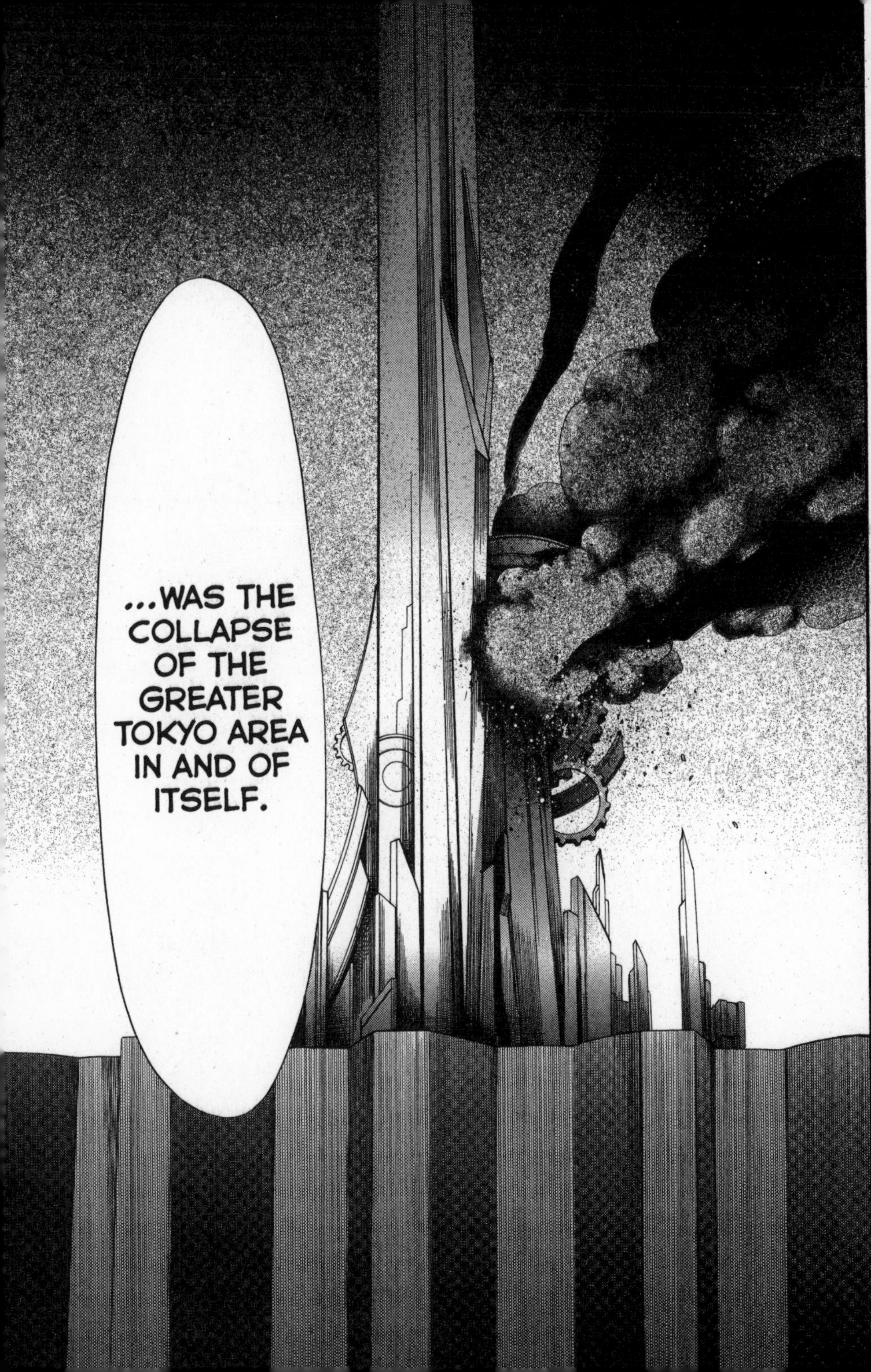
...WAS THE COLLAPSE OF THE GREATER TOKYO AREA IN AND OF ITSELF.

CLOCKWORK
PLANET

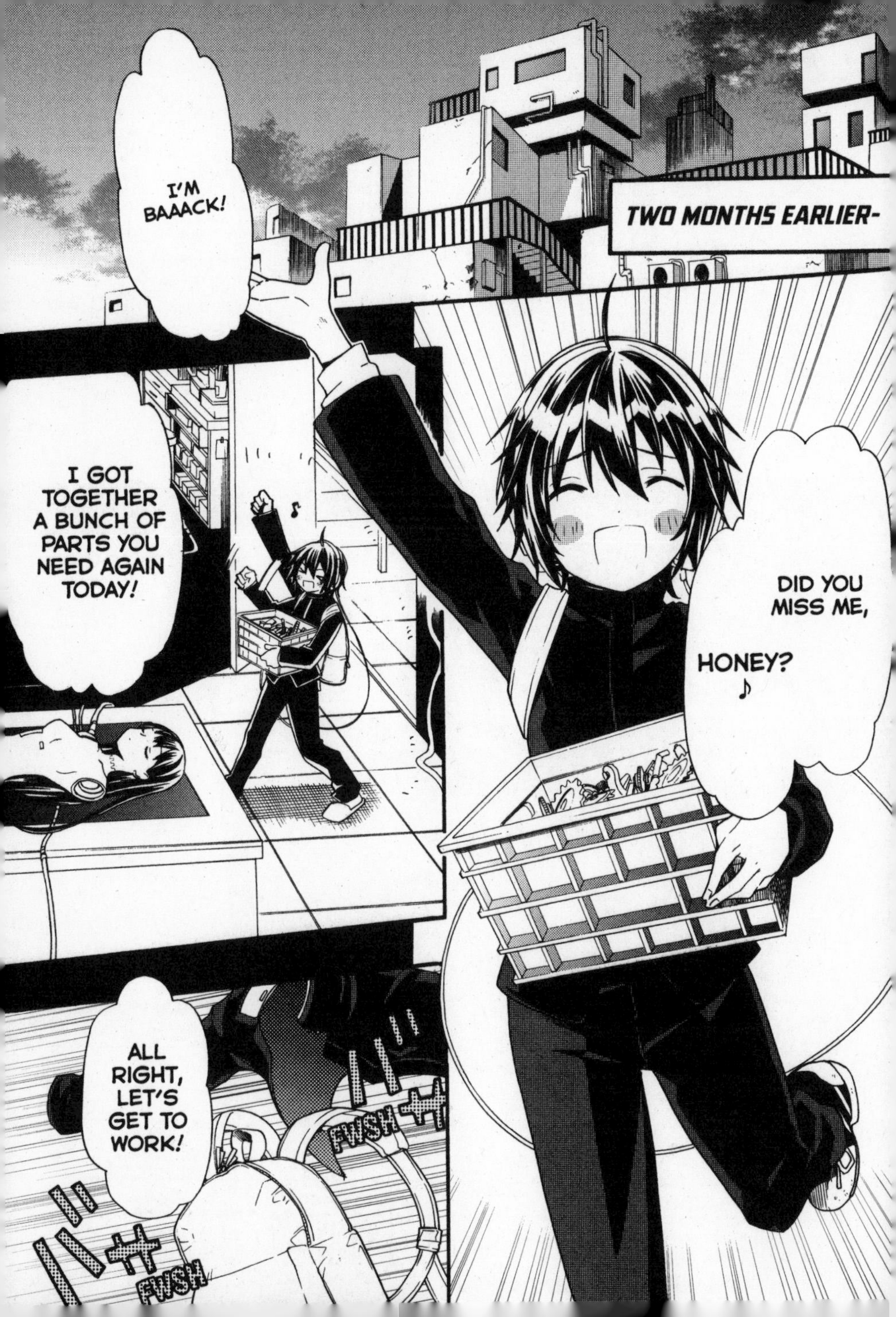
TWO MONTHS EARLIER-
I'M BAAACK!
DID YOU MISS ME, HONEY? ♪
I GOT TOGETHER A BUNCH OF PARTS YOU NEED AGAIN TODAY!
ALL RIGHT, LET'S GET TO WORK!
FWSH
FWSH

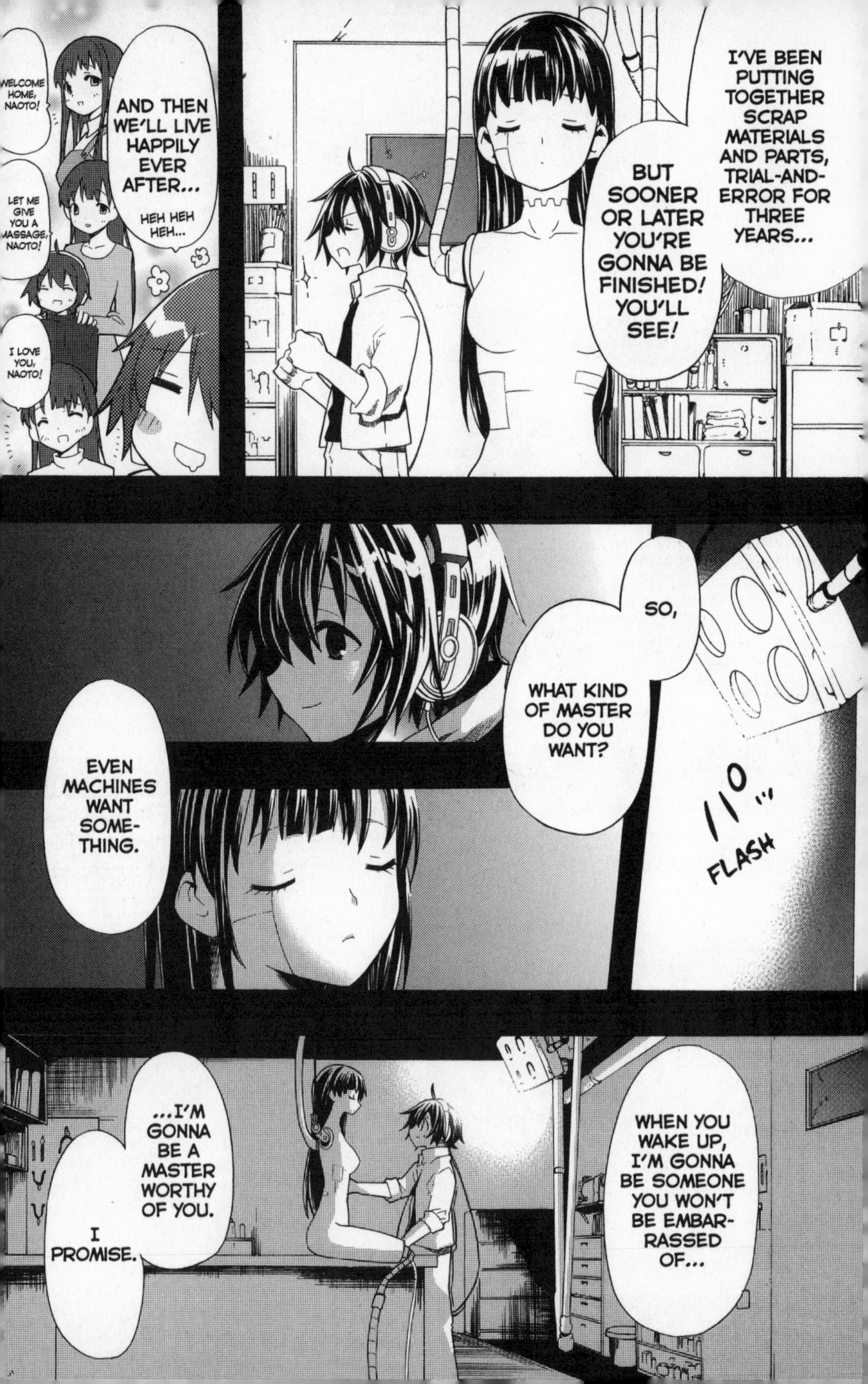
I'VE BEEN PUTTING TOGETHER SCRAP MATERIALS AND PARTS, TRIAL-AND-ERROR FOR THREE YEARS...
BUT SOONER OR LATER YOU'RE GONNA BE FINISHED! YOU'LL SEE!
AND THEN WE'LL LIVE HAPPILY EVER AFTER...
WELCOME HOME, NAOTO!
HEH HEH HEH...
LET ME GIVE YOU A MASSAGE, NAOTO!
I LOVE YOU, NAOTO!
SO,
WHAT KIND OF MASTER DO YOU WANT?
FLASH
EVEN MACHINES WANT SOMETHING.
WHEN YOU WAKE UP, I'M GONNA BE SOMEONE YOU WON'T BE EMBARRASSED OF...
...I'M GONNA BE A MASTER WORTHY OF YOU.
I PROMISE.

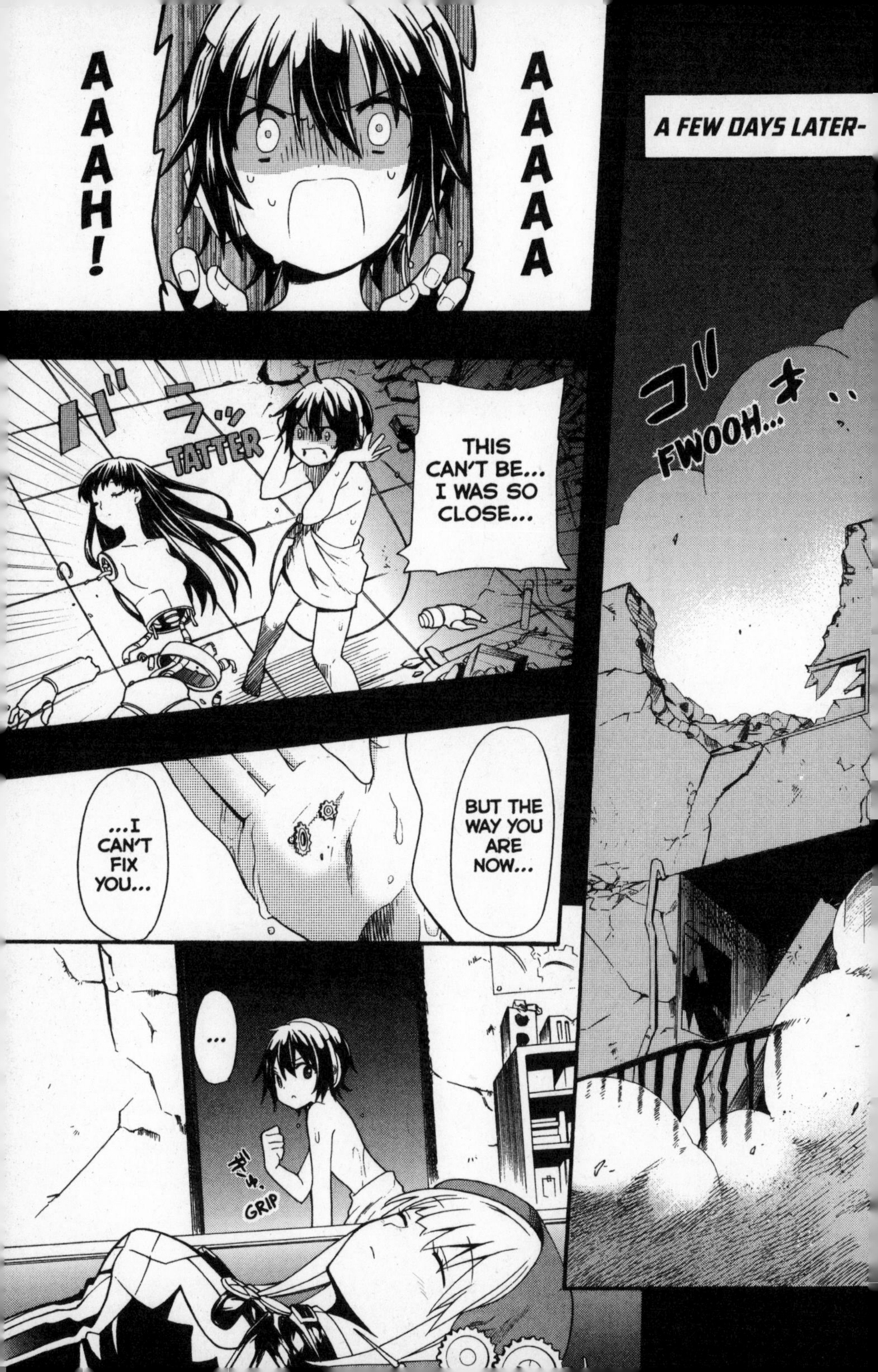
A FEW DAYS LATER-
FWOOH...
AAAAA
AAAAH!
TATTER
THIS CAN'T BE... I WAS SO CLOSE...
BUT THE WAY YOU ARE NOW...
...I CAN'T FIX YOU...
...
GRIP

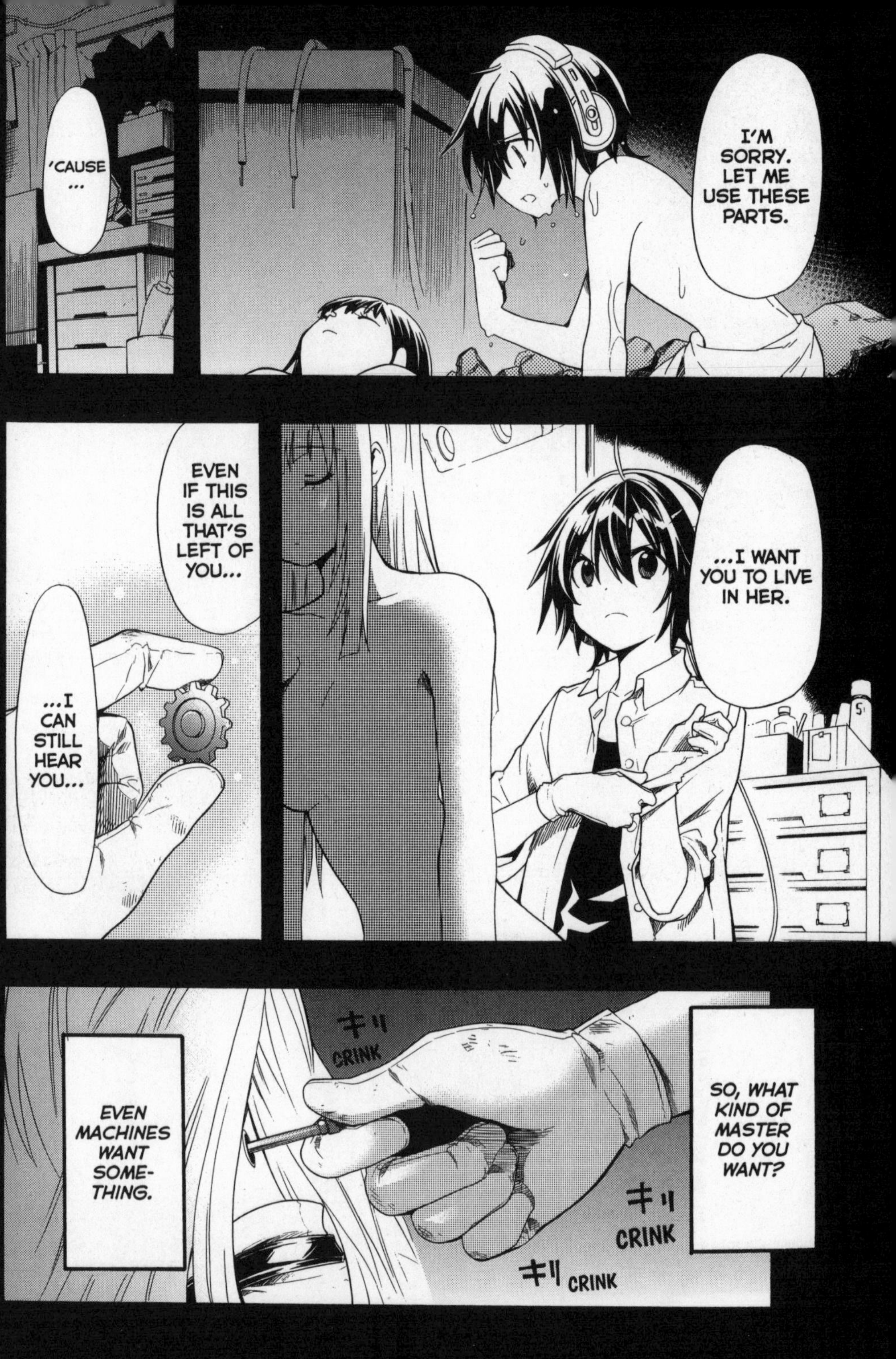
I'M SORRY. LET ME USE THESE PARTS.
'CAUSE ...
...I WANT YOU TO LIVE IN HER.
EVEN IF THIS IS ALL THAT'S LEFT OF YOU...
...I CAN STILL HEAR YOU...
SO, WHAT KIND OF MASTER DO YOU WANT?
キリ CRINK
キリ CRINK
キリ CRINK
EVEN MACHINES WANT SOME-THING.

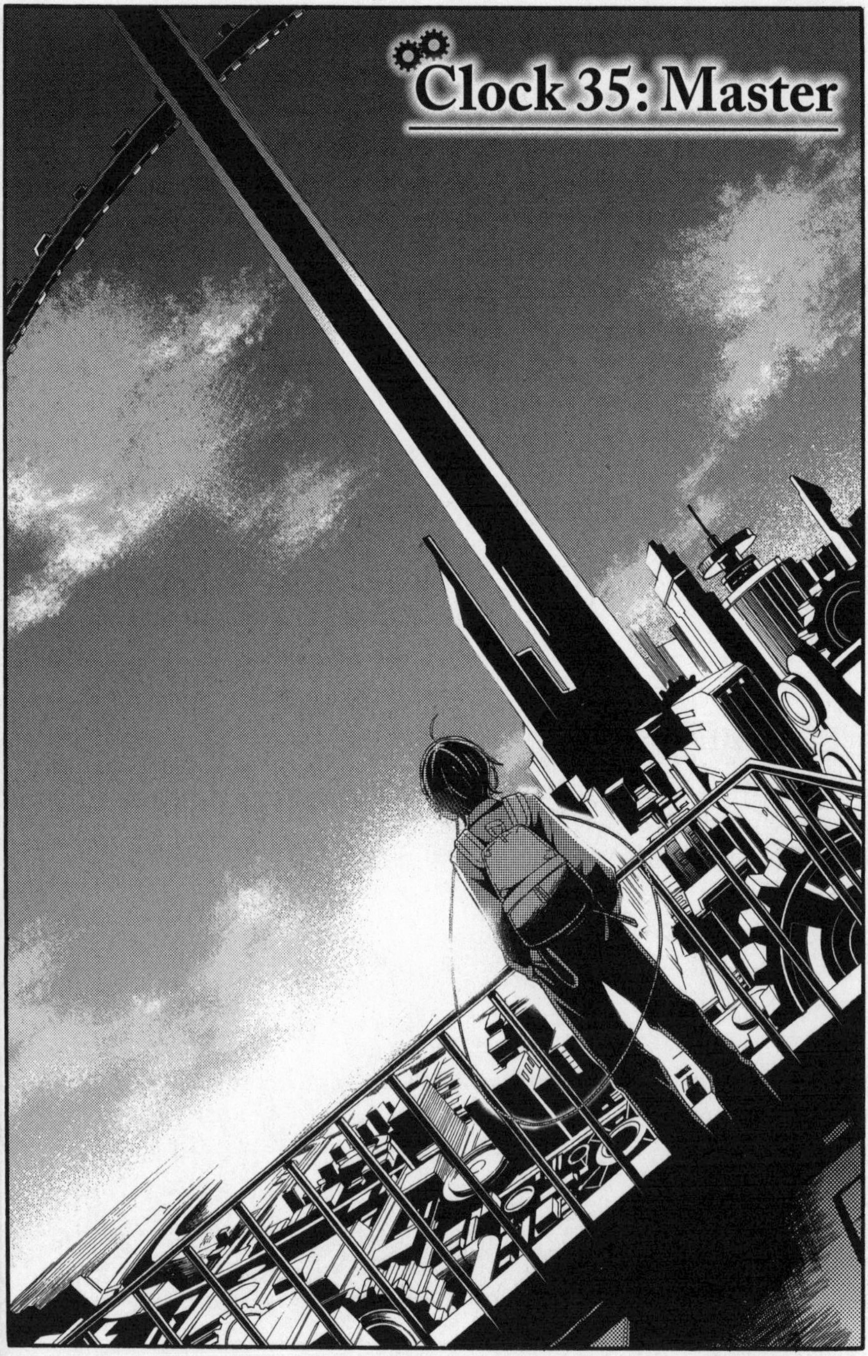
Clock 35: Master

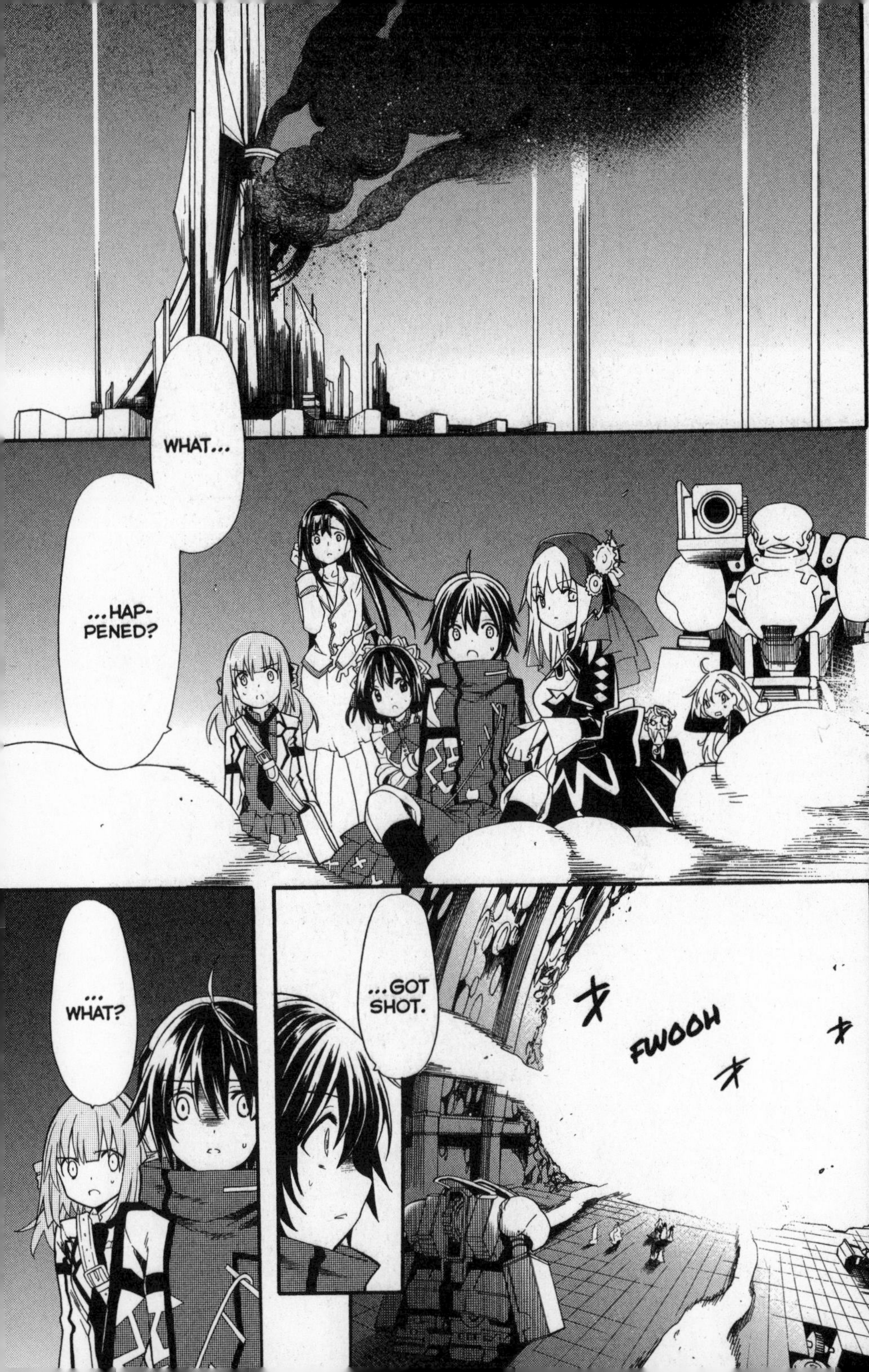
WHAT...
...HAP-PENED?
FWOOH
...GOT SHOT.
... WHAT?

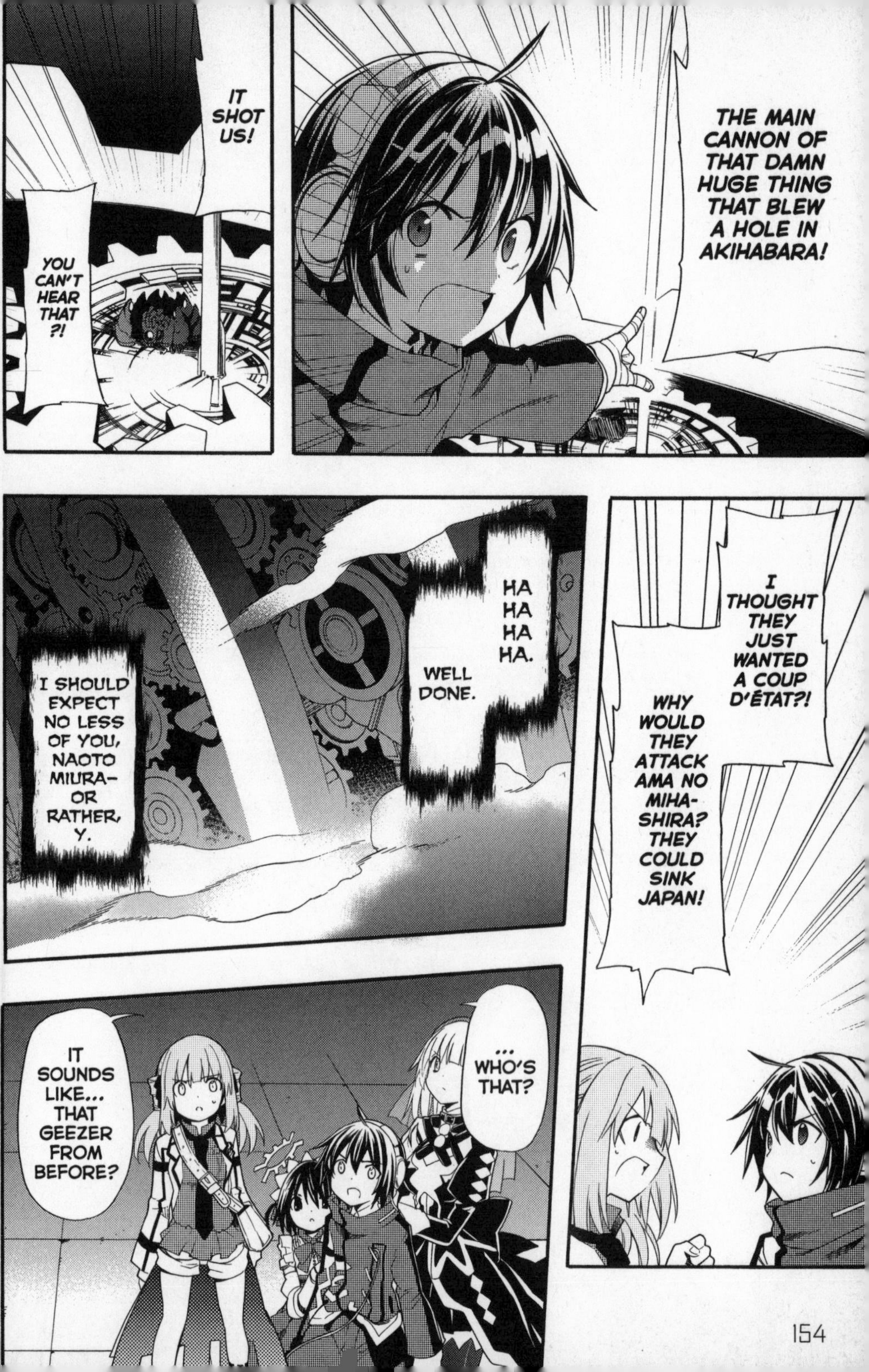
THE MAIN CANNON OF THAT DAMN HUGE THING THAT BLEW A HOLE IN AKIHABARA!
IT SHOT US!
YOU CAN'T HEAR THAT?!
I THOUGHT THEY JUST WANTED A COUP D'ÉTAT?!
WHY WOULD THEY ATTACK AMA NO MIHA-SHIRA? THEY COULD SINK JAPAN!
HA HA HA HA.
WELL DONE.
I SHOULD EXPECT NO LESS OF YOU, NAOTO MIURA- OR RATHER, Y.
... WHO'S THAT?
IT SOUNDS LIKE... THAT GEEZER FROM BEFORE?

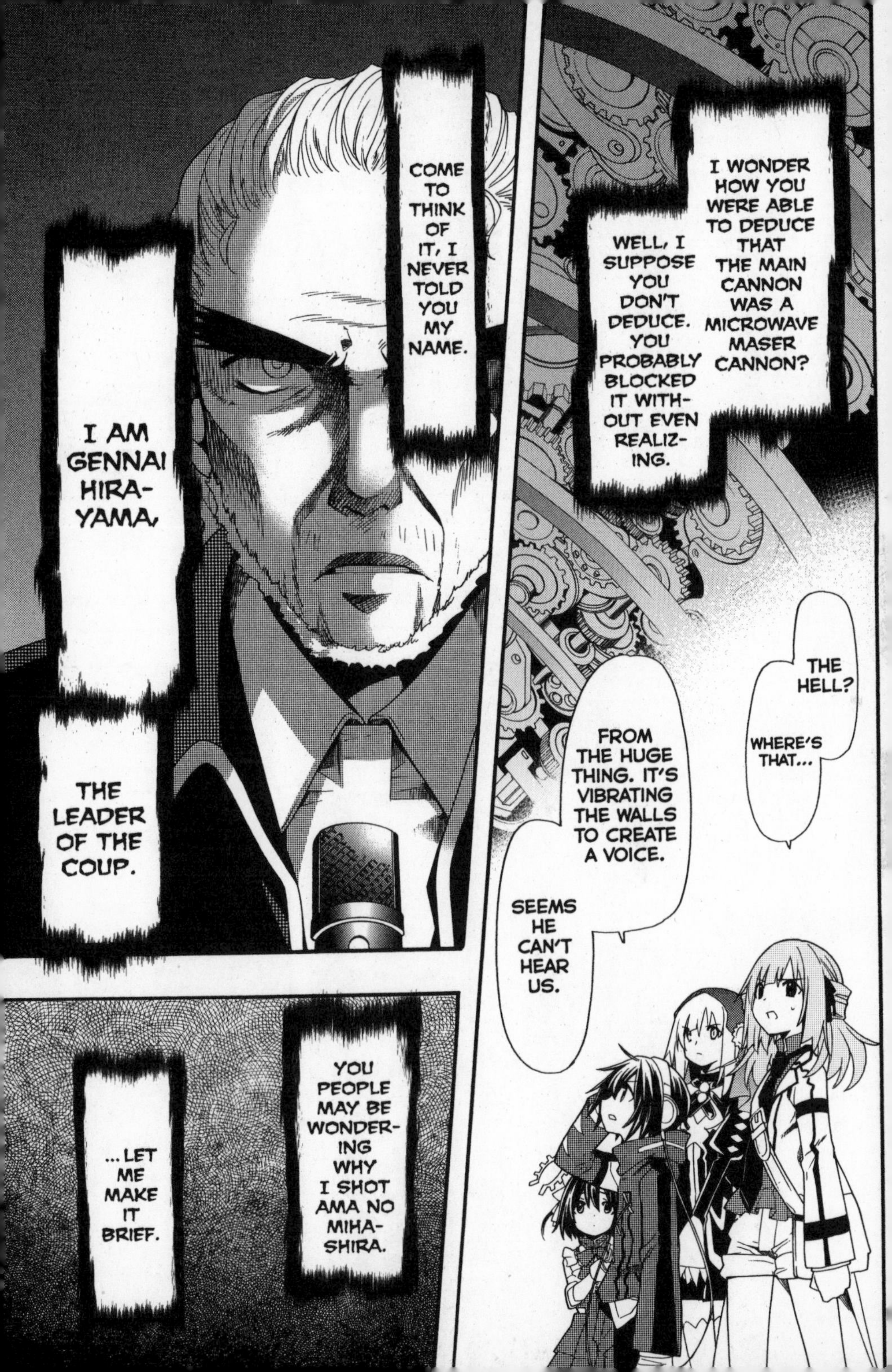
I WONDER HOW YOU WERE ABLE TO DEDUCE THAT THE MAIN CANNON WAS A MICROWAVE MASER CANNON?
WELL, I SUPPOSE YOU DON'T DEDUCE. YOU PROBABLY BLOCKED IT WITH-OUT EVEN REALIZ-ING.
THE HELL?
WHERE'S THAT...
FROM THE HUGE THING. IT'S VIBRATING THE WALLS TO CREATE A VOICE.
SEEMS HE CAN'T HEAR US.
COME TO THINK OF IT, I NEVER TOLD YOU MY NAME.
I AM GENNAI HIRA-YAMA,
THE LEADER OF THE COUP.
YOU PEOPLE MAY BE WONDER-ING WHY I SHOT AMA NO MIHA-SHIRA.
...LET ME MAKE IT BRIEF.

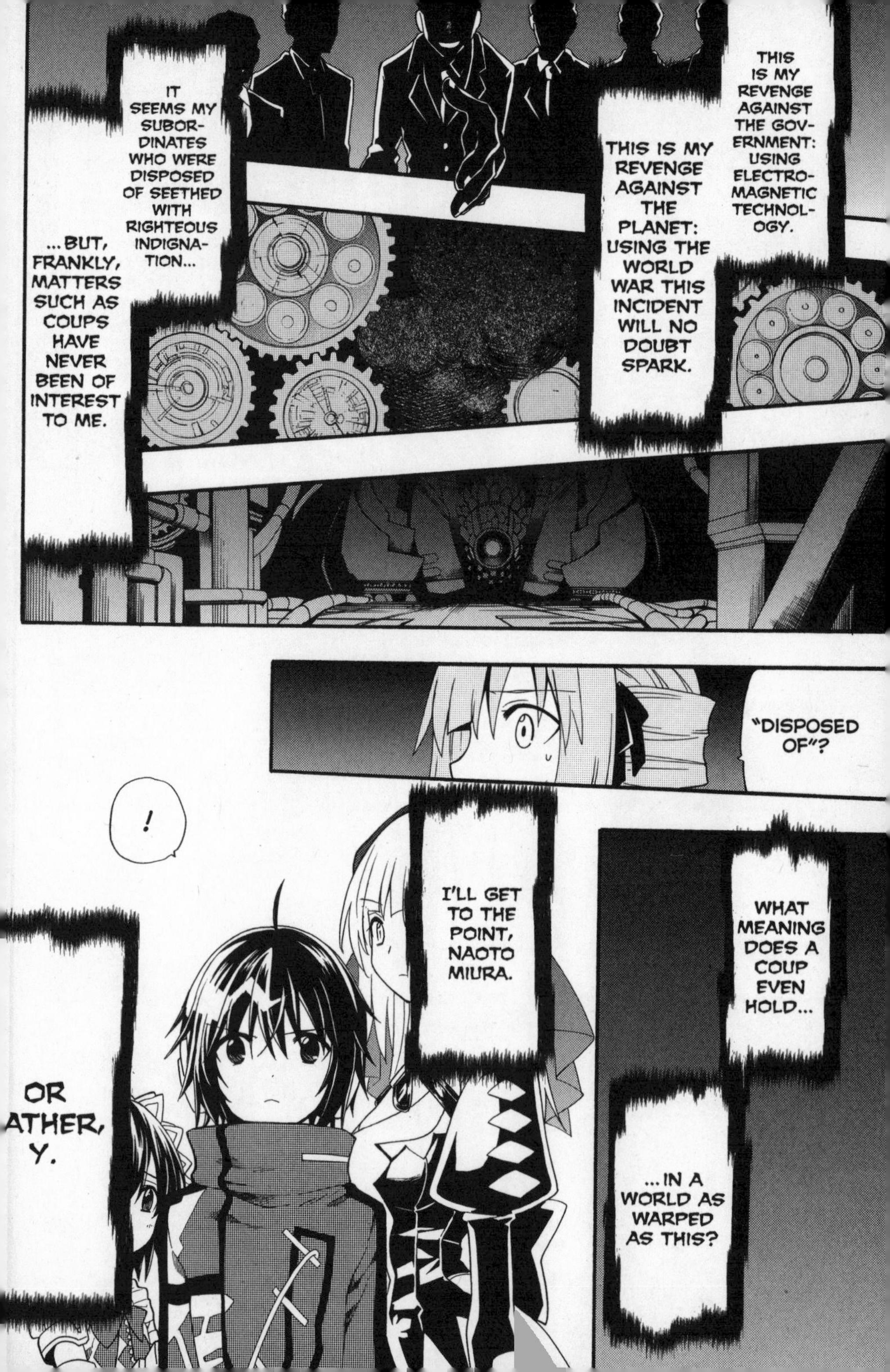
THIS IS MY REVENGE AGAINST THE GOVERNMENT: USING ELECTROMAGNETIC TECHNOLOGY.
THIS IS MY REVENGE AGAINST THE PLANET: USING THE WORLD WAR THIS INCIDENT WILL NO DOUBT SPARK.
IT SEEMS MY SUBORDINATES WHO WERE DISPOSED OF SEETHED WITH RIGHTEOUS INDIGNATION...
...BUT, FRANKLY, MATTERS SUCH AS COUPS HAVE NEVER BEEN OF INTEREST TO ME.
"DISPOSED OF"?
WHAT MEANING DOES A COUP EVEN HOLD...
...IN A WORLD AS WARPED AS THIS?
!
I'LL GET TO THE POINT, NAOTO MIURA.
OR ATHER, Y.

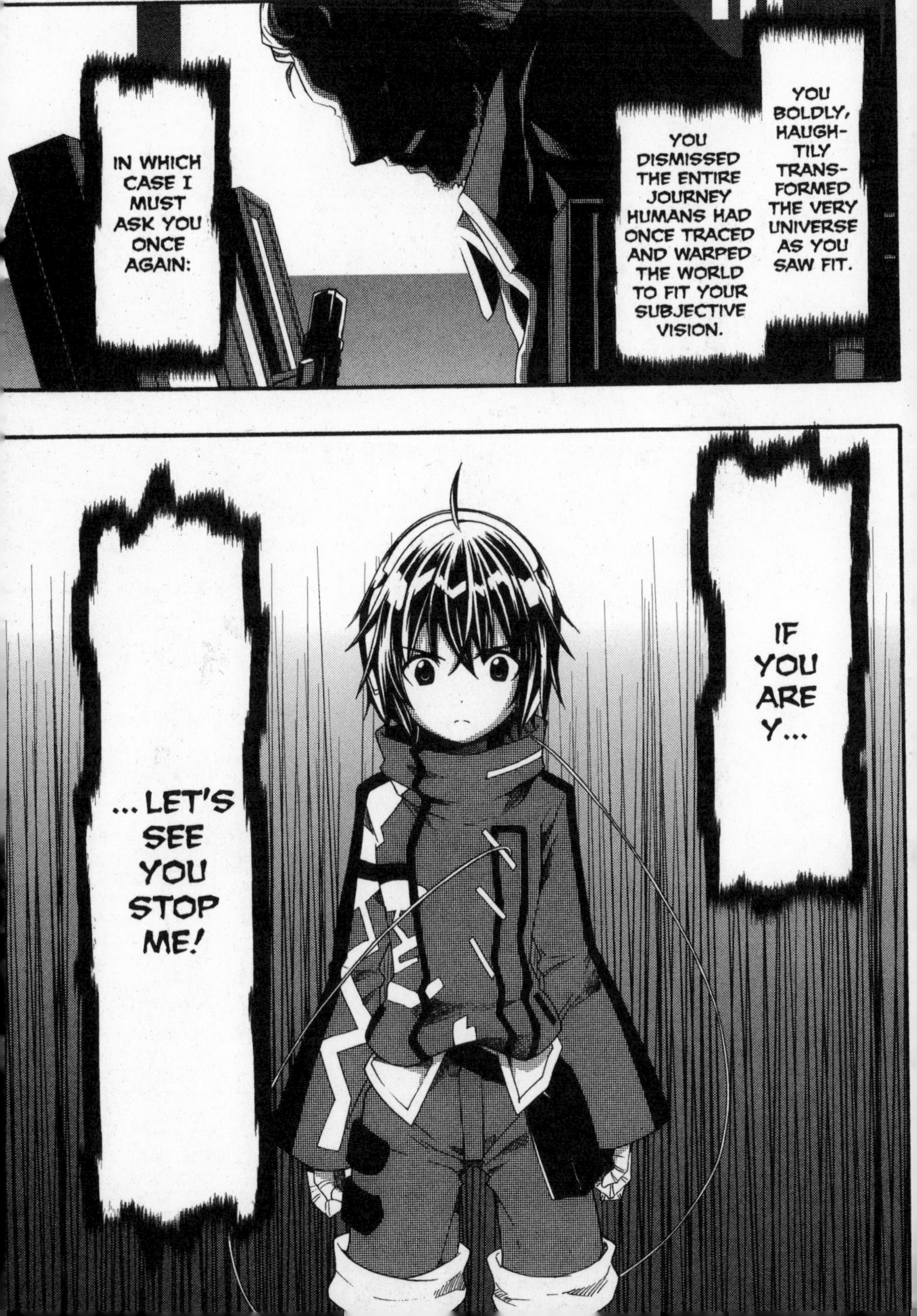
YOU BOLDLY, HAUGH-TILY TRANS-FORMED THE VERY UNIVERSE AS YOU SAW FIT.
YOU DISMISSED THE ENTIRE JOURNEY HUMANS HAD ONCE TRACED AND WARPED THE WORLD TO FIT YOUR SUBJECTIVE VISION.
IN WHICH CASE I MUST ASK YOU ONCE AGAIN:
IF YOU ARE Y...
...LET'S SEE YOU STOP ME!

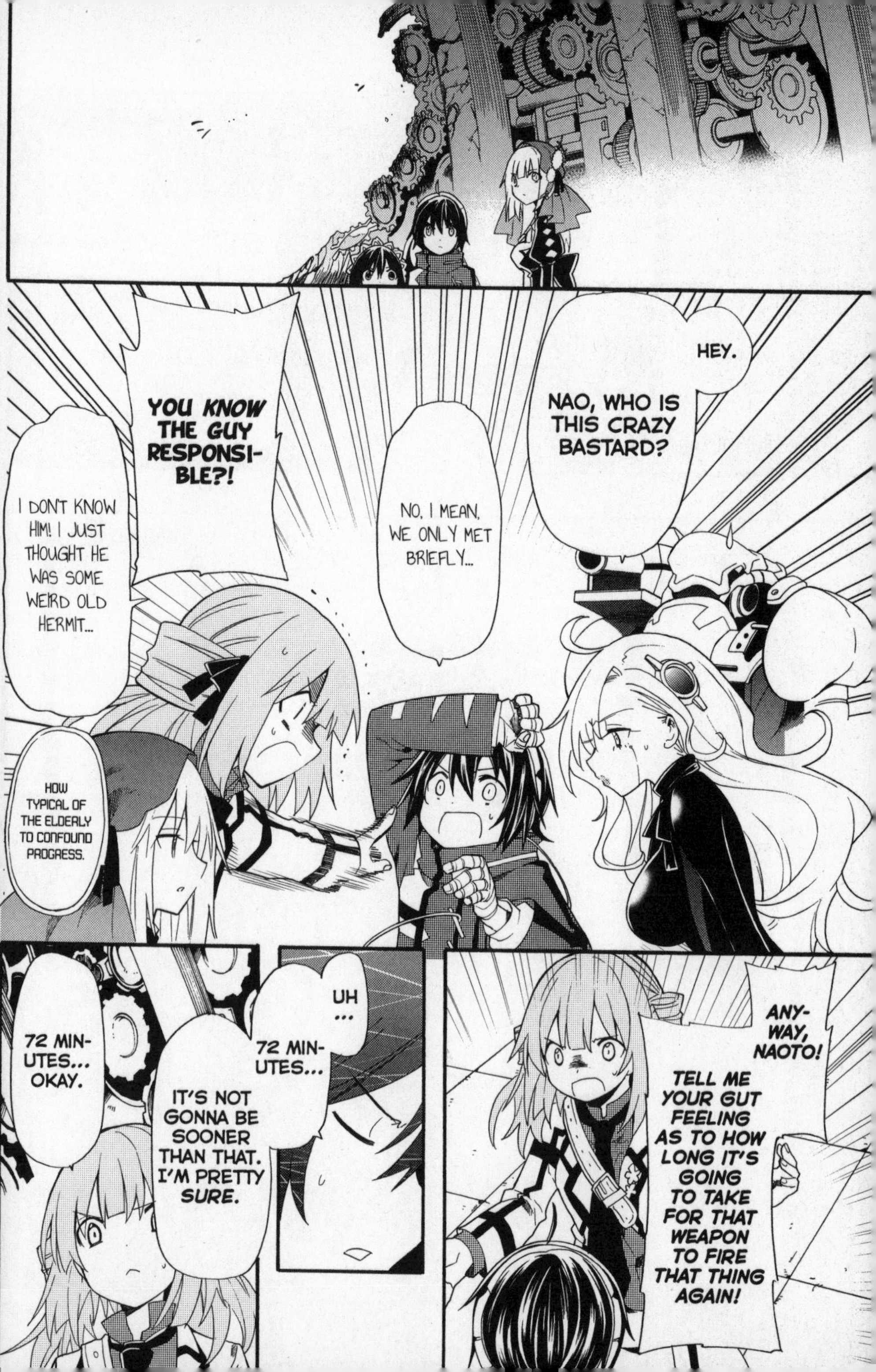
HEY.
NAO, WHO IS THIS CRAZY BASTARD?
YOU KNOW THE GUY RESPONSI-BLE?!
NO, I MEAN, WE ONLY MET BRIEFLY...
I DON'T KNOW HIM! I JUST THOUGHT HE WAS SOME WEIRD OLD HERMIT...
HOW TYPICAL OF THE ELDERLY TO CONFOUND PROGRESS.
ANY-WAY, NAOTO!
TELL ME YOUR GUT FEELING AS TO HOW LONG IT'S GOING TO TAKE FOR THAT WEAPON TO FIRE THAT THING AGAIN!
UH ...
72 MIN-UTES...
IT'S NOT GONNA BE SOONER THAN THAT. I'M PRETTY SURE.
72 MIN-UTES... OKAY.

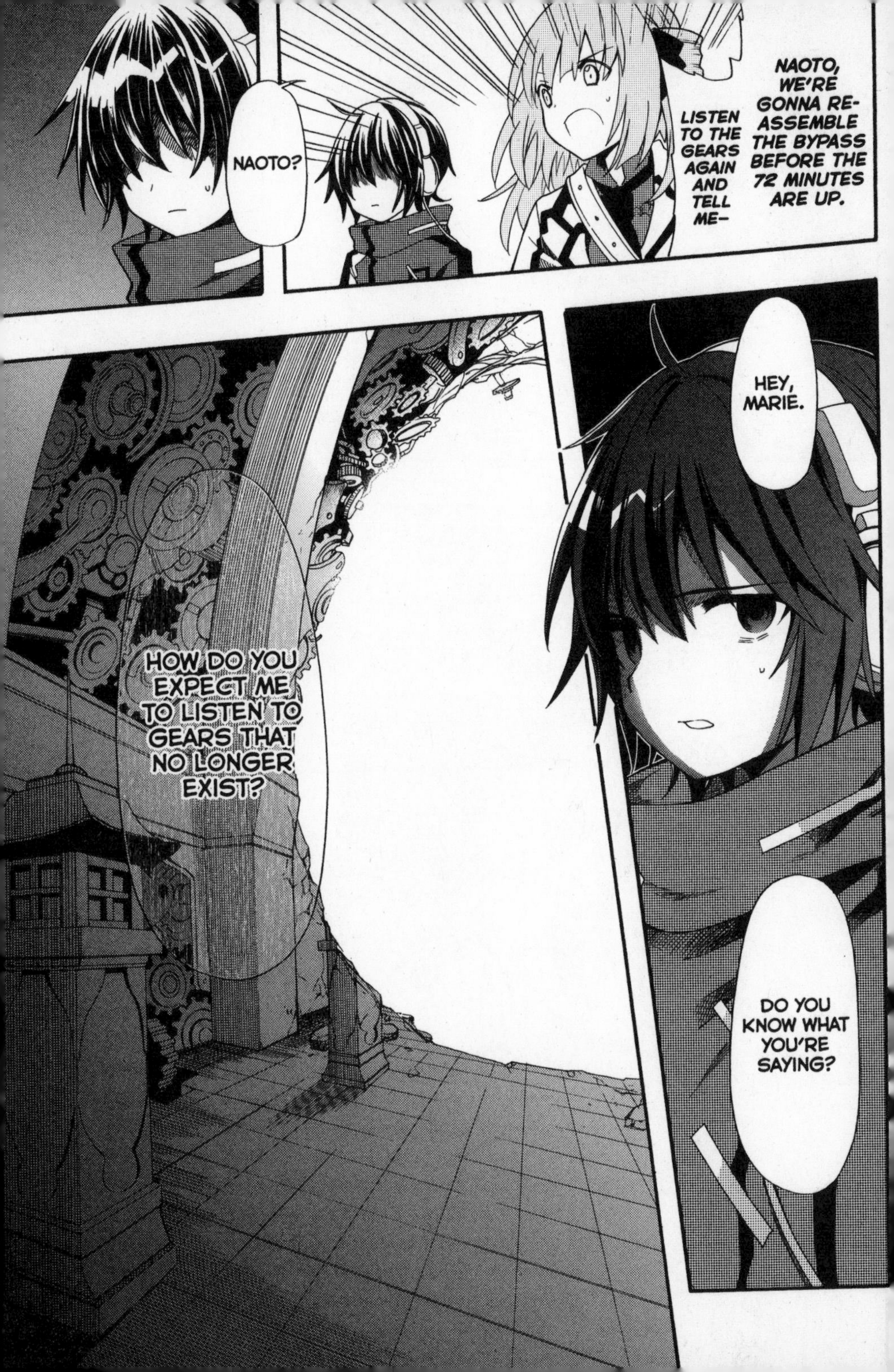
NAOTO, WE'RE GONNA RE-ASSEMBLE THE BYPASS BEFORE THE 72 MINUTES ARE UP.
LISTEN TO THE GEARS AGAIN AND TELL ME-
NAOTO?
HEY, MARIE.
DO YOU KNOW WHAT YOU'RE SAYING?
HOW DO YOU EXPECT ME TO LISTEN TO GEARS THAT NO LONGER EXIST?

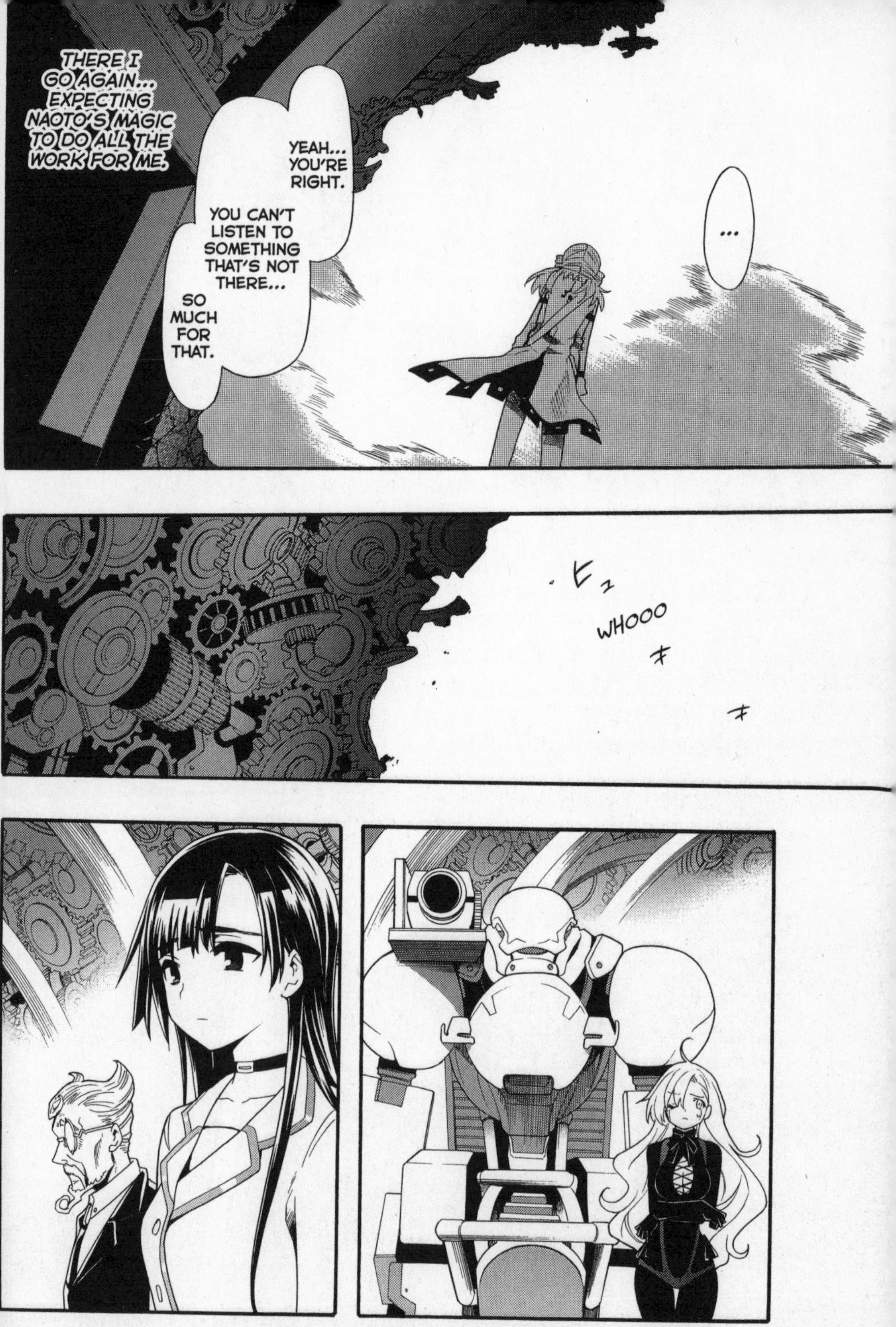
...
YEAH... YOU'RE RIGHT.
YOU CAN'T LISTEN TO SOMETHING THAT'S NOT THERE...
SO MUCH FOR THAT.
THERE I GO AGAIN... EXPECTING NAOTO'S MAGIC TO DO ALL THE WORK FOR ME.
WHOOO

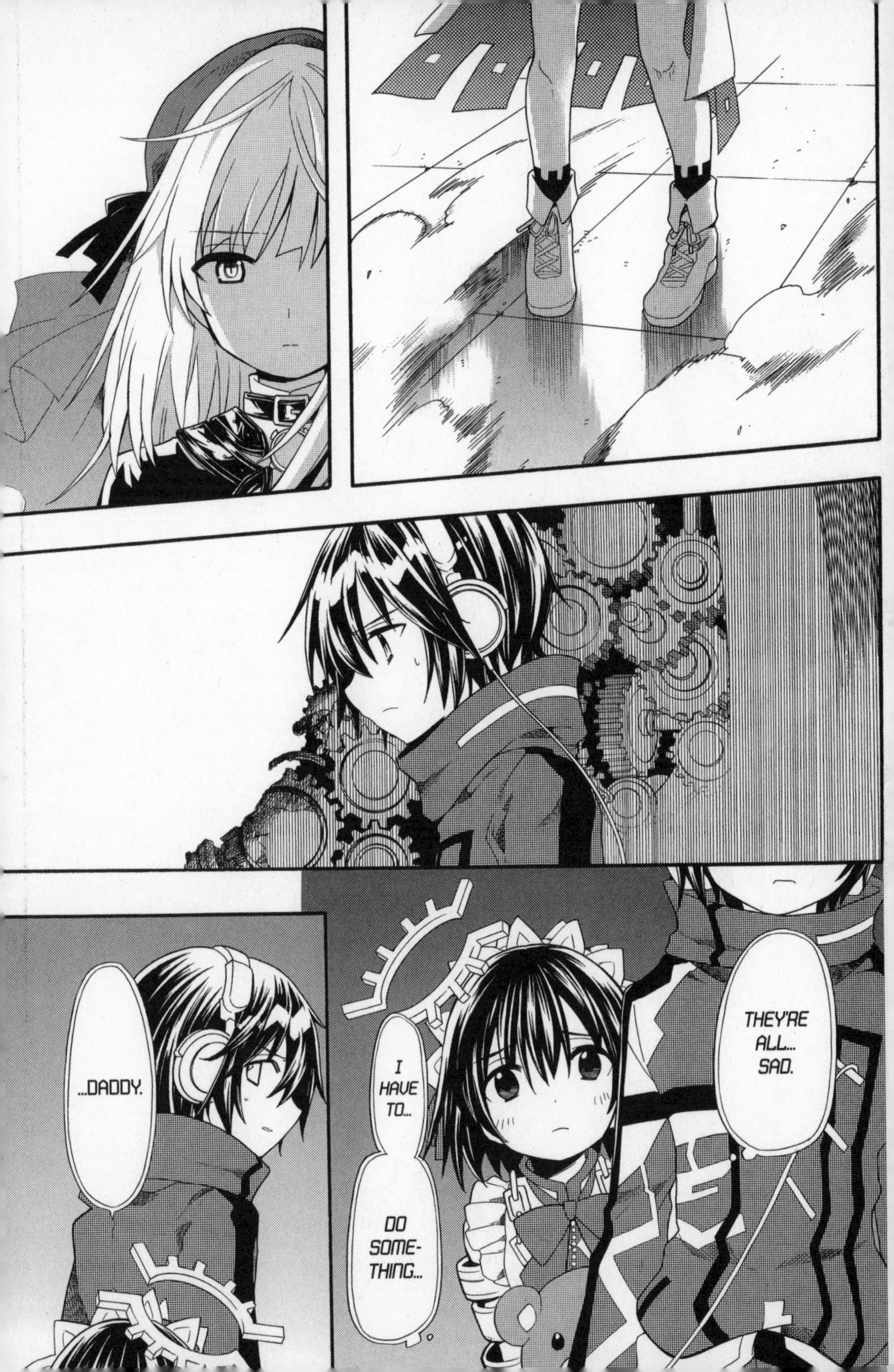
THEY'RE ALL... SAD.
I HAVE TO... DO SOMETHING...
...DADDY.

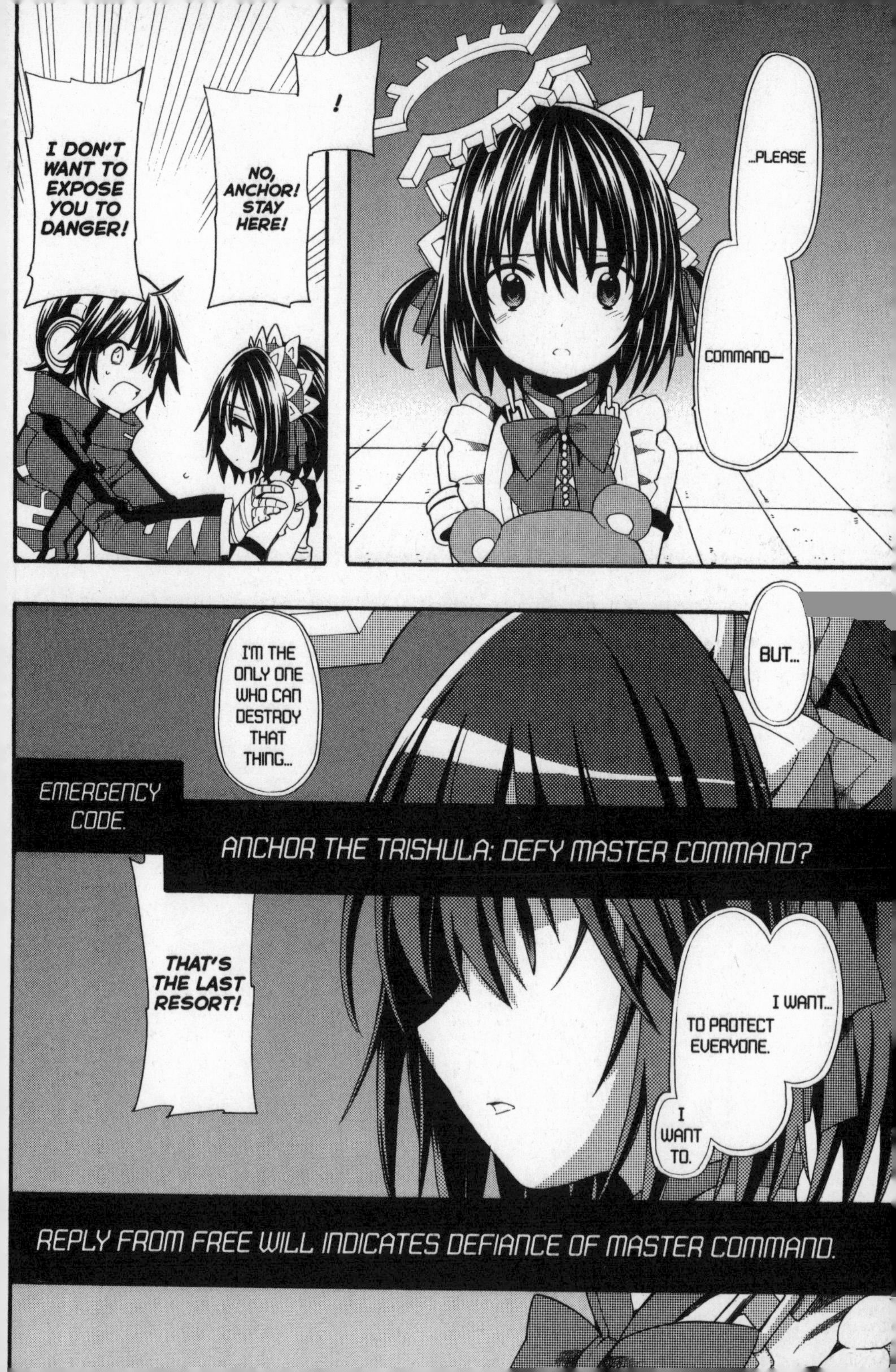
...PLEASE
COMMAND—
!
NO, ANCHOR! STAY HERE!
I DON'T WANT TO EXPOSE YOU TO DANGER!
BUT...
I'M THE ONLY ONE WHO CAN DESTROY THAT THING...
EMERGENCY CODE.
ANCHOR THE TRISHULA: DEFY MASTER COMMAND?
I WANT... TO PROTECT EVERYONE.
I WANT TO.
THAT'S THE LAST RESORT!
REPLY FROM FREE WILL INDICATES DEFIANCE OF MASTER COMMAND.

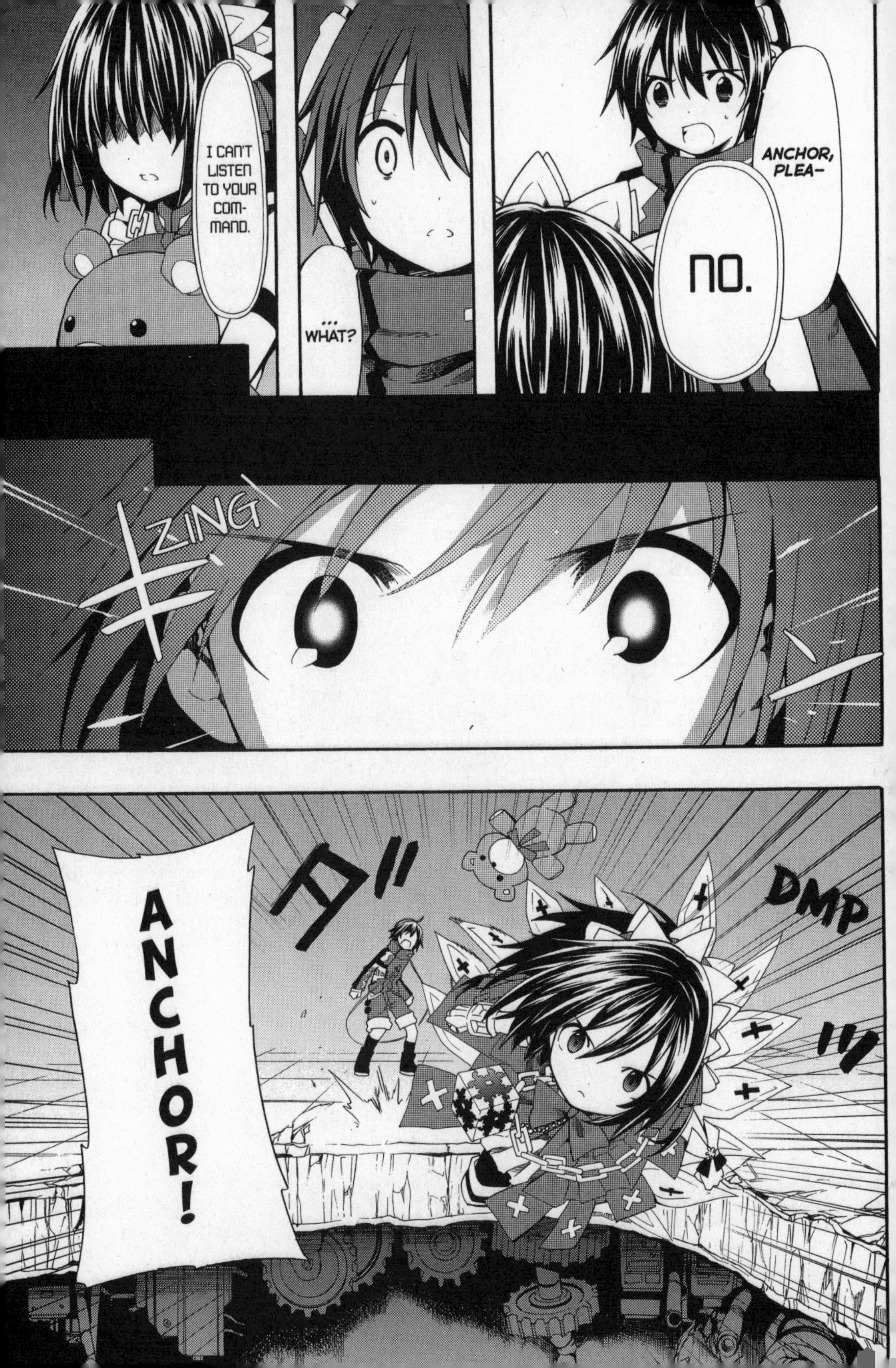
ANCHOR, PLEA-
NO.
... WHAT?
I CAN'T LISTEN TO YOUR COM-MAND.
ZING
DMP
!!!
ダ
ANCHOR!

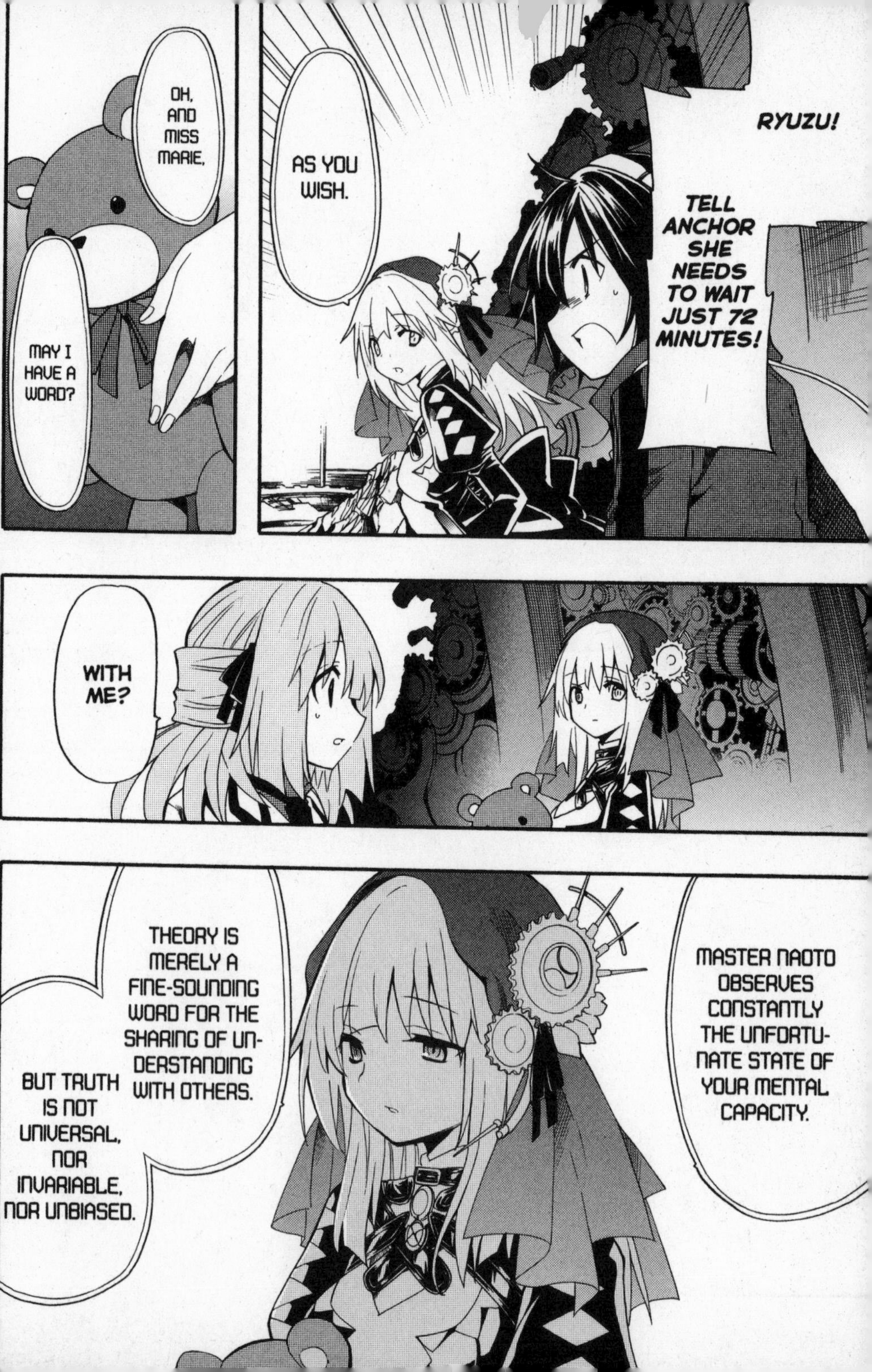
RYUZU!
TELL ANCHOR SHE NEEDS TO WAIT JUST 72 MINUTES!
AS YOU WISH.
OH, AND MISS MARIE,
MAY I HAVE A WORD?
WITH ME?
MASTER NAOTO OBSERVES CONSTANTLY THE UNFORTU-NATE STATE OF YOUR MENTAL CAPACITY.
THEORY IS MERELY A FINE-SOUNDING WORD FOR THE SHARING OF UN-DERSTANDING WITH OTHERS.
BUT TRUTH IS NOT UNIVERSAL, NOR INVARIABLE, NOR UNBIASED.

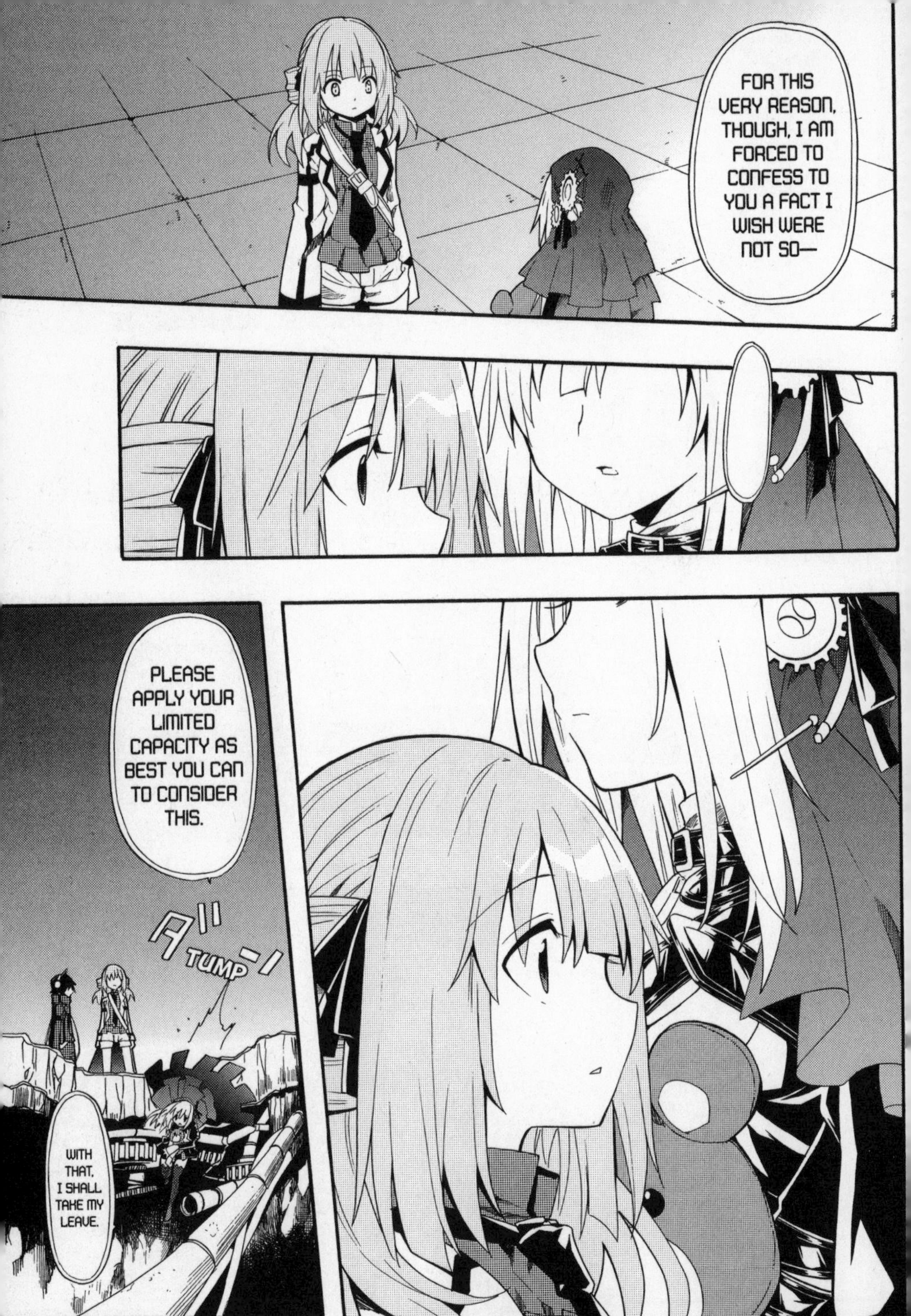
FOR THIS VERY REASON, THOUGH, I AM FORCED TO CONFESS TO YOU A FACT I WISH WERE NOT SO—
PLEASE APPLY YOUR LIMITED CAPACITY AS BEST YOU CAN TO CONSIDER THIS.
TUMP
WITH THAT, I SHALL TAKE MY LEAVE.

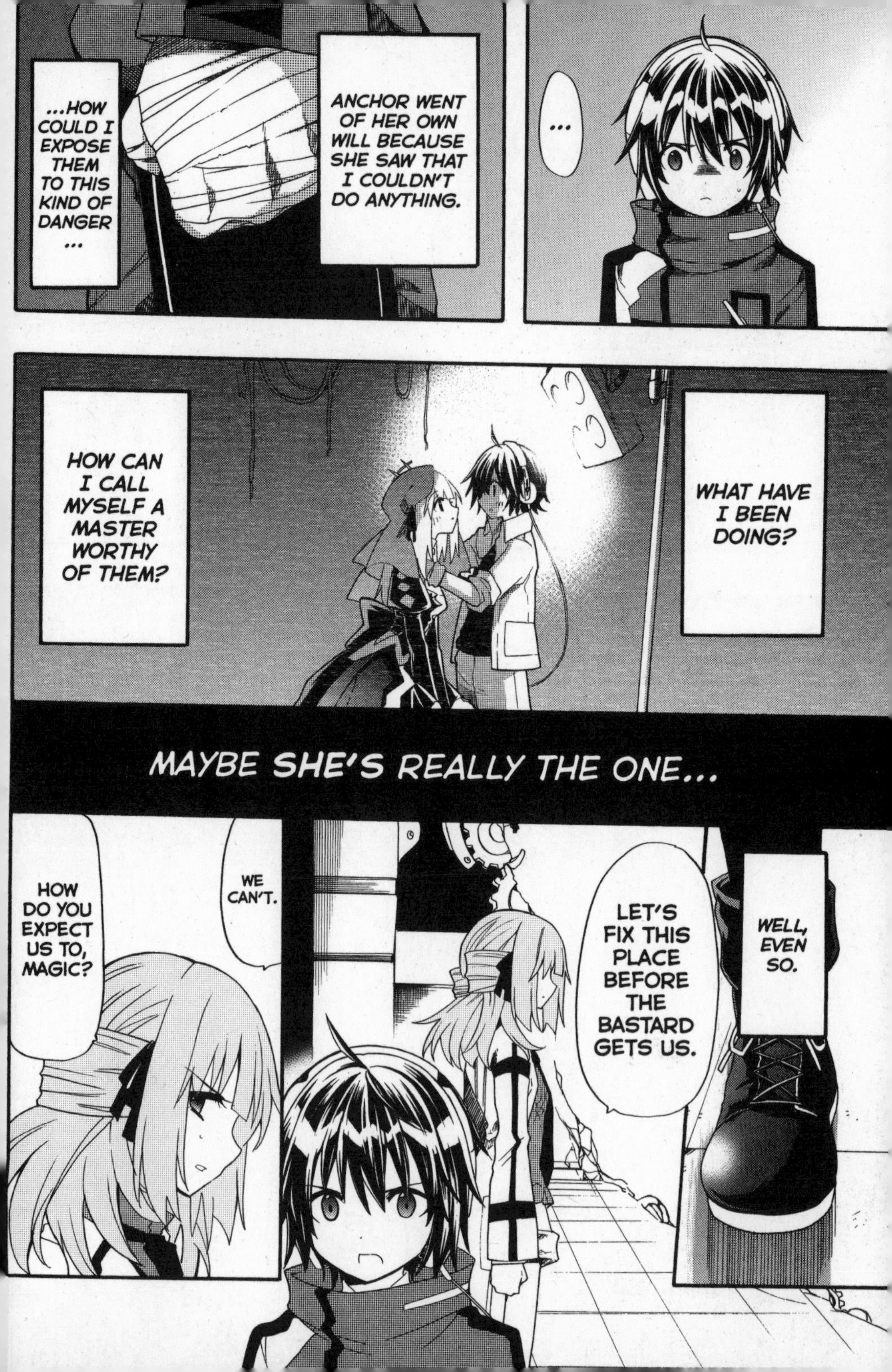
...
ANCHOR WENT OF HER OWN WILL BECAUSE SHE SAW THAT I COULDN'T DO ANYTHING.
...HOW COULD I EXPOSE THEM TO THIS KIND OF DANGER ...
WHAT HAVE I BEEN DOING?
HOW CAN I CALL MYSELF A MASTER WORTHY OF THEM?
MAYBE SHE'S REALLY THE ONE...
WELL, EVEN SO.
LET'S FIX THIS PLACE BEFORE THE BASTARD GETS US.
WE CAN'T.
HOW DO YOU EXPECT US TO, MAGIC?

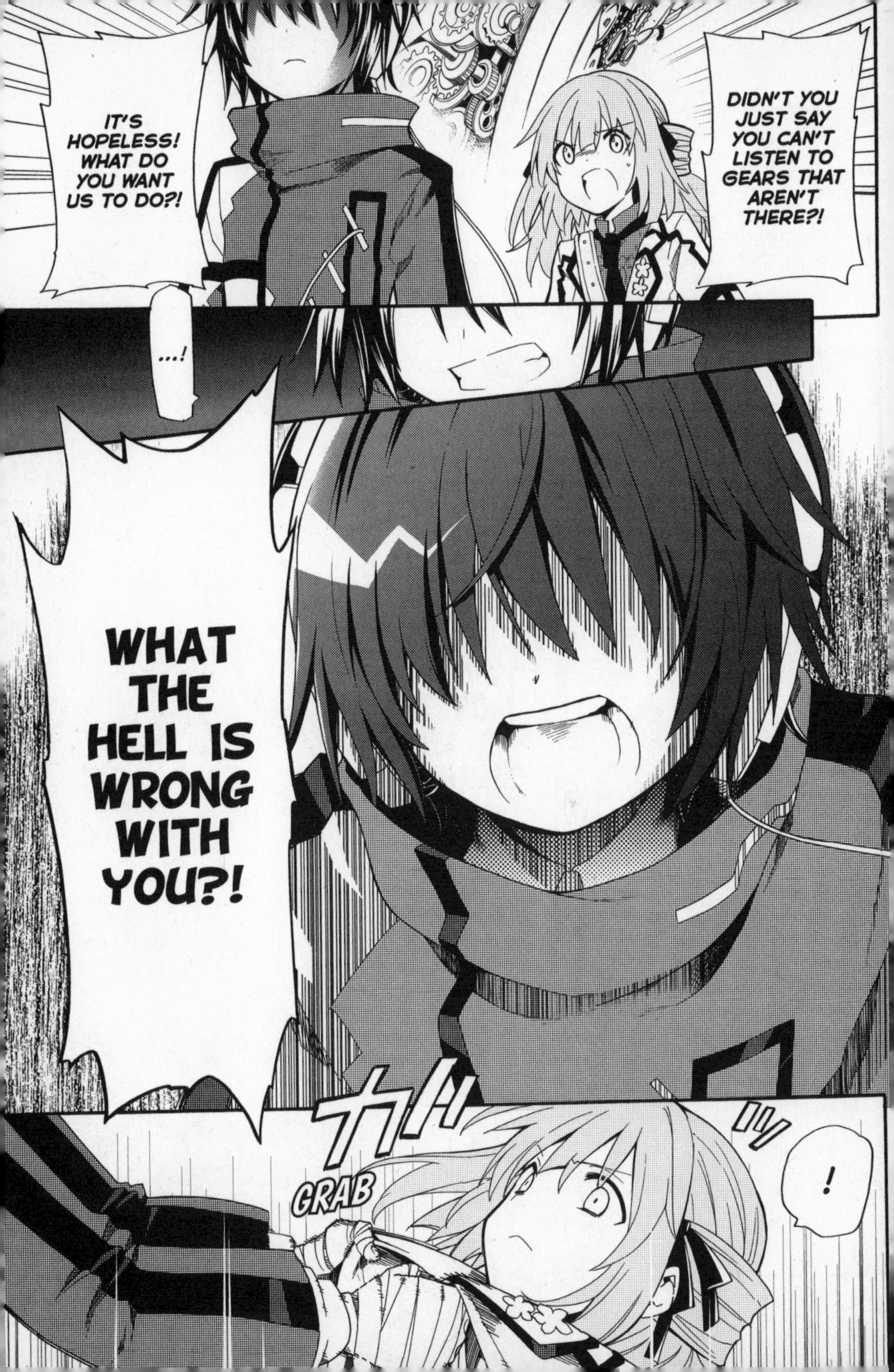
DIDN'T YOU JUST SAY YOU CAN'T LISTEN TO GEARS THAT AREN'T THERE?!
IT'S HOPELESS! WHAT DO YOU WANT US TO DO?!
...!
WHAT THE HELL IS WRONG WITH YOU?!
!
GRAB

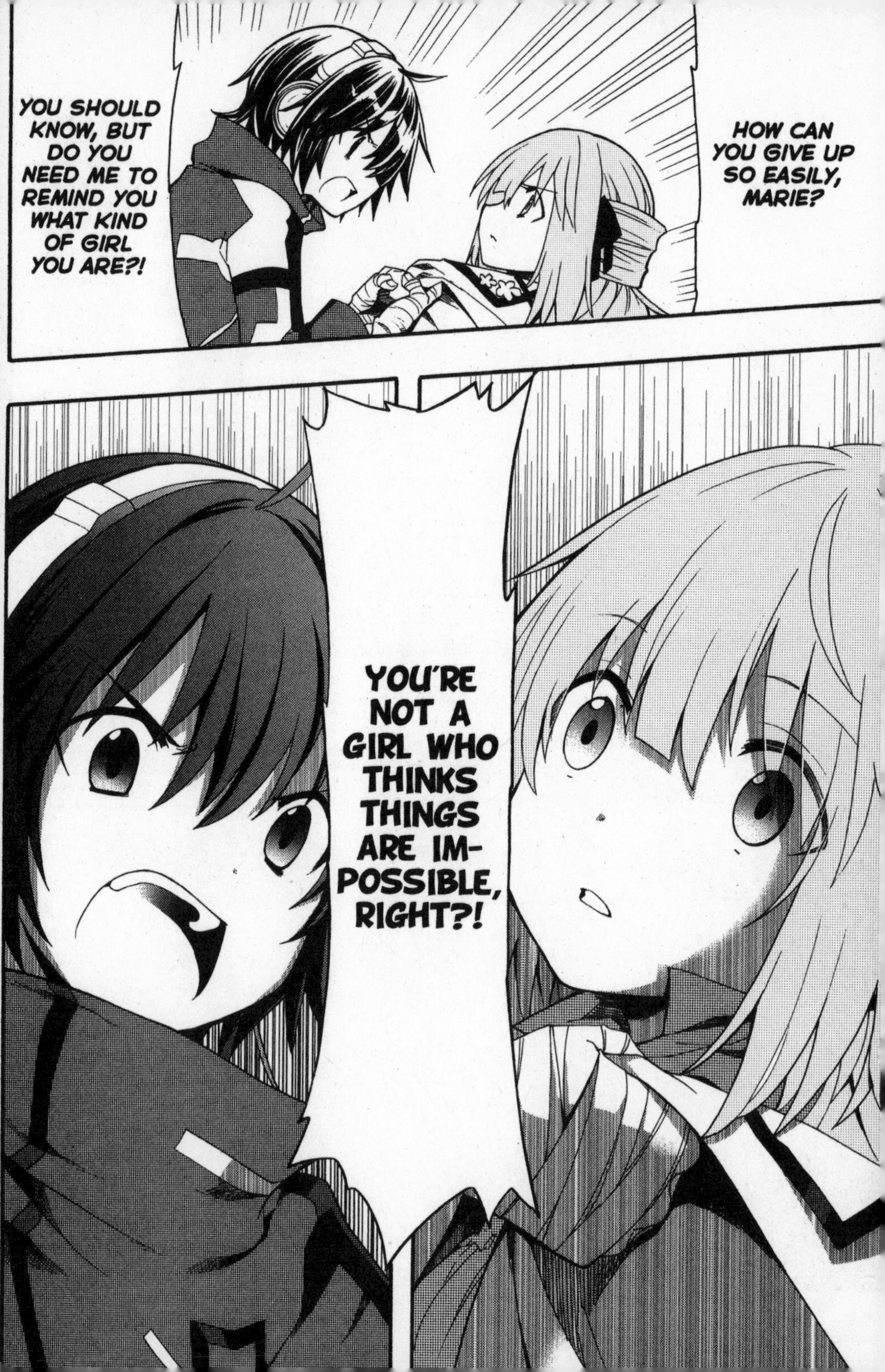
HOW CAN YOU GIVE UP SO EASILY, MARIE?
YOU SHOULD KNOW, BUT DO YOU NEED ME TO REMIND YOU WHAT KIND OF GIRL YOU ARE?!
YOU'RE NOT A GIRL WHO THINKS THINGS ARE IM-POSSIBLE, RIGHT?!

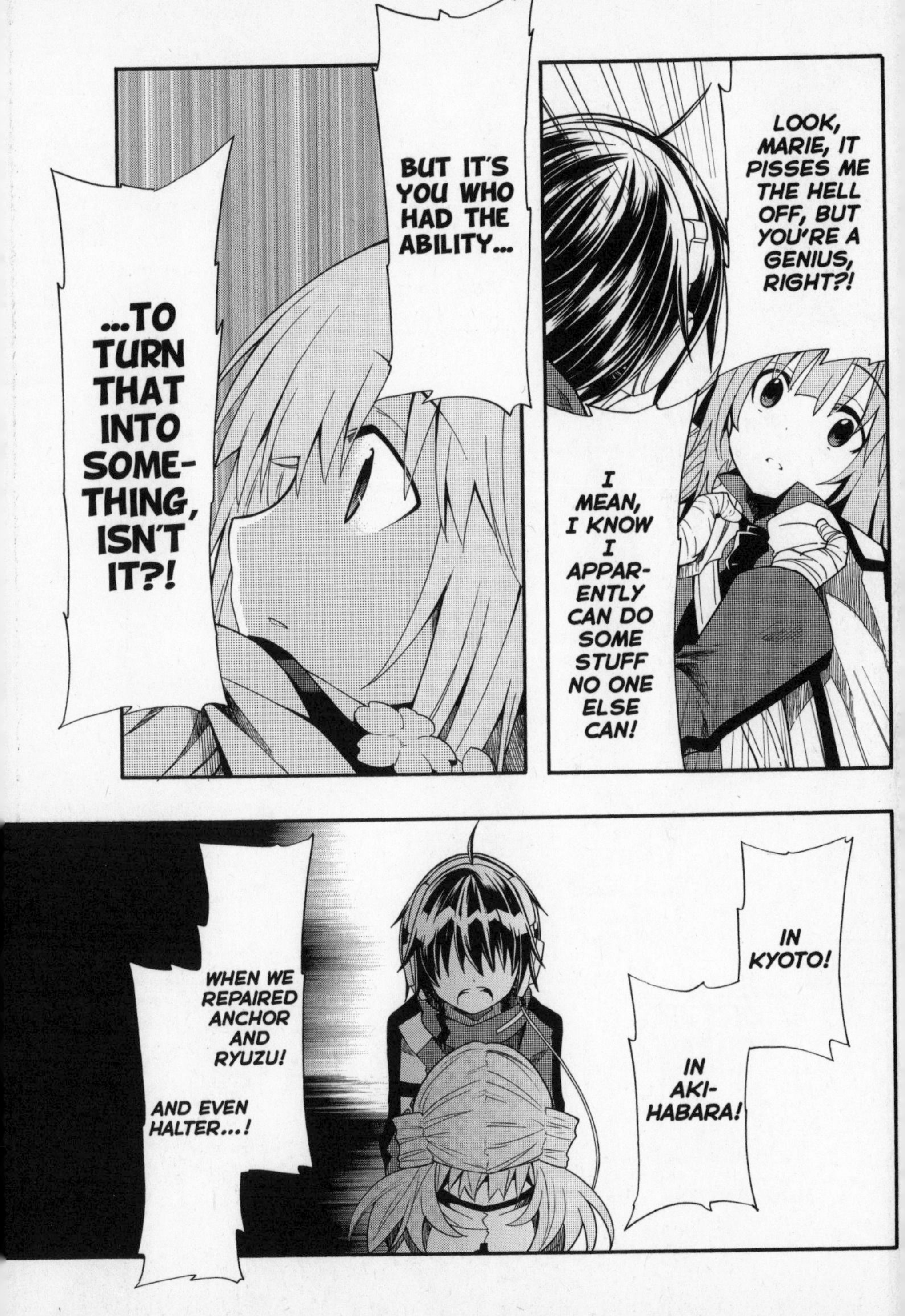
LOOK, MARIE, IT PISSES ME THE HELL OFF, BUT YOU'RE A GENIUS, RIGHT?!
I MEAN, I KNOW I APPARENTLY CAN DO SOME STUFF NO ONE ELSE CAN!
BUT IT'S YOU WHO HAD THE ABILITY...
...TO TURN THAT INTO SOME-THING, ISN'T IT?!
IN KYOTO!
IN AKI-HABARA!
WHEN WE REPAIRED ANCHOR AND RYUZU!
AND EVEN HALTER...!

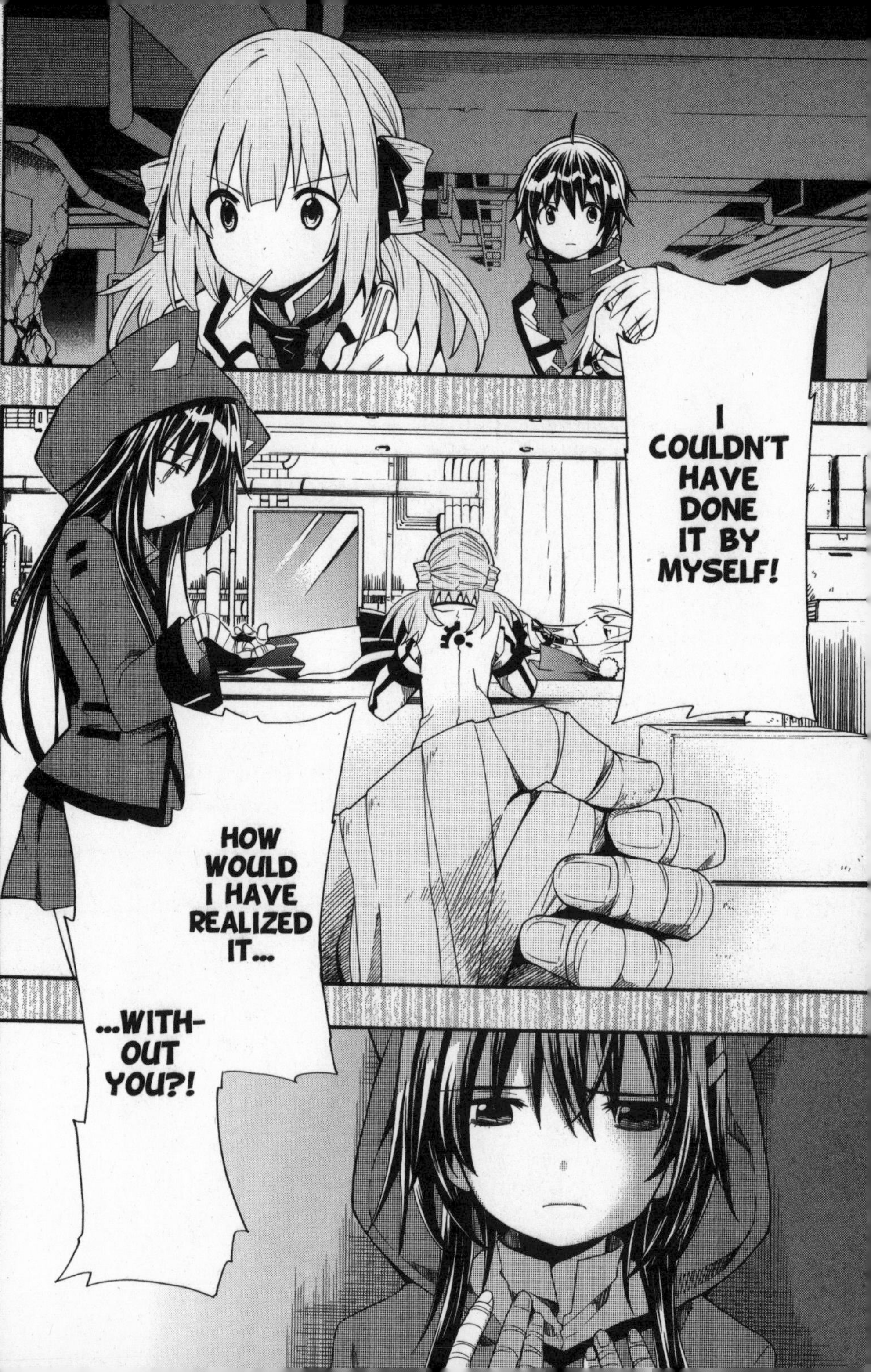
I COULDN'T HAVE DONE IT BY MYSELF!
HOW WOULD I HAVE REALIZED IT...
...WITH-OUT YOU?!

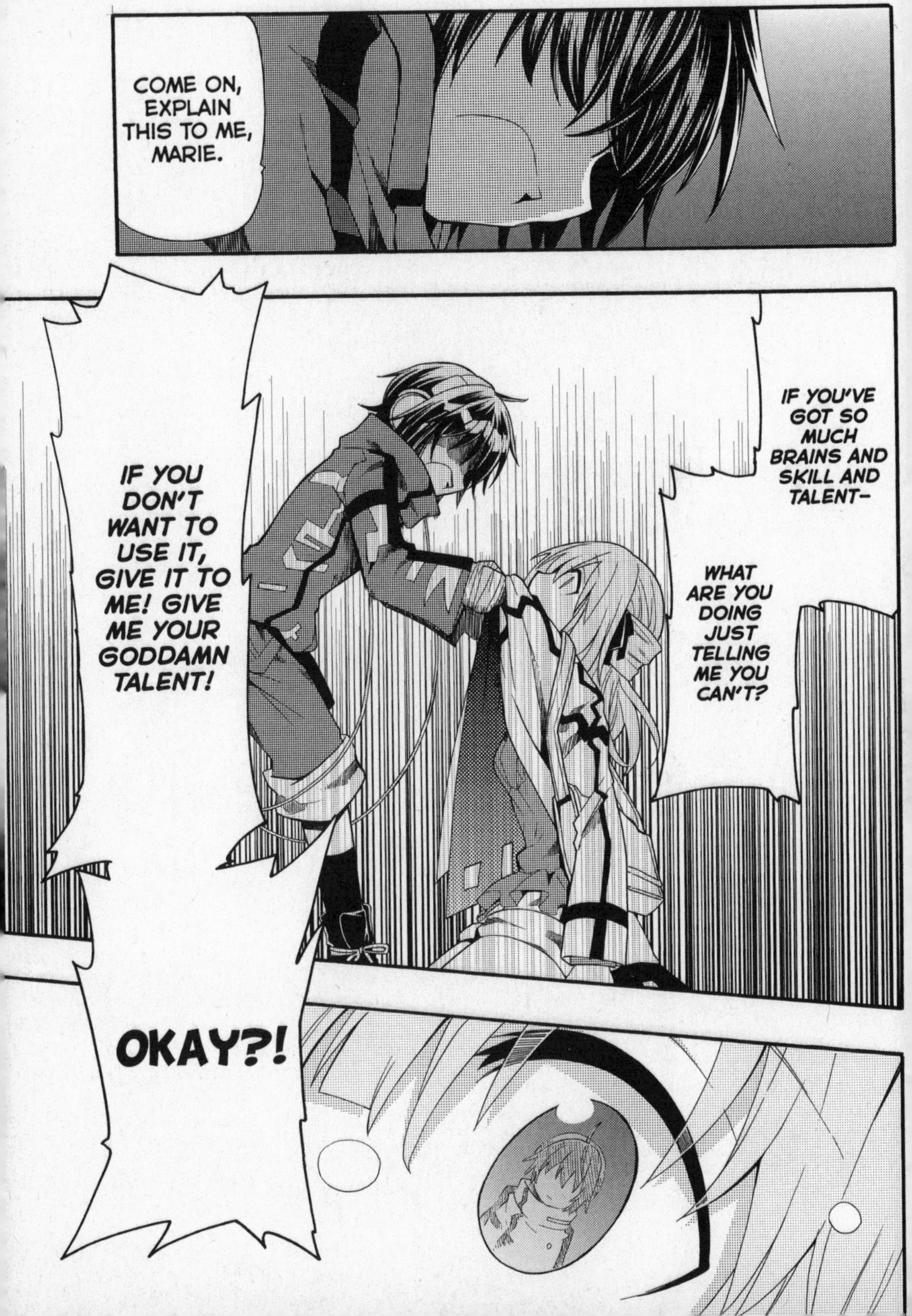
COME ON, EXPLAIN THIS TO ME, MARIE.
IF YOU'VE GOT SO MUCH BRAINS AND SKILL AND TALENT–
WHAT ARE YOU DOING JUST TELLING ME YOU CAN'T?
IF YOU DON'T WANT TO USE IT, GIVE IT TO ME! GIVE ME YOUR GODDAMN TALENT!
OKAY?!

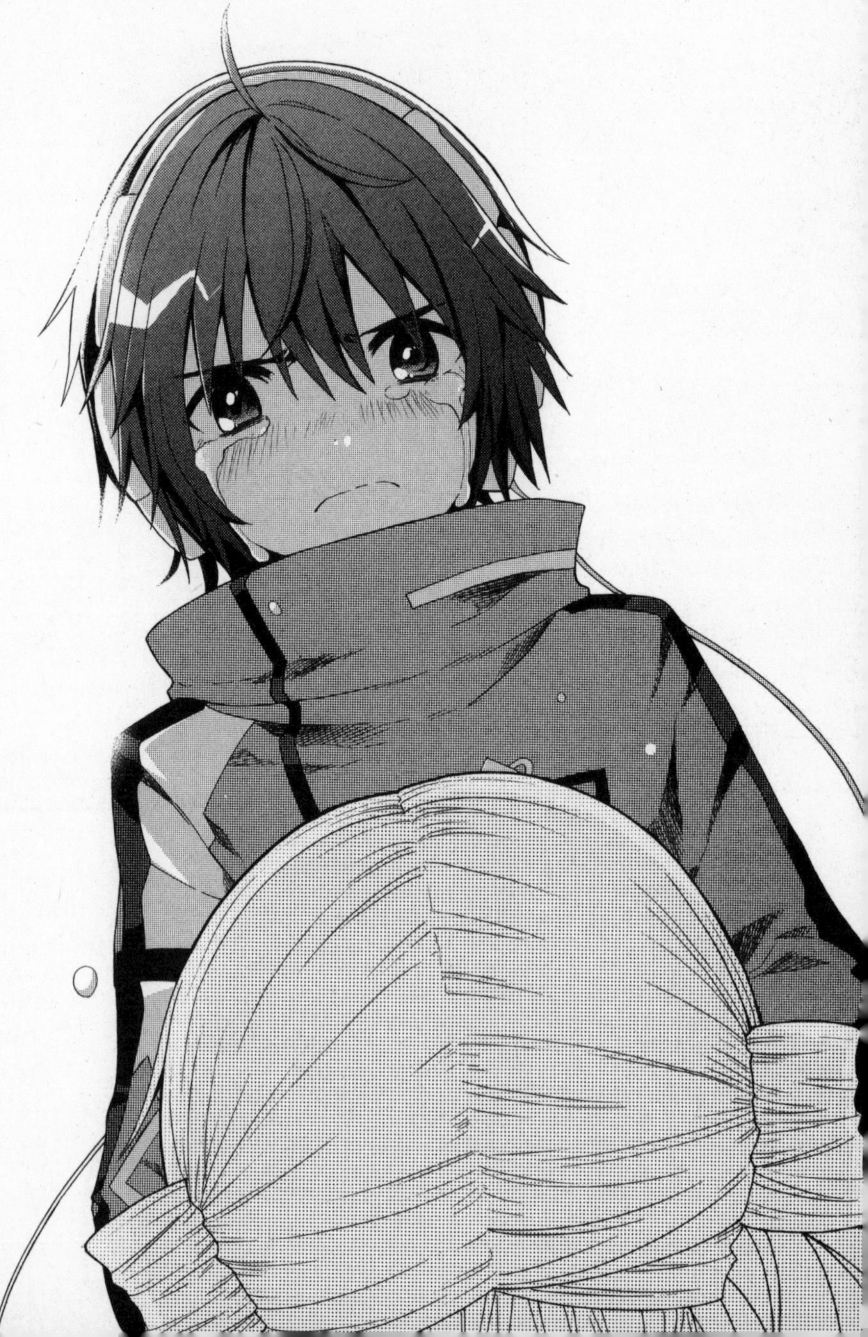

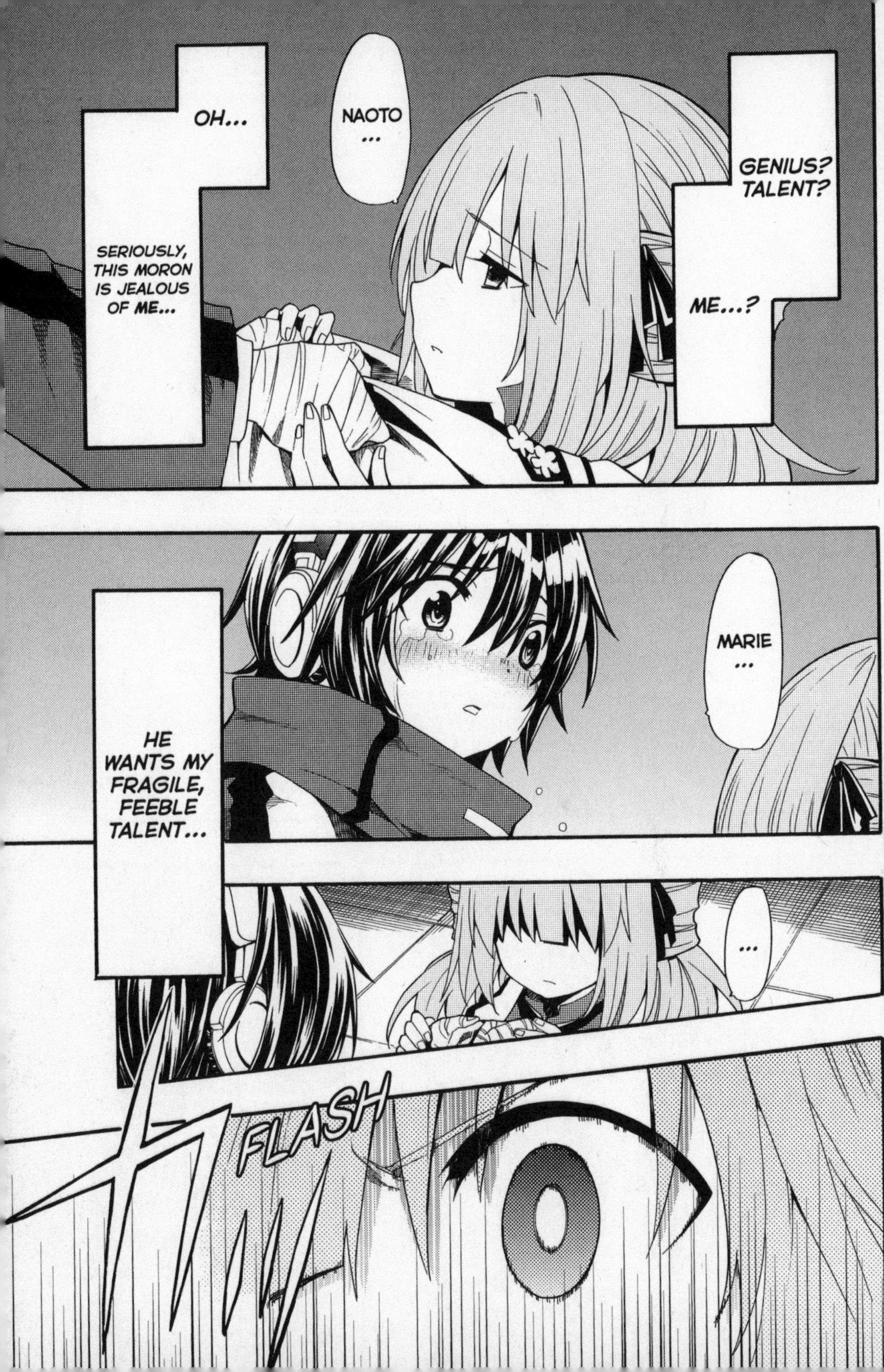
GENIUS? TALENT?
ME...?
NAOTO ...
OH...
SERIOUSLY, THIS MORON IS JEALOUS OF ME...
MARIE ...
HE WANTS MY FRAGILE, FEEBLE TALENT...
...
FLASH

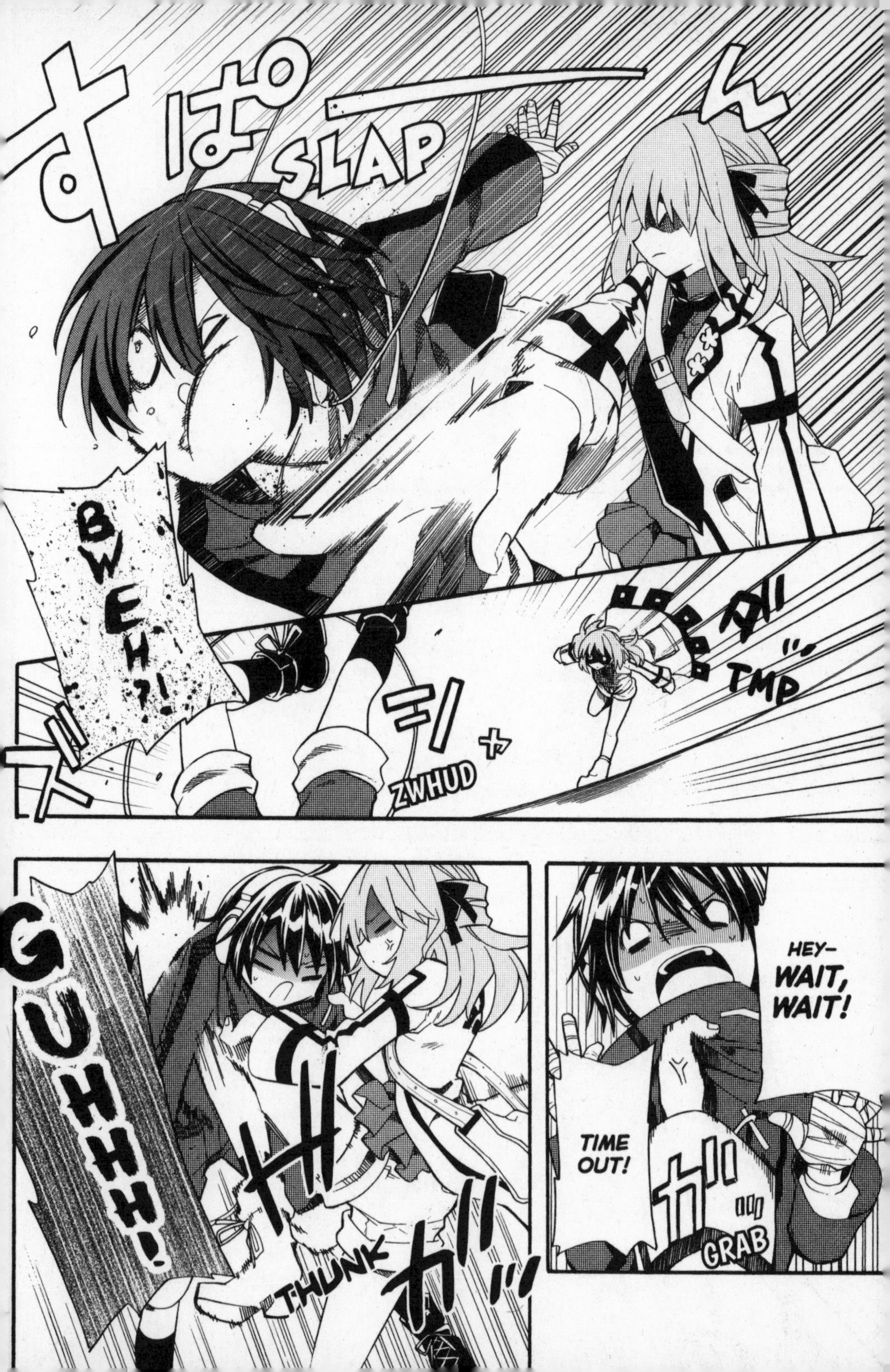
すぱーん
SLAP
BWEH?!
TMP
ZWHUD
HEY—WAIT, WAIT!
TIME OUT!
GRAB
GUHHH!
THUNK

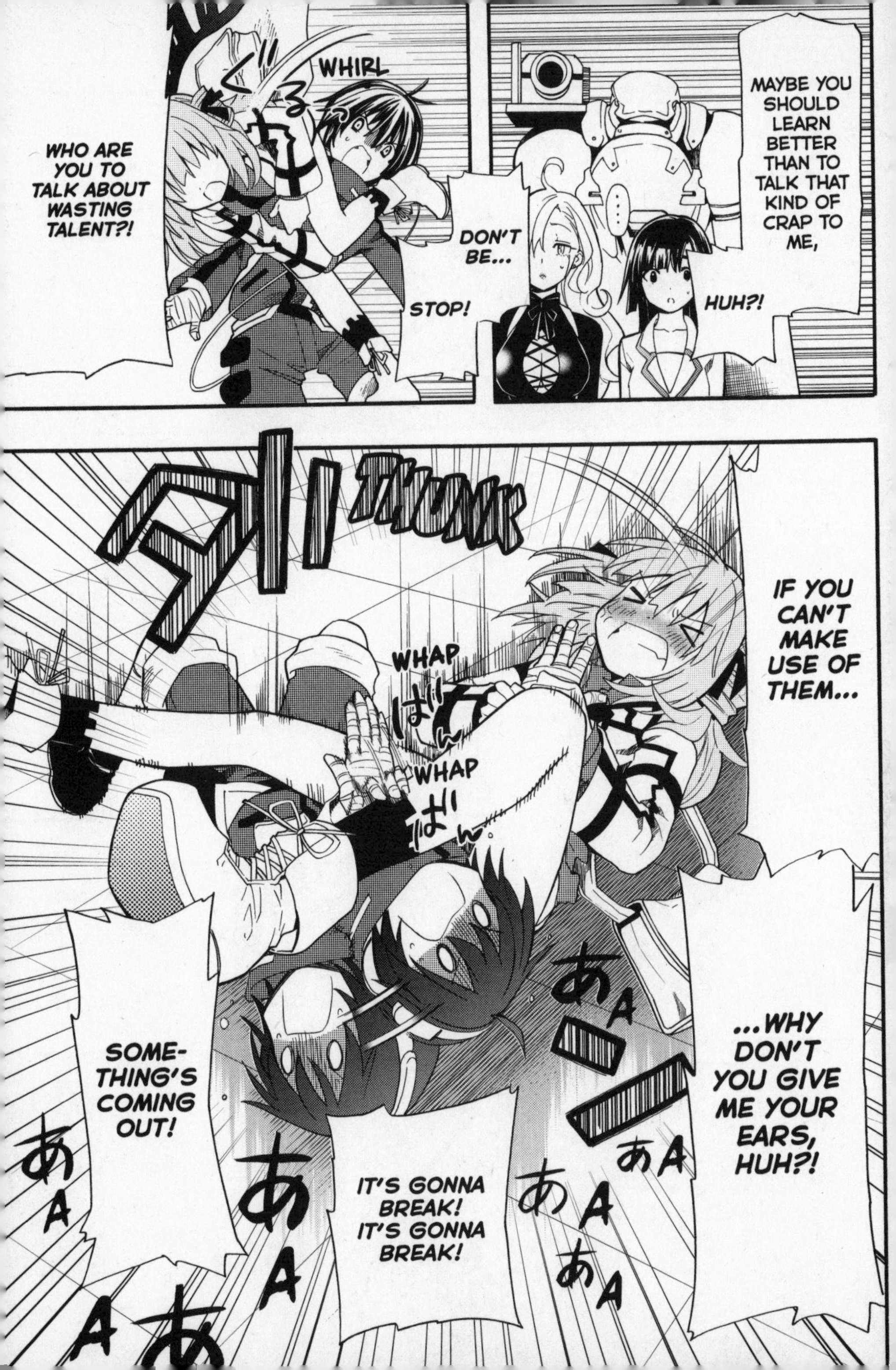
MAYBE YOU SHOULD LEARN BETTER THAN TO TALK THAT KIND OF CRAP TO ME,
HUH?!
DON'T BE...
STOP!
WHIRL
WHO ARE YOU TO TALK ABOUT WASTING TALENT?!
IF YOU CAN'T MAKE USE OF THEM...
THUNK
WHAP
WHAP
...WHY DON'T YOU GIVE ME YOUR EARS, HUH?!
A
A
A
A
IT'S GONNA BREAK! IT'S GONNA BREAK!
SOME-THING'S COMING OUT!
A
A
A

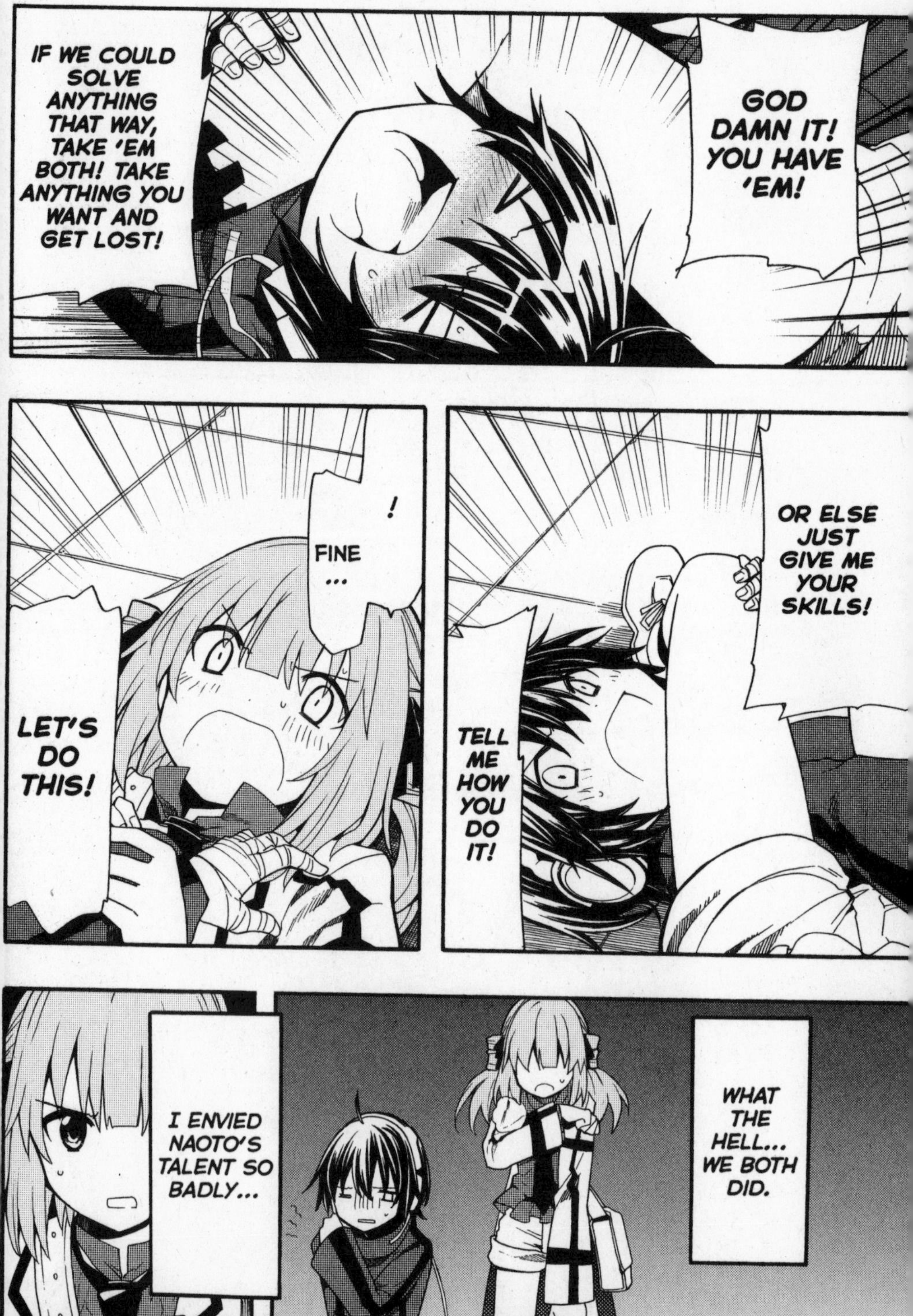
GOD DAMN IT! YOU HAVE 'EM!
IF WE COULD SOLVE ANYTHING THAT WAY, TAKE 'EM BOTH! TAKE ANYTHING YOU WANT AND GET LOST!
OR ELSE JUST GIVE ME YOUR SKILLS!
TELL ME HOW YOU DO IT!
! FINE...
LET'S DO THIS!
WHAT THE HELL... WE BOTH DID.
I ENVIED NAOTO'S TALENT SO BADLY...

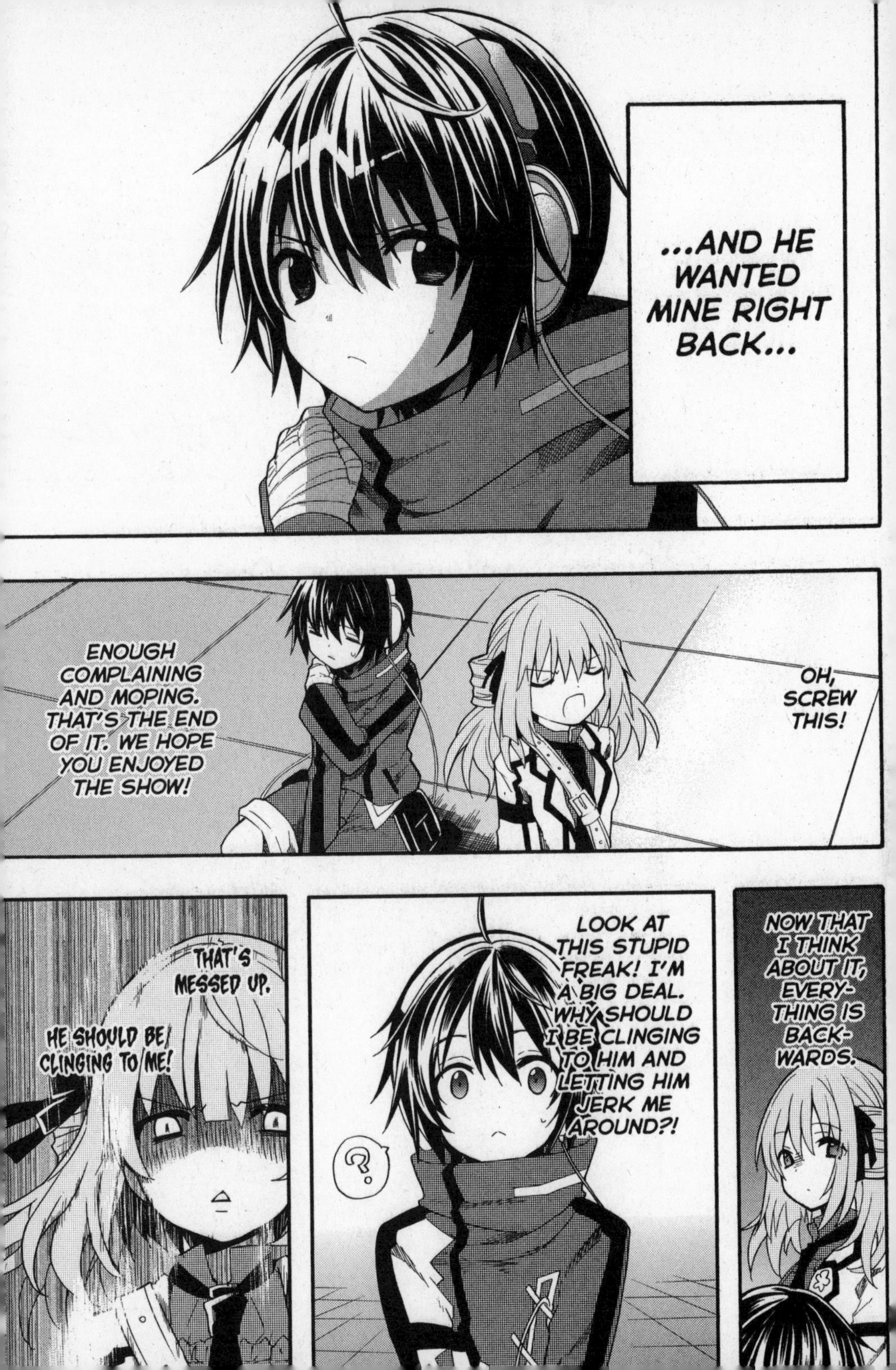
...AND HE WANTED MINE RIGHT BACK...
OH, SCREW THIS!
ENOUGH COMPLAINING AND MOPING. THAT'S THE END OF IT. WE HOPE YOU ENJOYED THE SHOW!
NOW THAT I THINK ABOUT IT, EVERYTHING IS BACKWARDS.
LOOK AT THIS STUPID FREAK! I'M A BIG DEAL. WHY SHOULD I BE CLINGING TO HIM AND LETTING HIM JERK ME AROUND?!
?
THAT'S MESSED UP.
HE SHOULD BE CLINGING TO ME!

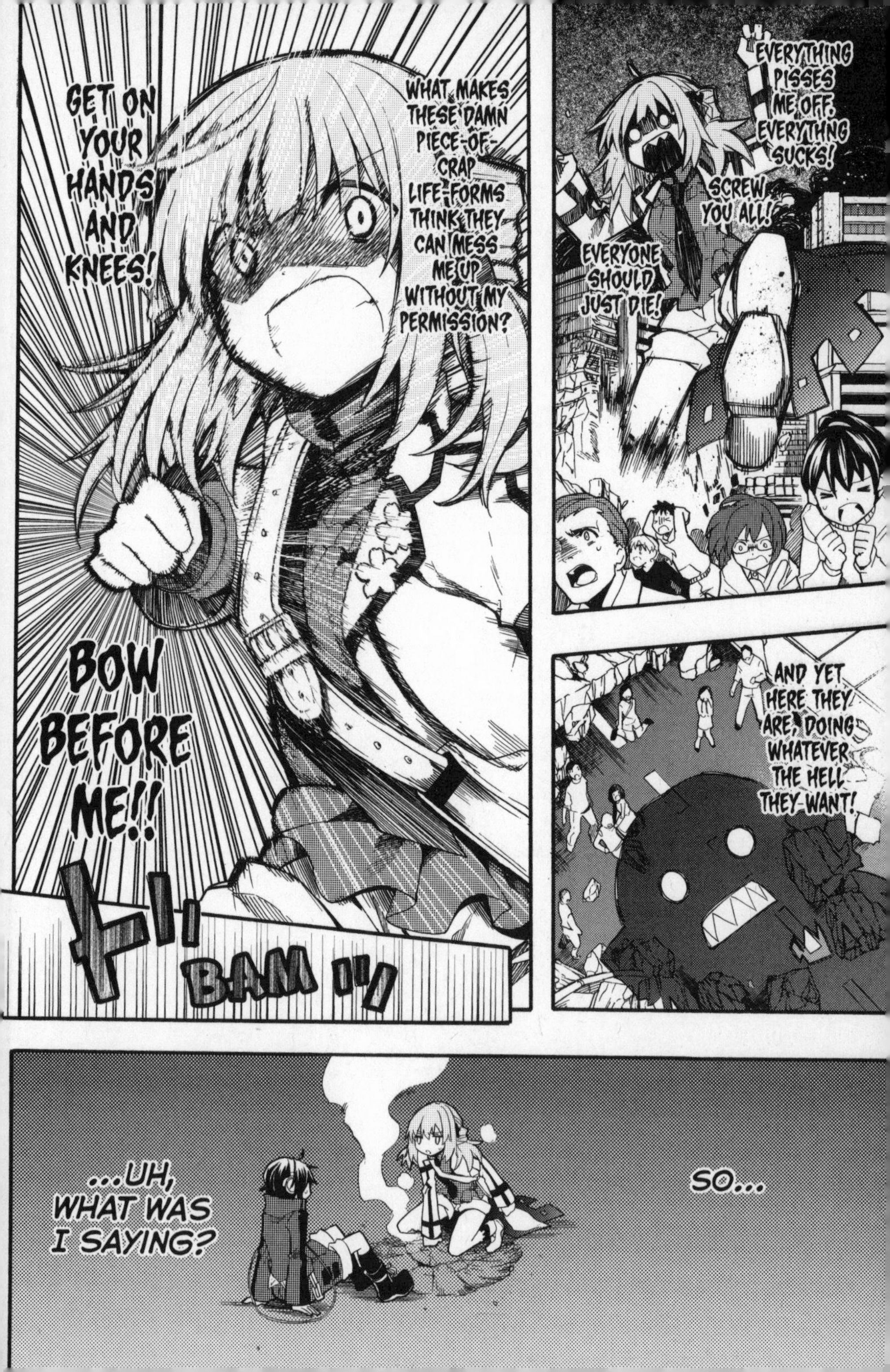
EVERYTHING PISSES ME OFF. EVERYTHNG SUCKS!
SCREW YOU ALL!
EVERYONE SHOULD JUST DIE!
AND YET HERE THEY ARE, DOING WHATEVER THE HELL THEY WANT!
WHAT MAKES THESE DAMN PIECE-OF-CRAP LIFE-FORMS THINK THEY CAN MESS ME UP WITHOUT MY PERMISSION?
GET ON YOUR HANDS AND KNEES!
BOW BEFORE ME!!
BAM!!
SO...
...UH, WHAT WAS I SAYING?

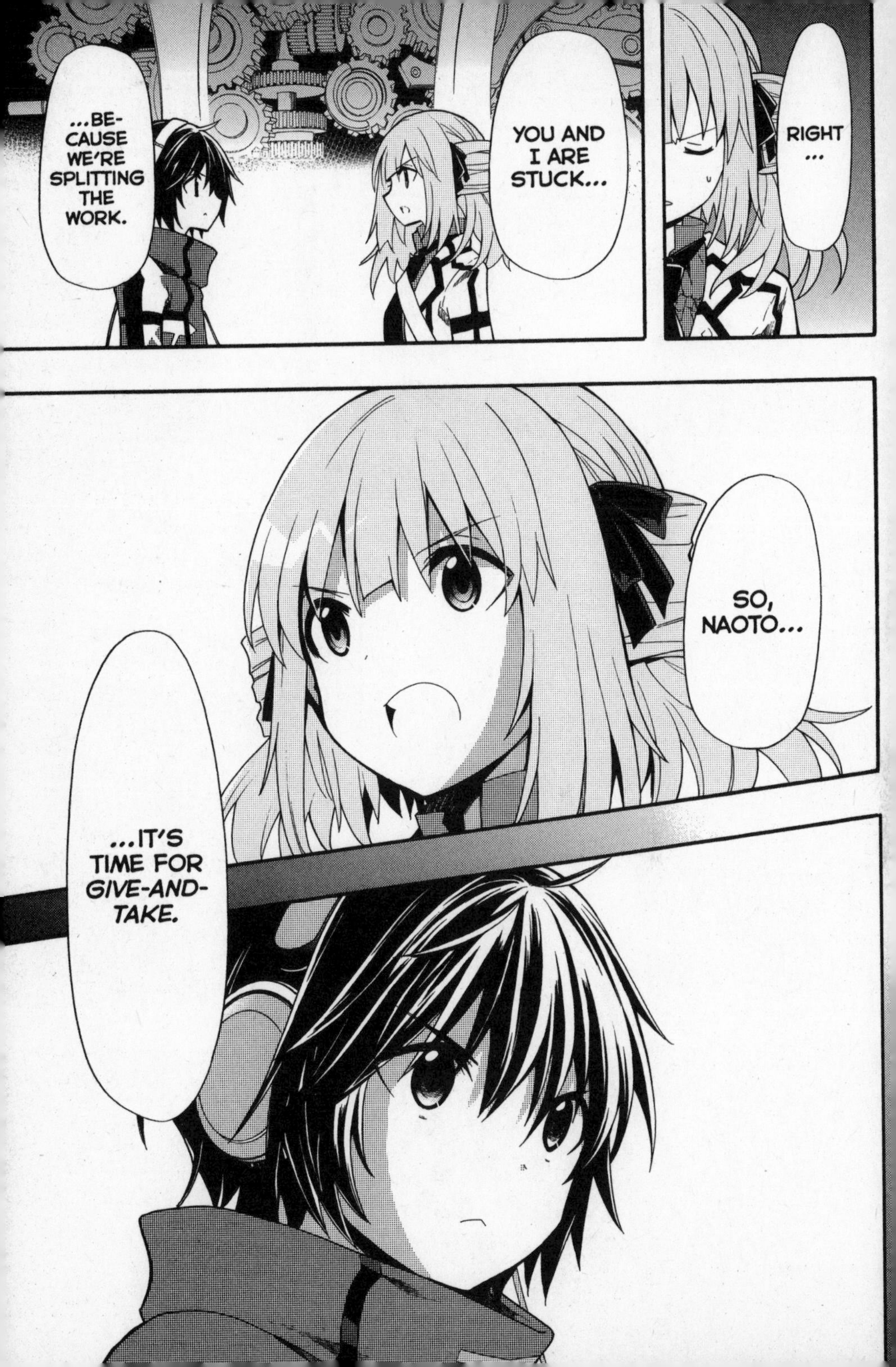
RIGHT...
YOU AND I ARE STUCK...
...BE-CAUSE WE'RE SPLITTING THE WORK.
SO, NAOTO...
...IT'S TIME FOR GIVE-AND-TAKE.

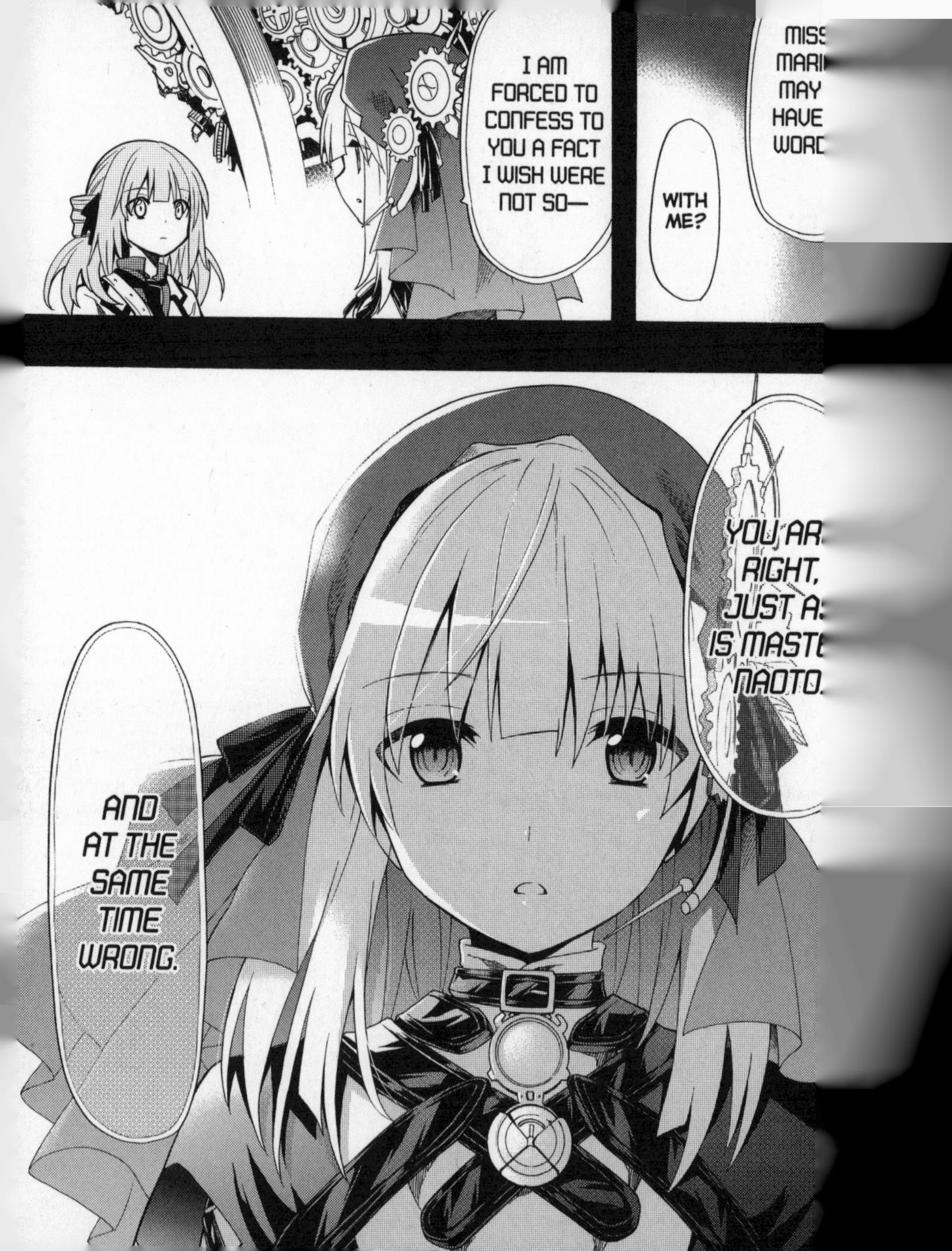
MISS MARI MAY HAVE WORD
WITH ME?
I AM FORCED TO CONFESS TO YOU A FACT I WISH WERE NOT SO—
YOU AR RIGHT, JUST A IS MASTE NAOTO.
AND AT THE SAME TIME WRONG.

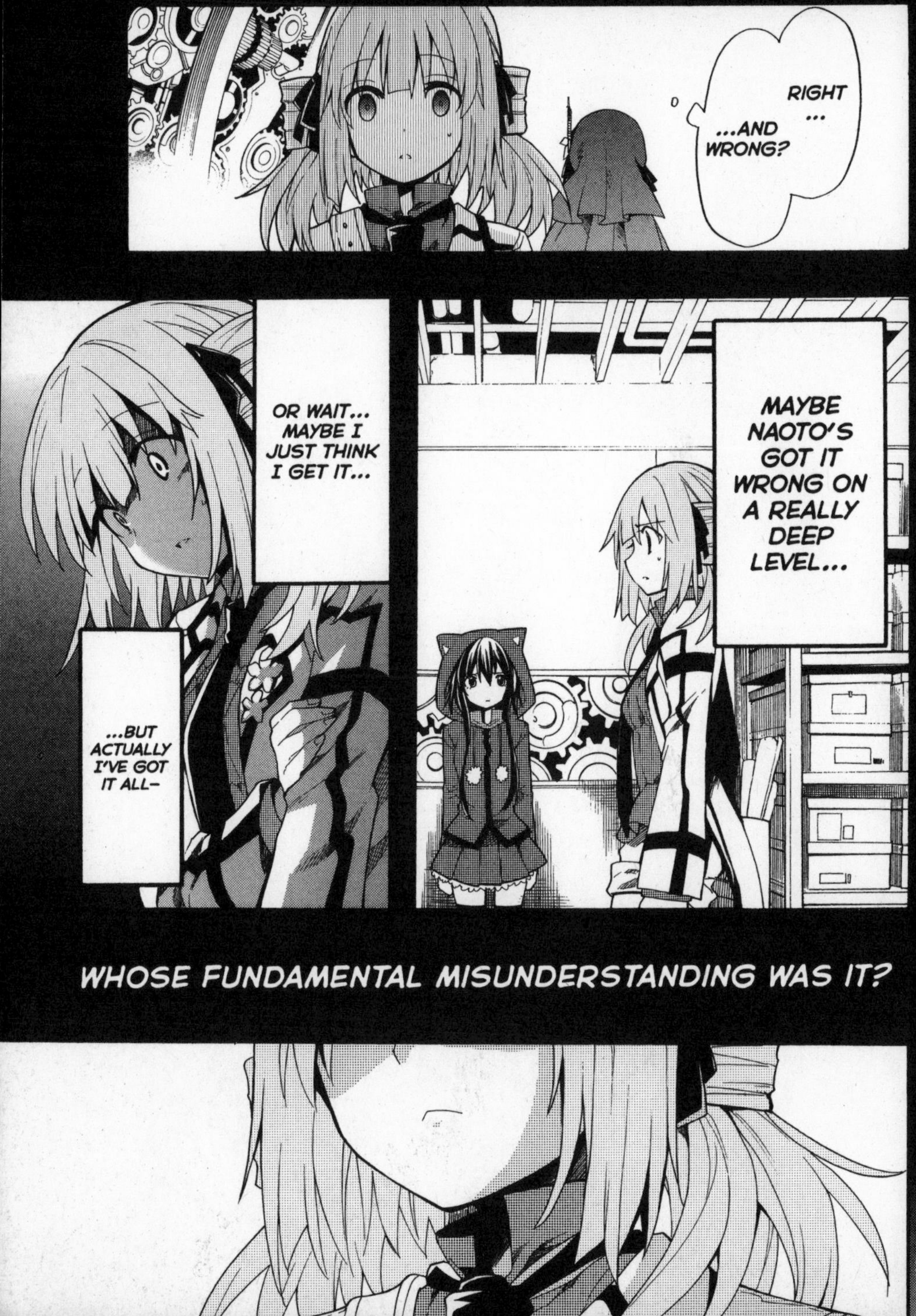
RIGHT... ...AND WRONG?
MAYBE NAOTO'S GOT IT WRONG ON A REALLY DEEP LEVEL...
OR WAIT... MAYBE I JUST THINK I GET IT...
...BUT ACTUALLY I'VE GOT IT ALL—
WHOSE FUNDAMENTAL MISUNDERSTANDING WAS IT?

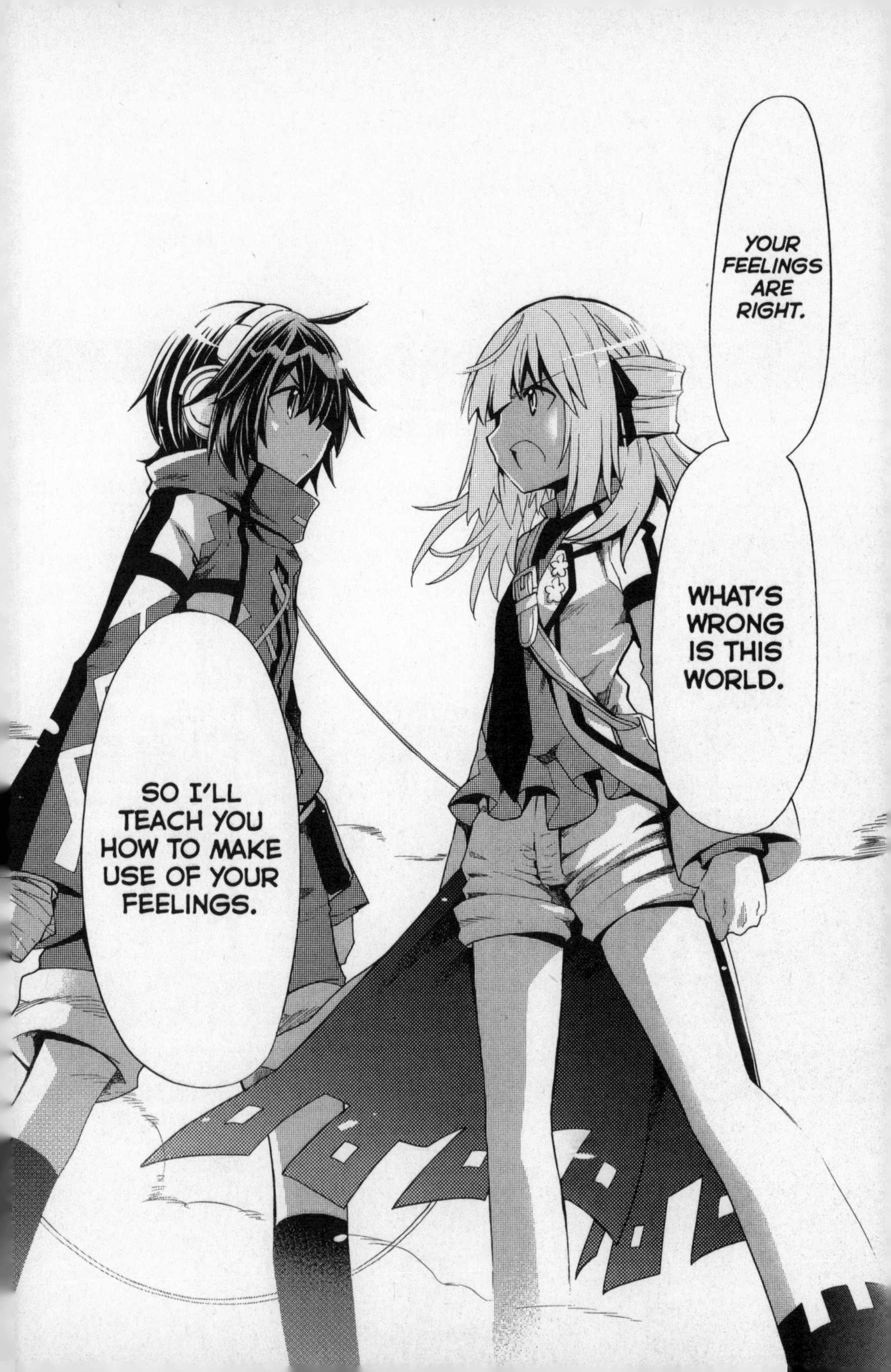

YOUR FEELINGS ARE RIGHT.
WHAT'S WRONG IS THIS WORLD.
SO I'LL TEACH YOU HOW TO MAKE USE OF YOUR FEELINGS.

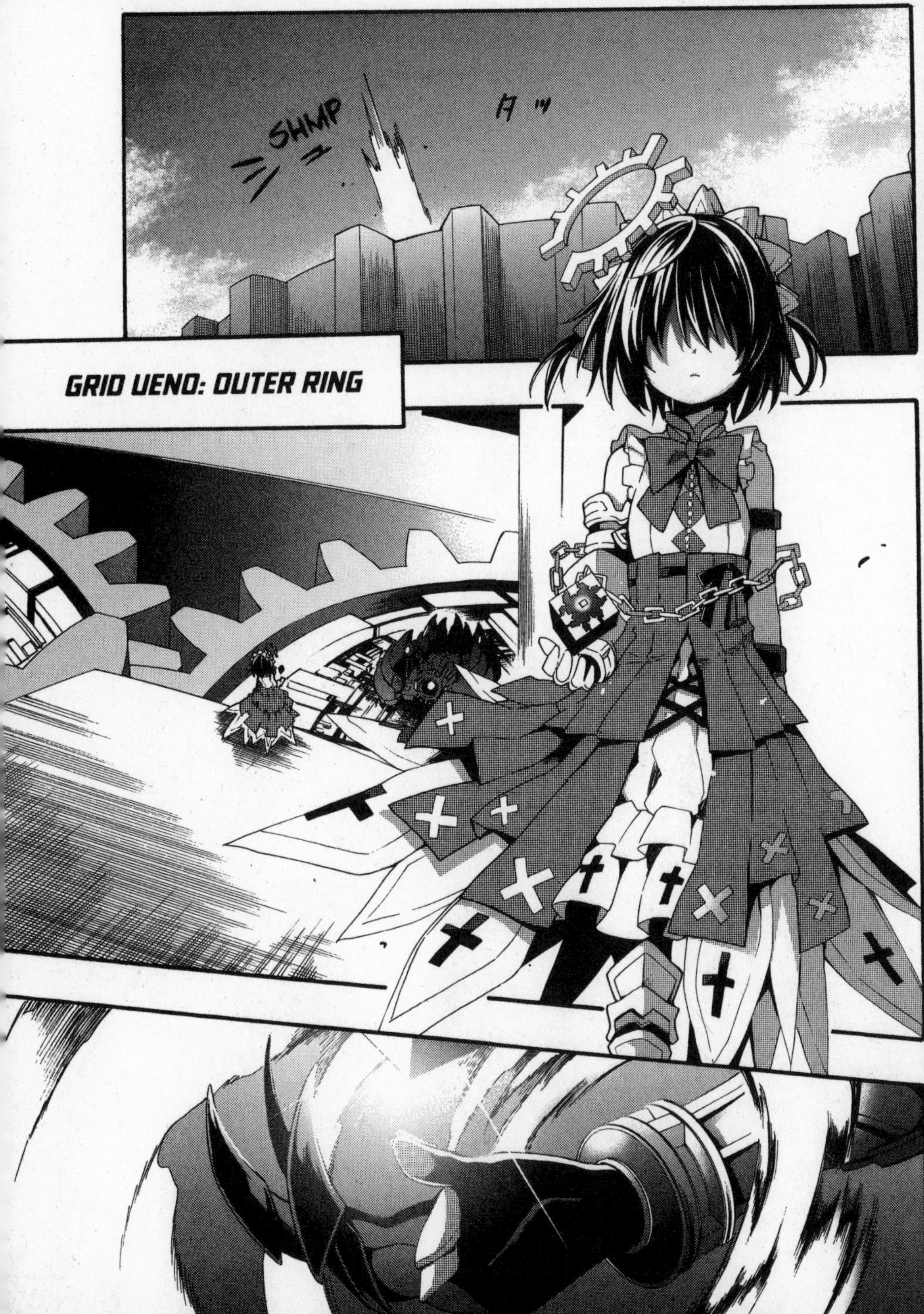
SHMP
GRID UENO: OUTER RING

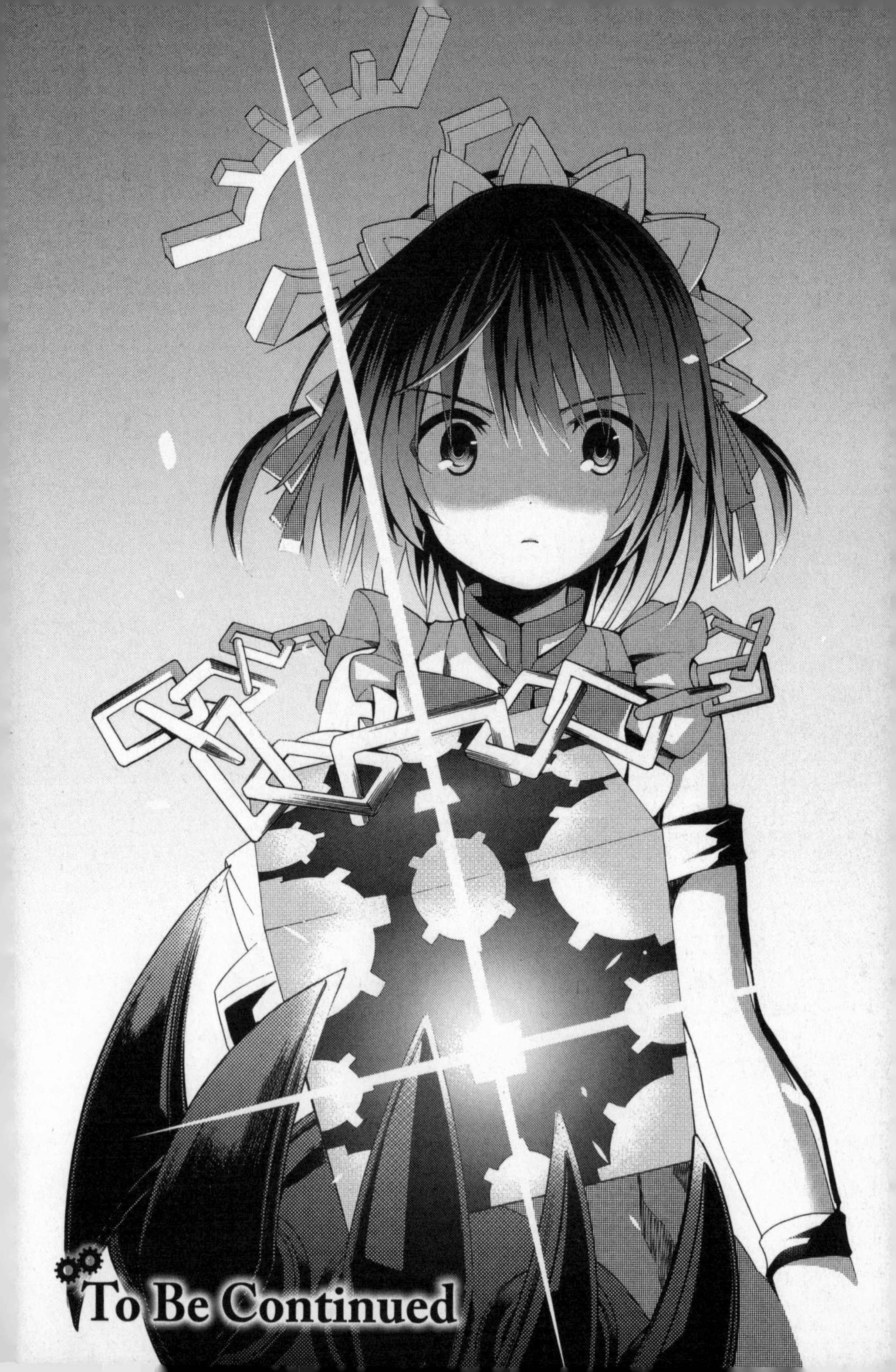
To Be Continued

CLOCKWORK PLANET

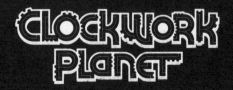

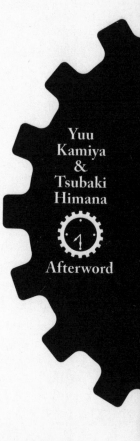

Yuu Kamiya & Tsubaki Himana Afterword

K: So. Another afterword, another "say something funny."

H: You know how they asked us to go live on Nico (an online video streaming site) in March? ditorial totally thinks of us as professional clowns now, don't they? But hey, I guess we have plenty talk about with the anime coming up.

K: Indeed! So let us begin with the topic of how I'm finally getting some.

H: What about the anime?! Uh, hello, Mrs. Kamiya? Your dork husband is talking about cheating n you or some crazy jealousy-inducing crap like that. Ha ha. Go to hell, you normies!

K: Yeah, don't worry. I've been to hell already.

H: Oh, so she already caught you? Awww yeah, suck on that!

K: She's been getting some from the same folks, so it's not cheating. Their ames are Rota, Noro, and Flu A and B.

H: Uh... Wait a second. Are you talking about...those things that aren't ulticellular organisms?

K: Yes! They're not even cells—they call them viruses, those mysterious on-organism mofos who can't even self-replicate and yet have the nerve leech onto organisms! They've been screwing us so hard since the end of st year that I haven't made it to a single one of the recording sessions! And hat were you doing while I was in hell? In what kind of craaazy, jealousy-ducing delights have you partaken? Tell me. Reveal it all to me, while I eep tears of blood in rapt attention; come on, give it to me! *(Weeps tears blood.)*

H: Uh, um... Well, you know. Yeah, I guess it was better than hell... But, ll, it was just like, for instance, some of the guy actors and Manga Editor and myself had some fun talking about adult videos; you know, that kind thing?

K: Dude! You want to send me deeper into hell? Don't start some legal ouble, all right?!

H: Huh? Wait a sec. On what charges?!

K: You can't talk about adult videos in public! What were you going to do if e of the actresses heard you? If this was America, they'd sue you for sexual rassment and win for sure! But since you haven't been sued, I guess they dn't... Damn, that was close.

H: W-wait, it was just, like, real light talk, like whose boobs we like the—

: Then let's consider a hypothetical scenario. What if the women were all pping about what adult video actor's "member" they like the best?

H: Wut? I sure would be curious.

: Oh, I forgot, you're gay. Bad example. Let's see...

H: Hey, wait, wait! What women think about adult videos—how can you find a better opportunity an this to be enlightened with views of great academic significance? One's personal sexual eferences aside, one must appreciate the value of the opinions herein presented and discuss them ch the intellectual curiosity that befits—

: So as you see, this is a borderless work in many ways. We hope—by the way, apparently Kuro ard you having that conversation. Kuro was like, "Those pigs, lol."

H: See you in the next vol—wait, what? I haven't heard about this. You—*(bzt)*

AFTERWORD

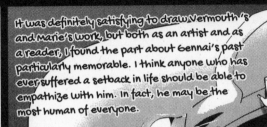

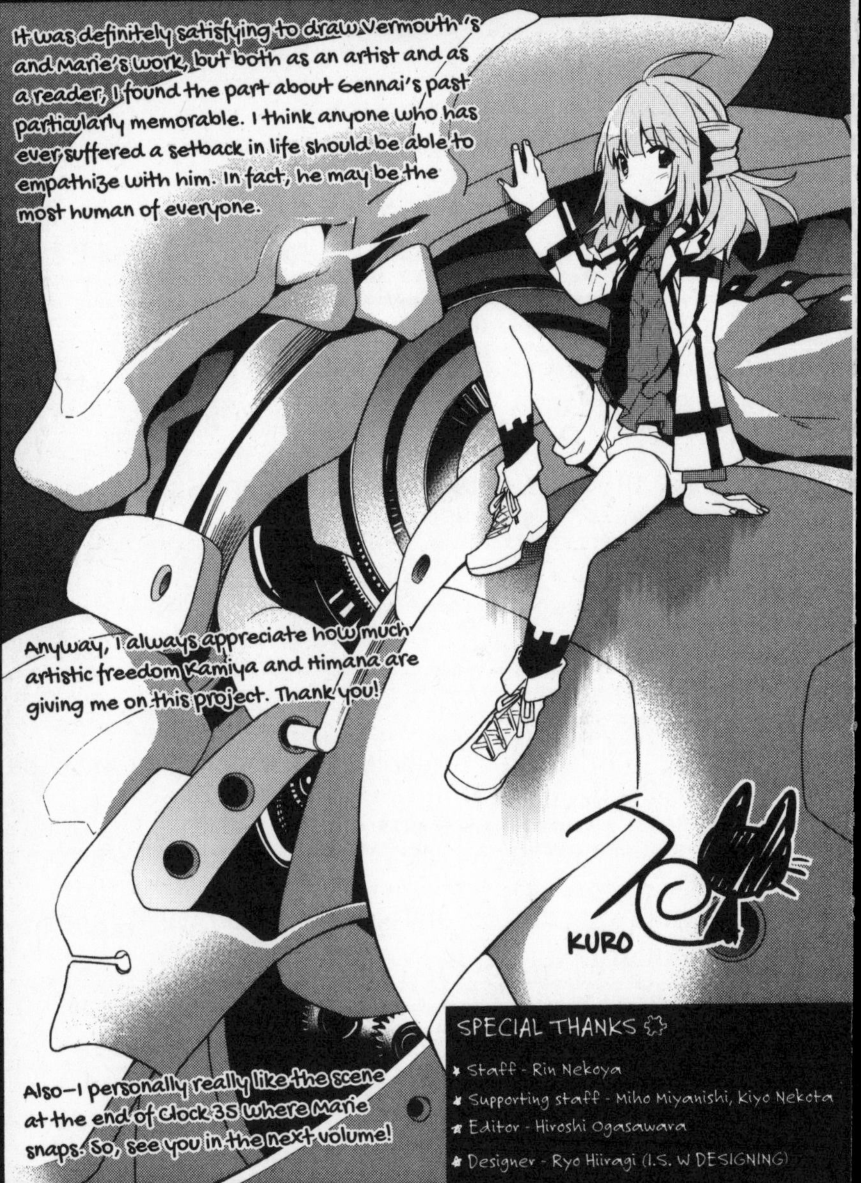

It was definitely satisfying to draw Vermouth's and Marie's work, but both as an artist and as a reader, I found the part about Gennai's past particularly memorable. I think anyone who has ever suffered a setback in life should be able to empathize with him. In fact, he may be the most human of everyone.

Anyway, I always appreciate how much artistic freedom Kamiya and Himana are giving me on this project. Thank you!

KURO

Also—I personally really like the scene at the end of clock 35 where Marie snaps. So, see you in the next volume!

SPECIAL THANKS

* Staff - Rin Nekoya
* Supporting staff - Miho Miyanishi, Kiyo Nekota
* Editor - Hiroshi Ogasawara
* Designer - Ryo Hiiragi (I.S. W DESIGNING)

Translation Notes

Raid, Rise, page 2
These both use the characters for "work," given a pronunciation meaning "war" for Clock 31 and "miracle" for Clock 32.

Genbu, page 11
Genbu (pronounced and occasionally spelled "Gembu") is the Japanese name of Xuanwu, literally "Dark Warrior," a figure in Chinese myth represented sometimes as a divine man and sometimes as a tortoise with a snake coiled about.

Komainu, page 13
Komainu, also known in English as lion-dogs, are guardian statues on either side of Shinto shrine entrances.

Tekki, page 13
Tekki means Iron Oni. An oni is a mythological Japanese creature similar to an ogre.

Your Imperial Highness the Princess Hoshi, page 77
In previous volumes, the correct spelling of the last name Hoshi was misrepresented as Hoshinomiya. We apologize for any confusion.

Jirai onna, page 122
In Japanese, *jirai onna* is made up of the words "land mine" and "woman." A *jirai onna* is a negative label for women who appear pleasant on the surface, but have "land mines" hidden beneath the surface. For more, see Volume 3.

How typical of the elderly to confound progress, page 158
Literally, "Is it not truly *rōgai*," wherein *rōgai* ("elderly harm") is a caustic word for the phenomenon of old executives or politicians abusing their authority in Japanese society to get in the way of progress.

Not universal, nor invariable, nor unbiased, page 164
All three of these adjectives are pronounced exactly the same in Japanese, as "*fuhen*."

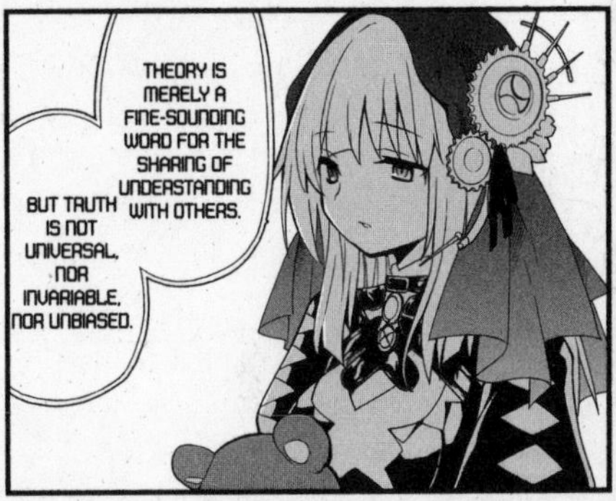
THEORY IS MERELY A FINE-SOUNDING WORD FOR THE SHARING OF UNDERSTANDING WITH OTHERS.
BUT TRUTH IS NOT UNIVERSAL, NOR INVARIABLE, NOR UNBIASED.

Normies, page 186
Riajū, a bitter slang word that is short for *riaru no seikatsu ga jūjitsu shite iru hito*, which translates to "people whose real lives are fulfilled."

From the bestselling creator of *NO GAME, NO LIFE* comes the original light novel that inspired the anime and manga

One day, the world ended--but it has been rebuilt anew! Everything on Earth, even gravity itself, is now powered by endlessly intricate clockwork. Young gearhead Naoto Miura dreams of becoming a master clocksmith, working with the wonders of this artificial planet. When one of those wonders comes crashing right through his ceiling, he gets more than he bargained for! Armed with a preternatural sense of hearing and a beautiful robotic ally, Naoto is the best shot his world has got at stopping a conspiracy that could end millions of lives.

CLOCKWORK PLANET

Story by YUU KAMIYA & TSUBAKI HIMANA
Illustrations by SINO

novel club

Available now in digital & print from **J-Novel Club** and **Seven Seas Entertainment**

"A fun adventure that fantasy readers will relate to and enjoy." —
Adventures in Poor Taste

Mikami's middle age hasn't gone as he
planned: He never found a girlfriend,
he got stuck in a dead-end job, and
he was abruptly stabbed to death in
the street at 37. So when he wakes
up in a new world straight out of a
fantasy RPG, he's disappointed, but
not exactly surprised to find that
he's facing down a dragon, not as a
knight or a wizard, but as a blind slime
monster. But there are chances for
even a slime to become a hero...

THAT TIME I GOT REINCARNATED AS A
SLIME

A Kodansha Comics Trade Paperback Original
Clockwork Planet volume 7 copyright © 2017 Yuu Kamiya/Tsubaki Himana/Sino/Kuro
English translation copyright © 2018 Yuu Kamiya/Tsubaki Himana/Sino/Kuro
All rights reserved.

Published in the United States by Kodansha Comics, an imprint of Kodansha USA Publishing, LLC, New York.

Publication rights for this English edition arranged through Kodansha Ltd, Tokyo.

First published in Japan in 2017 by Kodansha Ltd., Tokyo

ISBN 978-1-63236-542-2

Printed in the United States of America.

www.kodanshacomics.com

9 8 7 6 5 4 3 2 1
Translation: Daniel Komen
Lettering: David Yoo
Editing: Haruko Hashimoto
Kodansha Comics edition cover design by Phil Balsman